# Buying a Home
## in
# *Spain*
## *2003–04*

A Survival Handbook
by
David Hampshire

SURVIVAL BOOKS • LONDON • ENGLAND

First published 1997
Reprinted 1997
Second Edition 2000
Reprinted 2001, 2002
Third Edition 2003
Reprinted 2003

Copyright © Survival Books 1997, 2000, 2003

Survival Books Limited, 1st Floor,
60 St James's Street, London SW1A 1ZN, United Kingdom
☎ +44 (0)20-7493 4244, 🖺 +44 (0)20-7491 0605
✉ info@survivalbooks.net
🖥 www.survivalbooks.net
**To order books, please refer to page 360.**

British Library Cataloguing in Publication Data.
A CIP record for this book is available
from the British Library.
ISBN 1 901130 72 X

Printed and bound in Finland by WS Bookwell Ltd

# ACKNOWLEDGEMENTS

M y sincere thanks to those who contributed to the publication of the third edition of this book, in particular Joanna Styles (research and updating), Kerry & Joe Laredo (editing, proof-reading and desktop publishing – including the new style), and everyone else who provided information or contributed in any way. I would also like to thank John McManus (*Living Spain* magazine), Stacy Hamilton (Parador Properties) and Kerry Smith (Calahonda Select Properties) for providing photographs. Also a special thank you to Jim Watson for the superb illustrations, cartoons, maps and cover design.

## OTHER TITLES BY SURVIVAL BOOKS

**Living and Working Series**

Abroad; America; Australia;
Britain; Canada; France;
Germany; The Gulf States &
Saudi Arabia; Holland, Belgium
& Luxembourg; Ireland; Italy;
London; New Zealand; Spain;
Switzerland

**Buying a Home Series**

Abroad; Britain; Florida;
France; Greece & Cyprus;
Ireland; Italy; Portugal;

**Other Titles**

The Alien's Guide to Britain;
The Alien's Guide to France;
The Best Places to Live
in France;
The Best Places to Live
in Spain;
How to Avoid Holiday &
Travel Disasters;
Retiring Abroad;
Rioja and its Wines;
The Wines of Spain

*Order forms are on page 360.*

# WHAT READERS & REVIEWERS

When you buy a model plane for your child, a video recorder, or some new computer gizmo, you get with it a leaflet or booklet pleading 'Read Me First', or bearing large friendly letters or bold type saying 'IMPORTANT – follow the instructions carefully'. This book should be similarly supplied to all those entering France with anything more durable than a 5-day return ticket. It is worth reading even if you are just visiting briefly, or if you have lived here for years and feel totally knowledgeable and secure. But if you need to find out how France works then it is indispensable. Native French people probably have a less thorough understanding of how their country functions. – Where it is most essential, the book is most up to the minute.

LIVING FRANCE

Rarely has a 'survival guide' contained such useful advice. This book dispels doubts for first-time travellers, yet is also useful for seasoned globetrotters – In a word, if you're planning to move to the USA or go there for a long-term stay, then buy this book both for general reading and as a ready-reference.

AMERICAN CITIZENS ABROAD

It is everything you always wanted to ask but didn't for fear of the contemptuous put down – The best English-language guide – Its pages are stuffed with practical information on everyday subjects and are designed to complement the traditional guidebook.

SWISS NEWS

A complete revelation to me – I found it both enlightening and interesting, not to mention amusing.

CAROLE CLARK

Let's say it at once. David Hampshire's *Living and Working in France* is the best handbook ever produced for visitors and foreign residents in this country; indeed, my discussion with locals showed that it has much to teach even those born and bred in l'Hexagone. – It is Hampshire's meticulous detail which lifts his work way beyond the range of other books with similar titles. Often you think of a supplementary question and search for the answer in vain. With Hampshire this is rarely the case. – He writes with great clarity (and gives French equivalents of all key terms), a touch of humour and a ready eye for the odd (and often illuminating) fact. – This book is absolutely indispensable.

THE RIVIERA REPORTER

A mine of information – I may have avoided some embarrassments and frights if I had read it prior to my first Swiss encounters – Deserves an honoured place on any newcomer's bookshelf.

ENGLISH TEACHERS ASSOCIATION, SWITZERLAND

# HAVE SAID ABOUT SURVIVAL BOOKS

What a great work, wealth of useful information, well-balanced wording and accuracy in details. My compliments!

THOMAS MÜLLER

This handbook has all the practical information one needs to set up home in the UK – The sheer volume of information is almost daunting – Highly recommended for anyone moving to the UK.

AMERICAN CITIZENS ABROAD

A very good book which has answered so many questions and even some I hadn't thought of – I would certainly recommend it.

BRIAN FAIRMAN

We would like to congratulate you on this work: it is really super! We hand it out to our expatriates and they read it with great interest and pleasure.

ICI (SWITZERLAND) AG

Covers just about all the things you want to know on the subject – In answer to the desert island question about the one how-to book on France, this book would be it – Almost 500 pages of solid accurate reading – This book is about enjoyment as much as survival.

THE RECORDER

It's so funny – I love it and definitely need a copy of my own – Thanks very much for having written such a humorous and helpful book.

HEIDI GUILIANI

A must for all foreigners coming to Switzerland.

ANTOINETTE O'DONOGHUE

A comprehensive guide to all things French, written in a highly readable and amusing style, for anyone planning to live, work or retire in France.

THE TIMES

A concise, thorough account of the DOs and DON'Ts for a foreigner in Switzerland – Crammed with useful information and lightened with humorous quips which make the facts more readable.

AMERICAN CITIZENS ABROAD

Covers every conceivable question that may be asked concerning everyday life – I know of no other book that could take the place of this one.

FRANCE IN PRINT

Hats off to *Living and Working in Switzerland*!

RONNIE ALMEIDA

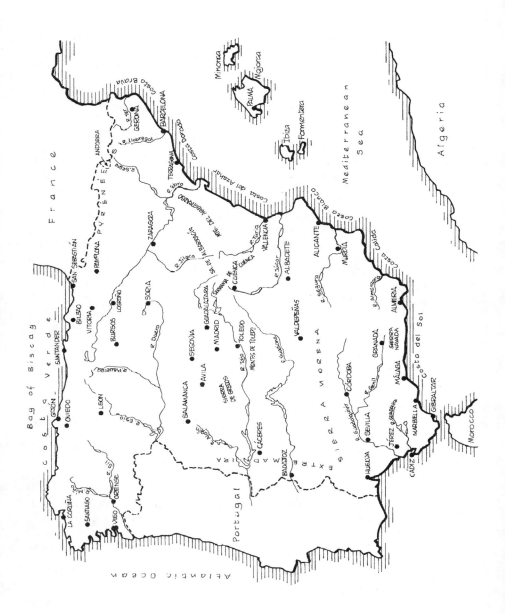

# CONTENTS

# IMPORTANT NOTE

Readers should note that the laws and regulations regarding buying property in Spain aren't the same as in other countries and are liable to change periodically. **I cannot recommend too strongly that you always check with an official and reliable source (not necessarily the same) and take expert legal advice before paying any money or signing any documents.** Don't, however, believe everything you're told or read, even, dare I say it, herein!

To help you obtain further information and verify data with official sources, useful addresses and references to other sources of information have been included in all chapters and in appendices A to C. Important points have been emphasised throughout the book in **bold** print, some of which it would be expensive or foolish to disregard. **Ignore them at your peril or cost!** Unless specifically stated, the reference to any company, organisation, product or publication in this book doesn't constitute an endorsement or recommendation. Any reference to any place or person (living or dead) is purely coincidental.

# THE AUTHOR

David Hampshire was born in the United Kingdom, where after serving in the Royal Air Force he was employed for many years in the computer industry. He has lived and worked in many countries, including Australia, France, Germany, Malaysia, the Netherlands, Singapore, Switzerland and Spain, where he now resides most of the year. It was while working in Switzerland that he wrote his first book, *Living and Working in Switzerland*, in 1987. David is the author of some 15 books, including *Buying a Home in France, Buying a Home in Italy, Buying a Home in Spain, Living and Working in France, Living and Working in Spain* and *Retiring Abroad*.

# AUTHOR'S NOTES

● Frequent references are made throughout this book to the European Union (EU), which comprises Austria, Belgium, Denmark, Finland, France, Germany, Greece, Ireland, Italy, Luxembourg, the Netherlands, Portugal, Spain, Sweden and the United Kingdom, and the European Economic Area (EEA), which includes the EU countries plus Iceland, Liechtenstein and Norway.

● **Prices quoted should be taken as estimates only**, although they were mostly correct when going to print and fortunately don't usually change overnight in Spain. Most prices in Spain are quoted inclusive of value added tax (*IVA incluido*), which is the method used when quoting prices in this book (unless otherwise indicated), although prices are sometimes quoted exclusive of tax (*más IVA*).

● Times are shown using am (Latin *ante meridiem*) for before noon and pm (*post meridiem*) for after noon. Most Spaniards don't use the 24-hour clock. All times are local, therefore you should check the time difference when making international calls.

● His/he/him also means her/she/her (please forgive me ladies). This is done to make life easier for both the reader and (in particular) the author, and **isn't** intended to be sexist.

● The Spanish translation of many key words and phrases is shown in brackets in *italics*.

● Warning and important points are shown in **bold** type.

● All spelling is (or should be) English, not American.

● The following symbols are used in this book: ☎ (telephone), ▤ (fax), 💻 (Internet) and ✉ (e-mail).

● Lists of **Useful Addresses**, **Further Reading** and **Useful Websites** are contained in **Appendices A** to **C** respectively.

● For those unfamiliar with the metric system of weights and measures, imperial conversion tables are included in **Appendix D**.

● Maps of Spain showing the regions and provinces, airports, the high-speed train (*AVE*) network, and motorways and other major roads are included in **Appendix E**, and a map showing the major cities and geographical features is on page 6.

● A table showing the scheduled airline services between Spain and the UK/Ireland can be found in **Appendix F**.

● A list of property, mortgage and other terms used in this book is included in a **Glossary** in **Appendix G**.

# INTRODUCTION

Since it was first published in 1997, *Buying a Home in Spain* has been the most comprehensive and up-to-date book for homebuyers in Spain. To make the information more accessible and helpful, we have totally re-designed and enlarged the third edition. Furthermore, commencing with this edition, *Buying a Home in Spain* will be published annually, thus ensuring that you always have the most up-to-date information at your fingertips.

Whether you want a villa, farmhouse, townhouse or an apartment, a holiday or permanent home, this book will help make your dreams come true. The purpose of *Buying a Home in Spain* is to provide you with the information necessary to help you choose the most favourable location and the most appropriate home **to satisfy your individual requirements**. Most importantly, it will help you avoid the pitfalls and risks associated with buying a home in Spain, which for most people is one of the largest financial transactions they will undertake during their lifetimes.

You may already own a home in your home country; however, buying a home in Spain (or in any foreign country) is a different matter altogether. One of the most common mistakes many people make when buying a home in Spain is to assume that the laws and purchase procedures are the same as in their home country. **This is almost certainly not the case!** Despite some reports to the contrary, buying property in Spain is generally safe and needn't be a lottery. However, if you don't obtain legal advice and follow the rules provided for your protection, a purchase can result in a serious financial loss, as many people have discovered to their cost.

Before buying a home in Spain you need to ask yourself exactly why you want to buy a home there? Is your primary concern a long-term investment or do you wish to work or retire there? Where and what can you afford to buy? Do you plan to let your home to offset the running costs? How will Spanish taxes affect your investment? *Buying a Home in Spain* will help you answer these and many other questions. It won't, however, tell you where to live, what to buy, or, having made your decision, whether you will be happy – that part is up to you!

For many people, buying a home in Spain has previously been a case of pot luck. However, with a copy of *Buying a Home in Spain* to hand you'll have a wealth of priceless information at your fingertips – information derived from a variety of sources, both official and unofficial, not least the hard won personal experiences of the author, his friends, colleagues and acquaintances. Furthermore, this book will reduce the risk of making an expensive mistake that you may bitterly regret later, and help you make informed decisions and calculated judgements, instead of costly mistakes and uneducated guesses (forewarned is forearmed!). **Most importantly, it will help you save money and repay your investment many times over.**

Buying a home in Spain is a wonderful way to make new friends, broaden your horizons and revitalise your life – and it provides a welcome bolt-hole to recuperate from the stresses and strains of modern life. I trust this book will help you avoid the pitfalls and smooth your way to many happy years in your new home in Spain, secure in the knowledge that you've made the right decision.

*¡Mucha suerte!*                                                          **David Hampshire**
                                                                              **May 2003**

# 1.

# MAJOR CONSIDERATIONS

Buying a home abroad is not only a major financial commitment, but also a decision that can have a huge influence on other aspects of your life, including your health, security and safety, your family relationships and friendships, your lifestyle, your opinions and your outlook. You also need to take into consideration any restrictions that might affect your choice of location and type of property, such as whether you will need (or be able) to learn another language, whether you will be able (or permitted) to find work, whether you can adapt to and enjoy the climate, whether you will be able to take your pets with you, and not least, whether you will be able to afford the kind of home (and lifestyle) that you want. In order to ensure that you're making the right move, it's as well to face these and other major considerations before making any irrevocable decisions.

## WHY SPAIN?

If you want guaranteed sunshine, miles of glorious sandy beaches, excellent food, an abundant choice of entertainment, and a wide choice of homes at affordable prices, then you will find Spain hard to beat. Although the vast majority of holidaymakers (and residents) come to recline on a beach, there's much more to the country than the *costas* and its islands. Spain offers infinite variety with something for everyone, including magnificent beaches for sun-worshippers; spectacular unspoilt countryside for nature lovers; an abundance of mountains and seas for sports fans; a vibrant night-life for the jet set; bustling sophisticated cities for 'townies'; superb wine and cuisine for gourmets; a wealth of art, culture and serious music for art lovers; numerous festivals and fiestas for inveterate party-goers and tranquillity for the stressed. Not for nothing do the Spanish claim to have 'Everything Under The Sun!' When buying a home there you aren't simply buying a home but a lifestyle, and as a location for a holiday, retirement or permanent home, Spain has few equals, particularly if you're seeking year-round sunshine.

There are many excellent reasons for buying a home in Spain, although it's important not to be under any illusions about what you can expect. The first and most important question you need to ask yourself is *exactly* why do you want to buy a home in Spain? For example, are you seeking a holiday or a retirement home (the Costa Blanca and Costa del Sol have the highest percentage of retired people in the world, when Spaniards and foreigners are included)? If you're seeking a second home, will it be used mainly for long weekends or for lengthier stays? Do you plan to let it to offset the mortgage and running costs? If so, how important is the property income? Are you primarily looking for a sound investment or do you plan to work or start a business in Spain?

Often buyers have a variety of reasons for buying a home in Spain, for example, many people buy a holiday home with a view to living there permanently or semi-permanently when they retire. If this is the case, there are many more factors to take into account than if you were 'simply' buying a holiday home that you will occupy for just a few weeks a year (when it's usually wiser not to buy at all!). If, on the other hand, you plan to work or start a business, you will be faced with a whole different set of criteria. The vast increase in cheap flights between Spain and other European countries, and the advent of the Internet means an increasing number of people also live in Spain and work in another European country, commuting back and forth.

Can you really afford to buy a home in Spain? What of the future? Is your income secure and protected against inflation and currency fluctuations? In the 1980s, many foreigners purchased holiday homes in Spain by taking out second mortgages on their family homes abroad and stretching their financial resources to the limits. Not surprisingly, when the recession struck in the 1990s many people had their homes repossessed or were forced to sell at a huge loss when they were unable to maintain the mortgage payments. Buying a home abroad can be a good, long-term investment, although it's possible to get your fingers burnt in the occasional volatile property market in some countries, including parts of Spain. For an overview of the cost of living and the cost of property in Spain see pages 26 and 24 respectively.

## Advantages & Disadvantages

There are both advantages and disadvantages to buying a home in Spain, although for most people the benefits outweigh any drawbacks. Among the many advantages are:

- guaranteed sunshine and high temperatures (in some areas, all year);
- one of the least polluted countries in the world (particularly in resort areas);
- good value for money; easy and inexpensive to get to (at least for most western Europeans);
- good rental possibilities (in most areas);
- good local tradesmen and services (particularly in resort areas);
- fine food and wine at reasonable prices; a relatively low cost of living;
- a slow, relaxed pace of life;
- the friendliness and warmth of the Spanish people;
- the dramatic and rugged beauty of Spain on your doorstep;
- a superb quality of life.

Naturally, there are also a few disadvantages, including:

- the relatively high purchase costs associated with buying property;
- unexpected renovation and restoration costs (if you don't do your homework);
- the dangers of buying a property with debts and other problems (if you don't take legal advice);
- a high rate of burglary and housebreaking in some areas;
- overcrowding in popular tourist areas during the peak summer season;
- traffic congestion and pollution in many towns and cities;
- the large number of taxes for non-resident homeowners;
- water shortages in some regions (particularly during the summer);
- the expense of getting to and from Spain if you own a home there and don't live in a nearby country (or a country with good air connections).

Before deciding to buy a home in Spain, it's advisable to do extensive research and read a number of books especially written for those planning to live or work there (like this one and *Living and Working in Spain*, also written by David Hampshire and *The Best Places to Buy a Home in Spain* by Joanna Styles, both published by Survival Books). It also helps to study specialist property magazines such as *Homes Overseas*, *International Homes* and *World of Property* (see **Appendix B** for a list), and visit overseas property exhibitions such as those organised by Outbound Publishing (1 Commercial Road, Eastbourne, East Sussex BN21 3XQ, UK, ☎ 01323-726040, ✉ outbounduk@aol.com).

> **SURVIVAL TIP**
> Bear in mind that the cost of investing in a few books or magazines (and other research) is tiny compared with the expense of making a big mistake. However, don't believe everything you read!

This chapter addresses the most serious concerns of anyone planning to buy a home and live in Spain, including the climate, economy, cost of property, cost of living, permits and visas, language, health and pets.

# BUYING FOR INVESTMENT

In recent years, Spanish property has been an excellent investment, particularly in the islands, on the *costas* and in the major cities. There are various kinds of property investment. Your home is an investment, in that it provides you with rent-free accommodation. It may also yield a return in terms of increased value (a capital gain), although that gain may be difficult to realise unless you trade down or move to another region or country where property is cheaper. Of course, if you buy property other than for your own regular use, e.g. a holiday home, you will be in a position to benefit from a more tangible return on your investment. There are essentially four main categories of investment property:

- **A holiday home**, which can provide a return in many ways. It can provide your family and friends with rent-free accommodation while (hopefully) maintaining its value, and you may be able to let it to generate supplementary income. It may also produce a capital gain if property values rise faster than inflation (as in recent years).

- **A home for your children or relatives**, which may realise a capital gain. This could also be let when not in use to provide an income.

- **A business property**, which could be anything from a private home with bed and breakfast or guest accommodation, to a shop or office.

- **A property purchased purely for investment**, which could be a capital investment or provide a regular income, or both. Many people have invested in property to provide an income on their retirement.

A property investment should be considered over the medium to long term, say a minimum of five and preferably 10 to 15 years. Bear in mind that property isn't always 'as safe as houses' and investments can be risky over the short to medium term. You also need to take into account income tax if a property is let (see **Income Tax for Property Owners** on page 229) and capital gains tax (see page 240) when you sell a second home. You also need to recoup the high purchase costs (see **Fees** on page 123) of around 10 per cent when you sell.

## Buying To Let

When buying to let, you must ensure that the rent will cover the mortgage (if applicable), running costs and void periods (when the property isn't let). Bear in mind that rental rates and competition varies depending on the region and town, and an area with high rents and occupancy rates today may not be so fruitful next year. Gross rental yields (the annual rent as a percentage of a property's value) are from around 5 to 10 per cent a year in most areas (although gross yields of 15 per cent or more are possible) and net yields (after expenses have been deducted) 2 to 3 per cent lower. Yields vary considerably depending on the region or city and the type of property. Note that there aren't special buy-to-let mortgages in Spain.

Before deciding to invest in a property, you should ask yourself the following questions:

- Can I afford to tie up capital in the medium to long term, i.e. at least five years?
- How likely is the value of the property to rise during this period?
- Can I rely on a regular income from my investment? If so, how easy will it be to generate that income, e.g. to find tenants? Will I be able to pay the mortgage if the property is empty, and if so, for how long?
- Am I aware of all the risks involved and how comfortable am I with taking those risks?
- Do I have enough information to make a rational decision?

See also **Mortgages** on page 183, **Taxation Of Property Income** on page 229, **Location** on page 73 and **Chapter 9** (Letting).

# CLIMATE

Hardly surprisingly, the overwhelming attraction of Spain for most foreigners is its excellent climate. Spain is the sunniest country in Europe and the climate (on the Costa Blanca) has been described by the World Health Organisation as among the healthiest in the world. Spain's Mediterranean coastline, from the Costa Blanca to the Costa del Sol, enjoys an average of over 300 days sunshine each year. When northern Europe is being deluged or is frozen, you can almost guarantee that the south of Spain will be bathed in sunshine. In general, May and October are considered the best months for touring as they're generally dry and not too hot in most regions. However, there's a price to pay for all those warm days, and in the summer of 1995 the reservoirs in central, southern and eastern Spain were almost empty after four years of severe drought, during which millions of people had to endure water rationing. The drought was broken in the winter of 1995/96, when torrential rain caused widespread flooding throughout the country. It was one of Spain's worst winters on record and many areas in the south of the country experienced over two months of almost constant heavy rainfall. More recently in early 2003, some areas in the east (including Alicante and Murcia) were declared 'emergency' areas due to widespread drought conditions, while at the same time vast areas of Aragon along the Ebro river in the north were affected by severe flooding. As the Spanish saying goes, 'it never rains to everyone's taste' (*nunca llueve a gusto de todos*).

Continental Spain experiences three climatic zones: Atlantic, Continental and Mediterranean, in addition to which some areas, particularly the Balearic and Canary Islands, have their own distinct micro-climates. In coastal areas there can be huge variations in the weather simply by travelling a few kilometres inland and up into the mountains. On some islands such as Majorca, rainfall varies from 300 to 400mm (12 to 16in) in the south to over 1,200mm (47in) in the north, and some areas experience strong winds in winter while others are sheltered.

The **Atlantic** or green zone (*costa verde*) embraces the north-west region of the country including Galicia (which has a mild and humid climate), the Cantabrian coast of Asturias, Cantabria, the Basque Country and the Pyrenees (dividing Spain and France). The region from Galicia's border with Asturias along the coast to the Pyrenees is the wettest area, although even here there are some 1,800 hours of sunshine a year (much more than in northern Europe). Summer coastal temperatures average around 25°C (77°F) and spring and autumn are mild. However, the region experiences high rainfall of from 900 to 2,000mm (35 to 79in) a year, particularly in winter on the coast, and inland it's cold with frequent snowfalls (Teruel and Soria provinces generally have the worst winter climate). Contrary to the popular saying, the rain in Spain certainly doesn't fall mainly on the plain – the plains are very dry and most rain falls along the northern and western coasts. Heavy snowfalls are common above 1,200m (3,937ft) in winter and although snow is rare outside the mountainous areas, most areas in the north of Spain and the Balearics occasionally experience snowfalls.

The **Continental** zone encompasses the central part of Spain, called the *meseta* (tableland), and the Ebro river valley. It embraces the provinces of Castile/La Mancha, Castile/Leon and Extremadura, plus part of Aragon and Navarra, and is baking hot in summer and freezing cold in winter. Madrid is in the centre of the *meseta* and has the lowest winter temperatures, ranging from 1°C (34°F) to 9°C (48°F) in January. Annual rainfall in Madrid is 300 to 600mm (12 to 16in). The further you travel south from Madrid in winter the warmer it becomes (except in mountainous regions), with, for example, Seville experiencing temperate winters. Seville also experiences the hottest summers, where the temperature averages around 34°C (93°F) in July and August and often exceeds 40°C (104°F). The temperature in Ecija, between Cordoba and Seville, has exceeded 47°C (117°F) and it's appropriately known as the frying pan of Andalusia (*la sartén de Andalucía*).

The **Mediterranean** zone embraces the coastal regions of Spain from the French to the Portuguese borders and is divided into three regions. Catalonia (including the Costa Brava) has relatively mild winters but is also quite humid, with 500 to 800mm (20 to 31in) of rain and between

2,450 and 2,650 hours of sunshine a year. Summers are pleasant without very high temperatures. The central eastern part of the Mediterranean coast, from around Alicante to Tarragona (known as the Levante) and including the Costa Blanca (plus Valencia and Murcia), is warmer in winter than Catalonia and has lower rainfall (300 to 425mm/12 to 17in). The annual hours of sunshine are between 2,700 to 3,000 and temperatures in summer can be over 30°C (86°F). The southern coast of Andalusia (including the Costa del Sol) has slightly higher temperatures than the eastern coast and between 2,900 and 3,000 hours of sunshine annually. Annual rainfall is just 230 to 470mm (9 to 19in). In winter the daytime temperature on the Costa Blanca and Costa del Sol often reaches a pleasant 15 to 20°C (59 to 68°F), when the Spanish habitually dress in overcoats and foreigners in shorts or bathing costumes! Andalusia includes the most arid part of Spain in the province of Almería and also the area with the highest rainfall in the whole of Spain in Grazalema in the province of Cádiz (Spain is a country of oases and deserts).

Most rain in Andalusia falls in the winter months, with some areas having as little as 200mm (8in) a year, which may all fall in one or two days, causing flash floods. The Mediterranean coast is also subject to cold winds from the north and north-east which bring snow to the Pyrenees and the meseta in winter. The Costa del Sol can be extremely windy in winter (it was originally called the 'windy coast' or *Costa de Viento* until the tourist ministry's marketing men got to work) and parts of the Atlantic coast of Cádiz experience a strong wind called the *levante*, which can blow for days at a time (great for windsurfers). The mountain ranges of the hinterland help to protect the coastal regions from climatic extremes and funnel warm air from the meseta to the coast in summer.

The **Balearic Islands** have a Mediterranean climate with mild winters and hot summers, tempered by cool sea breezes (the most pleasant summer climate in Spain). Annual sunshine is similar to the Levante, while annual rainfall is higher at between 450 and 650mm (18 to 26in).

The **Canary Islands** boast the best year-round climate with warm winters and temperate summers, and temperatures of 20 to 27°C (68 to 81°F) throughout the year. Hours of sunshine are similar to the Costa del Sol. Rainfall is low and varies from less than 100mm (4in) a year on Fuerteventura and Lanzarote to 750mm (30in) in the inland areas of Gran Canaria and Tenerife. The inland region of Tenerife experiences around 3,400 annual hours of sunshine – the highest in Spain.

# Natural Phenomena

Spain experiences many violent, cold/hot, dry winds, including the *terral* in the sout, the *tramontana* in Catalonia, Minorca (Balearics) and the

Pyrenees, and the *solano* in Cádiz. Although they're rare, the south is prone to earthquakes; however, the strongest usually measure a maximum of around 5.0 on the Richter scale and they rarely cause any damage or injuries. In summer, forest fires are a danger everywhere and along with droughts, pose a serious long-term threat to the landscape, which resembles a desert in many areas (some 15 per cent of the country's surface has a serious erosion problem). Flash floods can be dangerous, particularly in mountainous areas, e.g. over 80 people died in August 1996 when flash floods struck a campsite in Biescas (Huesca) in the north.

Approximate average daily maximum/minimum temperatures for major cities are shown below in Centigrade and Fahrenheit (in brackets):

| Location | Spring | Summer | Autumn | Winter |
| --- | --- | --- | --- | --- |
| Barcelona | 18/11 (64/52) | 28/21 (82/70) | 21/15 (70/59) | 13/6 (55/43) |
| Cádiz | 20/13 (68/55) | 27/20 (81/68) | 23/17 (73/63) | 15/9 (59/48) |
| Granada | 20/7 (68/45) | 34/17 (93/63) | 23/10 (73/50) | 12/2 (54/36) |
| Madrid | 18/7 (64/45) | 31/17 (88/63) | 19/10 (66/50) | 9/2 (48/36) |
| Malaga | 21/13 (70/55) | 29/21 (84/70) | 23/16 (73/61) | 17/8 (63/46) |
| Palma | 19/10 (66/50) | 29/20 (84/68) | 18/10 (64/50) | 14/6 (57/43) |
| Santander | 15/10 (59/50) | 22/16 (72/61) | 18/12 (64/54) | 12/7 (53/45) |
| Seville | 24/11 (75/52) | 36/20 (97/68) | 26/14 (79/57) | 15/6 (59/43) |
| Tenerife | 24/17 (75/62) | 28/20 (83/68) | 28/21 (82/69) | 20/14 (68/58) |
| Valencia | 20/10 (68/50) | 29/20 (84/68) | 23/13 (73/55) | 15/6 (59/43) |

Frequent weather forecasts (*pronósticos* or *el tiempo*) are given on television, radio and in daily newspapers. A quick way to make a **rough** conversion from Centigrade to Fahrenheit is to multiply by two and add 30. See also **Water** on page 307.

# ECONOMY

When considering buying a property in Spain, the financial implications of the purchase is usually one of the major factors that may influence your decision. This includes the state of not only the Spanish economy, but also that of your **home country** (or the country where your earn your income). The state of the economy in your home country (and your assets and job security there) may dictate how much you can afford to spend on the purchase, whether you can maintain your mortgage payments and the upkeep of a property, and how often you can afford to visit Spain each year. For example, in 2002 and early 2003 the German recession meant that many prospective German property owners could no longer afford to buy in Spain and numerous property owners were unable to travel as often as they wished. Your home country's economy is also important if you plan to retire to Spain and will be primarily living on a pension. If you intend to live and work in Spain, or more importantly plan to run a business, then the state of the Spanish economy will be a major consideration.

Spain currently has one of the strongest economies in Europe and has been transformed in the last few decades from a rural, backward agricultural country into a nation with a diversified economy and strong manufacturing and service sectors. After joining the European Union (EU) in 1986, Spain had one of the world's fasting-growing economies with annual growth averaging over 4 per cent until being hard hit by the recession in the early 1990s. A vastly improved balance of payments and economic reforms introduced by the new right-wing government in 1996 initiated a strong recovery and since 1997 Spain has had one of the highest growth rates in the EU, mainly due to the rapid expansion of industry and tourism. Growth, although slower (1.9 per cent in 2002), continues apace and remains higher than the EU average. Inflation, although 4 per cent in 2002, is relatively low and the government's austere public spending programme means that the budget deficit has fallen almost to zero (from 7.5 per cent in 1993). Unemployment, however, remains a concern and is among the highest in the EU at around 11 per cent, in spite of numerous government initiatives to reduce it.

Spain adopted the euro and the European Central Bank (ECB) interest rates along with eleven other EU countries in January 2002. One year later prices had generally risen across the board (in common with most other euro-zone countries), although not as much as popular perception would have you believe. To compensate, interest rates were at a all-time low (2.5 per cent in March 2003). Economic predictions for Spain forecast GDP growth of nearly 10 per cent between 2003 and 2005, considerably higher than that of the UK, France, Germany and Italy (Source: Economist Intelligence Unit). In general, the economic forecast for Spain is good and one of the best in the EU.

# COST OF PROPERTY

One of the major considerations (or **the** major consideration) for anyone contemplating buying a home in Spain is whether you can afford to buy a home there, and if so, what kind of home can you afford and where? Foreign buyers have traditionally been attracted by the relatively low cost of resort property compared with many other European countries. However, prices have risen considerably in the last five years and property in the most popular areas is no longer the bargain it once was, which can come as quite a shock to newcomers. Note also that although more Spaniards own their own homes than the inhabitants of most other European Union (EU) countries, they don't generally buy property as an investment and you shouldn't expect to make a quick profit when buying property in Spain. **You also need to take into account the fees (see page 123), which usually amount to around 10 per cent of the purchase price.**

If you're seeking a holiday home and cannot afford to buy one outright, you may wish to investigate a scheme that provides sole occupancy of a property for a number of weeks each year rather than buying a property. Schemes available include part-ownership, leaseback and timesharing (see **Timeshare & Part-Ownership Schemes** on page 143 for information).

 **Don't rush into any of these schemes without fully researching the market and before you're absolutely clear what you want and what you can realistically expect to get for your money.**

Property values generally increase at an average of less than 5 per cent a year or in line with inflation (with no increase in real terms), although in many fashionable resorts and developments prices rise much faster than average, which is usually reflected in much higher purchase prices. For example, prices have increased by up to 25 per cent a year on the Costa Blanca and Costa del Sol over the last few years and in many other resort areas prices have risen by an average of 15 to 20 per cent a year.

There's a stable property market in most of Spain (barring recessions), which acts as a discouragement to speculators wishing to make a fast buck, particularly when you consider that capital gains tax can wipe out much of the profit made on the sale of a home (especially a second home). You also need to recover the costs (around 10 per cent of the purchase price) associated with buying a home, when you sell.

 **You shouldn't expect to make a quick profit when buying property in Spain, but should look upon it as an investment in your family's future happiness, rather than merely in financial terms.**

There are some two million foreign property owners in Spain, which is Europe's favourite country for second homes, particularly among buyers from the Benelux countries, the UK, Germany and Scandinavia. Most foreigners are concentrated on the Mediterranean coastline (the *costas*) and in the Balearic and Canary Islands. Officially some 20 per cent of foreign property owners are residents, the majority of whom are retired, although the real figure is much higher as many foreigners fail to register. A slice of *la buena vida* needn't cost the earth, with 'old'

apartments and village homes available from as little as €50,000, modern apartments from €100,000 and detached villas from €150,000, although prices in some resort areas, especially the Costa del Sol, are considerably higher. However, if you're seeking a substantial home with a sizeable plot of land and a swimming pool, you will usually need to spend over €250,000 (depending on the area). For those with the financial resources the sky's the limit, with luxury apartments and villas costing hundreds of thousands (or even millions) of euros! In recent years prices have risen sharply throughout Spain – in both resort areas and the major cities – and it's now almost impossible to find a bargain on the most popular *costas* and islands.

# COST OF LIVING

No doubt you would like to try to estimate how far your euros will stretch and how much money (if any) you will have left after paying your bills. Spain is no longer the inexpensive Eldorado that it once was and the cost of living has risen considerably in recent years. Inflation is relatively low (4 per cent in 2002), although unemployment is high and many Spaniards have seen a drop in their standard of living in recent years. According to a survey conducted by the charity Caritas, some 20 per cent of the population (around 8 million people) live in poverty, defined as earning less than half the average income (around €1,250 per month). Around 5 per cent of the population live in extreme poverty with an income below €120 per month. There's a huge variation between average incomes in different regions of the country, e.g. GDP is an average of just €8,330 a year in Extremadura and €9,500 in Andalusia, compared with over €15,500 a year in Catalonia and even higher in Madrid, Navarra and the Basque Country.

In the last few decades, inflation has brought the price of many goods and services in line with that in most other European countries. Among the more expensive items in Spain are quality clothes and many consumer goods. However, many things remain cheaper than in northern European countries, including property (avoiding the hot spots), cars, rents, food, alcohol, hotels, restaurants and general entertainment.

With the exception of the major cities, where the higher cost of living is generally offset by higher salaries, the cost of living in Spain is lower than in most other western European countries, particularly in rural and coastal areas. Overall, the cost of living is lower than in the UK, France and Germany, and around the same as North America. A couple owning their home can 'survive' on a net income of as little as €400 a month (many pensioners actually live on less) and most can live quite comfortably on an income of €800 a month (excluding rent or mortgage payments). In fact many northern Europeans (particularly Scandinavians) who live modestly in Spain without over-doing the luxuries find that their cost of living is up to 50 per cent lower than in their home country.

It's difficult to calculate an average cost of living as it depends on each individual's particular circumstances and life-style. The actual difference in your food bill will depend on what you eat and where you lived before coming to Spain. Food generally costs around the same as in the USA, but is cheaper than in most northern European countries. Around €200 will feed two adults for a month, including (inexpensive) wine, but excluding fillet steak, caviar and expensive imported foods. Shopping for expensive consumer goods such as hi-fi equipment, electronic goods, computers and photographic equipment in other European countries or North America can also yield savings (you can also shop on the Internet).

A list of the approximate **MINIMUM** monthly major expenses for an average single person, couple, or family with two children are shown in the table below, although many live on less (most people will agree that the figures are either too HIGH or too LOW). When calculating your cost of living, you will need to deduct the appropriate percentage for social security contributions and income tax (see page 225) from your gross salary. The numbers (in brackets) refer to the notes following the table:

| | MONTHLY COSTS (€) | | |
|---|---|---|---|
| ITEM | Single | Couple | Couple with 2 children |
| Housing (1) | 300 | 400 | 550 |
| Food (2) | 160 | 200 | 350 |
| Utilities (3) | 60 | 60 | 100 |
| Leisure (4) | 100 | 125 | 200 |
| Transport (5) | 50 | 100 | 125 |
| Insurance (6) | 60 | 75 | 125 |
| Clothing | 100 | 150 | 200 |
| **TOTAL** | **830** | **1,110** | **1,650** |

1. Rent or mortgage payments for a modern or modernised apartment or house in an average small town or suburb, excluding major cities and other high-cost areas. The properties envisaged are a studio or one-bedroom apartment for a single person, a two-bedroom property for a couple, and a three-bedroom property for a couple with two children.

2. Doesn't include luxuries or liquid food (alcohol).

3. Includes electricity, gas, water, telephone, cable or satellite TV, and heating and air-conditioning costs.

4. Includes entertainment, dining out, sports and vacation expenses, plus newspapers and magazines.

5. Includes running costs for an average family car, plus third party insurance, annual taxes, petrol, servicing and repairs, but excludes depreciation or credit costs.

6. Includes 'voluntary' insurance such as inexpensive supplementary health insurance, household (building and contents), third party liability, travel, automobile breakdown and life insurance. Expensive private health insurance isn't included.

# PERMITS & VISAS

Before making any plans to buy a home in Spain, you must check whether you will need a visa or residence permit and ensure that you will be permitted to use the property whenever you wish and for whatever purpose you have in mind. While foreigners are freely permitted to buy property, they aren't allowed to remain longer than three months in succession without obtaining a 90-day extension (*permanencia*) or a residence permit. If there's a possibility that you or a family member may wish to live permanently or work in Spain, you should enquire whether it will be possible before making any plans to buy a home there.

**All foreigners except EU, EEA and Swiss nationals who live, work or study in Spain** need a residence permit to live there permanently, and non-EU nationals may need a visa to enter Spain, either as a visitor or for any other purpose. Citizens of non-EU countries must obtain a visa from a Spanish consulate in their home country before coming to Spain to work, study or live. There are various categories of visas, including employees, retired pensioners, investors, employees of multi-national companies (tranferees), students, extended holidays over 90 days, and those engaged in cultural or sporting activities. Non-EU nationals planning to reside permanently in Spain must obtain a 'residence visa' (*visado de residencia*) before entering the country. The visa is stamped in your passport, which must be valid for a minimum of six months.

When in Spain you should always carry your foreign identity card, passport or residence permit (or a copy certified by a Spanish police station). You can be asked to produce your identification papers at any time by the police or other officials, and if you don't have them with you,

you can be fined (though this is unlikely). A residence permit constitutes an identity card for foreigners, which Spaniards must carry by law. Spain is noted for its notoriously lax immigration controls and registration of foreigners, and many people live in Spain unofficially for years without becoming residents or paying taxes or social security.

 **Permit infringements are taken very seriously by the authorities and if you're discovered living illegally in Spain there are severe penalties, including fines and even deportation for flagrant abuses (which will mean being excluded from Spain for a number of years).**

# Visitors

Visitors with a permanent address in Spain, can remain for a maximum of 90 days in succession and a total of six months in a calendar year (the exception is visitors who are touring and staying in different places for short periods, who can remain in Spain for six months in succession). Visitors from EEA countries, North and South America, Andorra, Australia, Brunei, Costa Rica, Croatia, Cyprus, the Czech Republic, Estonia, Gibraltar, Grenada, Hungary, Iceland, Israel, Japan, South Korea, Latvia, Lithuania, Malaysia, Malta, Monaco, New Zealand, Norway, Poland, San Marino, Singapore, Slovakia and Switzerland **don't** need a visa for stays of up to 90 days. All other nationalities require a visa to visit Spain. Spanish immigration officials may require non-EU visitors to produce a return ticket and proof of accommodation, health insurance and financial resources.

Most visitors require a full passport to visit Spain, although EU nationals and nationals of Andorra, Monaco and Switzerland can enter Spain with a national identity card only. A non-EU visitor wishing to remain in Spain longer than 90 days must obtain a special entry visa (*visado especial de entrada*) at a Spanish consulate before coming to Spain. If you're a non-EU national, it isn't possible to enter Spain as a tourist and change your status to that of an employee, student or resident. Usually you must return to your country of residence and apply for a visa, although it's possible to obtain an exemption from the civil governor of the local province.

After 90 days, someone who entered Spain as a visitor can apply for a 90-day extension (*prórroga de estancia/permanencia*), which permits him to remain for another 90-days. An extension should be applied for at a local police station (*comisaría de policía*) with a foreigners' department (*departamento/oficina de extranjeros*) at least two weeks before the first 90-day period has expired. A visitor can also leave Spain briefly before the

90-day period has expired, e.g. by crossing to a neighbouring country, and return again for another 90-days. However, if you wish to prove you've left, you must have your passport stamped. This is legal, although your total stay must **not** exceed six months in any calendar year. After six months you **must** either leave the country or apply for a residence permit, although if you aren't legally employed in Spain or have insufficient financial means, your application will probably be refused.

Anyone who remains in the country for longer than six months in a calendar year without becoming a resident may be liable to a fine of €300 and being excluded from Spain for up to three years (although exclusion is highly unlikely for an EU national with the right to live there). However, the law isn't strictly enforced, particularly for EU nationals, many thousands of whom live illegally more or less permanently in Spain.

## Residence Permit

A foreigner residing in Spain for longer than six months must apply for a residence permit unless you're an EU, EEA or Swiss national coming to Spain to work (either as an employee or self-employed) or study full-time. If you come with the intention of remaining longer than six months (e.g. as an employee, student or a non-employed resident), you must apply for a residence permit within 15 days of your arrival. EU nationals who visit with the intention of finding employment or starting a business normally have up to six months to find a job. Note, however, that if you don't have a regular income or adequate financial resources, your application will be refused. Failure to apply for a residence permit within the specified time is a serious offence and can result in a heavy fine and even deportation.

# WORKING

An increasing number of people are looking to work in Spain, not only as English teachers, and it's becoming common for employees to commute from Spain to northern Europe or for the self-employed to run their businesses via the Internet or by phone.

If there's a possibility that you or any family members may wish to work in Spain, you must ensure that it will be possible before buying a home. If you don't qualify to live and work in Spain by birthright, family relationship or as a national of a European Economic Area (EEA) country, obtaining a work permit (*permiso de trabajo*) may be difficult or even impossible.

> ## IMPORTANT NOTE
> Under new legislation introduced in March 2003, EU, EEA and Swiss nationals who have legal employment (either as an employee or self-employed) no longer require a residence permit in Spain. In order to qualify for this exemption, employees must have a legal contract and pay monthly social security contributions and taxes, and the self-employed must fulfil all legal requirements. Dependants of both employees and the self-employed also no longer require a residence permit.

A non-EEA national who carries out an activity for monetary gain (*fines lucrativos*) in Spain requires a work permit and a residence permit (issued simultaneously for the same duration). A work permit for a non-EEA national is initially valid for one year, after which a two, three or five-year permit may be issued no longer restricting the holder by area, activity, employer or industry. The spouse and children under 21 years of age of a non-EEA work permit holder are also granted limited rights to work in Spain. A work permit isn't required to buy property, make an investment, start a Spanish company or to register a foreign company in Spain, although the person who's responsible for a company's activities must have a work permit.

Spain has a virtual freeze on the employment of non-EEA nationals, which has been strengthened in recent years by the high unemployment rate. Before granting or renewing work permits, certain factors are taken into account, including the level of unemployment in the relevant profession or activity, the number of vacancies in the profession or trade, and whether a reciprocal agreement exists between Spain and the applicant's country of origin. Certain non-EEA nationals are given preference, including those married to Spaniards; people closely related to a Spaniard or to someone who previously held Spanish nationality; nationals of Latin American countries, Andorra, the Philippines, Equatorial Guinea and Portugal; Jews of Spanish origin; the family of a work permit holder and those born and living legally in Spain or who have been resident there for the past five years.

Before moving to Spain to work, you should dispassionately examine your motives and credentials, for example:

- What kind of work can you realistically expect to do there?
- What are your qualifications and experience?
- Are they recognised in Spain?

- How good is your Spanish? Unless your Spanish is fluent, you won't be competing on equal terms with the Spanish. Most Spanish employers aren't interested in employing anyone without, at the very least, an adequate working knowledge of Spanish.
- Are there any jobs in your profession or trade in the area where you wish to live?

The answers to the above and many other questions can be quite disheartening, but it's best to ask them **before** moving, rather than after.

Many people turn to self-employment or start a business to make a living, although this path is strewn with pitfalls for the newcomer. **Most foreigners don't do sufficient homework before moving to Spain.** While hoping for the best, you should plan for the worst case scenario and have a contingency plan and sufficient funds to last until you're established (this also applies to employees). If you're planning to start a business, you must also do battle with the notoriously obstructive bureaucracy (*¡mucha suerte!*). **It's difficult for non-EEA nationals to obtain a residence permit to be self-employed in Spain.**

> **SURVIVAL TIP**
> If you intend to work in Spain, you should employ a *gestor* (see page 107) to apply for permits and licences on your behalf and do your paperwork for you. This will save you time and money in the long run and may prevent you falling foul of the law and incurring severe penalties.

For more information about self-employment and starting a business in Spain, see *Living and Working in Spain* (Survival Books).

# RETIREMENT

Retired and non-active EEA nationals don't require a long-stay visa before moving to Spain, but a residence permit (*residencia*) is necessary and an application should be made within one week of your arrival. Non-EEA nationals require a residence visa (*visado de residencia*) to live in Spain for longer than three months and you should make a visa application at your local Spanish Consulate well before your planned move. All non-employed residents must provide proof that they have an adequate income or financial resources to live in Spain without working. The minimum income necessary for EU nationals is roughly equivalent (there's no official figure) to the Spanish statutory minimum wage (*salario mínimo interprofesional*), which was €442.20 per month or €5,306.40 a year in 2003, although the recipient of an EU state pension will qualify.

A new residential visa (*visado de residencia sin finalidad lucrativa*) has been introduced in recent years for 'wealthy' foreigners. Applicants mustn't have a criminal record and must have sufficient funds or income for accommodation, living expenses and health care for their family. Non-EU pensioners need to show proof of an annual income in the form of a pension, in addition to owning a home in Spain. Non-EU nationals who aren't pensioners must be able to show an annual income of US$75,000, and proof of accommodation in Spain.

# LANGUAGE

Spanish (known as Castilian (*castellano*) in Spain) is one of the world's most widely-spoken languages. Note, however, that although all Spaniards speak Castilian, in some areas the regional language dominates and you may find integration into the local community considerably easier if you speak the local language as well as Castilian. As well as Castilian, there are three other official languages: Catalan (*catalán* or *català*), spoken in its pure form in Catalonia and in various dialects in the Balearics and the Comunidad Valenciana; Galician (*gallego* or *galego*), which is spoken by most people in Galicia in the north-west of Spain; and Basque (*euskera*), which is spoken in the Basque lands, although many Basques don't speak it. Note that other areas also have their own dialects (e.g. Asturias) or strong regional accents that may be hard to understand at first; for example, rural Andalusian is notoriously difficult to decipher even for native speakers! Wherever you choose to live, your efforts to speak in Spanish will be appreciated by the locals, who will invariably go out of their way to understand and help you.

## Learning Spanish

If you don't speak Spanish, it's advisable to take evening classes or a language course **before you leave home**, as you will probably be too busy for the first few months after your move when you most need the language. In any case, you should enrol in a course at a local language school as soon as possible after arriving in Spain.

It isn't always **essential** for retired residents and residents who live and work among the expatriate community to learn Spanish, but it certainly makes life easier and less frustrating, and you're unlikely to obtain a job interacting with Spaniards if you don't speak good Spanish. Unfortunately many residents (particularly British retirees) make little effort to learn Spanish beyond the few words necessary to buy the weekly groceries and order a cup of coffee, and live as if they were on a short holiday. Some even assume that everybody, whether Spaniards or other foreigners, speak their national language and don't even bother to ask before launching into their native tongue!

If you're a retiree, you should make an effort to learn at least the rudiments of Spanish so that you can understand your bills, use the telephone, deal with servicemen, and communicate with your local town hall. If you don't learn Spanish, you will be continually frustrated in your communications and will be constantly calling on friends and acquaintances to assist you, or even paying people (such as *gestores* – see page 107) to do jobs you could quite easily do yourself.

 **For anyone living in Spain permanently, learning Spanish shouldn't be seen as an option, but as a necessity. The most important and serious purpose of learning the language is that in an emergency it could save your life or that of a loved one!**

Learning Spanish also helps you to appreciate the Spanish way of life and make the most of your time in Spain, and opens many doors that remain firmly closed to resident 'tourists'.

Although it isn't easy, even the most non-linguistic (and oldest) person can acquire a working knowledge of Spanish. All that's required is a little hard work and some help and perseverance, particularly if you have only English-speaking colleagues and friends. You won't just 'pick it up' (apart from a few words), but must make a real effort to learn. Although learning any language isn't easy, learning basic Spanish is simpler than learning many other languages because it's written phonetically with all letters pronounced. Courses are available in most resort towns and major cities.

## HEALTH

One of the most important aspects of living in Spain (or anywhere else for that matter) is maintaining good health. The quality of health care and health care facilities in Spain is generally good and, at their best, are the equal of any country in Europe. Medical staff are highly trained and major hospitals are equipped with the latest high-tech equipment. Health care costs per head are around average in the EU, although Spain spends a relatively small percentage of its GDP on health (around 8 per cent). However, nursing care and post-hospital assistance are well below what most northern Europeans and North Americans take for granted, and spending on preventive medicine is low. Public and private medicine operate alongside each other and complement one another, although public health facilities are limited in some areas.

Spain has a public health system, providing free or low cost health care to those who contribute to Spanish social security, plus their families and retirees (including those from other EEA countries). If you don't qualify for health care under the public health system, it's essential to have private health insurance – in fact, you won't usually get a residence permit without it. This is often advisable in any case if you can afford it, due to the inadequacy of public health services and long waiting lists for specialist appointments and non-urgent operations in some areas, although reducing waiting lists has been a health service top priority for the last few years and in many areas waiting time has been spectacularly reduced. Visitors should have holiday health insurance (see page 260) if they aren't covered by a reciprocal arrangement.

The Spanish are among the world's healthiest people and have an average life expectancy of nearly 83 for women and 75 for men, the highest in the EU. The incidence of heart disease is among the lowest in the world, a fact partly contributed to their diet (which includes lots of garlic, olive oil and red wine), as is the incidence of cancers. They do, however, have a high incidence of liver problems and other complaints associated with excess alcohol. The infant mortality rate of around five deaths per 1,000 births is still a little high (although this has improved in recent years) and smoking-related ailments and deaths are a serious problem. Smoking is the leading cause of death among adults, directly causing some 56,000 deaths a year (Spain rates second highest after Greece in the number of smokers per capita in Western Europe).

Among expatriates, common health problems include sunburn and sunstroke, stomach and bowel problems (due to the change of diet and more often, water, but they can also be caused by poor hygiene), and various problems caused by excess alcohol, including a high incidence of alcoholism. Other health problems are caused by the high level of airborne pollen in spring (May is the worst month) in many areas which affects asthma and hay fever sufferers, and noise and traffic pollution (particularly in major cities). If you aren't used to Spain's fierce sun, you should limit your exposure and avoid it altogether during the hottest part of the day, wear protective clothing (including a hat) and use a sun block. Too much sun and too little protection will dry your skin and cause premature aging, to say nothing of the risks of skin cancer. Care should also be taken to replace the natural oils lost from too many hours in the sun and the elderly should take particular care not to exert themselves during hot weather.

The climate is therapeutic, particularly for sufferers of rheumatism and arthritis and those who are prone to bronchitis, colds and pneumonia. Spain's slower pace of life (plus the *siesta*) is also beneficial for those who are prone to stress (it's difficult to remain up-tight while lying in the sun), although it takes many foreigners some time to adjust. The climate and lifestyle in any country has a noticeable effect on mental health and people who live in hot climates are generally happier and more relaxed than those who live in cold, wet climates (such as northern Europe). When you've had a surfeit of Spain's good life, a variety of health cures are available at spas and health 'farms'.

Health (and health insurance) is an important issue for anyone retiring to Spain. Many people are ill-prepared for old age and the possibility of health problems. There's a shortage of welfare and home-nursing services for the elderly in Spain, either state or private, and many foreigners who are no longer able to care for themselves are forced to return to their home countries. There are few state residential nursing homes or hospices for the terminally ill, although there are an increasing number of private, purpose-built, retirement developments (see page 142). Spain's provision for handicapped travellers is also poor and wheelchair access to buildings and public transport is well below the average for western Europe.

There are no special health risks in Spain and no immunisations are required. However, it's important to avoid getting ill in August, when it seems that the country's entire medical staff is on holiday (although emergencies are covered). You can safely drink the water, although it sometimes tastes awful and many people prefer bottled water – when not drinking wine and sundry other alcoholic beverages (which aren't only tastier, but may even be beneficial to your health – when consumed in moderation!). *¡Salud!*

# PETS

If you plan to take a pet (*animal de compañía* or *mascota*) to Spain, it's important to check the latest regulations. Ensure that you have the correct papers, not only for Spain, but for all the countries you will pass through. Particular consideration must be given before exporting a pet from a country with strict quarantine regulations, such as the UK. If you need to return prematurely with a pet to a country with strict quarantine laws, even after a few hours or days in Spain, your pet must go into quarantine, e.g. for six months in the UK.

However, in March 2000, the UK introduced a pilot 'Pet Travel Scheme (PETS)' which replaced quarantine for qualifying cats and dogs. Under the scheme, pets must be micro-chipped (they have a microchip inserted in their neck), vaccinated against rabies, undergo a blood test and be issued with a 'health certificate' ('passport'). Note that the PETS certificate sometimes isn't issued until six months after the above have been carried out!

The scheme is restricted to animals imported from rabies-free countries and countries where rabies is under control – 22 European countries plus Bahrain, Canada and the USA. However, the current quarantine law will remain in place for pets coming from Eastern Europe, Africa (including the Spanish enclaves of Ceuta and Melilla), Asia and South America. The new regulations cost pet owners around £200/€300 (for a microchip, rabies vaccination and blood test), plus £60/€90 a year for annual booster vaccinations and around £20/€30 for a border check. Shop around and compare fees from a number of veterinary surgeons. To qualify, pets must travel by sea via Dover, Plymouth or Portsmouth, by train via the Channel Tunnel or via Gatwick or Heathrow airports (only certain carriers are licensed to carry animals). Additional information is available from the Department for Environment, Food and Rural Affairs (DEFRA, formerly MAFF, ☎ UK 020-7904 6000 or 020-7238 6951, ✉ pets.helpline@defra.gsi.gov.uk, 🖳 www.defra.gov.uk/animalh/quarantine/index.htm).

A maximum of two pets may accompany travellers to Spain. A rabies vaccination is usually compulsory, although this **doesn't** apply to accompanied pets (including dogs and cats) coming directly from the UK or for animals under three months old. However, if a rabies vaccination is given, it must be administered not less than one month or more than 12 months prior to export. A rabies vaccination is necessary if pets are transported by road from the UK to Spain via France. Pets over three months old from countries other than the UK must have been vaccinated against rabies not less than one month and not more than one year before being imported. If a pet has no rabies certificate it can be quarantined for 20 days. Two official certificates are also required: one signed and stamped by a vet declaring that the animal has been vaccinated against rabies and the second which is a signed declaration by the owner of the pet stating that the animal has been under his supervision for three months prior to its importation into Spain. Both certificates are in Spanish and English and are valid for **only** 15 days after they've been signed. The certificates can be obtained from Spanish consulates abroad and can also be downloaded from Spanish consulate websites. Some animals require a special import permit from the Spanish Ministry of Agriculture and pets from some countries are subject to customs duty.

British pet owners must contact their Local Animal Health Office to obtain an *Application for a Ministry Export Certificate for Dogs, Cats and Rabies Susceptible Animals* (form EXA1). Contact details are available via the Pet Travel Scheme run by the Department for Environment, Food and

Rural Affairs (DEFRA), Animal Health (International Trade) Area 201, 1A Page Street, London SW1P 4PQ, UK (☎ 0870-241 1710 or 020-7904 6000, ✉ www.defra.gov.uk/animalh/quarantine). The completed form should be sent to DEFRA at the above address. DEFRA will contact the vet you've named on the form and he will perform a health inspection. You will then receive an export health certificate, which must be issued no more than 15 days before your entry into Spain with your pet.

If you're transporting a pet by ship or ferry, you should notify the ferry company. Some companies insist that pets are left in vehicles (if applicable), while others allow pets to be kept in cabins. If your pet is of nervous disposition or unused to travelling, it's best to tranquillise it on a long sea crossing. A pet can also be shipped to Spain by air and animals are permitted to travel to most airports.

If you intend to live permanently in Spain, most vets recommend that you have a dog vaccinated against rabies before arrival. Dogs should also be vaccinated against leptospirosis, parvovirus, hepatitis, distemper and kennel cough, and cats immunised against feline gastro-enteritis and typhus. Note that there are a number of diseases and dangers for pets in Spain that aren't found in most other European countries. These include the fatal Leishmaniasis (also called Mediterranean or sandfly disease), processionary caterpillars, leeches, heartworm, ticks (a tick collar can prevent these), feline leukaemia virus, feline enteritis, rabies and poison (laid to control foxes and rodents). You should also consult a local vet about 'sand fly'; it isn't a fly and has nothing to do with sand, but it can be deadly to your dog in certain areas if you don't take precautions.

Take extra care when walking your dog, as some have died from eating poisoned food such as bread. Obtain advice from a veterinary surgeon (*veterinario*) on arrival about the best way to protect your pets.

Dog owners are required to register their dogs and have them either tattooed with their registration number in an ear or have a microchip inserted in their neck (a painless process, apart from the bill). Registration costs around €15 to €30 and there are fines for owners who don't have their dogs registered. Regardless of whether your dog is micro-chipped, it's advisable to have it fitted with a collar and tag with your name and telephone number on it and the magic word 'reward' (*recompensa*).

In response to several killings and maiming by dogs in Spain, the government introduced extensive legislation for dangerous dogs with strict regulations regarding ownership of such dogs. Under the legislation there are eight breeds defined as 'dangerous': Akita, American Staffordshire Terrier, Dogo Argentino, Fila Brasileiro, Japanese Tosa, Pit Bull, Rottweiler and Staffordshire Bull Terrier. 'Dangerous' breeds also include dogs that have all or most of the following characteristics: a strong and powerful appearance; a strong character; short hair; shoulder height between 50 and 70 cm **and** weight over 20kg (44lb); square and robust head with large jaws; wide and short neck; broad and deep chest; robust fore legs and muscular hind legs. If you're not sure whether your dog has most of these 'monster' characteristics, you should consult your vet. If your dog is 'dangerous' you will need a special licence. In order to obtain a licence (available from local councils) the owner must be aged over 18, have no criminal record, undergo psychological and physical tests and have compulsory third party insurance for €120,000. A 'dangerous' dog must be muzzled in public areas (also in private areas if it isn't securely enclosed) and kept on a lead no longer than two metres.

Dogs (with the exception of guide dogs) are prohibited from entering places where food is manufactured, stored or sold, including restaurants and cafés. They're also barred from sports and cultural events and beaches, although you can walk dogs on some beaches in winter. Note that there may be discrimination against pets when renting accommodation, particularly when it's furnished, and the statutes of community properties can legally prohibit pets. Many hotels accept pets such as cats and dogs, although they aren't usually permitted in restaurants, cafés or food shops (except for guide dogs). Guides to hotels accepting dogs and other animals, *Viajando con Perro* (Seiquer SL) and *Guía Atuim* (Cierto Punto), are available from bookshops. A useful publication for pet owners in Spain is *Caring for Your Pet in Spain* by Erny & Peter Harrison (Santana).

# 2.

# THE BEST PLACE TO LIVE

After having decided to buy a home in Spain, your first tasks will be to choose the region and what sort of home to buy. **If you're unsure about where and what to buy, the best decision is usually to rent for a period.** The secret of successfully buying a home is research, research and more research. You may be fortunate and buy the first property you see without doing any homework and live happily ever after. However, a successful purchase is much more likely if you thoroughly investigate the towns and communities in your chosen area, compare the range and prices of properties and their relative values, and study the procedure for buying property. It's a wise or lucky person who gets his choice absolutely right first time, although there's a much better chance if you do your homework thoroughly.

When choosing a location, take into account its popularity, which will greatly affect prices. Instead of the Costa del Sol, for example, where prices are soaring, why not consider the Costa de la Luz, the coast around Murcia and the Northern Atlantic coast. Bear in mind also the type of buyers in each area: for example, resorts which are popular with German owners (e.g. Denia on the Costa Blanca or Neja on the Costa del Sol) may be cheaper than in resorts where British, Irish or Dutch buyers are prevalent, as the German property market has been relatively weak in the last decade or so.

This chapter is designed principally to help you decide where to buy a home in Spain, as location is the most important aspect of buying a home. The chapter also includes useful information on getting to Spain (a vital consideration when choosing where to buy) and on getting around once you're there. This book's sister publication, *The Best Places to Buy a Home in Spain* by Joanna Styles, contains comprehensive surveys of the most popular regions to buy a home in Spain in addition to a wealth of information about each area's facilities and amenities.

# GEOGRAPHY

Spain, or the Kingdom of Spain (*Reino de España* or *Estado Español*), is the second-largest country in western Europe after France, and is often referred to as 'the old bull hide' (*la piel de toro*) because a map of the country resembles a stretched out bull hide. It covers an area of 492,463km² (190,154mi²) of the Iberian Peninsula or 504,749km² (194.898mi²), including the Balearics and the Canary Islands. The mainland is 805km (500mi) from north to south and 885km (550mi) from east to west. The Balearic Islands off the eastern coast comprise the islands of Majorca, Ibiza, Minorca and Formentera and cover an area of 5,014km² (1,936mi²), while the Canary Islands, situated 97km (60mi) off the west coast of Africa, cover an area of 7,272km² (2,808mi²). Spain also has two North African enclaves, Ceuta and Melilla, which are two separate autonomous regions. They've been held by Spain since the 15th century and are, not surprisingly, claimed by Morocco.

The Pyrenees in the north form a natural barrier between Spain and France and Andorra, while to the west is Portugal. To the north-west is the Bay of Biscay and the province of Galicia, with an Atlantic coast. In the east and south is the Mediterranean. The southern tip of Spain is just 16km (10mi) from Africa across the Straits of Gibraltar (a British territory claimed by Spain and a constant source of friction between the two countries). Spain's mainland coastline totals 2,119km (1,317mi).

The country consists of a vast plain (the *meseta*) surrounded by mountains and is the highest country in Europe after Switzerland, with an average altitude of 650m (2,132ft) above sea level. The vast plateau of the meseta encompasses an area of over 200,000km$^2$ (77,000mi$^2$) at altitudes of between 600m and 1,000m (2,000 to 3,300ft). Mountains hug the coast on three sides with the Cantabrian chain in the north (including the Picos de Europa), the Pénibetic chain in the south (including the Sierra Nevada with the highest peaks in mainland Spain) and a string of lower mountains throughout the regions of Catalonia and Valencia in the east. The highest peak on the peninsula is the *Pico de Mulhacén* in the Sierra Nevada range (3,482m/11,423ft), which is topped by Mount Teide (3,718m/12,198ft) on the Canary island of Tenerife.

Spain's main river is the Ebro, from which the Iberian peninsula gets its name, the only Spanish river flowing into the Mediterranean. Others include the Douro, Guadalquivir, Guadiana, Tagus and Tajo, all of which flow into the Atlantic. Half of Spain's soil is unproductive or barren and some parts of the south-east are almost desert (Spaghetti westerns are made in Almería). At the other extreme, the *huerta* of Valencia and the Guadalquivir valley are extremely fertile and the northern coast of Cantabria, Asturias and Galicia are green and lush, with abundant forests and pasturelands.

Spain is divided into 17 autonomous regions, most of which have genuinely distinct identities, forged in history and proclaimed in local laws, customs and values, although some have been created for political reasons. There's a map of the regions and provinces in **Appendix E** and a map showing major cities and geographical features is on page 6.

# REGIONS

## Andalusia (*Andalucía*)

Andalusia (from *Al Andalus*, the Arabic name for the region) is the second-largest region (after Castile and Leon), covering an area of 87,268km$^2$

(33,694mi$^2$) and contains the provinces of Almería, Cádiz, Córdoba, Granada, Huelva, Jaén, Malaga and Seville. It's Spain's most populated region (pop. 7.35 million), the most southerly and is just 14km/9mi from Africa (across the Straits of Gibraltar), where Spain has two North African enclaves, Ceuta and Melilla (administered by the provinces of Cádiz and Malaga). The historic British colony of Gibraltar guards the Straits of Gibraltar and the entrance to the Mediterranean, the ownership of which is a source of constant friction between Spain and the UK.

Andalusia's major towns include Algeciras, Almería, Antequera, Cádiz (the oldest city in western Europe), Córdoba, Granada, Huelva, Jaén, Jerez, Malaga (birthplace of Picasso and one of Spain's most underrated cities), Ronda (straddling a spectacular gorge) and Seville. Seville (the region's capital) is Spain's fourth-largest city and its only inland port. Host of the 1992 Expo World Fair, it's a fascinating, exciting city with a rich history, where the Alcázar bears witness to the city's eminence during the Moors' occupation of Spain. The region contains many popular coastal resorts including Almuñécar, Benalmádena (with an attractive marina), Estepona, Fuengirola, Malaga, Marbella (the region's most fashionable resort), Nerja (stunning caves), Torre del Mar and Torremolinos. Andalusia is also renowned for its picturesque whitewashed villages (*pueblos blancos*), which include Arcos de la Frontera, Benahavís, Casares, Cómpeta, Frigiliana, Gaucín, Istán, Mijas, Mojácar and Ojén.

Andalusia is Spain's most colourful region and the one that most represents the foreigners' stereotypical image of the 'real' Spain of bullfights, flamenco, gypsies, whitewashed hilltop villages, snow-capped *sierras*, sandy beaches, fiestas, fishing villages, Moorish architecture, horses, guitars and ancient traditions. The region encompasses the Costa del Sol (the sunny coast), Spain's most famous coastline (160km/99mi), which **roughly** equates to the coastline of the province of Malaga, extending from Nerja in the east almost to Gibraltar in the south. In eastern Andalusia the coastal area of the province of Granada is named the Costa Tropical (or Costa de Granada) and the Almería coast is the Costa de Almería. In the west, the Atlantic coast of Cádiz and Huelva provinces (from Tarifa at the southern tip of Spain to the Portuguese border) is called the Costa de la Luz (coast of light), which, along with the Costa de Almería, is the region's most authentic coastline, unspoilt by mass tourism. It's noted for its magnificent dunes, windswept marshes, sleepy villages and delicious seafood.

Despite its despoiled coastline, Andalusia contains a wealth of natural beauty, including 22 nature parks and Europe's largest nature reserve (15,000hectares/ 37,000acres), the Doñona National Park (Coto de Doñana) near Cádiz in the delta of the Guadalquivir River. The park is a stopover between Europe and Africa for millions of migrating bird colonies and is one of the most highly-protected areas in the world. Andalusia also has an abundance of spectacular hiking areas, including the Alpujarras and the Sierra Nevada in Granada, the Sierra de Grazalema, extending from Cádiz to Malaga, and the Serranía de Ronda. The highest peak on the Iberian peninsula is the *Pico de Mulhacén* in the Sierra Nevada range (3,482m/11,423ft). Andalusia has little industry and the main sources of income are tourism and farming, notably olives (it produces 20 per cent of the world's crop), almonds, grapes, vegetables and fruit. The warm fertile Guadalquivir Valley near Cádiz is one of the richest agricultural areas and Almería is noted for its numerous market gardens where early vegetables are grown. A wide variety of wines are produced in the region, including sweet dessert wines in Malaga and Córdoba, dry wines from Montilla, white fruity table wines in Cádiz, and Spain's most famous wine, sherry, which is produced in Jérez.

Andalusia has an abundance of fine beaches and sports facilities such as golf courses (over 60), which has led the Costa del Sol where there are over 30 to being dubbed the 'Costa del Golf', and offers a huge variety of restaurants, bars, entertainment and other attractions. Not surprisingly, it's one of Spain's most popular regions with foreign homebuyers (over half buy there), both for holiday and permanent homes, and it offers the widest choice of homes (from €30,000 to € millions). Although most of the coastline has been spoilt by development and mass tourism (it's the most widely developed coast), there are still a few pretty coastal villages, and inland there's a wealth of charming original villages and unspoilt countryside. Although house prices fell by up to 50 per cent during the recession in the early 1990s, there has been a strong recovery, particularly in popular coastal areas where prices have risen considerably.

Andalusia enjoys an average of 320 days sunshine a year and, with the exception of the Canaries, is the sunniest region, where even in mid-winter the daytime temperature averages around 16C (64F). Due to the low level of industry, atmospheric pollution is among the lowest in Europe. The region has good road (although few motorways) and rail connections, with the Spanish high speed train (*AVE*) running from Madrid to Seville (it will be extended to Malaga by 2005). There are major airports at Malaga and Seville, smaller airports at Almería and Jerez, and those travelling to southern Andalusia can also fly via Gibraltar.

The most popular areas with foreign property buyers in Andalusia are listed below.

## Costa del Sol

The heart of the Costa del Sol (population around 1.3 million) is in the province of Malaga, between Estepona and Nerja, where tourism is highly developed and the area's principal industry (some 10 million tourists visited the Costa del Sol in 2002). The area is also the second most popular with British property buyers after Majorca. The scenery is dramatic, the coastline is ringed by high mountain ranges along most of its length, including the Sierra Bermeja behind Estepona, the Sierra de las Nieves – with peaks rising to 3,000m (9,900ft) – which forms the backdrop to Marbella, and the high mountains of the Axarquía range, which flank much of the eastern Costa del Sol.

Most of the coast is green and lush (mainly thanks to intensive watering), and there are large wooded areas, mostly of pine and cork oaks. The eastern region is a centre for tropical fruit farming, with vast areas planted with avocados, custard apples and mango trees. Intensive 'hothouse' farming is also becoming popular and some areas around the Axarquía are under plastic. The far west of the coast is the least developed part, where there are still large stretches of virgin countryside dotted with cork oaks and cattle. From Estepona eastwards, however, the area becomes ever more built-up, although gardens and green areas provide some relief from the urban sprawl.

The main towns and cities in the area are Estepona, a medium-sized and relatively unspoilt town and probably one of the coast's most 'Spanish' tourist resorts; Marbella and its famous harbour, Puerto Banus, is one of the most fashionable areas and its famed coastal 'golden mile' contains some of the most expensive real estate in Europe; Sotogrande, competing with Marbella for the millionaire's attention, an exclusive estate and marina development of luxury villas, townhouses and apartments, many with their own private moorings on man-made waterways; Fuengirola and Torremolinos, both traditionally package-tour destinations and lively cosmopolitan towns; Benalmadena, one of the fastest growing localities on the coast; Malaga, the Costa del Sol's capital and main service centre, with its excellent amenities and facilities; Nerja, the main service centre for the eastern part of the Costa del Sol, is an attractive small town, which has managed preserve much of its original character. The area is dotted with stunning white villages, some of which such as Benahavís, Casares and Mijas are expensive and you pay a premium for a home, although there are numerous other attractive white villages further inland where property is considerably cheaper.

Advantages of the Costa del Sol include a year-round pleasant climate, excellent communications (Malaga airport offers a comprehensive flight service to numerous destinations in the UK and Europe) and a wide range of leisure activities and facilities. There's also a wide established expatriate community along much of the coast, which makes integration easier. Property prices have risen in the area steadily over the last six years and rose an average of 21 per cent in 2002 alone.

Prices vary tremendously depending on the location – a penthouse apartment costing €200,000 in Malaga city may cost €1m or more on the 'golden mile' – but start at €100,000 for a two bedroom apartment, at €120,000 for a three bedroom apartment and at €250,000 for a small villa. The sky's your limit for large villas, particularly in Sotogrande or on exclusive developments such as La Zagaleta near Marbella.

 **There's talk of extending the railway west from Fuengirola as far as Marbella, perhaps Estepona. Unless it's all built underground (which is unlikely, as it would be costly), this will impinge on many properties along the route.**

### Costa de Almería

The Costa de Almería (population around 500,000) lies in the south-eastern part of Andalusia and is one of contrasts, between busy tourist resorts and starkly beautiful, unspoilt land. It's also one of Spain's wealthiest regions, owing to the large agricultural industry: there are more than 10,000 ha (24,000 acres) of vegetables and flowers under plastic greenhouses. The area includes the national park of Cabo de Gata, a unique marine reserve with beautiful virgin beaches and rocky coves. Inland the landscape is practically uninhabited, comprising desert and sandstone rock formations, the setting for many Wild West movies. Main towns include Almería, a modern city and the main service centre for the region; Aquadulce, Almerimar and Roquetas del Mar are important holiday resorts with marina and holiday apartment blocks and Mojacar is an attractive white village perched in the mountains with a thriving summer resort on the coast. Inland are several villages such as Garrucha, Vícar and Enix set in the lower foothills of the Sierra de Gador.

The Costa de Almería enjoys an excellent climate and unspoilt countryside, which provides many leisure activities. Communications are improving and some flights are available to Almería airport from the UK. The area can be very quiet in the winter months. Property prices have risen in the last few years, but remain cheaper than the Costa del Sol. A two bedroom apartment costs from €65,000 and a villa from €180,000.

### Costa de la Luz

The Costa de la Luz is in south-western Andalusia on the Atlantic stretching from Tarifa, the southern tip of Spain, to the Portuguese border. The area has one of Spain's most 'authentic' coastlines, virtually untouched by mass tourism, although the area is gradually increasing in popularity with foreign property buyers, particularly the British. The Costa de la Luz is noted for its magnificent sand dunes, windswept marshes, sleepy villages and delicious seafood. Main towns in the area include Tarifa, one of the world's top windsurfing destinations; Conil, Chiclana and Zahara de los Atunes, all small towns but rapidly expanding with the demand for new property and Cadiz, one of Spain's great maritime cities with many fine monuments.

Advantages of the Costa de la Luz include a pleasant climate, although strong winds blow most of the year round, and peace and quiet. Communications are generally poor, although limited flights are available to the airports of Jerez and Seville from the UK. Property here is considerably cheaper than the neighbouring Costa del Sol, although prices have risen markedly in the last two years. A two bedroom apartment costs from €100,000 and a villa from €230,000.

**The Alpujarras**

The Las Alpujarras area, north of the Costa del Sol lies in the provinces of Granada and Almería, and has the perpetually snow-capped Sierra Nevada to the north, the dramatic Gador mountains to the east and the Mediterranean to the south. Average altitude is over 1,000m (3,300ft) and the area, one of the most beautiful in Spain, is increasingly popular with foreign property owners in search of the 'real' Spain. The main localities in the area are Lanjarón, famous for its spring water and spa, Orgiva, the 'capital', Albuñol and Berja. Las Alpujarras provide unique surroundings, tranquillity and the locals are renowned for their hospitality. It does, however, have a harsh climate, poor communications and few amenities. Property is generally cheap, although prices are rising, and townhouses cost from €30,000. *Cortijos* in good condition with mains electricity and water start at around €100,000. Ruins are considerably cheaper.

# Aragon (*Aragón*)

Aragon is a landlocked northern region containing the provinces of Huesca, Teruel and Zaragossa (Zaragoza), extending from the central Pyrenees across the valley formed by the Ebro river to the Iberian mountain range. The region consists of three distinct areas roughly corresponding to its three provinces: the Pyrenees (Huesca), the Ebro River Valley (Zaragossa) and the Iberian Mountains (Teruel). Although Aragon is one of Spain's largest regions (47,669km$^2$/18,405mi$^2$), it's also the most sparsely populated (1.2 million) with just 25 people per km$^2$. The most populated areas include the region's capital Zaragossa (pop. 700,000) and the surrounding area and the Ebro valley. Other major towns include Huesca, Jaca and Teruel. Zaragossa is a fine city with a beautiful medieval cathedral and the most magnificent Moorish structure (the Aljaferiá Palace) outside Andalusia. Huesca, in the foothills of the Pyrenees, is noted for its beautiful setting and Teruel has some of the best Mudéjar architecture in Spain. The region also has some of Spain's best-preserved medieval villages including Albarracín, Sos del Rey Católico and Tarazona.

Aragon was an independent kingdom until the 15th century and once ruled the Mediterranean in a union with Catalonia. It's best known through two famous natives, Catherine of Aragón (who fatefully married Henry VIII of England) and Ferdinand of Aragón, whose marriage to Isabella, queen of Castile-León, led to the unification of Spain. Today, it's neglected and largely untouched by tourism and noted for its relaxed pace of life (most people know it only as somewhere to drive through between Barcelona and Madrid). However, it encompasses a wealth of magnificent unspoilt countryside and some of the best mountain scenery in Spain, including the Ordesa National Park which is rich in flora and fauna. The region is mainly agricultural with little industry (centred on Zaragossa) and it produces strong red and good white wines, and is noted for its hearty mountain cuisine and game dishes.

Aragon's climate is a mixture of Continental and Mediterranean with cold winters and hot summers and little rain. It's milder in the central depression and cooler and wetter in the Pyrenees in the north. Heavy snowfalls are common above 1,200m in winter, when there's good skiing in the Pyrenees. Spring and autumn are pleasant and the best time to visit. Aragon has good rail and road connections with Madrid, Barcelona and Bilbao, and the high-speed train (*AVE*) line from Madrid to Zaragossa will open in 2004. There's a small regional airport at Zaragossa and limited flights are available from the UK in Girona in neighbouring Catalonia. Although generally of little interest to foreign homebuyers, it may appeal to skiers, hikers and climbers or anyone with a love of the outdoor life.

## (*Principado de*) Asturias

The region and principality of Asturias (the heir to the Spanish throne is the Prince of Asturias) is situated on the northern coast of Spain on the Cantabrian Sea (Bay of Biscay) and contains just one province of the same name. It's one of the smallest regions (10,565km$^2$/4,079mi$^2$) with a population of 1.06 million. The coastline (290km/180mi) of Asturias and neighbouring Cantabria is known as the Costa Verde (green coast) due to its lush, verdant vegetation. Main towns include Avilés, Gijón (Xixón in the Asturian dialect), the largest port on the Cantabrian coast, and Oviedo, the capital, with a beautiful Gothic cathedral. The coastline of

Asturias is the least spoilt and most beautiful, and is dotted with traditional picturesque fishing ports and villages with beautiful churches. Fertile valleys run along the coast which is noted for its deep bays and golden beaches. The region is most famous for its mountain scenery, notably the Picos de Europa, Spain's first national park (inhabited by brown bears and wolves), with peaks rising to 2,640m (8,660ft). It's one of the world's most spectacular mountain ranges with breathtaking panoramas and is a popular hiking, climbing and winter sports area.

Asturias is one of the most remote and isolated regions, an ancient land where important prehistoric cave paintings have been discovered. It differs markedly from the rest of Spain, particularly in its flora, fauna, customs, houses, food, drink (cider) and people. The region has a long mining (iron ore, coal) tradition in its inland villages and there are iron and steel works in Avilés. However, the region's main industry is farming, notably potatoes, corn, fruit, cattle and pigs. Like the rest of the northern coast, Asturias is one of the wettest regions, although it enjoys hot summers, and spring and autumn are generally mild. The region has poor communications with the rest of Spain, although there are modern motorways between the region's main towns and Leon to the south, and trains run along the coast between Santander and Oviedo. A year-round ferry service runs from Plymouth to Santander and there are flights from several UK airports to Bilbao. The region has traditionally been of little interest to foreign homebuyers, although this is gradually changing, particularly among the British and Dutch. Property prices start at around €50,000 for an apartment and at €60,000 for a country house with land.

## Balearics (*Islas Balearics*)

The Balearic Islands (5,015km$^2$/1,936mi$^2$) in the Mediterranean are both a region and a province, and consist of the islands of Ibiza, Majorca (Mallorca), Minorca (Menorca), Formentera and Cabrera (plus several other tiny islands). The islands have a fascinating chequered history, including colonisation by Carthaginians, Romans, Vandals, Byzantines, Vikings, Normans, Charlemagne, Moors, Britain (Minorca), France and Catalonia, until being integrated into a unified Spain in the 15th century. The Balearics are Spain's foremost tourist region accounting for over 40 per cent of overnight stays in Spain and some nine million visitors a year. They differ considerably in character, although they all have excellent clean beaches and exhibit a stark contrast between their bustling coastlines with large towns, and tranquil inland villages and hills. The three main islands are all popular with foreign property buyers, particularly British and German.

Until the 1960s agriculture was the main industry, when tourism began luring people away from the land, and today there's little agriculture left and most food is imported from the mainland. The islands have a Mediterranean climate with mild winters and hot summers, tempered by cool sea breezes. Annual sunshine is similar to the Levante (Valencia), while annual rainfall is higher at between 450 and 650mm (18 to 26in). The islands suffer from a perennial shortage of water, which is mostly extracted from deep wells and is expensive. Spanish (Castillian) is widely spoken, although the local language is a dialect of Catalan which varies from island to island, e.g. *Mallorquin* (Mallorca), *Menorquin* (Minorca) and *Ibizenco* (Ibiza). All three are similar in vocabulary with many words having their origin in Arabic, French, Italian, Latin and Portuguese.

## Majorca (*Mallorca*)

Majorca, situated 150km (93mi) off the mainland, is the largest island (3,640km$^2$/1,405mi$^2$), 95km (60mi) wide at its widest point. A rugged mountain range (Sierra de Tramontana) covers 20 per cent of the island, extending for 100km (62mi) along the north-western coast from Isla Dragonara to Cabo Formentor, with seven peaks over 1,000m (3,280ft), the highest of which is Puig Mayor (1,445m/4,750ft). In contrast to parts of the over-developed coastline, the rugged interior is empty and peaceful and completely unspoilt. Over half the island's population of 660,000 live in Palma de Mallorca (pop. 325,000), the capital of the Balearics and an attractive town with many architectural treasures, including a splendid cathedral. Majorca has a wealth of resort towns, the most popular of which are situated on Palma Bay (*Bahía de Palma*). However, most of these (such as El Arenal, Magaluf and Palma Nova) are prime examples of the worst kind of 1960s over-development, with a plethora of ugly high-rise buildings.

In stark contrast to Palma Bay the mountainous north-west coast is still relatively undeveloped and the east coast is also mostly unspoilt with many isolated beaches and coves (only some 10 per cent of the coastline has been sacrificed to tourism). Popular east coast resorts include Cala Bona, Cala Figuera, Cala Millor, Cala d'Or and Porto Cristo. There are also many attractive residential towns along the north-west coast including Andratz, Camp de Mar, Deya (home of the late British poet Robert Graves), Puerto de Pollensa, Sóller and Valdemosa. In the north on Alcudia Bay (*Bahía de Alcudia*), Alcudia and Ca'n Picafort are picturesque towns. The main inland towns are Inca and Manacor, centre of the island's artificial pearl industry. Railway enthusiasts can enjoy a trip on the vintage (circa 1900) train running from Palma to Sóller (the only other train in the Balearics runs from Palma to Inca), travelling through tunnels and mountains and offering some of the best views on the island. From Sóller an equally ancient tram runs through orange and lemon groves to Puerto de Sóller.

Majorca is the most favoured destination in Spain for British property buyers, although property on the island is among the most expensive in the country with prices for a small two-bedroom apartment starting at €150,000 and at €1 million for a villa. The ugly low-quality, high-rise buildings of the 1960s are now out of favour and new developments consist mainly of low-rise, low-density buildings. Planning laws mean it's now difficult to build on the island. Majorca is home to the international jet set and many of the world's rich and famous have homes there (luxury properties abound). The island has a bustling nightlife and an endless choice of bars, restaurants and night spots, and enjoys a high standard of living, exceeded in Spain only by Madrid and Barcelona. Majorca caters to millions of tourists annually, including some three million Germans (it has been dubbed Munich-on-the-Med) and nearly 3.5 million Britons.

Average temperatures are 10°C (50°F) in winter and 25°C (77°F) in summer, when the heat is moderated by cooling winds from the south. Most rain falls in November and December, when it can be torrential, and it also snows occasionally, although the mountains protect the island from the cold north winds from France. Majorca's San Juan airport (Palma) is the busiest in the whole of Spain and there are frequent ferry services from Alicante, Barcelona and Valencia, and to Ibiza, Mahón and Cabrera, plus Genoa (Italy) and Marseille (France) in summer.

### Minorca (*Menorca*)

Minorca, located 40km (25mi) north-east of Majorca, is 48km (30mi) long and 15km (9mi) wide, with a coastline of 189km (117mi). The island covers an area of 669km² (258mi²) and has a population of around 71,000. The main towns include the capital Mahón (Maó), an attractive town with a fine harbour, and Cuidadela (Ciutadella), the ancient former capital. There are a number of relatively new resorts on the south and east coasts at Binibeca, Cala'n Porter, El Grao, Santo Tomas, Son Bou and Villa Carlos, while popular north coast developments include Cala Morell and Fornells. The main inland towns include Alayor, Ferrerias and Mercadal. Minorca is noted for its rugged coastline, rolling green landscape and sandy beaches, although the general topography is bleak and monotonous. The island has over 120 beaches, most in secluded coves, regarded by many as the best in the Balearics. It has a slow, relaxing pace of life and isn't the place for those who want to rave all night long.

Old houses in Mahón and Ciudadela have an abundance of character and are much prized by foreign buyers. The island's traditional Mediterranean island architecture has an English influence (it was ruled on and off by the British in the 18th century), which can be seen in the Georgian architecture, houses without balconies, sash windows, door knockers and latches. Not surprisingly, Minorca is popular with the British, who have traditionally been the main foreign homebuyers, although in recent years it has become popular with Germans. With the exception of a few eyesores, it's largely unspoilt and there are few high-rise buildings, with low-level, Moorish-style architecture predominating. The less exposed south coast is primarily given over to purpose-built holiday homes and isn't best suited for permanent residents. Property on the island is expensive, although cheaper than both Majorca and Ibiza, and there's generally a shortage of resale property. Prices for a two-bedroom apartment start at €100,000 and at €250,000 for a small villa. As on the other islands, new construction on Minorca is subject to strict regulations. Minorca has a fine summer climate, but is very windy in winter (actually from October to April) when the cold *Tramontana* wind often blows. There is an international airport in Mahón, although flights are greatly reduced in winter and you may have to travel via the mainland airports of Barcelona or Valencia. Minorca has ferry connections with Palma and Barcelona.

## Ibiza (*Eivissa*)

Ibiza is located 83km (52mi) from the mainland and 40km (25mi) south-west of Majorca, covering an area of 572km$^2$ (220mi$^2$) with a coastline of 179km (105mi). The resident population is around 87,000, most of whom live in the capital, Ibiza Town, which enjoys a stunning location and has a well preserved and attractive old walled town (Dalt Vila). Ibiza is a beautiful island, almost Greek in appearance, with fine beaches and a rugged coastline with steep cliffs and barely accessible coves. Inland, there's fine unspoilt countryside with fields of olive, almond and carob trees, melons and vines.

Ibiza is noted for its excellent restaurants and vibrant nightlife and has Europe's biggest and boldest dance clubs (the spiritual home of the Euroraver). The island's visitors and foreign residents are renowned for their excess, and note that the island has a large gay population and nude bathing is commonplace. Ibiza is the most fashionable Balearic island, having been discovered by the international jet set and artists in the early 1960s, since when it has never looked back. Mass tourism followed in the mid-1960s, although the over-development which ran riot in Majorca and on the mainland's *costas* was avoided thanks to strict planning controls.

However, although Ibiza hasn't been ruined by high-rise buildings, like Majorca it's plagued by drunken tourists in summer and certain areas (e.g. San Antonio) are best avoided during the peak summer months.

Property is generally more expensive in Ibiza than in the other Balearic islands and luxurious millionaire's homes abound. The coast between Ibiza Town (pop. around 23,000) and Santa Eulalia is particularly attractive and property is consequently very expensive. The largest towns include Santa Antonio Abad and Santa Eulalia del Rio, both of which are ugly and over-developed. The northern rural half of the island around the villages of San Carlos and San Mateo is the least developed. Popular residential resorts include Cala Longa and Roca Lisa, while Portinatx is an attractive resort. Like Majorca, Ibiza has become increasingly popular with the Germans, who along with the British, are the main property buyers. Two-bedroom apartments cost from €200,000 (from €160,000 in San Antonio) and villas start at €600,000. The island authorities have imposed strict controls and quotas on building, which is now very limited on the island.

The island has good roads, which were rebuilt in the mid-1980s, and the infrastructure and services have been upgraded in the last few decades. It has an international airport handling over four million passengers a year, although flight frequency is much reduced in winter and options are often limited to (expensive) flights via the mainland airports of Barcelona and Valencia. Ibiza is served by ferries from Barcelona, Denia and Valencia on the mainland, and also from Majorca.

**Formentera**

Formentera is just 7km (3.5mi) from Ibiza, although it's a one-hour ferry or 20-minute catamaran trip due to the strong currents (take your seasickness pills). It's the smallest of the inhabited Balearics (14km/9mi long) with an area of 115km$^2$ (44mi$^2$) and a population of just 5,000. The island has some of Spain's longest, whitest and least developed beaches, although inland it's completely barren, with the few remaining crops requiring protection from the strong winter winds. The capital is San Francisco Javier (*Sant Francesc Xavier*) situated in the middle of the island. Due to the island's acute shortage of water, there are very few homes for sale (and almost nowhere to stay) and it's of little interest to foreign homebuyers.

# Basque Lands (*País Vasco*)

The Basque Lands (pop. 2.08 million) cover an area of 7,261km$^2$ (2,800mi2) in the north of Spain bordering the Bay of Biscay. (Note that the Basque Country extends through the region of Navarra and into France.) The region contains the provinces of Alava, Guipuzcoa and Vizcaya. The main towns include Bilbao, San Sebastián (Donostia) and Vitoria (Gasteiz), the region's capital, renowned for its fine old quarter. San Sebastian is a beautiful city with an attractive old town, a sweeping bay, fine beaches (on the Costa Vasca), wide boulevards, and a cosmopolitan and distinguished air. It's a fashionable resort popular with Madrileños and a former favourite of the Spanish aristocracy. In stark contrast to San Sebastian, Bilbao is an ugly industrial city, although it has an interesting old town and is home to the futuristic Guggenheim Art Gallery. Picturesque fishing villages such as Lekeittio and Ondarroa dot the magnificent Basque coast.

The Basque Lands are one of Spain's wealthiest regions and one of its most heavily industrialised (farming, fishing, commerce and tourism are also important) and most densely populated, particularly the province of Guipuzcoa. It's also one of Spain's most beautiful and picturesque regions with Alpine-like country (it has been called 'Switzerland by the sea') bordered by the Pyrenees in the east and the Cantabrian mountains in the west. It's noted for it rugged, dramatic mountain scenery (with wooden chalet-style houses perched precariously on steep slopes), green river valleys, rolling farmland, lively fishing ports, sandy beaches and bustling resorts. Basque cuisine is the finest in Spain and is best sampled in the old quarter of San Sebastian.

The Basques are a fiercely independent people with their own architecture, dress, language, cuisine, customs, sports (e.g. *pelota*) and folklore. Many of Spain's 600,000 Basques live in the neighbouring province of Navarre, with a further 80,000 living in France. The Basque (*euskera* in Basque or *vascuence* in Spanish) language is spoken by around 500,000 inhabitants of the Basque Lands, mostly in rural areas. It's an ancient tongue of unknown origin that first appeared in Latin texts in the 9th century and bears no relation to any other European language and is thought to be the only remaining representative of a pre-Indo-European language. To foreigners and almost anyone but a native speaker it's unfathomable, full of Ks, Xs and Zs and cluttered with other consonants.

The region's climate is varied, experiencing both Atlantic and Continental on the coast, and cold and wet in the mountains. The Basque Lands has excellent communications, with some of the best and most dramatic motorways in Spain, and is well served by rail and air links. Bilbao airport is served by flights from several UK airports. Bilbao also has a twice-weekly ferry service to Portsmouth in the UK. The region is of little interest to most foreign homebuyers, although it's a good location for a summer holiday home for those who cannot bear the more extreme heat in some other regions.

# Canary Islands (*Islas Canarias*)

The Canary Islands (or Canaries) are located in the Atlantic 95km (60mi) off the west coast of Africa and 1,150km (700mi) from the Spanish mainland. They consist of seven inhabited islands (in order of size): Tenerife, Fuerteventura, Gran Canaria, Lanzarote, La Palma, Gomera and Hierro, with a total population of around 1.7 million and a total area of 7,272km² (2,808mi²). The islands are divided into eastern and western administrative provinces: the greener, western province of Santa Cruz de Tenerife includes the islands of Tenerife, La Palma, Gomera and Hierro, while the more arid eastern province of Las Palmas de Gran Canaria embraces Gran Canaria, Fuerteventura and Lanzarote. The islands are volcanic in origin with imposing geological formations and spectacular vegetation, and are among the most dramatic in the world. They were colonised by Spain in the 15th century, prior to which the inhabitants (the *Guanches*) were said to have been living in the 'Stone Age'. The Canaries attract a potpourri of foreign residents, although the Germans and British (the first Caucasian settlers) predominate (the *lingua franca* is English).

The islands enjoy a climate described as eternal spring (the Romans called them the Fortunate Islands) and they're one of the principal, year-round holiday destinations for Europeans (particularly in winter), attracting over seven million visitors a year. The Canaries enjoy mild, warm winters and temperate summers, with daytime temperatures usually between 20°C and 27°C (68°F to 81°F) throughout the year. The inland region of Tenerife experiences around 3,400 annual hours of sunshine, the highest in Spain. Rainfall (mostly between November and February) is low and varies from less than 100mm (4in) a year on Fuerteventura and Lanzarote, to 750mm (30in) in the inland areas of Gran Canaria and Tenerife. The 'best climate in the world' is reportedly found 91m (300ft) above sea level in the south of Gran Canaria (Fuerteventura and Lanzarote are similar). Not surprisingly, the islands have a shortage of natural drinking water, particularly Fuerteventura and Lanzarote, much of which is provided by desalination plants. The main industry is tourism, although there are also major farming and fishing industries. An added attraction of the Canaries is that they aren't incorporated into the EU tax system and enjoy lower taxes than the mainland.

The main islands of Tenerife, Lanzarote and Gran Canaria have international airports and are well served by inexpensive charter flights from the mainland, the UK, Germany and other European countries. Ferry services operate from Cádiz on the mainland to Tenerife, Las Palmas, Lanzarote and Fuerteventura, and there are large sea ports at Las Palmas and Santa Cruz accepting cruise ships. A frequent inter-island ferry and jetfoil service operates throughout the islands.

# Tenerife

Tenerife is the largest and best known of the Canaries (2,053km²/793mi²) with a population of around 700,000 (the islanders are called *Tinerfeños*), including a large number of foreign residents. There's intense rivalry between Tenerife and Gran Canaria, who have fought over the leadership of the islands for centuries. The capital, Santa Cruz de Tenerife, is a smaller, quieter and altogether nicer town than Las Palmas (Gran Canaria), although it isn't much favoured by foreign homeowners. The island is home to the Canaries' university at La Laguna, the island's former capital. Tenerife is split in two by the mountains; the south is arid with sandy beaches, while the north is lush with banana trees and a dramatic, rugged coastline, ancient woodland and black sandy beaches in Taganana in the far north-east. Tenerife is noted for its wealth of natural beauty, rich sub-tropical vegetation, and an extraordinary range of flora and landscape. The Orotava Valley and Las Cañadas National Park are national treasures and include Spain's highest mountain, the snow-capped Pico del Teide (3,718m/12,198ft).

The island is highly developed with many hotels and apartment complexes. The most popular resorts are along the west coast and include Playa de Las Américas, Puerto de la Cruz, Los Gigantes and Los Cristianos, while El Beril, Ouerto Santiago and Playa Paraiso are quieter. The beautiful Oratava valley was the centre of early tourism and remains popular with foreign residents. Tenerife offers a vast range of facilities and everything you could wish for from a popular holiday destination. New roads have vastly improved communications and the island has two airports. There are frequent year-round flights from the UK. The island is popular with holiday homeowners and also has numerous time-share developments. The property market is good and there's a shortage of resale property in the popular southern resort areas. Two-bedroom apartments start at €90,000 and three-bedroom at €120,000.

# Gran Canaria

Gran Canaria with a population of around 745,000 is the third-largest island with an area of 1,532km² (592mi²). The capital, Las Palmas (pop. 350,000), is the largest town in the Canaries (with the largest port in Europe) and is the region's capital and seat of government. It's a bustling cosmopolitan town with an interesting old quarter, a 7km (4mi) coastline and a large foreign population. The north (the most beautiful part of the island) and west coasts are rugged and remote with steep cliffs, while the south is noted for its excellent long beaches such as La Playa del Inglés, Playa Canteras, Playa de San Augustin and Playa de las

Maspalomas, interspersed with traditional fishing villages. Huge modern resorts dominate the south coast, most of which are ugly and lacking in charm (one of the few exceptions is Mogán Port). Inland, there are stark mountains and tranquil valleys cultivated with sugar canes, banana plantations (in the north), papaya and mango trees. The island is also famous for its magnificent sand dunes.

Gran Canaria has a stable property market, although property is more expensive than on the other islands and it's difficult to find a two-bedroom apartment below €125,000. Three-bedroom villas generally start at €400,000.

Gran Canaria has good communications between the airport, the capital and the southern resort areas. The airport has frequent year-round flights to many destinations, particularly Britain and Germany. Ferries from the capital sail to neighbouring islands and mainland Spain (Cadiz).

## Lanzarote

Lanzarote with a population of 65,000 is the fourth-largest island covering an area of 813km² (314mi²). Arrecife, the island's capital and main port, is a rundown, unattractive modern town. The old capital of Teguise 11km (7mi) inland is more interesting and there are also a number of unspoilt inland villages. The island has a unique character and is noted for its whitewashed houses with bright green doors and shutters, profusion of exotic flowers, vineyards, palm trees, camels and fine white beaches (some say that Playa Famara is the best beach in the Canaries). Lanzarote is famous for its spectacular Fire Mountains and their lunar landscapes, stark volcanic rocks and over 300 extinct volcanoes, which form the Timanfaya National Park (covering around a third of the island). Unlike Tenerife and Gran Canaria, Lanzarote isn't overdeveloped, although it has grown hugely in popularity in the last decade and there are a number of massive new coastal developments (timeshare developments abound). Locals are now, however, strongly opposed to new developments and the island's authorities have introduced strict planning regulations. The island's resorts are mostly located in the east of the island and include Arrecife, the Costa Teguise and Playa de los Pocillos, while new developments include El Puerto del Carmen and Playa Blanca (on the southern coast).

The property market is presently booming in Lanzarote and property here is considered a good investment, particularly as it's likely that construction will severely limited in the future leading to a shortage of resale properties. A two-bedroom apartment in a resort area costs from €105,000 and a small three-bedroom villa from €300,000.

Lanzarote has good communications and there are year-round flights from its airport (one of Spain's busiest) to several UK destinations. Frequent ferries connect the island with the other Canary islands.

## Fuerteventura

Fuerteventura has a population of 54,000 and is the second-largest island after Tenerife, covering an area of 1,688km$^2$ (652mi$^2$). Puerto del Rosario, the island's capital and major port, has a lively fishing industry and is home to the Spanish foreign legion. The island is tranquil and unspoilt with long white sandy beaches (the best in the Canaries, some say the world), and is noted for its excellent fishing, windmills, camels, surfing and windsurfing. The island has almost no rainfall and little vegetation, and its arid terrain is reminiscent of the desert landscape of north-west Africa with its Sahara-like sand dunes. Most resorts are situated along the 25km (16mi) of southern beaches south of the airport, although Corralejo in the north (a fishing port with superb beaches) is becoming a popular resort. Fuerteventura is virtually undiscovered by the tourist hordes and is an ideal spot for a relaxing holiday away from it all. Communications are reasonable, although out of season the frequency of flights is greatly reduced and except for the capital and resort areas, roads are poor. There's a ferry service between the capital and Gran Canaria.

The property market on the island is currently booming and growing by some 20 per cent a year with a corresponding rise in prices, although property on Fuerteventura is still cheaper than Tenerife and Gran Canaria. Prices for a two-bedroom apartment start at €100,000 and for a villa with a small garden at around €200,000. Unlike the other islands, Fuerteventura has a wide choice of building plots available.

## La Palma

La Palma is the most westerly island and with a population of around 79,000 it is the fifth largest island. It is 20 minutes by air from Tenerife and covers an area of 728km$^2$ (281mi$^2$). The capital is Santa Cruz de la Palma, an attractive, unspoilt town which is noted for its colonial architecture. La Palma is the greenest of the islands with the most varied landscape and is renowned for its majestic mountains (reaching 2,426m/7,959ft at Roque de los Muchachos, site of one of Europe's most important observatories); lush woodlands; terraced hillsides (where crops are grown); beautiful coastline and its huge volcanic crater (one of the world's largest at 9km/5.5mi in diameter), the Caldera de Taburiente, which is a national park. La Palma was a latecomer to package tourism due to its thriving, self-supporting agricultural industry. The island has a small airport with flights to Tenerife, Gran Canaria, Madrid and some German destinations, but none directly to the UK, although connecting flights are available. Seats are in short supply and early booking is advisable. Ferries run from La Palma to Tenerife (7 hours) and Gran Canaria.

## Gomera

Gomera has a population of 16,000 and is the second-smallest island in the Canaries covering an area of 535km$^2$ (207mi$^2$). The capital, San Sebastian, is where Christopher Columbus set sail from on his voyage to discover America in 1492. The island is almost totally unspoilt with stunning valleys and mountains reaching 1,487m (4,879ft) on Mount Garajonay (Garajonay National Park). It's noted for its steep cliffs, extraordinary rock formations, lush valleys, litchen-covered rain forests, terraces, date palms, fertile red soil and the natives' strange whistling language used to communicate over long distances. It's becoming more popular with foreign residents looking for a quieter life than is available on Tenerife. Gomera's airport was completed in 1999, although it's very small and only offers flights to Tenerife (Los Rodeos) and Gran Canaria. The island can also be reached by ferry from Tenerife, La Palma and El Hierro.

## El Hierro

El Hierro is the smallest of the inhabited islands with around 7,000 inhabitants (and once the farthest westerly point known to man) with an area of 278km$^2$ (107mi$^2$). The main town is Valverder, the only Canary island capital that's situated inland, while the island's beaches are located along the southern, inaccessible coastline (*El Julan*). Its dramatic landscape is wild and remote, containing a massive crater, and the island is almost totally undeveloped and rarely visited by tourists. Cattle and livestock farming are the mainstays of the local economy and the island produces wine (considered the best in the islands). El Hierro has a small airport offering a few weekly flights to Tenerife and Gran Canaria only. There's a daily ferry service between the island and Tenerife.

The property market on all three islands has grown in recent years, although resale property is in short supply and new construction is very limited. Prices have risen and are expected to do so for the immediate future, and are higher on La Palma. A two-bedroom apartment costs from €80,000 (€110,000 on La Palma) and a country property with a large plot costs from €200,000.

# Cantabria

Like its neighbour Asturias, Cantabria, once part of the Castile and Leon region, is situated on the northern green coast (Costa Verde) on the Cantabrian Sea (Bay of Biscay) and contains just one province: Santander. The region covers an area of 5,289km$^2$ (2,042mi$^2$) with some 535,000 inhabitants. The Cantabrian mountain range, which divides the region from the more arid landscapes of Castile and Leon, gave rise to the region's colloquial name, *La Montaña* (the mountain). The region's main towns include Comillas, Laredo (an ancient port and Cantabria's biggest resort), Santander (the region's capital) and Santillana del Mar. Santander is an important port and a fine town, situated on a lovely bay boasting a number of excellent beaches such as El Sardinero. The coast has a number of popular summer resorts, including Laredo, where the population of 10,000 increases ten-fold in August, drawn by the beautiful Salvé Beach. The region also contains a wealth of pretty villages such as Comillas, Los Tojos and Santillana del Mar. Cantabria is a stunning unspoilt region noted for its dramatic mountains that fall to the sea, lush countryside and meadows, fine sandy beaches, picturesque fishing villages, historical inland villages, and typical stone and slate-roofed houses. The region's main industry is dairy farming and food production.

Santander has a regular ferry service to Plymouth and good rail connections, and the region's road connections have improved greatly in recent years due to the completion of the Cantabrian Highway in the region. If you're travelling south from Santander it's quicker (although more expensive) to take the toll motorway (A67/A68/A1) via Bilbao and Miranda de Ebro, rather than the mountainous N623 to Burgos. Bilbao airport is accessible and offers flights to several destinations in the UK. The region is of little interest to most foreign homebuyers, although it may appeal to hikers and climbers and those seeking tranquillity, and in recent years many Britons and Dutch have shown an interest in the area. Property is generally inexpensive (with the exception of Santander where property is among the most expensive in Spain).

# Castile-La Mancha (*Castilla-La Mancha*)

Castile-La Mancha (New Castile) is situated in central Spain and contains the provinces of Albacete, Cuenca, Ciudad Real, Guadalajara and Toledo. Castile-La Mancha and Castile and León historically comprised the ancient kingdom of Spain (Castile), occupying most of the central plain from the Cantabrian Mountains in the north to the Sierra Morena chain in the south (north of Córdoba). The area was divided into two autonomous regions in 1978. Castile-La Mancha contains 10 per cent of Spain's landmass (79,226km²/30,589mi²) with just 4 per cent of its population (1.76 million). Its main towns include Albacete, Cuenca (famous for its 'hanging houses'), Ciudad Real (the traditional capital of La Mancha), Guadalajara and Toledo (the former capital of Spain and one of its most striking and historic cities).

Castile-La Mancha encompasses the vast tableland of the southern *meseta* and consists mainly of flat plains of cereal fields, saffron, olives and vines, surrounded by mountains. It contains Spain's largest wine-growing region, where low-priced wines such as Valdepeñas are produced and is famous for its cheese (*queso manchego*). The region has a Continental climate with long cold winters and short hot summers and low rainfall. It's mainly agricultural with little industry and the rural exodus in the last 50 years has left many areas abandoned and desolate, particularly in the central mountain chain. Castile-La Mancha is of little interest to foreign homebuyers.

## Castile & Leon (*Castilla y León*)

The region of Castile and Leon (Old Castile) is the largest in Spain (94,147km²/36,350mi²) encompassing one-fifth of Spain's northern *meseta*. Despite its vast area, the region is one of the least populated in Spain with a total population of just 2.5 million and a population density of 27 people per km², one of the lowest in Spain. Castile and Leon occupies the northern half of the old Kingdom of Castile, containing the provinces of Avila, Burgos, León, Palencia, Salamanca, Segovia, Soria, Valladolid and Zamora, which are also the names of the region's principal towns (Valladolid is the region's capital). It's a region with a rich historical and architectural heritage, noted for its majestic castles and magnificent, perfectly-preserved towns and cities. Castile and Leon's most famous towns include Avila (one of the best-preserved medieval towns in Spain with imposing city walls); Burgos (the birthplace of El Cid); Salamanca (a majestic, welcoming city with an ancient university, dubbed the city of gold after its golden sandstone) and Segovia with its incomparable Roman aqueduct. Like Castile-La Mancha, Castile and Leon's rural areas have suffered greatly from depopulation (many villages have a frontier feeling) as the young have left to seek work in the cities.

The region consists almost entirely of the Duero basin, a seemingly endless limestone plain surrounded by mountains, and is noted for its wide valleys, rocky pinnacles, gentle rolling hills and vast plateau. It also takes in the Sierra de Gredos, a spectacular unspoilt area that has hardly changed in centuries. It's mainly an agricultural region where grain crops dominate (it's the bread basket of Spain), with some livestock and vegetables, although it also has some important industries, including mines and nuclear power stations. The Ribera de Duero area (on the banks of the Duero river) in Burgos province reputedly produces the best red wines in Spain (they're certainly some of the most expensive) and among the best in the world. Castile and Leon has a Continental climate with long cold winters and short hot summers with low rainfall (the climate has been described as nine months of winter and three of hell). The region is of little interest to foreign homebuyers.

## Catalonia (*Cataluña*)

Catalonia (pop. 6.34 million) is situated in the extreme north-east of Spain bordering France and Andorra. It encompasses the provinces of Barcelona, Girona, Lleida and Tarragona. The region's main towns include Barcelona (Spain's second-largest city and the region's capital), Girona (with its stunning medieval centre), Lleida and Tarragona, which was the capital (*Tarraco*) of Roman Spain. Barcelona (host to the 1992 Olympic Games) is one of the world's great cities (pop. 1.5 million) and an important port. It's a beautiful, cultured, fascinating city with a wealth of outstanding architecture, both modern (e.g. Antonio Gaudí) and ancient. It's also famous for its cuisine, nightlife, shopping and culture, and is considered by many to be Spain's most exciting city. An added attraction in recent years has been the creation of the vast Port Aventura theme park in Tarragona, one of the largest in Europe.

Catalonia covers an area of 31,930km$^2$ (12,328mi$^2$) and its varied relief produces a profusion of diverse and beautiful landscapes, from the green, wooded mountainous north (where the Pyrenees reach 3,000m/9,800ft) to the rocky Costa Brava (the rugged coast) with its many beautiful bays and inlets. The coastline in Catalonia is particularly attractive and unspoilt on the Costa Brava in the province of Girona, where the mountains fall to the sea forming cliffs (and leaving little room for urban sprawl). South of Blanes, the coast becomes flat and straight only to rise again south of Castelldefells and flatten out towards Tarragona on the Costa Dorada (golden coast) as far as the Ebro delta.

Catalonia is Spain's industrial powerhouse, producing some 20 per cent of its GDP, and one of Europe's most important industrial regions. Some 85 per cent of companies are located in Barcelona, which is also home to half of the foreign multi-national companies in Spain. The region is also famous for its wine (Penedes is the most prestigious wine-growing area), particularly *cava*, Spain's celebrated sparking wine. Catalonia is Spain's most nationalistic region, seeing itself as a country within Spain rather than a mere region. It has its own language, Catalan (*Catalán*), spoken by some 6.5 million people in Catalonia, the Balearics, the principality of Andorra and parts of the French Pyrenees. It's by far the predominant language in Catalonia and is particularly noticeable in schools and universities, where all lessons are conducted in Catalan. Although more people speak Castillian fluently than Catalan, many Catalonians are reluctant to speak to anyone but foreigners in Castillian.

Catalonia has relatively mild winters but is also quite humid, with 500 to 800mm (20 to 31in) of rain and between 2,450 and 2,650 hours of sunshine a year. Summers are pleasant without very high temperatures and winters are mild in coastal areas, although they're harsh inland, particularly in the northern mountainous areas. The region has excellent communications with the rest of Spain and Europe, including many modern (toll) motorways, good rail services (to be connected to Madrid by 2004 and northern Europe by high-speed trains by 2007), and international airports in Barcelona and Girona, both of which have flights from the UK. Like Madrid, Barcelona also has an underground railway (*metro*) system.

Property prices vary enormously depending on the area and are naturally at their highest in Barcelona, although even here there are huge variations depending on the district. A luxury apartment on the fashionable La Rambla, Barcelona's most famous street, will set you back over €600,000, while a reasonable apartment (50 to 100m²) in the port district of the old city (*Ciutat Vella*) can be purchased for under €150,000. Prices have risen steadily over recent years and rose by 19 per cent in 2002 alone and land prices at an average of €2,500 per m² are now on a par with those in Madrid. Girona is reportedly one of the best places to live in the whole of Spain and frequently tops the annual 'Quality of Life' index carried out by La Caixa savings bank. Catalonia, particularly its two coasts (see below) will appeal to those seeking a home with close proximity to both sea and mountains (e.g. the ski resorts in the Spanish Pyrenees and Andorra), although it isn't the best region for those seeking year-round sunshine.

## Costa Brava

The Costa Brava (where package tourism started in the 1950s) runs along the north-east coast from the frontier town of Le Perthus to Blanes and contains a curious mixture of long stretches of wild, rugged coastline, sprawling holidays resorts (e.g. Blanes, Lloret de Mar and Tossa) and picturesque fishing villages (such as Tamariu, Sa Tuna, Aigua Blava and Sa Riera). The Dalí Museum (*Museu Dalí*) in Figueres (birthplace of the artist), housed in a building as surreal as the exhibits within, is the most visited museum in Spain after the Prado (Madrid). The Costa Brava is one of Spain's top tourist destinations and is growing in popularity annually with both foreign and Spanish visitors.

The Costa Brava has good communications and is served by four airports, Montpelier and Perpignan (both in France), Girona and Barcelona, all of which have charter flights to and from the UK. Road communications are excellent, although road access to more remote parts of the coast is often poor and the journey time long. The property market is currently buoyant in the area, which is one of the few places on the Spanish coast where you can still buy a bargain, although increased interest in the area from Dutch, German and, to a lesser extent, British property buyers means that this won't last! Prices for a two-bedroom apartment start at €60,000 (although front-line beach properties are at least double this price) and at €80,000 for a three-bedroom townhouse. Building plots are widely available in the area.

### Costa Dorada

The Costa Dorada runs along the southern Catalonia coast from Castelldefels (a large commuter town for Barcelona in the north to L'Hospitalet in the south. The landscape is generally flat with long golden beaches (hence the coast's name), some of which are Spain's best. Salou and Sitges are both picturesque resorts with many foreign residents and good amenities and leisure activities. The area isn't as popular as Spain's other coasts and outside July and August, many resorts are very quiet with facilities and amenities closed.

Communications are generally good with two airports, Reus (limited flights) and Barcelona, and a comprehensive road network. The Costa Dorada property market currently offers many bargains, particularly compared to other coasts, although prices have risen somewhat in recent years. Property generally consists of apartments (from €90,000 for two bedrooms) and modern villas (from €180,000). There's little land for sale in the area.

# Extremadura

Extremadura (pop. 1.06 million) covers an area of 41,602km$^2$2 (16,064mi$^2$) in the extreme west of Spain, bordering Portugal and contains the provinces of Badajoz and Cáceres. Main towns include Badajoz, Cáceres, Cuidad Rodrigo, Guadaloupe, Mérida (the capital), Placencia, Trujillo (birthplace of Trujillo) and Zafra. It's the most wild and isolated region, and the poorest, although its remoteness (and the protection afforded by the surrounding mountains) has helped preserve it from invaders and the modern world. Today it's the purest, most Spanish region (the best of 'old' Spain), birthplace of many of the conquistadors (such as Cortés and Pizarro) who explored and conquered South America.

Extremadura is noted for its abundance of stunning wild landscapes, ancient towns virtually untouched by modernity, and authentic country food. It has a rich history and a wealth of historic, unspoilt towns such as Cáceres (ringed by Moorish walls and watchtowers), one of the best preserved towns in Spain, and Mérida, one of the most important cities in Roman Spain with a plethora of well-preserved Roman remains, including a beautiful theatre. Extremadura is one of the most attractive and unspoilt regions where the verdant northern sierras run south into rolling hills, forests and reservoirs, abounding with rare wildlife, wild thyme and eucalyptus. In spring, the Jerte Valley is a sight not to be missed, when a million cherry trees are in blossom.

The main industry is dry (not irrigated) farming such as olives, cork, cotton, tobacco and vines, plus livestock grazing, wheat, fruit and vegetables, food processing and diverse trade with Portugal. It's Spain's main production area for beef and pork (plus sheep farming) and the source of its most prized hams, the celebrated *pata-negra*. Extremadura (which aptly means 'severe extremes') is very hot in summer with little rain and experiences severe winters, when it rains frequently in the mountains and snows in the Sierra Guadalupe and the Peña de Francia. Although neglected by most foreigners (the ability to speak Spanish is a must), it's a fascinating area to visit. The region has poor communications with the rest of Spain, although these are improving (albeit slowly) and is of little interest to foreign homebuyers.

# Galicia

Galicia (pop. 2.7 million) in the extreme north-west of Spain contains the provinces of La Coruña, Lugo, Orense and Pontevedra. The main towns include Corunna (A Coruña, the region's capital), Lugo, Orense (Ourense), Pontevedra, Santiago de Compostela and Vigo (the most important port). Galicia was the original cradle of Christian Spain and was the only region not to be conquered by the Moors. Santiago de Compostela is one of the most important holy places in Christendom (it once rivalled Rome) and has been a place of pilgrimage since the ninth century when the tomb of St. James (Spain's patron saint) was 'discovered'. It contains a wealth of fine and interesting buildings, not least its Romanesque cathedral.

Galicia covers an area of 29,500km² (11,390mi²) and is a land of stunning panoramas, verdant green forests and pasturelands, rugged mountains, and a wild Atlantic coastline (380km/240mi), with landscapes more common to northern Europe than Spain. The coastal area is divided into two sections, distinguished by their deep inlets or estuaries (*rías*). The upper rias (*rías altas*) of Ribadeo and O Barqueiro are wild, while the lower rias (*rías bajas*) of Pontevedra and Vigo are gentler, with the sea embraced by sloping hills. The region is famous for its romantic mists, superstitions and shipwrecked sailors off the aptly named 'Costa de la Muerte' (coast of death), where in late 2002 the oil tanker *Prestige* broke in half and sank covering hundreds of beaches in inches of tar and ruining the livelihoods of thousands of Galicians.

Galicians are a fiercely independent people, descendants of Celtic invaders in 1000 BC, with their own language (*Gallego*), customs (bagpipes, *gaitas*, are a traditional instrument), cuisine, dress and architecture. In the last century, Galicians populated most of Hispano-America, particularly Argentina, and those who return are still called *americanos* (the area is also infamous for its Columbian drug connections). Galicia's most famous son was General Francisco Franco (born in El Ferrol), although he turned his back on the region after he came to power and even banned the use of the local language. Galician (*gallego*) is a mixture of Spanish and Portuguese and is today spoken by some 80 per cent of the population (around 2.2 million people), 40 per cent of whom (mostly in the countryside) speak it exclusively. Like Catalan, Galician is a recognised language and not a dialect, although three dialects are spoken.

The main industries are agriculture and fishing, while timber production and shipbuilding are also important. Some 60 per cent of Spain's huge fishing fleet is based in Galicia, where there's a close relationship between the people and the sea. Galicia is noted for its fine cuisine and the best fish and seafood in Spain (it also makes what many consider to be the best white wines in Spain). The region has a mild and humid climate, with warm summers. However, it's also the wettest region in Spain, particularly in winter, when most rain falls along the northern and western coasts (in contrast the plains are very dry). Average temperatures are around 13°C (55°F) and average rainfall 1000mm (40in). The region has poor communications with the rest of Spain, although these have improved in recent years and it's a fascinating place to visit, but of little interest to foreign homebuyers.

# Community of Madrid (*Comunidad de Madrid*)

Madrid (pop. 5.42 million), situated in the centre of Spain, is a region, province and the capital city of Spain (since the 16th century). It embraces an area of 7,995km² (3,087mi²) and its main towns include Alcalá de Henares, Aranjuez, Getafe and San Lorenzo de Escorial (with its imposing palace-monastery). The city of Madrid (founded by the

Moors) is Europe's highest capital (600m/2,000ft above sea level) and the third-largest city in the European Union (after London and Paris). It's one of Europe's great cities with a wealth of museums (the Prado houses one of the world's best collections) and art galleries, magnificent parks and gardens, striking architecture, lively theatres, fine restaurants and fashionable night-spots.

It's a friendly, free-wheeling, densely-populated city of some 3 million inhabitants (known as *Madrileños*), bursting with art treasures and culinary delights, and has been dubbed the capital of joy and contentment (it never sleeps – a *siesta* is essential for ravers). Madrid stages the most famous bullfighting event in Spain, the fiesta of San Isidro in May, with 23 consecutive days of *corridas*, which take place at the Las Ventas bullring (the largest in Spain seating 25,000). Madrid is also home to Spain's (and one of the world's) most famous football clubs, Real Madrid, although it has been overshadowed in recent years by the success of its arch rival, Barcelona.

Madrid is a sprawling metropolis (with the highest population density in Spain) and its suburbs almost engulf the neighbouring towns of Segovia and El Escorial. It's a major manufacturing centre which includes the production of flour, sugar, wood, chemicals, textiles, iron and steel, and cement, with an important agricultural sector (mainly vegetable and livestock farming). The region has a harsh Continental climate with very cold winters (there's skiing in the nearby Guadarrama mountains) and scorching summers. Located at the geographical centre of Spain, Madrid is the centre of the country's road, rail and air networks and also has an underground railway (*metro*) system. Property prices are the highest and have increased dramatically in recent years after hitting a low during the recession in the early 1990s. Property prices vary greatly depending on the district and a two-bedroom apartment costs from €150,000 to €500,000, and a small house with a garden from €350,000 to over €2.5 million. Property in Madrid is of little interest to foreign homebuyers, except perhaps for those working there.

# Murcia

Murcia (pop. 1.2 million), located in the extreme south-east, is both a region and a province. It's one of the smallest regions covering an area of 11,317km² (4,369mi²) and became an autonomous region only because when the regions were created post-Franco, nobody wanted poor Murcia! Main towns include Cartagena, Lorca (the prettiest town in Murcia) and the capital Murcia, plus a number of coastal resorts, including Aguilas, Mazarrón and Mar Menor. Murcia is a lively Baroque town with a fine cathedral and university, and the site of prominent Carthaginian and

Roman settlements. Cartagena, the region's main port and an important naval base, is an interesting historic town of Roman origin (over 2,000 years old) which was the major city of the Carthaginians in Spain. In general, it's a flat, parched, character-less region with a lot of industry. However, agriculture is the main industry and includes fruit, vegetables (early produce is grown under plastic) and cereals, pig and goat farming, silkworm farms, plus iron and steel works in Cartagena. The region has a Mediterranean climate with mild winters and hot summers, similar to the southern Costa Blanca and Almería. Murcia is served by the international airport at Almería and Murcia airport, although most flights are seasonal charter flights, and the region has poor access by modern standards. There are trains to Alicante, Barcelona, Madrid and Valencia (which also has bus connections). Property prices are low in Murcia due to its relative obscurity and lack of development, although it may suit those seeking somewhere off the beaten track.

### Costa Cálida

The coast of Murcia, known as the Costa Cálida (the warm coast, an indication of the climate), is mostly unattractive, although there are some fine beaches and includes the Mar Menor, the largest salt water lake in Europe with excellent beaches and water sports. The Mar Menor is all but surrounded by residential developments, the main one being La Manga (Spanish for 'the sleeve') Club resort, an exclusive sports and leisure development located a narrow wedge of land between the Mar Menor and the Mediterranean. The area is popular with summer visitors (it can be extremely crowded in July and August) and is increasingly with foreign property buyers attracted to the coast's reasonable prices and improved communications. The San Javier airport has recently increased its flights, particularly to destinations in the UK. Alicante airport is also reasonably near the Mar Menor. The property market in the area is currently booming, reflecting the increased interest by foreign buyers, although in the Mar Menor area there's a short supply of resale property. Prices are rising, although they're considerably cheaper than many other coasts. A two-bedroom apartment costs from €90,000 and a three-bedroom villa on a small plot in La Manga from €220,000.

# Navarre (*Navarra*)

Navarre (pop. around 555,000) is located in the north of Spain, sharing a border with France. It's both a region and a province covering an area of 10,421km² (4,024mi²). Navarre is an ancient medieval kingdom and despite being the battleground of invading armies throughout history, has managed to preserve its own government and identity. Unlike most provinces, it chose to keep its old name rather than use the name of its major city, Pamplona, for the province. Pamplona (pop. 180,000), the region's main town and capital, is immortalised in Ernest Hemingway's book *The Sun Also Rises*. It's a historic university town (named after the Roman general Pompey) with a fine cathedral, although it's most famous for the running of the bulls during the Feast of San Fermín in July. Other important towns include Aoiz, Estella, Tafalla and Tudella.

The Pyrenees extend along the region's northern border, which includes some of the most beautiful mountain scenery in the Pyrenees, notably the Toncal and Salazar Valleys. The main industries of Navarre include dairy and livestock farming, fruit and vegetables, forestry and a few other minor industries. It's also a prominent wine-producing region famous for its rosé wines, widely considered to be the best in the world. The climate is a mixture of Continental and Mediterranean, with cold winters and warm summers. In winter it snows heavily in the mountains in the north, while the south is milder and drier. Spring and autumn are generally pleasant. Navarre has good road and rail connections with the rest of Spain and there's an airport at Pamplona (and San Sebastian is close by). The region is ignored by most foreign homebuyers, although it may appeal to keen hikers, climbers and skiers.

# La Rioja

La Rioja is situated in the north of Spain between the Ebro Valley and the Iberian Mountains and consists of just one province, Logroño. It's the smallest autonomous region in Spain covering an area of 5,034km$^2$ (1,944mi$^2$) with around 275,000 inhabitants. La Rioja lies on the western side of the beautiful Ebro valley (the region takes its name from the River Oja, a tributary of the Ebro) and is mountainous in the north and west and flat elsewhere. Half of all Riojans live in Logroño, the region's capital, a prosperous commercial town. Calahorra is the capital of lower Rioja and the second most important town in Rioja. Rioja has many interesting towns such as the walled town of Santo Domingo de la Calzada, a stop on the ancient pilgrimage route to Santiago de Compostela, and Laguardia, a medieval city ringed by ramparts, towers and fortified gateways.

Rioja is Spain's (and one of Europe's) foremost wine-growing areas, producing world-renowned wines, with some 48,000 hectares of vines (almost 120,000 acres) under cultivation. La Rioja is divided into three sub-zones: Rioja Alta (Upper Rioja), where the best wines are made, Rioja Alavesa (actually situated in Alava province in the Basque Lands), and Rioja Baja (lower Rioja), whose coarser wines are used mostly for blending. Haro, in the upper Rioja, is the principal town of the wine district and is packed with wine bodegas, most of which welcome visitors but generally require advance notice. Apart from wine production, the region's main industry (in lower Rioja) is farming, notably early vegetables such as asparagus, artichokes, peppers and tomatoes, most of which are tinned. The region has a Continental-Mediterranean climate, with cold winters and hot summers, although it varies markedly between the humid mountainous north and the flat southern area. Rioja has good road and rail connections, but no commercial airports. It's of little interest to foreign homebuyers, although it may appeal to wine *aficionados* and gourmets, and those with a love of the outdoor life (it's a popular hiking, climbing, hunting and fishing area).

## Community of Valencia (*Comunidad Valenciano*)

The Community of Valencia (pop. 4.2 million) in the far east contains the provinces of Alicante, Castellón and Valencia, and embraces an area of 23,305km² (8,998mi²). The main towns include Alcoy, Alicante, Castellón, Elche and Valencia (Spain's third-largest city). Valencia is a large industrial and commercial centre with shipyards, textile, chemical, metal and tin industries (it also produces Spain's most famous porcelain, *Lladró*). It's most famous for its fiesta of Saint Joseph in March known as *Las Fallas*, which culminates in a parade and ritual burning of enormous *papier mâché* figures, although the city offers many more attractions such as the new eye-catching avant-garde Arts Palace complete with Europe's largest aquarium. The region has its own language, Valenciano (a dialect of Catalan), and although Spanish is spoken by almost everyone, Valenciano is used in official communications by the regional government and local municipalities.

The region's coastal area includes the renowned Costa Blanca (white coast) bordering the province of Alicante and the Costa del Azahar (orange blossom coast) of Castellón and Valencia, famous for its bountiful citrus harvest. The land along the coast is low-lying and consists of dunes and offshore sand bars which form lagoons, such as the *La Albufera* south of Valencia, a beautiful inland sea that's a haven for over 250 species of birds. A chain of mountains run parallel to the coast, which has large fertile plains and *huertas* (irrigated regions or market gardens). Valencia is famous for its citrus fruit, particularly its oranges, which are grown in the *Huerta de Valencia*, an area irrigated by the Turia River. Table wine is produced in inland areas, which, although palatable enough, isn't among Spain's best. There are salt mines on the coast of Alicante. Tourism is the region's main industry, although farming is important to the local economy and includes fruit, vegetables and rice.

The region has a Mediterranean climate with mild winters and hot summers and enjoys an average of 320 days sunshine a year (between 2,700 to 3,000 hours annually), with summer temperatures often exceeding 30°C (86°F). The climate on the Costa Blanca has been described by the World Health Organisation (WHO) as among the healthiest in the world. The region has excellent communications with the rest of Spain, including modern motorways, main railway lines, and major airports at Alicante and Valencia. There are also ferry services to the Balearics from Alicante, Denia and Valencia.

## Costa Blanca

The Costa Blanca (population 750,000) is one of Spain's most popular coastal resorts among foreigners visitors and residents, and stretches for 100k (63mi) along the east coast, mainly in Alicante province. Geographically, the Costa Blanca has two clearly defined sections. The northern part, known as the Marina Alta and Marina Baja areas, enjoys a dramatic backdrop of high mountains, such as Montgó at Denia and Puig Campana at Benidorm. There are cliffs and sandy coves along the coast, while inland, there are many picturesque villages with panoramic views of the surrounding orange, lemon and almond groves, such as Orbeta, Orba and Tormos and others in the Jalon Valley (a conservation area where housing is strictly controlled). The southern coast, comprises lowlands, with flat salt plains backing long sandy beaches. The main towns and cities in the Marina Alta and Baja areas include Altea, an attractive unspoilt village; Benitachell, an inland village; Calpe, an attractive and lively town home to the symbol of the Costa Blanca, the famous 'Rock of Ifach'; Denia, the capital of Marina Alta with extensive amenities and facilities; Javea is one of the Mediterranean's most attractive sea ports and known as the 'Pearl of the Costa Blanca. The town is home to a huge expatriate community, of whom the majority are British; Moraira; and Benidorm (meaning 'good sleep') is infamous for its ugly, high-rise apartment blocks and hotels, and is a prime example of coastal development at its worst. However, it's a popular resort, both in the summer and winter, when northern Europe's retirees flock there. The city of Alicante is the capital of the Costa Blanca and is a thriving and cosmopolitan city with good amenities and services. South of Alicante is Torrevieja, one of the most popular resorts in the area and one of Spain's fastest growing towns, which has seen massive expansion and construction in recent years.

The Costa Blanca offers a wealth of leisure and sports facilities, including numerous golf courses, although not as many as the Costa del Sol. Advantages of the area include a year-round pleasant climate, good communications (Alicante airport has frequent flights from many destinations in the UK and Europe) and attractive property prices. The area also has a well-established expatriate community (mostly British), which can help integration. The resort property business in Spain started on the Costa Blanca in the mid-1960s, although low-rise buildings are more common than high-rise apartment blocks (Benidorm excepted) and the property market is currently buoyant (prices rose by 21 per cent in 2002 alone) and demand for resale property is high. Property on the Costa Blanca is generally cheaper than on the Costa del Sol, although prices are similar for villas in the north around Altea, Moraira and Javea. A two-bedroom apartment costs from €80,000 and new, detached, bungalow-style villas start at around €250,000, although luxury villas in prime positions cost over €1.6 million.

### Costa del Azahar

The Costa del Azahar (Orange Blossom Coast) lies north of the Costa Blanca and runs from Benicássim in the north to Gandía in the south. The city of Valencia lies in the centre of the coast. The area is famous for its acres of orange groves, whose intoxicating scent is carried for miles in early spring, its long sandy beaches and the Albufera, a vast freshwater marshland home to unique bird-life and Valencia's rice growing industry. Main towns in the area are Gandía, a large town and service centre with a beach resort; Cullera, a family resort; Vinarós; the historic Benicarló; the beautiful town of Peníscola, famous for its perfectly preserved medieval centre perched on a rock over the sea; and Benicássim, the largest resort in the northern part of the coast. The area is popular with German and Spanish visitors and property owners, although Britons are now increasingly interested in the area. The property market is buoyant and there's a good supply of resale property. Prices are cheaper than in the Costa Blanca and start at €60,000 for a two-bedroom apartment and at €175,000 for a villa on a large plot.

The most popular regions among foreigners are described in further detail in this book's sister publication, *The Best Places to Buy a Home in Spain* by Joanna Styles.

# LOCATION

The most important consideration when buying a home is usually its location – or as the old adage goes, the **three** most important points are location, location and location! **This is particularly important if you're buying for investment or plan to let a property.** A property in a reasonable condition in a popular area is likely to be a better investment than an exceptional property in a less attractive location. There's usually no point in buying a dream property in a terrible location. Spain offers almost anything that anyone could want, but you must choose the right property in the right spot.

 **The wrong decision regarding location is one of the main causes of disenchantment among foreigners who have purchased property in Spain.**

Where you buy a property in Spain will depend on a range of factors, including your personal preferences, your financial resources and, not least, whether you plan to work or not. If you have a job in Spain, the location of your home will probably be determined by the proximity to your place of employment. However, if you intend to look for employment or start a business, you must live in an area that allows you the maximum scope. Unless you have good reason to believe otherwise, it would be foolish to rely on finding employment in a particular area. If, on the other hand, you're looking for a holiday or retirement home, the whole of Spain is your oyster. The most popular areas are the *costas*, particularly the Costa del Sol and the Costa Blanca, and the Balearic and Canary islands. When seeking a permanent home, don't be too influenced by where you've spent an enjoyable holiday or two. A town or area that was adequate for a few weeks' holiday may be totally unsuitable for a permanent home, particularly regarding the proximity to shops, medical services, and sports and leisure facilities. If you're looking for a holiday home that you also plan to let then you will need to look in an area attractive to holiday makers and the property should have a pool and be within easy reach of an airport (see **Chapter 9**).

If you have little idea about where you wish to live, read as much as you can about the different regions of Spain (see **Regions** on page 43 and this book's sister publication *The Best Places to Buy a Home in Spain* by Joanna Styles) and spend some time looking around your areas of interest. Note that the climate, lifestyle and cost of living can vary considerably from region to region (and even within a region). Before looking at properties it's important to have a good idea of the type of property you want and the price you wish to pay, and to draw up a short list of your areas or towns of interest. Most importantly make a list of what you want and don't want in a property – if you don't do this you're likely to be overwhelmed by the number of properties to be viewed.

The 'best' area in which to live depends on a range of considerations including the proximity to your place of work, schools, bar, country or town, shops, public transport, bar, coast or inland, entertainment and sports facilities, swimming pool, bar, etc. There are beautiful areas to choose from, most within easy travelling distance of a town or city.

Don't, however, believe the travelling times and distances stated in adverts and quoted by estate agents. According to many developers and agents, everywhere in the south of Spain is handy for Malaga airport and everywhere on the Costa Blanca is a stone's throw from Alicante airport. When looking for a home, bear in mind travelling times and costs to your place of work, shops and schools (and the local bar/restaurant). If you buy a remote country property, the distance to local amenities and services could become a problem, particularly if you plan to retire to Spain. If you live in a remote rural area you will need to be much more self-sufficient than if you live in a town. Don't forget that Spain is a **BIG** country and if you live in a remote rural area you will need to use the car for everything (which will increase your cost of living).

If possible you should visit an area a number of times over a period of a few weeks, both on weekdays and at weekends, in order to get a feel for the neighbourhood (it's often better to walk rather than drive around). A property seen on a balmy summer's day after a delicious lunch and a few glasses of *vino tinto* may not be nearly so attractive on a subsequent visit **without** sunshine and the warm inner glow. If possible, you should also visit an area at different times of the year, e.g. in both summer and winter, as somewhere that's wonderful in summer can be forbidding and inhospitable in winter (or vice versa if you don't like extreme heat). If you're planning to buy a winter holiday home, you should view it in the summer, as snow can hide a multitude of sins! In any case, you should view a property a number of times before deciding to buy it. If you're unfamiliar with an area, most experts recommend that you rent for a period before deciding to buy (see **Renting Before Buying** on page 112). This is particularly important if you're planning to buy a permanent or retirement home in an unfamiliar area. Many people change their minds after a period and it isn't unusual for buyers to move once or twice before settling down permanently.

If you will be working in Spain, obtain a map of the area and decide the maximum distance you will consider travelling to work, e.g. by drawing a circle with your work place in the middle. Obtain a large scale map of the area and mark the places that you've seen, at the same time making a list of the plus and minus points of each property. If you use an estate agent, he will usually drive you around and you can then return later to the properties that you like best at your leisure (providing that you've marked them on your map!). If you're looking at properties at your leisure in the Spanish countryside, it's sensible to take a mobile phone with you in case you get lost! Note that agents may be reluctant to give you the keys to visit a property on your own.

There are many points to consider regarding the location of a home, which can roughly be divided into the local vicinity, i.e. the immediate surroundings and neighbourhood, and the general area or region. Take into account the present and future needs of all members of your family.

## Accessibility

Is the proximity to public transport, e.g. an international airport, port or railway station, or access to a motorway important? Don't believe all you're told about the distance or travelling times to the nearest airport, railway station, motorway junction, beach or town, but check yourself.

 **Although it isn't so important if you're buying a permanent home in Spain and planning to stay put, one of the major considerations when buying a holiday home is communications (e.g. air links) with your home country.**

If you're buying a home with a view to retiring, check the local public transport as you may not always be able (or wish) to drive. There's little point in choosing an isolated spot or somewhere with a limited public transport system, when in a few years' time you may have to rely on local bus, taxi or train services to get about. You should also consider the terrain of your chosen home, as a location with lots of hills or steps could become an insurmountable problem if you have mobility problems or become disabled. A home in a town is usually a much better proposition for retirees than a country home. See also **Location** on page 73.

## Amenities

What local health and social services are provided? How far is the nearest hospital with an emergency department? Are there English-speaking doctors and dentists and private clinics or hospitals in the area?

What shopping facilities are provided in the neighbourhood? How far is it to the nearest sizeable town with good shopping facilities, e.g. a supermarket? How would you get there if your car was out of action? Note that many rural villages are dying and have few shops or facilities so they aren't usually a good choice for a retirement home.

## Climate

Do you want or need winter **and** summer sunshine? If you want it to be really warm all year-round, then the only choice is the Canaries. Note that although the Costa Blanca and Costa del Sol are mild and pleasant in winter with daytime temperatures around 15 to 20°C (60 to 68°F), this may seem quite cool if you're accustomed to the blazing heat of high summer. In winter, it's too cold for sea bathing anywhere except the

Canaries. Bear in mind both the winter and summer climate, position of the sun, average daily sunshine, plus the rainfall and wind conditions (see **Climate** on page 20). The orientation or aspect of a building is vital and if you want morning or afternoon sun (or both) you must ensure that balconies, terraces and gardens are facing south (some people take a compass when house hunting). Bear in mind that properties facing north will receive practically no sun at all except in the height of summer.

## Community

Do you wish to live in an area with many other expatriates from your home country or as far away from them as possible (practically impossible in many areas)? If you wish to integrate with the local community, avoid the foreign 'ghettos' and choose a Spanish village or an area or development with mainly local inhabitants. However, unless you speak fluent Spanish or intend to learn it, you should think twice before buying a property in a village, although residents in rural areas who take the time and trouble to integrate into the local community are invariably warmly welcomed. If you're buying a permanent home, it's important to check on your prospective neighbours, particularly when buying an apartment. For example, are they noisy, sociable or absent for long periods? Do you think you will get on with them? **Good neighbours are invaluable, particularly when buying a second home in a village.**

On the other hand, if you wish to mix only with your compatriots and don't plan to learn Spanish, then living in a predominantly foreign community may be ideal. Note that many developments and towns are inhabited largely by second homeowners and are like ghost towns for most of the year. In these areas many facilities, businesses and shops are closed outside the main tourist season, when even local services such as public transport and postal collections may be severely curtailed.

## Crime

What is the local crime rate? In many resort areas the incidence of housebreaking and burglary is extremely high, which also results in more expensive home insurance. Check the crime rate in the local area, e.g. burglaries, housebreaking, stolen cars and crimes of violence. Is crime increasing or decreasing? Note that professional crooks love isolated houses, particularly those full of expensive furniture and other belongings that they can strip bare at their leisure. You're much less likely to be the victim of thieves if you live in a village, where crime is virtually unknown (strangers stand out like sore thumbs in villages, where their every move is monitored by the local populace).

# Employment

How secure is your job or business and are you likely to move to another area in the near future? Can you find other work in the same area, if necessary? If there's a possibility that you may need to move in a few years' time, you should consider renting or at least buy a property that will be relatively easy to sell and recoup the cost.

If necessary, make sure that a property has a telephone line installed (or that you can quickly get one installed) and that you can get access to the Internet and ADSL (broadband) if required (see page 297). This is particularly important if you will be working from home or running a business. You may also wish to check whether mobile phone reception is possible in the local area (reception is poor in some areas).

# Garden

If you're planning to buy a country property with a large garden or plot of land, bear in mind the high cost and amount of work involved in its upkeep. If it's to be a second home, who will look after the house and garden when you're away? Do you want to spend your holidays mowing the lawn and cutting back the undergrowth? It's best to choose low-maintenance gardens with little lawn, plenty of paved areas and drought-loving plants. Do you want a home with a lot of outbuildings? What are you going to do with them? Can you afford to convert them into extra rooms or guest accommodation?

# Local Council

Is the local municipal council well run? Unfortunately many are profligate and simply use any extra income to hire a few more of their cronies or spend it on grandiose schemes. What are the views of other residents? If the municipality is efficiently run you can usually rely on good local social and sports services and other facilities. In areas where there are many foreign residents, the town hall may have a foreign residents' department (*departamento de extranjeros*).

# Natural Phenomena

Check whether an area is particularly prone to natural disasters such as floods, storms or forest fires. If a property is located near a waterway, it may be expensive to insure against floods (or flash floods), which are a threat in some areas. Note that in areas with little rainfall there may be frequent droughts, severe water restrictions and high water bills.

# Noise

Noise can be a big problem in Spain, the noisiest country in Europe! Although you cannot choose your neighbours, you can at least ensure that a property isn't located next to a busy road, industrial plant, commercial area, building site, discotheque, night club, bar or restaurant. Spanish people generally keep later hours than north Europeans and revelries may continue into the early hours (or even until dawn!). If you like a quiet life, don't buy an apartment in a block where there are lots of Spaniards or properties rented out to short-term holidaymakers, who can be equally noisy, especially during school holidays.

Look out for objectionable neighbouring properties that may be too close to the one you're considering and check whether nearby vacant land has been zoned for commercial activities. In community developments (e.g. apartment blocks) many properties are second homes and are let short-term, which means you may have to tolerate boisterous holidaymakers as neighbours throughout the year (or at least during the summer months). In towns, traffic noise, particularly from motorcycles, can continue all night!

# Parking

If you're planning to buy in a town or city, is there adequate private or free on-street parking for your family and visitors? Is it safe to park in the street? Note that in cities it's important to have secure off-street parking if you value your car.

 **Parking is a huge problem in most cities and large towns, and private garages or parking spaces may be unobtainable or prohibitively expensive. In out-of-town developments there may be inadequate parking for residents and visitors, particularly in summer, so it's advisable to ensure that you have a private garage or a reserved parking space close to your home.**

Traffic congestion is a problem in many towns and resorts, particularly during the high season. Bear in mind also that an apartment or townhouse in a town or community development may be some distance from the nearest road or car park. How do you feel about carrying heavy shopping hundreds of metres to your home and possibly up several flights of stairs? If you're planning to buy an apartment above the ground floor, you may wish to ensure that the building has a lift (that works!).

# Property Market

If you're planning to buy a property mainly for investment (see page 18), you should base your decision regarding the location and type of property on the investment potential, rather than your own preferences. If you plan to let a property (see **Chapter 9**) you will need to ensure that it's in a popular area, preferably with year-round letting potential, with good access to a beach and other facilities. It should have, or have access to, a pool and be within easy travelling distance of an airport (most holidaymakers don't want to travel for more than 30 minutes by car from the airport).

# Schools

Consider your children's present and future schooling? What is the quality of local schools? Are there any bi-lingual or international schools nearby? Note that even if your family has no need or plans to use local schools, the value of a home may be influenced by the quality and location of schools.

# Sports & Leisure Facilities

What's the range and quality of local leisure, sports, community and cultural facilities? What's the proximity to sports facilities such as beaches, golf courses, ski resorts or waterways? Note that properties in or close to ski and coastal resorts are considerably more expensive, although they also have the best letting potential. If you're a keen skier you may want to be close to the Sierra Nevada (Granada) or the Pyrenees, although there are also smaller skiing areas in other regions.

# Tourists

Bear in mind that if you live in a popular tourist area, i.e. almost anywhere on the Mediterranean coast or the islands, you will be inundated with tourists in the summer. They won't only jam the roads and pack the beaches and shops, but even occupy your favourite table at your local bar or restaurant! Bear in mind that while a 'front-line' property on the beach sounds attractive and may be ideal for short holidays, it isn't always the best solution for permanent residents. Many beaches are hopelessly crowded in the peak season, streets may be smelly from restaurants and fast food joints, parking may be impossible, services stretched to breaking point, and the incessant noise may drive you crazy. You may also have to tolerate water shortages, power cuts and sewage problems. Some people prefer to move inland to higher ground, where it's less humid, you're isolated from the noise and can also enjoy excellent views. On the other hand, getting to and from hillside properties is often precarious and the frequently poorly-maintained roads (usually narrow and unguarded) are definitely for sober, confident drivers only.

## Town or Country?

Do you wish to be in a town or do you prefer the country? Inland or by the sea? How about living on an island? Life on an island is more restricted and remote, e.g. you cannot jump into your car and drive to Barcelona or Madrid or 'pop' over the border into Andorra, France, Gibraltar or Portugal. Bear in mind that if you buy a property in the country you will have to tolerate poor public transport, long travelling distances to a town of any size, solitude and remoteness, and the high cost and amount of work involved in the upkeep of a country house and garden. You may find that builders and other professionals are reluctant to travel long-distances to your property. You won't be able to pop along to the local shop for fresh bread, drop into the local bar for a glass of your favourite tipple with the locals, or have a choice of restaurants on your doorstep. In a town or large village, the weekly market will be just around the corner, the doctor and pharmacy close at hand, and if you need help or run into any problems, your neighbours will be near by.

On the other hand, in the country you will be closer to nature, will have more freedom (e.g. to make as much noise as you wish) and possibly complete privacy, e.g. to sunbathe or swim *au naturel*. Living in a remote area in the country will suit those looking for peace and quiet who don't want to involve themselves in the 'hustle and bustle' of town life. If you're after peace and quiet, make sure that there isn't a busy road or railway line nearby or a local church within 'DONGING!' distance. Note, however, that many people who buy a remote country home find that the peace of the countryside palls after a time and they yearn for the more exciting city or coastal night-life. If you've never lived in the country, it's advisable to rent before buying. Note also that while it's cheaper to buy in a remote or unpopular location, it's usually much more difficult to find a buyer when you want to sell.

# GETTING THERE

Although it isn't so important if you're planning to live permanently in Spain and stay put, one of the major considerations when buying a holiday home is the cost of getting to Spain from your home abroad.

How long will it take to get to a home in Spain, taking into account journeys to and from airports, ports and railway stations? How frequent are flights, ferries or trains at the time(s) of year when you plan to travel? Are direct flights or trains available? Is it feasible to travel by car? What is the cost of travel from your home country to the region where you're planning to buy a home? Are off-season discounts or inexpensive charter flights available? Are costs likely to rise or fall in the future?

If a long journey is involved, you should bear in mind that it may take you a day or two to recover. Obviously, the travelling time and cost of travel to a home in Spain will be more important if you're planning to spend many long weekends there, rather than a few long stays each year. Note that you should include the price of getting to and from Spain in your budget when considering a property purchase, particularly if you're planning to make several visits a year. If you plan to let a property, it will be more popular if it's within easy reach of an airport with a range of flights, particularly budget and charter flights, from the UK.

Always allow plenty of time to get to and from airports, ports and railway stations in Spain, particularly when travelling during peak hours, when traffic congestion can be horrendous.

## Airline Services

Most major international airlines provide scheduled services to Madrid and many also fly to Barcelona and other major cities. The Spanish state-owned national airline, Iberia, is Spain's major international carrier. Although it isn't rated as one of the world's best airlines, Iberia has an excellent safety record and its standard of service has improved in recent years. Its fares have also become more competitive, although, like most European carriers, it still makes huge losses.

Nowadays there's a wide range of flights from airports in the UK (and Ireland to a lesser extent) to many airports in Spain, although some regions are less well-served than others (see **Appendix F**). The Costa Blanca, Costa del Sol and the Canaries are the best served with year-round flights from several airlines, while destinations such as the north of Spain (excluding Catalonia) and the Costa de la Luz have fewer flight options. Note that flights to the Balearics (especially Minorca) are greatly reduced in winter and you may need to travel via the mainland, which will increase the cost. Note also that the instability of the airline business means that airlines can (and do) merge or go bankrupt, which often results in a cut-back of services or the disappearance of a route. Budget airlines also frequently change their routes and prices. You therefore shouldn't invest in a property if you need to rely on cheap flights to a local airport (e.g. to Jerez). Bear in mind that it's relatively easy to reach regional airports in Spain via Madrid or Barcelona, but domestic flights (see page 97) are invariably expensive and time consuming.

## Scheduled Flights

Iberia provides good connections to Central and South America and throughout Europe, but few connections to North America (New York and Miami only) and the rest of the world apart from a few cities such as Cairo, Tangier, Tel Aviv and a number of countries in North and West Africa. However, Iberia is a member of the One World alliance along with British Airways, American Airlines, Cathay Pacific and Qantas, among others. This allows them to offer flights to most destinations in the world via other airlines in the alliance at competitive fares. Most transatlantic flights from North America are routed via Madrid. If you're unable to get a direct flight to Spain from North America or Asia, it's usually advisable to fly via London, from where there are inexpensive daily flights to airports throughout Spain. British Airways and its subsidiary, GB Airways, also operate daily flights to the main Spanish airports from several destinations in the UK. Fares on scheduled flights to Spain have fallen in recent years due to increased competition, although they're still high compared with charter fares. Increased competition from airlines such as Air Europa (Spanish owned) on many routes has forced Iberia to reduce its fares, particularly on domestic routes.

## Charter Flights

Inexpensive charter flights to Spain are common from many European countries, particularly the UK and Germany. Around 70 per cent of people visiting Spain from the UK do so on charter aircraft (the UK and Spain are the only two countries in the world with such a high percentage of charter flights). In recent years the number of so-called 'no-frills' budget airlines has also increased greatly and competition is fierce. The cheapest Spanish destinations from the UK are Malaga, Alicante and Palma de Mallorca, with one-way fares from as little as £40 in the low season rising to £150 to £200 in the peak season (mid-June to mid-September). If you're travelling from the UK to the western Costa del Sol or the Costa de la Luz, you can also fly via Gibraltar (fares are similar to flights to Malaga), although you will need to allow extra time to enter and leave Gibraltar where queues for passport and customs checks can be long. Charter flights from New York to Madrid cost around $350. It may be cheaper for North Americans and others travelling on intercontinental flights to fly to London and get a charter flight from there, particularly outside the summer season. Fares from other European cities to Spain are generally more expensive than those from the UK and Ireland (and Germany), and may cost up to 50 per cent more.

Two large charter companies operating from the UK, Britannia and Avro, offer good flight deals to Spain from a wide range of airports in the UK. Avro (☎ UK 0870-458 2841, 🖥 www.avro.com), awarded the UK's Best Seat Only Operator in 2003 by travel agents, provides flights from many UK airports to most resorts in Spain, including the Balearics and Canaries. It also has a limited number of seats on regional flights within Spain. Avro operates an 'Avro Flying Club' scheme targeted at frequent flyers and property owners abroad, whereby members (£19.99 a year) are entitled to 5 per cent off flights booked with Avro as well as discounts on Monarch scheduled flights, car hire and travel insurance. Britannia (☎ UK 0800-000 747, 🖥 www.britanniadirect.com) offers charter flights from many airports in the UK, particularly during the summer when flights are available from smaller airports such as Aberdeen and Exeter. Note, however, that during the winter months Britannia reduces its service considerably. Charter flights are available to most Spanish resorts.

**Budget Airlines**

The introduction of 'no-frills' flights into the Spanish holiday market has been revolutionary and has provided some welcome competition, forcing British Airways and Iberia to reduce their prices. Budget airlines offer several advantages, including Internet and/or telephone booking, ticket-less flights and no seat allocation. Fares are generally lower, although they have risen in recent months and in many cases are no cheaper than scheduled flights (particularly if you're able to take advantage of special offers from British Airways and Iberia, where the price includes a newspaper, drinks and meal!). Budget airlines often advertise very cheap seats, although these are usually limited and involve travelling at unsociable times (e.g. EasyJet has a cheap flight to Malaga that arrives and leaves at around 2am) or at short notice. Flights in high season or on popular routes are generally as expensive as those offered by scheduled airlines, but you can save money by travelling out of high season and avoiding weekends. Note that budget airline advertised prices usually don't include airport taxes, which can be high (e.g. €17.50 from Luton) and you will probably be charged for using a credit card, e.g. €5 to €7. Food and drinks on budget airlines are also expensive.

# Airports

This section contains a survey of Spain's major international flights, plus a few in neighbouring countries convenient for Spain, and lists the UK airports serving them. A table showing the Spanish airports with flights from the UK and Ireland is shown in **Appendix F.**

## Andalusia

**Almería:** Almería at the eastern end of Andalusia has a small airport with a modest number of flights, mainly from the UK and Germany, which has recently been 'discovered' by the budget airlines, who now offer several flights weekly. There's also a limited domestic flight service from the major Spanish airports, although flights are expensive. Almería is served by regular flights from the UK from London-Gatwick (GB Airways) and London-Stansted (Ryanair) airports. Britannia (☎ UK 0800-000 747, 🖥 www.britanniadirect.com) provides seasonal flights to Almería from Birmingham, London-Gatwick and Manchester. Airport Information is available on ☎ 950 213 709. Note that Murcia airport (see page 90) is also an option for the Costa de Almería.

**Faro:** Situated on the Algarve Coast in Portugal, Faro airport is served by a wide range of charter and budget flights and provides good communications to the western Costa de la Luz. Road communications along the Algarve to the province of Huelva are excellent and fast. Note, however, that if you wish to reach the Costa de la Luz east of Doñana National Park from Faro airport, you must make a lengthy detour inland via Seville. Flight information is available on ☎ 289 800 800 and 🖥 www.ana-aeroportos.pt.

**Gibraltar:** Gibraltar airport also serves the Costa del Sol, although there are few flights and they're almost exclusively to and from the UK. Queues to leave Gibraltar are often long and customs checks lengthy. There's no public transport to Gibraltar from the Costa del Sol except taxis. **You may require a visa to enter Spain from Gibraltar.** Gibraltar airport is served by regular flights from the UK from London-Gatwick (GB Airways) and London-Luton (Monarch) airports. Flight information is available on ☎ +350-73026 from abroad or ☎ 956 773 026 from Spain.

**Jerez:** The small Jerez airport, situated just outside Jerez de la Frontera, is convenient for the Costa de la Luzand. However, it offers only a limited number of flights and public transport is poor. Jerez airport is served by regular flights from the UK from London-Gatwick (Britannia) and London-Stansted (Ryanair). Airport information is available on ☎ 956 150 000.

**Malaga:** The region's main airport is Malaga's Pablo Picasso (8km/5mi to the west of Malaga city), the third-busiest in Spain handling some 10 million passengers a year. It's well served by domestic and international flights, particularly from the UK, Germany and Ireland, with between 50 and 100 flights daily. Scheduled flights operate from most major European destinations throughout the year and charter flights are also widely available, although flights from some destinations (such as Edinburgh and Exeter in the UK) are suspended during the winter months. The airport was modernised in the 1990s and is spacious and generally efficient. A new control tower was completed in 2001 and a second terminal is under construction with a second runway planned. Bus and train services link the airport with Malaga and the rest of the Costa del Sol, and taxis and car hire companies are plentiful.

Malaga airport is served by regular flights from the UK and Ireland from Birmingham, Bristol, Cardiff, Dublin, the East Midlands, Edinburgh, Glasgow, Leeds/Bradford, London-Gatwick, London Heathrow, London-Luton, London-Stanstead, Liverpool and Manchester airports. Britannia (☎ UK 0800-000 747, 🖥 www.britannia direct.com) provides seasonal flights to Malaga from Belfast, Birmingham, Bristol, Cardiff, Edinburgh, Glasgow, Humberside, Leeds/Bradford, London-Gatwick, London-Luton, London-Stanstead, Liverpool, Manchester and Newcastle. Flight information is available on ☎ 952 048 804 and 🖥 www.aena.es/aeropuertos/malaga.

**Seville:** The city's San Pablo airport is small but modern, situated 12km/7.5mi from the city centre. Domestic flights are plentiful but international flights are limited and are currently only available from the UK from London-Gatwick (GB Airways) and London-Heathrow (Iberia) airports. Seville has excellent communications by public transport links with the rest of Andalusia and Spain, including high-speed trains (*AVE*) to Madrid. Airport information is available on ☎ 954 449 023.

**Balearics**

The three main islands have airports, which are among the busiest in Europe during the summer months.

**Majorca:** San Juan airport in Majorca (situated 11km/7mi east of Palma) is Spain's second-busiest, handling around 20 million passengers a year. Flights are available from most major European cities, particularly in the UK and Germany, most of which are are charter flights. Flights from mainland Spain are also frequent, the least expensive being from Barcelona and Valencia.

Palma airport is served by regular flights from the UK from Birmingham, Bristol, Cardiff, the East Midlands, Edinburgh, Glasgow, Leeds/Bradford, Liverpool, London-Gatwick, London-Heathrow, London-Luton, London-Stanstead and Manchester airports. Britannia (☎ UK 0800-000 747, 🖥 www.britanniadirect.com) provides seasonal flights to Palma from Aberdeen, Belfast, Birmingham, Bristol, Cardiff, East Midlands, Edinburgh, Exeter, Glasgow, Humberside, Leeds/

Bradford, London-Gatwick, London-Luton, London-Stansted, Liverpool, Manchester, Newcastle and Teeside. Airport information is available on ☎ 971 789 099 and 🖥 www.aena.es/aeropuertos/mallorca.

**Minorca:** Minorca has a small international airport situated just south of the capital, Mahon. There are charter flights from several European capitals, although they're concentrated during the high season, and in winter there are no direct flights from some destinations. Domestic flights to mainland Spain are also available, although fares are high. Mahon airport is served by regular flights from the UK from London-Gatwick (British Airways) and London-Luton (Monarch) airports. Britannia (☎ UK 0800-000 747, 🖥 www.britannia direct.com) offers seasonal flights to Mahon from Belfast, Birmingham, Bristol, East Midlands, Glasgow, Leeds/Bradford, London-Gatwick, London-Luton, London-Stanstead, Liverpool, Manchester, Newcastle and Teeside. Airport information is available on ☎ 971 157 000.

**Ibiza:** Ibiza airport mainly handles charter flights from the UK and Germany, which are greatly reduced in the winter. Flights to mainland Spain are mostly via Barcelona and Valencia, and are expensive. Ibiza airport is served by regular flights from the UK from East Midlands (BMi Baby) and London-Stansted (EasyJet) airports. Britannia (☎ UK 0800-000 747, 🖥 www.britanniadirect.com) provides seasonal flights to Ibiza from Belfast, Birmingham, Bristol, Cardiff, Edinburgh, Exeter, Glasgow, Humberside, Leeds/Bradford, London-Gatwick, London-Luton, London-Stanstead, Liverpool, Manchester, Newcastle and Teeside. Airport information is available on ☎ 971 809 000.

## Canary Islands

All the inhabited islands have airports, but the smaller islands of El Hierro, La Gomera and La Palma are served by tiny airports with virtually no international flights and only a limited number of flights from Gran Canaria or Tenerife. To date no budget airlines fly to the Canaries, although numerous charter flights are available.

**Tenerife:** Tenerife has two airports, Reina Sofía in the south near the Costa del Silencio and Los Rodeos in the north near the capital, which has recently been refurbished and has a new terminal. Los Rodeos handles mainly domestic and inter-island flights, while Reina Sofía handles most international traffic with an abundance of charter flights, mostly from the UK and Germany. A second runway is planned. Public transport to the capital and resort areas is generally good, and taxis and hire cars are plentiful.

Reina Sofía airport is served by regular flights from the UK from London-Gatwick (GB Airways) and London-Luton (Monarch) airports.

Britannia (☎ UK 0800-000 747, 🖳 www.britanniadirect.com) provides seasonal flights to Tenerife from Aberdeen, Belfast, Birmingham, Bristol, Cardiff, East Midlands, Edinburgh, Exeter, Glasgow, Humberside, Leeds/Bradford, London-Gatwick, London-Luton, London-Stanstead, Liverpool, Manchester, Newcastle and Teeside. Airport information is available on ☎ 922 759 200 (Reina Sofía) and 🖳 www.aena.es/aero puertos/tenerifesur, and ☎ 922 635 998 (Los Rodeos).

**Gran Canaria:** Gando airport on the east coast of the island is one of the busiest in Spain. It's served by frequent charter and scheduled flights from mainland Spain and Europe, particularly the UK and Germany. Flights are inexpensive and available all year round. There are also flights to the other Canary islands. The airport is well connected with both the north and south of the island, and public transport to the capital and southern resorts is good. Taxis and hire cars are plentiful. Gando airport is served by regular flights from the UK from London-Gatwick (GB Airways) airport. Britannia (☎ UK 0800-000 747, 🖳 www. britanniadirect. com) offers seasonal flights to Gran Canaria from Birmingham, Bristol, Cardiff, East Midlands, Exeter, Glasgow, London-Gatwick, London-Luton, London-Stanstead, Liverpool, Manchester and Newcastle. Airport information is available on ☎ 928 579 000 and 🖳 www.aena.es/aeropuertos/gcanaria.

**Fuerteventura:** Fuerteventura has an international airport to the south of the capital. There are frequent flights from Barcelona, Madrid and many European cities during the summer, although flights are considerably reduced during the rest of the year. Britannia (☎ UK 0800-000 747, 🖳 www.britanniadirect.com) provides seasonal flights to Fuerteventura from Birmingham, Bristol, East Midlands, Glasgow, London-Gatwick, London-Luton, London-Stanstead and Manchester. Airport information is available on ☎ 928 860 500.

**Lanzarote:** Lanzarote's Guacimeta airport is situated just outside the capital and has frequent services to the other islands, mainland Spain and Europe, particularly the UK and Germany. Public transport links the airport with the capital and the main resorts. Britannia (☎ UK 0800-000 747, 🖳 www.britanniadirect.com) provides seasonal flights to Lanzarote from Birmingham, Bristol, Cardiff, East Midlands, Glasgow, London-Gatwick, London-Luton, London-Stanstead, Manchester and Newcastle. Airport information is available on ☎ 928 811 450.

## Catalonia

**Barcelona:** The region's main airport is Barcelona's El Prat de Llobregat, located 14km/9mi from the city centre. It was extensively modernised for the 1992 Olympic Games and is one of the best in Spain. The airport is very busy and offers a wide range of chartered and scheduled flights to both domestic and international destinations. Note that weekend flights to Barcelona from the UK are in high demand and can be expensive. Public transport from the airport to the city is quick and efficient, although getting to the Costa Brava and Costa Dorada from El Prat can be slow due to traffic congestion.

Barcelona airport is served by regular flights from the UK and Ireland from Birmingham, Bristol, Dublin, East Midlands, Edinburgh, Glasgow, Leeds/Bradford, London-Gatwick, London-Heathrow, London-Luton, London-Stanstead, Liverpool and Manchester airports. Airport information is available on ☎ 932 983 838 and 🖥 www.aena.es/aeropuertos/barcelona.

**Girona:** Girona has a small international airport (28km/17.5mi from Blanes), which serves as the gateway to the Costa Brava. It offers both charter and budget flights from the UK and Germany, although the number of flights is considerably reduced outside the summer months. Girona airport is served by regular flights from the UK from London-Gatwick (GB Airways) and London-Stansted (Ryanair). Britannia (☎ UK 0800-000 747, 🖥 www.britanniadirect.com) provides seasonal flights to Girona from Birmingham, Cardiff, East Midlands, Glasgow, London-Gatwick, London-Luton, London-Stanstead, Manchester and Newcastle. Airport information is available on ☎ 972 186 600.

**Reus:** Reus airport (near Tarragona) is one of Spain's smallest, although its passenger numbers are increasing annually and it now handles scheduled and charter flights to many Spanish and European destinations. Reus airport is handy for resorts on the Costa Dorada and a good alternative to Barcelona. Brittania (☎ UK 0800-000 747, 🖥 www.britanniadirect.com) provides seasonal flights to Reus from Belfast, Bristol, Cardiff, East Midlands, Leeds/Bradford, London-Gatwick, London-Luton, London-Stanstead, Manchester and Newcastle. Airport information is available on ☎ 977 779 847. Note that the northern resorts on the Costa Brava can also be easily reached from Montpellier and Perpignan airports across the border in France, both of which are served by budget airlines from the UK (e.g. Ryanair from Stansted).

## Costa Blanca

**Alicante:** The Costa Blanca is served by three airports: El Altet (Alicante), Manisses (Valencia) and San Javier (Murcia). The main one and international gateway to the Costa Blanca is El Altet (11km/7mi from Alicante city centre), which is one of Spain's busiest airports. It provides a wide range of flights (mostly charter) to over 20 countries, although most are from the UK and Germany, plus a range of domestic flights. Communications to both the north and south regions of the Costa Blanca are good, and taxis and hire cars are plentiful.

Alicante airport is served by regular flights from the UK and Ireland from Birmingham, Bristol, Cardiff, Dublin, East Midlands, Leeds/Bradford, London-Gatwick, London-Heathrow, London-Luton, London-Stanstead, Liverpool, Manchester and Newcastle airports. Britannia (☎ UK 0800-000 747, 💻 www.britanniadirect.com) provides seasonal flights to Alicante from Birmingham, Bristol, Cardiff, East Midlands, Edinburgh, Glasgow, Humberside, Leeds/Bradford, London-Gatwick, London-Luton, London-Stanstead, Liverpool, Manchester, Newcastle and Teeside. Airport information is available on ☎ 966 919 000 and 💻 www.aena.es/aeropuertos/alicante.

**Valencia:** The second airport serving the Costa Blanca is Manisses, some 8km/5mi from Valencia city centre, which handles many regular domestic flights plus scheduled flights to some European cities. Manisses airport is the most convenient for the Costa del Azahar and is a good alternative to El Altet (Alicante) for the northern part of the Costa Blanca, although traffic congestion around Valencia tends to increase journey times. Valencia airport is served by regular flights from the UK from London-Gatwick (GB Airways) and London-Heathrow (Iberia) airports. Airport information is available on ☎ 961 598 500.

**Murcia:** The third airport serving the Costa Blanca, especially the southern resorts, is Murcia's San Javier airport (see page 90).

## Madrid

Madrid's Barajas airport is Spain's busiest, handling some 34 million passengers a year, and the main Spanish airport for intercontinental flights as well being the hub of domestic flights. The airport (15km/9.3mi to the east of the city) has been extensively modernised and a new terminal is currently under construction that will double the passenger capacity. The city centre is easily accessible by public transport, including the metro. Madrid airport is served by regular flights from the UK and Ireland from Birmingham, Dublin, Glasgow, London-Gatwick, London-Heathrow, London-Luton, Liverpool and Manchester airports. Airport information is available on ☎ 913 058 343 and 💻 www.aena.es/aeropuertos/barajas.

## Murcia

Murcia's San Javier airport serves the southern part of the Costa Blanca and the Costa Cálida, and is also useful for reaching the northern region of Almería. San Javier is a small airport, although air traffic has increased considerably in recent years, and offers a growing number of charter and

*Apartment, Canaries* ▶
(© Living Spain)

*Finca, Mallorca* (© Living Spain)

◀ *Mazarrón, Costa Cálida* (© Parador Properties)

◀ *Costa Brava* (© Living Spain)

*Villa, Costa Blanca* (© Living Spain) ▶

*Alicante, Costa Blanca* (© *Parador Properties*)

▲ *Denia, Costa Blanca* (© *Parador Properti*

▲ *Costa Blanca* (© *Parador Propertie*

(© *Living Spain*)

▲ *Alicante* (© *Parador Propertie*

Golf Development, Costa Blanca *(© Parador Properties)* ▶

▲ House, Canaries *(© Living Spain)*

Villa, Costa Blanca *(© Living Spain)* ▶

▼ Alicante, Costa Brava
*(© Parador Properties)*

Puerto Banus, Costa del Sol *(© Living Spain)* ▼

▲ *Mazarrón, Costa Cálida (© Parador Properties)*

*(© Living Spain)*

◀ *Finestrat, Costa Blanca (© Parador Properties)*

▼ *Altafulla, Costa Dorada*
*(© Parador Properties)*

▲ *Costa Blanca (© Parador Properties)*

budget flights to airports in the UK and Germany, as well as Dublin. Murcia airport is served by regular flights from the UK from Birmingham, East Midlands, London-Stanstead and Manchester. Airport information is available on ☎ 968 172 000.

### Northern Spain

The Atlantic and Cantabrian coasts in the north of Spain are poorly served by international flights from mainland Europe, although there are domestic flights from Madrid and Barcelona to the region's major airports at Santiago de Compostela, Avilés, Santander and Bilbao.

**Bilbao:** Bilbao is served by flights from the UK from London-Gatwick (GB Airways), London-Heathrow (Iberia) and London-Stanstead (EasyJet). Road connections to the rest of the Basque Lands and Cantabria are good, although Asturias and Galicia are several hours away by car. Airport information is available on ☎ 944 869 664.

# International Rail Services

There are direct trains to Spain (Barcelona or Madrid) from many European cities, including Lisbon, Montpellier, Oporto, Paris, Milan and Zurich, although train travel is slow and relatively expensive compared to air travel. At the Spanish border it may be necessary to change trains due to Spain's wider gauge than the rest of Europe (except on *Talgo* and TEE trains, which have adjustable axles). International trains usually have two classes, first (*gran clase*) and tourist (*turista*), plus sleeping cars (*coches camas*) with a choice of individual compartments or couchettes. Note that some international services run only at night.

The Spanish high speed train service, known as *AVE* (*Alta Velocidad Española*), runs on special lines travelling at speeds of up to 300kph/185mph. It's currently being extended and when the network is completed (planned for 2007) all provincial capitals will be under four hours from Madrid and all provinces under six and a half hours from Barcelona. The *AVE* line currently runs between Madrid and Seville (journey time 2 hours 35 minutes) and is to be extended from Madrid to Barcelona (by 2004) and to Malaga and Valencia (by 2005), and will eventually comprise part of a Europe-wide, high-speed rail network when the line connects with the French *TGV* service at the border in 2007.

# International Bus Services

There are regular international bus services from many European cities to Spain's major cities and resorts. For example, Eurolines runs coach services from the UK to some 45 destinations in Spain. Journeys are very long, e.g. from London it's 26 hours to Barcelona and 28 to Madrid, and fares are often little cheaper than flying (it's worth comparing bus fares with the cheapest charter flights). Unless you have a fear of flying or a love of coach travel, you may find one or two days spent on a bus a nightmare. Buses are, however, comfortable, air-conditioned, and equipped with toilets and video entertainment. Most services operate daily during the summer and three or four times a week at other times. Discounts are provided for students and youths on some routes. Bookings can be made at travel agents in Spain and abroad. Typical return fares with Eurolines are Barcelona-London around €120 and Madrid-London around €140. Apex returns are considerably cheaper.

## International Ferry Services

Regular car and international ferry services operate year round between Spain and the UK (and Morocco), and domestic ferries run between the mainland and the Balearics, the Canaries, and Spain's North African enclaves of Ceuta and Melilla. Spain's most important ports are Algeciras, Almería, Barcelona, Bilbao, Cádiz, Las Palmas (Gran Canaria), Palma de Mallorca, Santander, Santa Cruz (Tenerife) and Valencia. Two companies, Brittany Ferries and P&O, operate ferry services between the UK and Spain (to Santander and Bilbao respectively). There's little to choose between them for comfort, services and fares. Ships provide a variety of facilities and services, including a choice of bars and restaurants, swimming pool, Jacuzzi, sauna, cinema, shops, hairdressing salon, photographic studio, medical service, children's playroom and evening entertainment, including a night-club, casino, discotheque and live music.

Travelling between the UK and Spain by ferry will save you around 1,200km (750mi) of driving compared with travelling by road via France. Ferries can also be a cheaper way to travel, particularly with children and a car, as you don't pay expensive air fares for children and, if you bring your car with you, you save on car rental. Travelling from the UK to southern Spain by road (via France) entails spending at least two full days driving and one or two nights in a hotel en route, plus meals and petrol costs, although it can work out cheaper than the ferry. Note that the seas can be rough between Spain and the UK (the Bay of Biscay is famous for its storms) and travel isn't advisable during bad weather if you're a bad sailor. When seas are rough, there's absolutely no respite from sea sickness and the journey will be a nightmare (if you take a mini-cruise during bad weather you will have just a few hours relief before having to endure the return journey!). Check the weather report and be prepared to travel via France or fly. If you do travel by ferry, keep a good supply of seasickness pills handy!

Note that fares are only published in brochures and although you can book via the Internet, you don't have access to the full range of tickets and can only find the price by using the (time-consuming) booking form or quote facility. Note also that when you book your ticket, you must also book some form of accommodation.

**Brittany Ferries:** Brittany Ferries operate an almost year-round, once or twice-weekly service between Plymouth in the UK to the Spanish port of Santander. The days and times of sailings vary depending on the time of year. The journey time is 24 hours between Plymouth and Santander, when one night is spent on board ship. The ferry serving the route is the 32,000 tonne *Val de Loire*, with a capacity of 2,140 passengers and 570 cars.

Brittany Ferries have five fare tariffs (depending on the time of the year) and offer a choice of single fares, mini-cruises (spending around five hours in Spain or the UK), mini-breaks (four or five days abroad), ten-day returns (up to ten days abroad) and standard return fares. Children aged under four travel free and those aged from four to 14 travel for half fare. It's advisable to book well ahead when travelling during peak periods and at any time when you require a luxury cabin. If possible, it's best to avoid travelling during peak times, when ships can be uncomfortably crowded.

The cost (2003) for a standard return for a car, motor home, minibus or van (up to 5m in length), including driver is from €256 low season, from €380 mid season and from €512 during the high season. The cost of a cabin isn't included in the fare and is from €27 to €37 sharing a four-berth cabin, and from €93 to €168 for a two to four-berth private cabin, which is well worth the extra cost. The best cabins are in the Salon Commodore (Commodore Class) consisting of 14 luxurious wood-panelled suites (€209 to €264) with an exclusive lounge bar overlooking the bow. Reclining seats are also available at a cost of €7 to €10. Foot passengers pay from €91 to €161 for a standard return. Food and drinks are quite expensive, particularly bar drinks and snacks, although Brittany ferries has better food and restaurants than P&O. For reservations ☎ UK 0870-536 0360 or Spain ☎ 942 360 611 or you can book via the Internet (🖳 www.brittany-ferries.com). Brittany Ferries operate a Spanish Property Owners Club (☎ 0870-514 3555) for frequent travellers, offering savings of up to one-third off single and standard return fares.

**P&O Ferries:** P&O Ferries (voted the 'Best Ferry Operator' in 2002 by *Travel Weekly*) operate a year-round, once or twice-weekly service between Portsmouth in the UK to the Spanish port of Bilbao (the ferry port is actually at Santutzi, around 13km/8mi to the north-west of the city centre). The route is served by the P&O ferry *Pride of Bilbao*, the largest cruise ferry operating out of the UK (capacity 2,500 passengers, 600 cars). Departures from Portsmouth are at 8pm on Tuesdays and Saturdays, arriving in Bilbao at 8am on Thursdays and Mondays respectively. Departures from Bilbao are 12.30pm on Mondays and Thursdays arriving in Portsmouth at 4.30pm on Tuesdays and Fridays respectively. The journey time is 35 hours from Portsmouth and 29 hours from Bilbao. Ferries operate throughout most of the year.

Like Brittany Ferries, P&O offer luxury cabins with a double bed, two easy chairs, writing desk, TV, shower, toilet, washbasin, two large windows and room service. Children under four travel free and there are discounts for children aged between 4 and 15. For reservations ☎ UK 0870-242 4999 or book via the Internet (🖥 www.poportsmouth.com). P&O preference shareholders receive discounts of up to 50 per cent on P&O fares, although there are strict qualifying conditions and discounts vary depending on the route and the time of sailings.

## Driving To Spain (Via France)

Driving from the UK to Spain through France involves a long journey. If you use motorways, it's around ten hours' driving – less from the Normandy ports, more from Calais or Boulogne – from the Channel to the Spanish border, plus a further ten hours to the south of Spain. You must also take into account the cost of a cross-Channel ferry (see below), and expense of toll fees (around €65 from Calais to the Spanish border) and at least one overnight stop. It's a practical option if you wish to bring large amounts of luggage with you or wish to have the use of your car in Spain, and it may be quicker and cheaper than travelling by ferry to northern Spain. Some people like to turn the journey into a mini-holiday and take their time enjoying the delights of France and Spain on the way.

Once you reach Spain, there are two main motorway routes into Spain. If you're travelling to the Coast Brava or Costa Blanca (Spain's east coast), you can cross the border at La Jonquera and take the A7, which runs along the coast as far as Alicante (extremely busy during the summer months). The route for the west and central Spain, Madrid and the Costa del Sol is along the Atlantic in France and via San Sebastian. Note that traffic congestion is chronic around Madrid, especially at weekends (Sunday evenings should be avoided) and holiday periods.

Motorway information in France (including toll fees) is available from 🖥 www.autoroutes.fr and general traffic information is available from 🖥 www.bison-fute.equipement.gouv.fr (in French only). Spanish motorway information (including toll fees) is available from 🖥 www. aseta.es and general traffic information can be found on 🖥 www.dgt.es (in Spanish only).

Note that, if you drive to Spain, you must ensure that your car insurance covers travel abroad (most do, although you may need to obtain a 'green card') and you should also have breakdown recovery insurance for France and Spain. If you choose to drive to Spain via France, you should take it easy and make regular rest stops or share the driving.

Due to the high cost of ferry and road travel and the long travelling time by road between the UK and Spain, you may be better off flying and hiring a car on arrival. Many people who visit Spain frequently or for long periods, leave a car at their Spanish home.

**Crossing the Channel:** There's a wide choice of routes for travellers between France and Britain, depending on where you live and the route intended, but only one for Irish travellers. These are (from east to west):

- Dover/Dunkerque (Norfolk Line, 🖳 www.norfolkline.com);
- Dover/Calais (Hoverspeed, 🖳 www.hoverspeed.co.uk, P&O Ferries, 🖳 www. poferries.com, and Sea France, 🖳 www.seafrance.co.uk);
- Dover/Boulogne (Speed Ferries, 🖳 www.speedferries.com) – a new five-times daily fast ferry service starting in May 2003;
- Newhaven/Dieppe (Hoverspeed and Transmanche Ferries, 🖳 www. transmancheferries.com);
- Portsmouth/Le Havre (P&O Ferries);
- Portsmouth/Caen (Brittany Ferries, 🖳 www.brittany-ferries.co.uk);
- Portsmouth/Cherbourg (P&O Ferries);
- Portsmouth/Saint-Malo (Brittany Ferries);
- Poole/Cherbourg (Brittany Ferries);
- Poole/Saint-Malo via Guernsey and Jersey (Condor Ferries, 🖳 www. condorferries.co.uk);
- Weymouth/Saint-Malo via Guernsey and Jersey (Condor Ferries);
- Plymouth/Roscoff (Brittany Ferries);
- Cork/Roscoff (Brittany Ferries).

The most scenic route is via western France (Brittany or Normandy), although the lack of motorways on some parts of the journey slows the journey. The ferry routes entailing the least number of hours driving (and on the best roads) are via Saint-Malo, from where it's possible to reach the Spanish border in around eight hours.

Fares across the Channel have risen in recent years and except for special deals or last minute fares, they're no longer cheap on any routes. If you're travelling to Spain, you probably won't be able to take advantage of economy returns, which are usually valid for five days only. Fares vary greatly depending on the time of day and when you travel, with peak fares during July and August. Ferry companies offer different deals and discounts for advance bookings and most have loyalty schemes, usually based on points-allocation. Brittany Ferries, Eurotunnel and P&O Portsmouth have special schemes for property owners abroad, which may be worth joining if you plan to travel to Spain by car on a frequent basis, although there are high membership fees and/or restrictive conditions.

Shop around for the best deal, which is probably best done by a travel agent who has access to fares from all companies or a company specialising in discount Channel crossings. Two such companies are Channel Travel (💻 www.channel-travel.com) and Cross-Channel Ferry Tickets (First Floor Offices, 3 Queens Road, Brighton BN1 3WA, UK, 💻 www.cross-channel-ferry-tickets.co.uk) whose search engine provides a listing of the cheapest crossing for the dates and times you choose. It's difficult to look at fares online, as you don't have access to the full range and can only find the price by using the (time-consuming) booking form or quote facility. Brochures rarely include fares.

**Other International Ferry Services**

There are frequent car ferry services from Algeciras to Tangier and Ceuta. There's an hourly service from Algeciras to Tangier taking two and a half hours; however, there are long delays in summer when thousands of North Africans return home. There's also a ferry service from Gibraltar to Tangier, a hydrofoil service from Tarifa to Tangier, and ferry services to Melilla (North Africa) from Almería and Malaga. Ferry services also operate from Barcelona to Livorno and Sicily (Italy) and from Palma de Mallorca and Ibiza to Sète in France (June to September only).

# GETTING AROUND

Public transport (*transporte público*) services in Spain vary considerably depending on where you live. Public transport is usually good in Spanish cities, most of which have efficient urban bus and rail services, some also supplemented by underground railways (*metros*) and trams. Spanish railways (RENFE) provide an efficient and reasonably fast rail service, particularly between cities served by *AVE* high-speed trains (see page 91). Spain has comprehensive intercity bus and domestic airline services and is also served by frequent international coaches, trains and excellent air links. On the negative side, rail services are non-existent in many areas and buses can be infrequent in coastal resorts and rural areas, where it's often essential to have your own transport. Taxis are common in resort areas and cities, and are a cheap form of transport, especially if there are a number of passengers.

Urban public transport in major cities (such as Madrid and Barcelona) is inexpensive and efficient, and rates among the best in the world. Services include comprehensive bus routes, *metros* and extensive suburban rail networks. Systems are totally integrated and the same ticket can be used for all services (a range of commuter and visitor tickets are also available). There are travel agencies (such as *Viajes Marsans, Halcón Viajes* and *Viajes Meliá*) in major cities and large towns, and specialist agencies for young travellers such as *Viajes TIVE*. Students with an International Student Identity Card (ISIC) receive discounts on some Iberia flights and some buses. A free travel map (*mapa de comunicaciones*) is available from the SNTO.

## Domestic Flights

There are a number of airlines providing domestic flights in Spain, including Iberia, Air Europa, Spanair and various small airlines such as Binter Canarias and Air Nostrum (subsidiaries of Iberia). Air Europa and Spanair operate most of the same routes as Iberia and are generally cheaper, although the competition has forced Iberia to reduce its prices. Single flights are available to most domestic destinations from €65 (from €95 to the Canaries) and cheaper night (*nocturno*) flights are available to some cities. Youth fares are also available at large discounts. Flights to the Balearics from the mainland are only slightly more expensive than ferries, although you need to reserve well in advance during the summer season.

Most domestic flights are routed via Madrid or Barcelona, so it can be difficult to get a direct flight between regional cities. There are frequent flights between Spain's international airports and regional airports, with Iberia operating flights from Barcelona and Madrid to around 20 domestic airports. There's a half-hourly or hourly 'air bridge' (*puente aéreo*) shuttle service between Barcelona and Madrid, carrying over two million passengers a year. Tickets for Iberia domestic flights can be purchased from machines at airports (using a credit card) and all companies have telephone and Internet booking facilities: Air Europa (☎ 902 401 501, 🖳 www.air-europa.com – tickets can also be purchased at Halcón Viajes travel agencies); Air Nostrum (☎ 902 400 5000, 🖳 www.airnostrum.es); Binter Canarias (☎ 928 579 601, 🖳 www.binter canarias.es); Iberia (☎ 902 400 500, 🖳 www.iberia.com) and Spanair (☎ 902 131 415, 🖳 www.spainair.com). Residents in the Balearics and Canaries receive discounts on Air Europa flights between the islands and the mainland. Private aircraft and helicopters can be rented from most Spanish airports to almost anywhere in Spain.

# Domestic Rail Services

The Spanish rail network is operated by the state-owned company *Red Nacional de los Ferrocarrilas Españoles (RENFE)* which operates 14,738km (9,158mi) of track and 2,500 stations. The RENFE network takes in most major cities, although it doesn't run to many small towns, and is supplemented by a few suburban networks such as the FFCC city lines in Barcelona and private narrow-gauge railways. Like most state-owned businesses in Spain, the railways were grossly under-funded under Franco and RENFE remains western Europe's most idiosyncratic railway (many lines are still single track), despite huge investments in new rolling stock. Spain's railway network is below average by European standards, particularly regarding punctuality, although it's also one of the continent's cheapest. However, RENFE has undergone a comprehensive modernisation programme in the last decade, during which journey times have been reduced by up to 50 per cent.

In 1992, a high speed *Tren de Alta Velocidad Española (AVE)* service was introduced between Madrid and Seville (2 hours 35 minutes) for the World Fair. The *AVE* (which means big bird in Spanish) employs 'disguised' French *TGV* trains running on special lines and travelling at speeds of up to 300kph (185mph). The *AVE* service is being extended from Madrid to Barcelona (by 2004) and to Malaga and Valencia (by 2005), and will eventually comprise part of a Europe-wide, high-speed rail network (unlike other Spanish trains, *AVE* trains run on European standard-gauge tracks). Other first-class, long-distance *(largo recorrido)* trains include the *Talgo 200,* which has first and tourist class seats and is similarly equipped to *AVE* trains (although slower).

Tickets can be purchased at station ticket windows (*taquillas de billetes*), from ticket machines (*máquinas de billetes*) accepting cash and credit cards, RENFE offices and from RENFE-appointed travel agents. Tickets can also be purchased online (💻 www.renfe.es), although the secure booking service requires a codename and password, which can only be obtained by calling RENFE first (☎ 902 157 507). RENFE also provides a telephone booking service (☎ 902 240 202) from 5am to 11.50pm, although tickets can be delivered only to addresses in Barcelona, Madrid, Seville and Valencia. The RENFE website (💻 www.renfe.es) provides information on fares and timetables plus a wealth of other useful information.

# Domestic Bus Services

There are excellent bus (*autobús*) services in major cities and towns in Spain and comprehensive long-distance 'coach' (*autocar*) services between major cities. Buses are the cheapest and most common form of public transport in Spain and most coastal towns and rural villages are accessible only by bus. The quality and age of buses varies considerably from luxurious modern buses in major cities to old ramshackle museum pieces in some rural areas. Private bus services are often confusing and uncoordinated, and buses usually leave from different locations rather than a central bus station (*estación de autobúses*), e.g. Madrid has eight bus stations and most cities have two or more, possibly located on the outskirts of a town.

Long-distance bus companies include Alsa-Enatcar (the largest), Auto Res and Continental-Auto. Fares on most routes are reasonable, with typical return fares from Madrid to Alicante around €40 and from Madrid to Barcelona around €55. Most major bus companies provide telephone helplines and comprehensive websites with on-line booking. Further information can be obtained from Alsa-Enatcar (☎ 902 422 242, 🖳 www.alsa.es), Auto Res (☎ 902 020 603, 🖳 www.auto-res.net) and Continental-Auto (☎ 902 330 400, 🖳 www.continental-auto.es).

## Spanish Roads

Motoring in Spain has changed dramatically in the last few decades, during which the number of cars has increased considerably, e.g. the traffic on Spanish roads doubled between 1980 and 1990, and between 1995 and 2000 increased by a further 27 per cent (heavy goods traffic by 37 per cent). The road network covers over 300,000km (200,000mi), of which around 8,000km (5,000mi) are motorways (*autopistas*) and dual carriageways (*autovías*). Although motorways cover a smaller proportion of the country than those in most northern European countries, there are plans to extend the network (dual carriageways) to all major towns and cities by 2007.

Spanish motorways are mostly toll roads built by private companies and are among Europe's finest roads. Unfortunately, they're also among the world's most expensive roads and consequently main trunk roads (*carreteras*) are jammed by drivers who are reluctant (or cannot afford) to pay the high motorway tolls. The road-building programme and provision of parking spaces has, however, failed to keep pace with the increasing number of cars on Spanish roads (it's hard to believe that Spain has a lower density of vehicles than most other European countries). In contrast to the excellent *autopistas* and fine trunk roads, roads in rural areas and small towns are often dreadful or even dangerous, and full of potholes.

Driving in Spain is usually cheaper than using public transport, particularly when your car runs on diesel, the costs are shared between a number of people and you avoid motorways. In any case, unless you're travelling between major cities you will have little choice but to drive, as public transport is generally poor in rural areas. However, if you're travelling long distances, you will find it quicker and certainly less stressful to take the train or fly. If you live in or near a city, particularly Madrid or Barcelona (where public transport services are excellent), a car is a liability, while in rural areas it's a necessity.

Driving is generally enjoyable in rural areas, particularly outside the tourist season, when it's possible to drive for miles without seeing another motorist (or a caravan!). However, driving in major cities and towns is a nightmare and to be avoided if at all possible (and parking is impossible). As a result of the *siesta*, Spain has four rush hours (*horas punta*): 8 to 9.30am, 12.30 to 2.30pm, 3.30 to 4pm and 6.30 to 8pm; the quietest period is usually between 2.30 and 4.30pm when many people are having their *siesta*. Traffic jams (*atascos*) are particularly bad in cities such as Madrid and Barcelona, where the rush 'hour' lasts all day.

Madrid, where the average traffic speed has fallen from over 50 kph (31 mph) in 1980 to below 20 kph (11 mph) in recent years, is to be avoided at any time. There is, however, a positive side to traffic jams, which reduce traffic speeds, thus contributing to the Spaniards' longevity. Bottlenecks and traffic jams are horrendous at the start and end of holiday periods and at weekends, particularly on major roads around Madrid and Barcelona. Some areas and roads (e.g. the N332 around Torrevieja and Orihuela Costa) are to be avoided in July and August, when millions of Spaniards and foreigners take to the roads on their annual holidays.

General road information can be obtained on ☎ 900 123 505 or via the Internet (🖳 www.dgt.es), although at weekends and peak holiday periods both the phone lines and Internet are overloaded and it can be impossible to get through. Road assistance is available from the *Real Automobil Club de España* (RACE, ☎ 902 120 441, 🖳 www.race.es), the largest and most famous, and *Real Automobil Club de Catalunya* (RACC, ☎ 902 414 143). Services are similar (RACC has cheaper fees) and both have agreements with foreign organisations such as the AA, AAA, ACI, ADAC, AvD, DTC, RAC and the TCI. Note that many car manufacturers in Spain such as Renault and Ford also provide breakdown assistance for members and most car insurance policies include road assistance (the telephone number should be included in your insurance policy).

# 3.

# YOUR DREAM HOME

Once you've considered possible locations for your dream home in Spain, you must decide on the type of property that will best suit your requirements and consider the purchase options and the fees associated with buying.

When buying a home anywhere, it isn't advisable to be in too much of a hurry – and Spain is no exception. It's a wise or lucky person who gets his choice absolutely right first time, which is why most experts recommend that you rent before buying unless you're absolutely sure of what you want, how much you wish to pay and where you want to live. Have a good look around in your chosen region(s) and obtain an accurate picture of the types of properties available, their relative prices and what you can expect to get for your money. However, before doing this, you should make a comprehensive list of what you want (and don't want) from a home, so that you can narrow the field and save time on wild goose chases. In most areas, properties for sale include derelict farmhouses, unmodernised village homes, modern townhouses and apartments with all mod cons, and a wide choice of detached villas. You can also buy a plot of land and have an individual, architect-designed house built to your own specifications.

To reduce the chances of making an expensive error when buying in an unfamiliar region, it's often prudent to rent a house for a period (see **Renting Before Buying** on page 112), taking in the worst part of the year (weather-wise). This allows you to become familiar with the region and the weather, and gives you plenty of time to look around for a home at your leisure. There's no shortage of properties for sale in Spain (indeed, in many resort areas there's a glut) and whatever kind of property you're looking for, you will have an abundance from which to choose. Wait until you find something you fall head over heels in love with and then think about it for another week or two before rushing headlong to the altar! One of the advantages of buying property in Spain is that there's often another 'dream' home around the next corner – and the second or third dream home is often even better than the first. Better to miss the 'opportunity of a lifetime' than end up with an expensive pile of stones around your neck. **Don't dally too long as good properties at the right price don't remain on the market for long.**

If you're looking for a holiday home (*segunda residencia*), you may wish to investigate mobile homes or a scheme that restricts your occupancy of a property to a number of weeks each year. These include shared ownership, leaseback and time-sharing (*multipropriedad*). Don't rush into any of these schemes without fully researching the market and before you're absolutely clear about what you want and what you can realistically expect to get for your money.

# RESEARCH

The secret of successfully buying a home in Spain is research, research and more research. A successful purchase is much more likely if you thoroughly investigate the various regions (see our sister publication *The Best Places to Buy a Home in Spain*), the type of properties available, prices and relative values, and the procedure for buying property.

The more research you do before buying a property in Spain the better, which should (if possible) include advice from those who already own a home there, from whom you can usually obtain invaluable information (often based on their own mistakes). Although it's a common practice, mixing a holiday with property purchase isn't advisable, as most people are inclined to make poor decisions when their mind is fixed on play rather than business.

 **Some people make expensive (even catastrophic) errors when buying a home in Spain, often because they don't do sufficient research and are simply in too much of a hurry – often setting themselves ridiculous deadlines such as buying a home during a long weekend or a week's holiday.**

## Publications & Exhibitions

Property exhibitions are now commonplace in the UK and Ireland, and are increasingly popular with prospective buyers who can get a good idea of what's available and make contact with estate agents and developers. **Appendix A** includes a list of the main exhibition organisers in the UK and Ireland. **You may be charged an admission fee.** Outbound Publishing (1 Commercial Road, Eastbourne, East Sussex BN21 3XQ, UK, ☎ 01323-726040, ✉ outbounduk@aol.com) publish *World of Property*, a quarterly publication containing many properties for sale in Spain (and other countries) and organise exhibitions in the south and north of England. Property is also advertised in many newspapers and magazines in Spain and abroad (see **Appendix B**) and on the Internet.

## Independent Advice & Information

A useful source of information for foreign property buyers in Spain is the Foundation Institute of Foreign Property Owners (Fundación Instituto de Propietarios Extranjeros/FIPE, Apartado de Correos 418, 03590 Altea (Alicante), ☎ 965 842 312, 🖳 www.fipe-altea.org). The FIPE publishes an English-language magazine (*Boletín*) for members containing valuable information, including an early warning system for owners who are the subject of official municipal notices regarding tax and other debts. The FIPE is the 'the voice of foreign homeowners in Spain' and provides free advice to members about buying and renting property, a free document check and legal scrutiny of contracts (for a fee). They can also help you choose an agent or lawyer and help you avoid the crooks, and publish a wealth of information, much of which is free to members and available on the website.

This chapter is designed to help you decide what sort of home to buy and to help you avoid problems (see below). It also contains information about renting, estate agents, cost of property, fees, buying a resale or a new home, community properties, timeshare and part-ownership schemes, retirement homes, buying for investment, inspections and surveys, renovation and restoration, and building your own home.

# AVOIDING PROBLEMS

The problems associated with buying property abroad have been highlighted in the last decade or so, during which the property market in many countries has gone from boom to bust and back again. From a legal viewpoint, Spain isn't one of the safest places in which to buy a home, although buyers have a relatively high degree of protection under Spanish law. In the last few decades, buying property in Spain has been the subject of much adverse publicity, both in the foreign and Spanish media. Some commentators have even gone so far as to advise people **not** to buy in Spain! However, although the pitfalls must never be ignored, buying property in Spain needn't be a gamble. There are nearly 2 million foreign property owners in Spain and many millions of Spanish owners, the vast majority of whom are happy with their purchases and encountered few or no problems when buying their homes. This should be borne in mind when you hear or read horror stories concerning foreign buyers in Spain. The possible dangers haven't been highlighted in order to discourage you, but simply to ensure that you go into a purchase with your eyes open and to help you avoid problems.

## Legal Advice

It cannot be emphasised too strongly that anyone planning to buy property in Spain must take expert, independent legal advice.

**SURVIVAL TIP**
Never sign anything, or pay any money, until you've sought legal advice in a language in which you're fluent, from a lawyer who's experienced in Spanish property law.

If you aren't prepared to do this, you shouldn't even think about buying a property! It has been estimated that some 80 per cent of buyers in Spain don't obtain independent legal advice. Most people who experience problems take no precautions whatsoever when purchasing property and of those that do take legal advice, many do so only after having already paid a deposit and signed a contract (or when they hit problems).

You will find that the relatively small price – in comparison with the cost of a home – of obtaining legal advice to be excellent value for money, if only for the peace of mind it affords. Trying to cut corners to save on legal costs is foolhardy in the extreme when tens or hundreds of thousands of euros are at stake. However, be careful whom you engage, as some lawyers are part of the problem rather than the solution (overcharging is also rife)!

Don't pick a lawyer at random, but engage one who has been highly recommended by someone you can trust.

 **There are many people in Spain who claim to be lawyers (often estate agents or accountants), although this is highly illegal and leaves you with no protection should anything go wrong.**

You should check that the lawyer is a member of the provincial lawyer's association (*Colegio de Abogados*) – you can easily telephone the association and check by giving the lawyer's name – membership of which is compulsory and all members are covered by professional indemnity insurance. The only professionals legally qualified and permitted to give legal advice in Spain are lawyers and you should take legal advice from no one else. Many estate agents will work hard to persuade you not to employ a lawyer on the grounds that they're not necessary, expensive and hold purchases up. Although it may seem expensive and legal checks on a property may mean you have to wait extra before buying, you should not attempt a purchase without legal advice and in any case, the lawyer's fees will be a small percentage of the estate agent's commission!

However, if money is tight and you really cannot afford a lawyer, in many areas you can hire a 'conveyancer' who will do the paperwork for a fixed fee (which may be 'as little' as 1,000 euros) irrespective of the price of the property that you're buying. Conveyancers often work with or for a *gestor* (see below) and generally do a good job for a fraction of the fee charged by a lawyer. Note, however, that conveyancers aren't licensed in Spain, unlike, for example, in the UK. Therefore you won't have any legal redress if things go wrong, as you would with a lawyer.

**Gestor**: A *gestor* is an official agent licensed by the Spanish government as a middleman between you and the bureaucracy. It isn't compulsory to employ a *gestor*, but without one you will usually need to speak fluent Spanish (or have an interpreter), possess boundless patience and stamina, and have unlimited time to deal with the mountains of red tape and obstacles. A *gestor's* services aren't generally expensive. Note, however, that the quality of service provided by *gestores* varies and that they cannot always be relied upon to do a professional job (some have been known to take money from clients and do absolutely nothing).

## Employing Professionals

There are professionals speaking English and other languages in most areas of Spain, and many expatriate professionals (e.g. architects, builders and surveyors) also practice there. However, don't assume that because you're dealing with a fellow countryman that he'll offer you a better deal or do a better job than a Spaniard (the contrary is often true). It's wise to check the credentials of all professionals you employ, whatever their nationality.

 **It's never advisable to rely solely on advice proffered by those with a financial interest in selling you a property, such as a developer or estate agent. Avoid 'cowboy' agents and anyone who does property deals on the side – such as someone you meet in a bar – as dealing with them often leads to heartache and it could also be dangerous!**

## Problems

Among the myriad problems experienced by buyers are properties bought without a legal title; properties built illegally without planning permission; properties sold that are subject to embargoes; properties sold with forged deeds; properties with missing infrastructure; builders or developers going bust; developer's loans being undischarged after completion; undischarged mortgages from the previous owner; intermediaries disappearing with the seller's proceeds; overcharging by vendors (particularly when selling to foreigners); properties sold to more than one buyer and even properties sold that don't exist! On the other hand, buyers must also accept their share of the blame. It's a common adage in Spain that many buyers 'leave their brains behind at the airport' and it's true that some people do incredibly irresponsible things, such as (on occasion) literally handing over bags full of cash to agents or owners without any security. In cases such as these it's hardly surprising that people are defrauded!

In the past, many properties in Spain were built without planning permission, weren't constructed according to the approved plans or were built on land that wasn't zoned for building in the first place. Even when planning permission was obtained, developers often built more homes than were approved. A system of 'legalising' unauthorised constructions by fines is used by many municipalities, although in extreme cases illegal buildings or extensions have been demolished. In some cases, areas have even been retroactively re-zoned as green zones (*zonas verde*) years after planning permission was approved and homes were built! In most cases, the property owners were the innocent parties and received derisory compensation, while the crooks got away scot free. Some municipalities turn a blind eye to (or even collude in) the building of illegal urbanisations and then levy owners (sometimes thousands of euros) for improving the infrastructure (e.g. roads, sewage, water, etc.), which was already paid for in the cost of their homes. Note that local officials have dictatorial powers in planning matters and some municipalities treat the victims of crooked builders and developers like criminals.

# Mistakes

Common mistakes made by buyers include:

- buying in the wrong area (rent first!);
- buying a home that's difficult to resell;
- buying a property for renovation and grossly underestimating the restoration costs;
- not having a survey done on an old property;
- not taking legal advice;
- not including the necessary conditional clauses in the contract;
- buying a property for business, e.g. to convert to self-catering accommodation, and being too optimistic about the income and taking on too large a mortgage.

It's common practice in Spain to declare a lower price in the title deed (*escritura*) than actually paid, although you must take care that you don't declare too low a price (see **Fees** on page 123). Checks must be carried out both before signing a contract (*contrato privado de compraventa*) **and** before signing the deed of sale (*escritura*). **If you get into a dispute over a property deal it can take years to get it resolved in Spanish courts, and even then there's no guarantee that you will receive satisfaction.**

# Subrogation

One of the Spanish laws that property buyers should be aware of is the law of subrogation, whereby property debts, including mortgages, local taxes and community charges, remain with a property and are inherited by the buyer. This is an open invitation to dishonest sellers to 'cut and run'. It's possible, of course, to check whether there are any outstanding debts on a property and this should be done by your legal advisor and/or the notary when signing the preliminary contract and again a few days before the completion, although the system isn't foolproof (see **Conveyancing** on page 190). The notary should always obtain an up to date notification from the Land Registry on the day of completion.

# Buying Off Plan

Many problems can arise when buying off plan, i.e. unbuilt properties, or a property on an unfinished development (urbanisation). Because of the problems associated with buying off plan, such as the difficulty in ensuring that you actually get what's stated in the contract and that the developer doesn't go broke, some experts have advised buyers against buying an unfinished property. However, this isn't practical, because in a seller's market it's essential to buy off plan if you wish to buy a home in a popular development. It's worth remembering that although there are many satisfied buyers of off plan property, the process is generally more time-consuming and stressful than buying a resale property. A 'finished' property is a property where the building is complete in every detail (as confirmed by your own lawyer or architect), communal services have been completed, and **all** the infrastructure is in place such as roads, parking areas, external lighting, landscaping, water, sewerage, electricity and telephone services. A builder is supposed to provide buyers purchasing off plan through stage payments with an insurance policy or banker's 'termination' guarantee, which protects them against the builder going broke before construction is completed. Note, however, some builders fail to obtain insurance and it has even been found to be forged!

# Buying Land

Before buying building land, ensure that is has planning permission or that planning permission will be a formality. Don't take the vendor's word for this, but make it a condition of the purchase of a building plot.

See also **Building Your Own Home** on page 159.

# Take Your Time

Many people have had their fingers burnt by rushing into property deals without proper care and consideration. It's all too easy to fall in love with the attractions of a home in the sun and to sign a contract without giving it sufficient thought. If you aren't absolutely certain, don't allow yourself to be rushed into making a hasty decision, e.g. by fears of an imminent price rise or of losing the property to another buyer who has 'made an offer' (note, that estate agents often pressurise by claiming there are several other clients about to make an offer). Although many people dream of buying a holiday or retirement home in Spain, it's vital to do your homework thoroughly and avoid the 'dream sellers' (often fellow countrymen), who will happily prey on your ignorance and tell you anything in order to sell you a home.

# Summary

The authorities have learnt a few lessons from the myriad disasters that have befallen many foreign (and Spanish) buyers, although changes in the law are painfully slow and the authorities have been slow to close loopholes. In the last decade changes have included better planning controls, tighter laws concerning urban matters, compulsory checks by notaries, and new rules requiring developers to provide full financial guarantees before beginning construction. New regulations concerning building in the vicinity of the coast and green belts, population densities and the height of developments have also been introduced. Although planning infringements still occur, they're generally dealt with more harshly than before. However, prosecutions of corrupt or incompetent officials, professionals, developers and builders are still extremely rare. Despite the improvements, the authorities and everyone concerned with the property industry in Spain still have some way to go to match the security provided in most other western European countries.

### The Valencian Urbanisation Regulations

The Urban Development Legislation (*Ley Reguladora de Actividad Urbanística/LRAU*) introduced in 1994 in the region of Valencia is currently the centre of a highly-publicised dispute between developers and hundreds of property owners, who are being forced to pay huge sums of money either for infrastructure development or for the repurchase of their own land. If the owners don't (or cannot) pay, developers can legally seize the land and pay owners compensation at a fraction of the market price.

When it was introduced in 1994, the LRAU's objective was to promote urban development in the region where town planning faced continual obstacles mainly from landowners who refused to participate in development projects. As a result, towns and cities could not expand or build low-cost housing or essential public services. Under the LRAU, landowners must participate in development projects backed by town councils by paying for contributions towards infrastructure such as roads, mains supplies and street lighting. In the city of Valencia, the LRAU has worked well and the city and suburbs have benefited hugely from new development for housing (relieving the chronic shortage), green areas and public services such as hospitals and schools. Control in and around the city has been strict and development highly regulated. However, in other parts of the region, particularly the Costa Blanca, the LRAU has been systematically abused by corrupt local authorities and developers who stand to make huge profits by developing rural land for villas. Most of the development plans in this area carried out under the auspices of the LRAU provide little or no public benefit.

Many owners, both Spanish and foreign, of semi-rural or rural properties in the area are affected by the LRAU, particularly as developers now move further inland away from the coast where there's a shortage of building land. As a result, many owners are facing large bills (up to €75,000) or are forced to sell their property. The LRAU has been challenged before the Spanish Constitutional Court as a breach of essential property rights, although a decision by the court is not expected at least until the end of 2003. Meanwhile, you're advised not to buy rural or semi-rural land in the region of Valencia without taking comprehensive professional advice, preferably from a lawyer who can thoroughly explain all the implications of such a purchase. Note that the *LRAU* only affects property situated on land that hasn't been developed.

# RENTING BEFORE BUYING

If you're uncertain about exactly what sort of home you want and where you wish to live, it's advisable to rent a furnished property for a period in order to reduce the chances of making a costly error, particularly when you're planning to buy in an unfamiliar area.

> **SURVIVAL TIP**
> Renting before buying is even more important for those planning to live permanently or set up a business in Spain, when it isn't wise to buy a home until you're sure that the business will be a success.

If possible, you should rent a similar property to that which you're planning to buy, during the time of year when you plan to occupy it. Renting allows you to become familiar with the weather, the amenities and the local people, to meet other foreigners who have made their homes in Spain and share their experiences, and, not least, to discover the cost of living at first hand.

If you plan to live in Spain permanently or for long periods, you should rent for at least six months and preferably a year. An area that'is quiet and relaxing between November and March can become noisy, congested and stressful between April and October, particularly in package holiday regions. Conversely, a place that's attractive in the summer can 'close' in the winter. If you can't rent for that long, try to visit for two-week periods in each of the four seasons.

Provided you still find Spain alluring, renting 'buys' you time to find your dream home at your leisure. You may even wish to consider renting a home long term (or even 'permanently') as an alternative to buying, as it saves tying up your capital and can be surprisingly inexpensive in many regions. Some people let out their family homes abroad and rent one in Spain, in which case it's possible to make a profit!

If you're looking for a rental property for a few months, e.g. three to six months, it's best not to rent unseen, but to rent a holiday apartment for a week or two to allow yourself time to look around for a longer-term rental. Properties for rent in Spain are advertised in local newspapers and magazines, particularly expatriate publications, and can also be found through property publications in many countries (see **Appendix B** for a list). Many estate agents offer both short and long-term rentals and developers may also rent properties to potential buyers. A rental contract (*contrato de arrendamiento*) is necessary when renting any property, whether long or short-term, where rental contracts are usually standard, state-sponsored agreements available from tobacconists' (*estancos*).

## Long-Term Rentals

Spain doesn't have a flourishing long-term (i.e. one year or longer) rental market in resort areas, where it's more common for people to buy, and it can be difficult to find good long-term rentals for a reasonable rent. Most rental properties in resort areas, whether long or short-term, are let furnished (*amueblado*) and long-term unfurnished (*sin muebles*) properties are difficult to find. However, in major cities, long-term rental properties are usually let unfurnished and furnished properties are in short supply. Rental costs vary considerably depending on the size (number of bedrooms) and quality of a property, its age and the facilities provided. However, the most significant factor affecting rents is the region, the city and the particular neighbourhood. A small, one or two-bedroom, unfurnished apartment (e.g. 50 to 75m²) which rents for up to €1,200 per month in Madrid or Barcelona, costs around 50 per cent less in most rural and resort areas outside the main tourist season. Many homeowners are reluctant to sign long-term rental contracts, as a contract for a primary residence (*arriendos de viviendas*) can be extended for five years after the initial letting period (although it can be terminated earlier by a tenant as specified in the contract) and provides tenants with much more security than a short-term contract.

## Short-Term Rentals

Short-term rentals are always furnished and are usually for holiday lets or periods of up to a year. A short-term or temporary contract (*contrato de arrendamiento de vivienda por temporada*) is necessary, which provides tenants with fewer rights than a long-term contract. There's an abundance of self-catering properties to rent in Spain including apartments, cottages, farmhouses, townhouses and villas. Rents for short-term rentals are usually higher than for longer lets, particularly in popular holiday areas where many properties are let as self-catering holiday accommodation. However, many agents let self-catering properties in resort areas at a considerable reduction (except for the Canaries) during the 'low season', which may extend from October to May. Some holiday letting agents divide the rental year into three seasons, e.g. low (October to March), medium (April to June) and high (July to September). You may also get a better deal if you offer to rent 'long-term' (e.g. two or three months) over the summer months.

The rent for an average one or two-bedroom furnished apartment or townhouse during the low season is usually between €400 and €650 a month for a minimum one or two-month let. Rent is usually paid one month in advance with one month's rent as a deposit. Lets of less than a month are more expensive, e.g. €275 a week for a two-bedroom apartment in the low season, which is some 50 per cent (or less) than the rent charged in the high season. Many hotels and hostels also offer special low rates for long stays during the low season (see below). Note, however, that when the rental period includes the peak letting months of July and August, the rent can be prohibitively high. Standards vary considerably, from dilapidated, ill-equipped apartments to luxury villas with every modern convenience. Always check whether a property is fully equipped (which should mean whatever you want it to mean) and whether it has central heating if you're planning to rent in winter. Rentals can be found by contacting owners advertising in the publications listed in **Appendix B** and through estate agents in most areas, many of whom also handle rentals. See also **Chapter 9**.

# Hotels & Motels

Hotel rates vary depending on the time of year, the exact location and the individual establishment, although you may be able to haggle over rates outside the high season and for long stays, for which many hotels offer special rates. Hotels located in large towns and cities, coastal resorts and spa towns are the most expensive and rates in cities such as Madrid and Barcelona are similar to other major European cities. However, inexpensive hotels can be found in most towns, where a single room (*habitación individual*) can usually be found for €15 to €20 and a double (*habitación doble*) for €20 to €30 (usually without a private bath or shower).

Minimum and maximum rates are fixed according to the facilities and the season, although there's no season in the major cities or in the Canaries, and in ski resorts the low season is the summer. Rates are considerably higher in tourist areas during the high season (*temporada alta*) of July and August, when rooms at any price are hard to find. On the other hand, outside the main season, particularly in winter, many hotels offer low half or full board rates, when a double room with a bath including dinner (buffet) and breakfast can be found for €35 for two (even better rates are offered for stays of a week or longer). Hotels aren't a cost-effective, long-term solution for home hunters, although there's usually little choice if you need accommodation for a short period. Bed and breakfast accommodation is also available, although it isn't usually budget accommodation, in which case you need to choose a hostel.

# Home Exchange

An alternative to renting is to exchange your home abroad with one in Spain for a period. This way you can experience home living in Spain for a relatively small cost and may save yourself the expense of a long-term rental. Although there's always an element of risk involved in exchanging your home with another family, most agencies thoroughly vet clients and have a track record of successful swaps. There are home exchange agencies in most countries, many of which are members of the International Home Exchange Association (IHEA). There are many home exchange companies in the USA including HomeLink International with over 12,500 members in around 50 countries (☎ 813 975 9825, 💻 www.swapnow.com). Two long-established home exchange companies in the UK are HomeLink International, Linfield House, Gorse

Hill Road, Virginia Water, Surrey GU25 4AS, UK (☎ 01344-842642, 🖳 www.homelink.org.uk), which publishes a directory of homes and holiday homes for exchange, and Home Base Holidays, 7 Park Avenue, London N13 5PG, UK (☎ 020-8886 8752, 🖳 www.homebase-hols.com).

# HOUSE HUNTING

There are many ways of finding homes for sale in Spain, including the following:

- Newspapers and magazines, including the English-language publications listed in **Appendix B** and many property newspapers published in Spanish such as *Llave en Mano* (weekly and distributed free in supermarkets, shops and cafés in resort areas) and *De Primera Mano* (monthly and available in the Canaries, Madrid and Malaga province);
- Property exhibitions (see **Appendix A** for further details);
- The Internet, where there are literally thousands of sites dedicated to property in Spain. These can be found by typing in 'Spanish property' or 'Costa del Sol property' in a search engine such as Google (🖳 www.google.com) or Altavista (🖳 www.altavista.com). Note that most of the property sites belong to or are linked to an estate agent;
- Visiting an area. Many property owners in Spain sell privately to avoid paying agent's commission and put up 'For Sale/ *Se vende*' signs outside the property. This is particularly common in rural areas where properties may also be advertised in bars. You can also ask the locals if they know of any properties for sale;
- Estate agents (see below). Most property owners sell through an estate agent.

# ESTATE AGENTS

The vast majority of property sales in Spain are handled by estate agents (*inmobiliarias*), particularly those where non-resident foreign buyers are involved. It's common for foreigners in many countries, particularly the UK and Germany, to use an agent in their own country who works in co-operation with Spanish agents and developers. Many Spanish agents also advertise abroad, particularly in the publications listed in **Appendix B**, in expatriate magazines and newspapers in Spain, and many also have extensive websites, some of which include virtual tours of property. Most Spanish agents have staff who speak English and other foreign languages, so don't be discouraged if you don't speak Spanish. If you want to find an agent in a particular town or area, you can look under *inmobiliarias* in the local Spanish yellow pages.

## Qualifications

Spanish estate agents are regulated by law and must be professionally qualified and licensed. You should choose an agent who's a member of a professional association such as the *Agente de Propiedad Inmobiliaria (API)* or *Gestor Intermediario en Promociones de Edificiones (GIPE)*, members of which have professional indemnity insurance (although it may be minimal). Ask to see an agent's registration number and have someone check it if you aren't convinced that it's genuine. You may also be afforded extra protection if the agent is a member of an international organisation, such as the European Federation of Estate Agents.

Note that few Spanish agents are bonded or have malpractice insurance (if they do it's limited to a paltry sum such as €300). The rules for estate agents also apply to foreigners, who cannot sell property in Spain without a full Spanish licence (although some Spanish agents are little more than sleeping partners in foreign-owned companies). However, there are many unlicensed, amateur 'cowboy' agents operating

in Spain (particularly in resort areas), who should be avoided. Among the many scams practised by unlicensed agents is increasing the price of a house above that agreed with the owner and pocketing the difference.

## Fees

There are no government controls on agents' fees in Spain, where an agent's commission is usually paid by the vendor and included in the purchase price. The commission charged by agents is usually between 5 and 10 per cent, which is included in the sale price and therefore effectively paid by the buyer. Commission charged on new properties is usually 10 per cent and on rural properties it can be as high as 25 per cent! Commission charged by agents varies and properties may be advertised at different prices in different agencies. In some areas many agents belong to a multiple listing service (MLS) whereby agents advertise the same properties and selling agent splits the fee with the original listing agent. Foreign agents located abroad often work with Spanish agents and share the standard commission, so buyers usually pay no more by using them. However, check in advance whether this is the case and how much you're required to pay. Note also that the same property is often on the books of different estate agents at different prices, reflecting different commissions, so shop around. When buying, also check whether you need to pay commission or any extras in addition to the sale price (apart from the normal fees and taxes associated with buying a property in Spain).

## Viewing

If possible, you should decide where you want to live, what sort of property you want and your budget **before** visiting Spain. Obtain details of as many properties as possible in your chosen area and price range, and make a shortlist of those you wish to view. Usually the details provided by estate agents are sparse and few agents provide detailed descriptions of properties. Often there's no photograph and even when there is, it usually doesn't do a property justice. Note that there are no national property listings in Spain, where agents jealously guard their list of properties, although many work with overseas agents in areas that are popular with foreign buyers and there are property networks in some areas used by several agents. Spanish agents who advertise in foreign journals or who work closely with overseas agents usually provide coloured photographs and a full description, particularly for the more expensive properties. The best agents provide an abundance of information. Agents vary enormously in their efficiency, enthusiasm and professionalism. If an agent shows little interest in finding out exactly what you want, you should look elsewhere. If you're using a foreign agent, confirm (and reconfirm) that a particular property is still for sale and the price, before travelling to Spain to view it. Many estate agents have websites, so you can check what's on offer from the comfort of your home, although sites won't show all properties for sale or the latest properties on their books and some sites require prior registration.

A Spanish agent may ask you to sign a document (*nota de encargo*) before showing you any properties, which is simply to protect his commission should you obtain details from another source or try to do a deal with the owner behind his back. In Spain you're usually shown properties personally by agents and won't be given the keys (especially to furnished properties) or be expected to deal with tenants or vendors directly. You should always make an appointment to see properties as agents don't usually like people just turning up. If you make an appointment, you should call and cancel it if you cannot keep it. If you are on holiday it's okay to drop in unannounced to have a look at what's on offer, but don't expect an agent to show you properties without an appointment. If you view properties during a holiday, it's better to do so at the start of it so that you can return later to inspect any you particularly like a second or third time. **Agents don't usually work during lunch hours and most are closed on Saturday afternoons and Sundays.**

You should try to view as many properties as possible during the time available, but allow sufficient time to view each property thoroughly, to travel between properties and for breaks for sustenance (it's **mandatory** to have a good lunch in Spain). Although it's important to see sufficient properties to form an accurate opinion of price and quality, don't see too many properties in one day (around four to six is usually a manageable number), as it's easy to become confused over the merits of each property. If you're shown properties that don't meet your specifications, tell the agent immediately. You can also help an agent narrow the field by telling him exactly what's wrong with the properties you reject. It's advisable to make notes of both the good **and** bad features and take lots of photographs of the properties you like, so that you're able to compare them later at your leisure (but keep a record of which photos are of which house!). It's also advisable to mark each property on a map so that should you wish to return later on your own, you can find them without getting lost. The more a property appeals to you, the more you should look for faults and negative points – if you still like it after stressing the negative points, it must have special appeal.

### Viewing Trips

Most agents and developers arrange viewing trips with inexpensive accommodation for prospective buyers and usually refund the cost if you buy a property. By all means take advantage of inspection flight offers, but don't allow yourself to be pressured into buying on a viewing trip. Note that inspection trips inevitably only look at a limited number or certain type of property and in order to show the area in its best light, agents will endeavour to take you via the most attractive routes and wine and dine you at the best places. Bear in mind that there's always more to an area than what you see on an inspection trip. Always allow yourself sufficient time to view and compare properties offered by a number of agents and developers. A long weekend isn't sufficient time to have a good look around, unless you already know exactly what you want to buy and where, or are coming to view just one or two properties.

Some agents advertise 'free' inspection flights, which you then have to pay for if you don't buy anything. Check the small print and conditions of inspection flights as well as the reputation of the estate agents offering them before you sign up. Note that reputable estate agents will probably vet you and how serious you are about buying before accepting you on an inspection trip, which are expensive to lay on. Most agents offer after sales services and will help you arrange legal advice, insurance, utilities, and interior decorators and builders, and may offer a full management and rental service on behalf of non-resident owners. Note, however, that agents may receive commissions for referrals and therefore you may not receive independent advice.

## Legal Advice

Never allow yourself to be pressurised into a purchase and always take independent expert legal advice. Some agents pressurise clients into signing contracts and paying deposits quickly, alleging there are queues of other clients waiting to buy the property (which may be true!). Some even claim legal advice is unnecessary or provide it themselves, which is both illegal and unethical. Your chances of solving any problems are greater if you take legal advice and registered lawyers have professional indemnity insurance. There are a large number of complaints concerning fraud and malpractice against estate agents in Spain, particularly from foreign buyers, and there's little consumer protection. There are, however, many reputable estate agents in Spain (such as those advertising in this book!) who provide an excellent service.

# PROPERTY PRICES

Property prices soared throughout Spain in the 1980s, particularly in the major cities where prices rose by up to 40 per cent a year. In resort areas, rising prices were fuelled by the high demand for holiday homes, particularly from foreigners. However, as the effects of the world-wide recession struck Spain in the late 1980s and early 1990s, prices in most resort areas plummeted as the stream of buyers dried up, leaving developers and agents with a glut of unsold properties. In contrast, prices in the major cities remained fairly stable, being less dependent on foreign buyers and the vagaries of the world economic climate.

However, by 1999, property prices in most resort areas had fully recovered and many regions such as the Costa del Sol, Costa Blanca and Balearics are now experiencing a property boom the likes of which has never been seen before. Prices have been rising steadily for the past six years (1998-2003) and have increased by over 100 per cent during this period in many areas, where they now far exceed those of the heady days of the boom in the late 1980s. Prices nation-wide rose by 18 per cent in 2002 alone, although this figure was higher in areas such as Madrid, Barcelona and the Costa del Sol. There has been a flood of new developments in the last few years in the most popular areas, despite which there's often insufficient properties to meet the demand. The market has been boosted in recent years by an increasing number of buyers from Eastern Europe (particularly Russians), Hong Kong and South Africa, and it remains a seller's market in many areas. Prices are expected to continue to rise during 2003 and into 2004, albeit at a slower rate, although still well above inflation (4 per cent in 2002).

In stark contrast to the wild fluctuations of the last decade, property prices in Spain generally rise slowly and steadily, and are usually fairly stable, particularly away from resort areas and in rural areas where there's little local demand and few non-resident owners. Apart from obvious factors such as size, quality and land area, the most important consideration influencing the price of a home is its location. The closer a property is to a major city, the more expensive it will be; for example, an average quality two-bedroom apartment in a reasonable area costing €60,000 in a town will cost two or three times as much in a major city or a fashionable coastal resort. Property is cheapest in rural areas, where a farmhouse with outbuildings and land may cost the same as a studio apartment in Madrid or Marbella, although prices in rural areas situated relatively near popular resorts have risen spectacularly in recent years. The quality of properties varies considerably in respect to materials, fixtures and fittings, and workmanship. Value for money also varies considerably and you should compare at least five to ten properties to get a good idea of their relative values. You usually pay a premium for a beachside or golf course 'front-line' property.

When property is advertised in Spain, the total living area in square metres (*metros cuadrados*), written as $m^2$, and the number of bedrooms (*dormitorios*) are usually stated. When comparing prices, compare the cost per square metre of the habitable or built (*construidos*) area, usually referred to as *metros útiles*, excluding patios, terraces and balconies, which should be compared separately. If you're in any doubt about the size of rooms you should measure them yourself, rather than rely on the measurements provided by the vendor or agent. Note that a garage (*garaje*) is rarely provided with apartments or townhouses, although there may be a private parking space or a communal off-road parking area. Some apartment blocks have underground garages, and lock-up garages can often be purchased separately for apartments and townhouses for €10,000 to €20,000 in resort areas. Villas usually have their own car port or garage. Note that without a garage, parking can be a nightmare, particularly in cities or busy resort towns and urbanisations in summer (or at any time of the year in some places).

For those seeking the sun and who can choose where they want to live in Spain, the cheapest properties are on the lesser known *costas*, such as the Costa de la Luz, Costa Brava, Costa Almería and Costa Dorada. Prices on Spain's most popular *costas*, the Costa Blanca and the Costa del Sol, have risen dramatically in the last few years and it's now almost impossible to find a bargain. The Costa del Sol has some of Spain's most expensive real estate, particularly along Marbella's 'golden mile' where you have to pay at least €1.5 million for a fashionable address. Prices on the Costa Blanca start at €50,000 for a resale studio apartment, €80,000 for two bedrooms, and from €150,000 for a two-bedroom villa. Prices on the Costa del Sol are usually around 25 to 50 per cent dearer than the Costa Blanca, although they vary considerably depending on the area and town. Prices are generally slightly lower on the less popular eastern Costa del Sol than at the western end, i.e. west of Malaga city.

Property in the Balearics is generally around 25 to 50 per cent more expensive than on the *costas*, and Ibiza and Majorca have some of Spain's most expensive real estate. Prices in the Canaries (which have year-round letting potential) are slightly more expensive than on the mainland, except on the smaller and less accessible islands. Island properties generally command a premium over their mainland counterparts due to stricter building controls, the higher cost of building land and the smaller market. Approximate prices on the *costas* are shown below:

| Property | Price Range (€) |
| --- | --- |
| Studio | 50,000–100,000 |
| 1-bedroom apartment | 60,000–200,000 |
| 2-bedroom apartment | 60,000–200,000+ |
| 3-bedroom apartment | 90,000–400,000+ |
| 1-bedroom townhouse | 60,000–150,000 |

| 2-bedroom townhouse | 90,000–200,000+ |
|---|---|
| 3-bedroom townhouse | 120,000–350,000+ |
| 2-bedroom detached villa | 150,000–350,000+ |
| 3-bedroom detached villa | 175,000–500,000+ |
| 4/5-bedroom detached villa | 200,000–1,000,000+ |

Bear in mind that the more expensive your home, the more you will have to pay in property taxes, wealth tax and the deemed income tax on letting income (see **Chapter 4**), which are based on a property's *catastral* value. Community fees for a communal property (see page 139) also rise in direct relation to the value of a property.

# FEES

A variety of fees are payable when you buy a property in Spain, which usually add a total of around 10 per cent to the purchase price, which is higher than in many other EU countries. Fees are slightly higher (e.g. plus 1 or 1.5 per cent) on new properties than resale properties. Most fees are based on the 'declared' value of the property, which was traditionally much lower than the actual price paid. However, under the 'law of public fees' (*Ley de Tasas*, 1989), it's no longer possible to declare a very low figure and there are severe penalties for gross under-valuation. Local authorities maintain tables to calculate the current fiscal value (*valor catastral*) of properties and it's this price (or the actual price paid) which should be declared. However, if you get an absolute bargain, it may be wise to declare the market value rather than the price paid! In any case the tax authorities (*Agencia Tributaria*) can still reassess a property's value for tax purposes. It's generally recognised that the figure in the sales deed should be around 1.6 times the fiscal value (which should still be well below the actual sales price) and in any case not less than 20 per cent below the sale price.

If the authorities discover that the declared value is lower than their valuation they can levy a surcharge of 6 per cent on the difference, plus administration charges. If the value declared in the sales deed (*escritura*) is under-declared by over €12,000 or 20 per cent less than the actual market value, the buyer can be taxed on the difference between the declared value and the authority's estimated value, as if it were a gift (see **Inheritance & Gift Tax** on page 243). If you grossly under-value a property by 50 per cent less than the official valuation, the authorities also have the right to buy it within two years at the under-valued price. Reviews of declared values (*hoja de valoración*) are common nowadays and it's risky to make too low a declaration. A revaluation can be made up to four years and six months after the date of purchase. If a property is revalued, the revaluation must name the architect or surveyor who performed the valuation and the reason for the increase. If you disagree with the valuation you can lodge a protest, which must be done within a limited period.

The fees payable when buying a property in Spain may include the following:

- transfer tax (resale properties only);
- legal document tax;
- value added tax (new properties only);
- land tax;
- notary's fees;
- stamp duty (new properties only);
- legal fees;
- deed registration fee;
- surveyor's fee (optional);
- selling agent's fees;
- utility fees (new properties only).

Most taxes are paid by the buyer, with the exception of land tax (*plus valía*) and the selling agent's fees. However, a contract may state that the buyer is liable for all expenses (*todos los gastos*), including *plus valía*. This is legal, provided the buyer agrees, as the law stipulates simply that expenses will be divided when they aren't set out in the contract and who pays what fees is often a matter of negotiation. Always ensure that you know exactly what the total fees will be before signing a contract.

## Transfer Tax

Property buyers must pay transfer tax (*Impuesto de Transmisiones Patrimoniales/ITP*) of a certain percentage when buying a resale property. The percentage varies depending on the region where the property is situated, e.g. 7 per cent in Andalusia, Aragón, Balearics, Catalonia, Galicia, Madrid, Murcia and Valencia, and 6 per cent in the remaining regions. *ITP* actually consists of 5.5 or 6 per cent of the assessed value, plus a 0.5 or 1 per cent legal document fee (see below). Note that most regions provide a reduction in *ITP* for first-time resident buyers (e.g. in Andalusia first-time buyers under 35 purchasing their permanent residence pay 3.5 per cent instead of 7 per cent), large families or the disabled.

## Legal Document Tax

A tax on 'documented legal acts' (*Impuesto sobre Actos Jurídicos Documentados*) of 0.5 per cent (1 per cent in Andalusia, Aragón, Balearics, Catalonia, Galicia, Madrid, Murcia and Valencia) is levied on property transfers. For resale properties it's included in the transfer tax of 6 per cent (see above), but for new properties it's payable in addition to VAT (see below).

## Value Added Tax

Value added tax (*IVA*) of 7 per cent (4.5 per cent in the Canaries) is levied on new properties purchased from a developer or builder and being sold for the first time (including a garage or swimming pool constructed at the same time). *IVA* is 16 per cent on building land (*terreno urbanizable*) bought without any immediate plans to construct a dwelling and 7 per cent on agricultural land (*terreno rústico*). *IVA* is also 16 per cent on the building of a garage or a swimming pool that isn't constructed at the same time as a dwelling.

## Land Tax

'Land tax' (*impuesto municipal sobre el incremento del valor de los terrenos*, usually called *plus valía*) is a municipal tax on the increase in the value of land (excluding any buildings), since the last change of ownership. Traditionally it's paid by the vendor as he is the one who has made the profit, although in many areas it's common practice for the buyer to pay it. *Plus valía* depends on the population of the municipality in which the land is located and the number of years the vendor has owned the land, and bears no relation to the value of any buildings on the land. *Plus valía* is low on modern properties such as apartments and townhouses in urbanisations, where land values have increased little since the properties were built and little land is involved. It can, however, be high if you buy a large plot or a detached house with a few hectares of prime building land which hasn't changed hands for decades. If you're liable for *plus valía*, you can find out how much it will be before signing a contract by enquiring at the local municipal tax office (*recaudación municipal*). Note that most developers of new properties insist the buyer pays the *plus valía* tax and this will be stated in the contract.

# Notary's Fees

The fees for the notary who officiates at a sale are fixed by law and are based on a sliding scale depending on the sale price, except for when the *escritura* doesn't include one (i.e. when the property is a gift), when there are fixed fees for each document. The fees are usually from €320 to €600. If you're buying a plot in order to build a house, you will have to pay fees for two *escrituras*; one for the land and another for the building.

# Stamp Duty

Stamp duty of 0.5 per cent of the declared price is payable on a new property that has never been inhabited.

# Legal Fees

Legal fees for the conveyancing (see page 190) involved in a sale are usually around 1 to 1.5 per cent of the purchase price for an average property. The actual fee may depend on the work involved, although there's usually a minimum charge, e.g. €1,000, and it may be negotiable on 'expensive' properties. Fees, which should be agreed in writing beforehand, are much lower (e.g. €300) if a lawyer is engaged to vet the sales contract only. Legal fees are payable only after you've received the final *escritura pública* after registration at the property register, although many lawyers demand a pre-payment (*provisión de fondos*). Engaging a lawyer and paying legal fees is optional, but it's highly recommended.

# Deed Registration Fee

This is usually between €180 and €300, although the first amount paid is a deposit and is often over-estimated, so you may receive a small refund.

# Surveyor's Fee

If you employ a surveyor to inspect a building or plot of land, the fee will depend on the type of survey, any special requirements and the value of the property or land. A homebuyer's survey and valuation costs from €500 to €2,000.

# Selling Agent's Fees

The selling agent's fees are usually between 5 and 10 per cent (up to 25 per cent in rural areas) of the selling price, depending on the cost of the property and the type of contract, and are paid by the vendor. However, they're usually allowed for in the asking price, so in effect are paid by the buyer. Agents' often add their fee to the price required by the seller and therefore you may see the same property advertised by a number of agents for a different selling price.

## Utility Fees

If you buy a new property you usually need to pay for electricity, gas and water connections, and the installation of meters. You should ask the builder or developer to provide the cost of connection to services in writing. In resale properties you will probably have to pay for the cost of new contracts, particularly water.

## Running Costs

In addition to the fees associated with buying a property, you should also take into account the running costs. These include local property taxes (rates); annual wealth tax, income tax on deemed letting income, and a fiscal representative or tax consultant's fees; rubbish tax; community fees for a community property (see page 139); garden and pool maintenance (for a private villa); building and contents insurance (see page 257); standing charges for utilities (electricity, gas, telephone, water); plus a caretaker's or management fees if you leave a home empty or let it. Annual running costs usually average around 2 to 4 per cent of the cost of a property.

## TYPES OF PROPERTY

Spain offers a wealth of different properties, from small holiday apartments to huge country mansions set in acres of land, with just about everything in between. Each region has a typical type of property, for example a *cortijo* (large white-washed country house in Andalusia), a *masía* (a large stone country houses in Cataluña) or a *pazo* (typical country house) in Galicia. The purchase and restoration of these typical country homes is becoming increasingly popular among foreigners, especially those keen to establish small hotels or bed and breakfast businesses. However, the vast majority of foreigners purchase on the Spanish *costas* or islands where most property generally consists of apartments, townhouses or villas, most of which are purpose-built for the holiday-home market.

Below is a brief guide to the types of property available, including country properties.

# Apartments

Apartments and flats (*apartamento* or *piso*) abound in Spain and the vast majority of Spaniards live in apartment blocks, particularly in large towns and cities. Resorts such as Benidorm, Lloret del Mar, Magaluf and Torremolinos are smothered to the point of saturation with apartment blocks purpose-built for the holiday market and it's now difficult to find a stretch of popular coastline without a sky-line of apartment blocks (and high-rise hotels). Construction of apartment blocks have continued unabated throughout Spain (as the numerous cranes dotting the horizon testify) since the late 1960s, and there's still a good market for both buyers and sellers.

The quality and size varies enormously, from tiny studio apartments crammed into multi-storey blocks with 1970s-style bathroom fittings to spacious marble-floored apartments complete with all mod-cons. They may be situated in small side streets and be dark and cramped, while others are spacious front-line beach or golf developments with views stretching as far as the eye can see. Prices range from €60,000 for a small one-bedroom apartment in a less popular resort (e.g. on the Costa Dorada or Costa Cálida) to over €1 million on Marbella's new Golden Mile with just about everything in between. Bargain apartments are few and far between in popular areas and lower-priced properties usually require extensive modernisation and refurbishment.

Note that under Spanish law all owners of apartments (regardless of their number or size) in Spain are members of the community of owners (*comunidad de propietarios* – see page 136) and as such must abide by the community's rules and regulations and pay community fees.

Advantages of apartments include low maintenance (once you've carried out any necessary work), security (especially if the block has 24-hour security or a *concierge/portero*) and the use of communal gardens and pool (and possibly other facilities such as tennis courts). Apartments situated in towns also have the added advantage of local facilities and amenities within walking distance. Disadvantages are noisy neighbours, poorly-maintained communities and crowded complexes during holidays.

# Townhouses

Townhouses (*casa adosada*) are generally rows of terraced houses, often in typical regional style set around communal gardens with a pool. Townhouse complexes are increasingly popular around large towns and cities, particularly Madrid, where there are vast suburbs lined with row upon row of townhouses. In coastal resorts townhouses are often built in a style known as the 'Mediterranean village' (*pueblo Mediterráneo*) and houses may be white-washed or, as is increasingly popular nowadays, painted in shades of blues and yellows. Townhouses are usually spacious and often have three or four 'floors', including a basement for a garage and storage, and a roof area with a roof terrace known as a *solarium*. Townhouses generally have little outside space or garden except for a small patch at the front and back, often paved as a patio. Construction tends to be recent and is generally of reasonable to good quality.

Note that townhouses usually form part of a community property (see page 136) and owners must abide by the community's rules and regulations and pay community fees.

Townhouses are generally located on the outskirts of resorts and towns or within urbanisations (see below), with prices ranging from €60,000 for a one-bedroom townhouse in a less popular area, e.g. Costa de la Luz, to over €350,000 for three bedrooms in a top quality resort. Advantages include low maintenance, plenty of living and storage space, use of communal gardens and pool without the upkeep, and community living with fewer neighbours than in an apartment. On the other hand, you may suffer from noisy neighbours, poorly-maintained communities, crowded complexes during holidays and exhaustion from climbing the endless flights of stairs!

# Villas

In general, the Spanish don't live in detached houses (*casa*, *chalé* or *villa*) and in many large towns and cities it's difficult to find a large house unless it's a mansion or palace belonging to the local aristocracy. On the coast, however, detached houses abound and are generally owned by foreigners or wealthy Spaniards who use them as second homes. Some villas form part of a complex and may share communal gardens and a pool, and are situated on small individual plots, while others are set in huge grounds. Villas built in the 1960s and 1970s tend to be single-storey and often need extensive renovation work, particularly if they've only been used as holiday homes and not properly maintained. Construction quality may be poor in older properties, although the quality is usually excellent in newer properties, which tend to be at least two storeys and more spacious than older villas. Prices start at €150,000 for a small two-bedroom villa in a less popular area, although villas in exclusive parts of the Costa del Sol, the northern part of the Costa Blanca, and Ibiza and Majorca can cost a million euros or more.

Note that if a villa forms part of a community property (see page 136) owners must abide by the community's rules and regulations, and pay community fees.

# Urbanisations

Urbanisations (*urbanizaciós*) are purpose-built estates or developments which may include apartments, townhouses and villas. They form an essential part of Spanish resort landscapes and cities and most popular areas are packed with them. Some have been part of the holiday home market since the first sun-worshippers arrived in Spain in the 1960s, although most are more recent. Some are small with a limited number of properties, while others are huge complexes, almost towns in their own right, such as Sitio de Calahonda on the Costa del Sol, the largest urbanisation with a population of some 15,000. Property available on urbanisations is varied and caters for different needs and price ranges, and many urbanisations contain a mixture of apartment blocks and individual villas. Facilities and amenities vary greatly from extensive shopping facilities, transport systems and sports complexes to little more than a local bar (which may only be open in summer). Some urbanisations have permanent resident populations while others turn into ghost towns outside the high season. Many urbanisations are populated mainly by foreigners and some tend to cater for one nationality only, e.g. British or German, particularly on the Costa del Sol, Costa Blanca and the islands.

Advantages include general tranquillity, pleasant surroundings, good security (if the urbanisation has private security) and a ready-made foreign community often with a good social scene. Disadvantages are few amenities and facilities, limited public spending (local councils collect rates and local taxes enthusiastically, but invest as little as possible in urbanisations) and a possibly claustrophobic ex-pat atmosphere.

Note that most urbanisations are community properties (see page 136), and owners, who automatically form a community of owners, must abide by the community's rules and regulations and pay community fees. In some cases, the property may belong to a sub-community within the larger community of the urbanisation.

# Country Properties

As property prices have risen on the coast and resort areas have become more crowded, foreigners are increasingly looking further inland to the Spanish countryside in their search for property. Property here, popularly known as *fincas* – a term loosely used to describe just about anything from a shepherd's hut to a well-preserved farmhouse – is generally cheaper than resort property and widely available except in areas in the immediate vicinity of coastal resorts. *Fincas* range from a ruin set in a large area of land to cottages or large country homes, sometimes together with working farmland. Almost all *fincas* come with large plots of land and may include fruit trees, olive groves or pasture. Renovation is almost always necessary unless you pay a premium and buy a property that's already been modernised.

Advantages of country properties include cheaper prices, peace and quiet, low local taxes and the opportunity to live in the 'real' Spain. On the other hand, rural properties usually involve extensive maintenance as well as restoration work, utilities may be poor or non-existent, amenities and facilities are often some distance away and you don't have the advantage of a ready-made community. The good news is that Spanish village communities are generally among the friendliest and most welcoming in the world!

---

**IMPORTANT NOTE**

The purchase of a rural property in Spain is potentially open to numerous legal complications and is therefore the most risky (see **Avoiding Problems** on page 106). Although legal advice is highly recommended in all property purchases, if you plan to buy a rural property, independent legal advice is essential. You (or preferably, your lawyer) should check that planning permission will be granted for any work you wish to do (contrary to popular expatriate belief, you **don't** automatically receive planning permission to restore a ruin in Spain – see page 154). If you plan to buy a rural property or a property in an undeveloped area in the *Comunidad Valenciana* (including the Costa Blanca), you **must** obtain legal advice regarding the implications of the *LRAU* (see page 111).

---

See also **Buying A Resale Home** on page 135, **New Homes** on page 131, **Renovation & Restoration** on page 154 and **Building Your Own Home** on page 159.

## BUYING A NEW HOME

New properties are widely available in Spain and include coastal and city apartments and townhouses, sports (e.g. skiing or golf) developments, and a wide range of individually-designed villas. Most new properties are part of purpose-built developments, particularly on the *costas* and in the Balearic and Canary islands. Note, however, that many developments are planned as holiday homes and may not be attractive as permanent homes. If you're buying an apartment or house that's part of a community development, check whether your neighbours will be mainly Spanish or foreigners. Some foreigners don't wish to live in a community consisting mainly of their fellow countrymen (or other foreigners) and this may also deter buyers when you wish to sell. On the other hand, some foreigners don't want to live in a Spanish community, particularly if they don't speak Spanish.

Prices of new properties vary considerably depending on their location and quality:

- from around €60,000 for a studio or one-bedroom apartment in a resort;
- from €60,000 for a two-bedroom apartment or townhouse;
- from €90,000 for a three-bedroom apartment or townhouse;
- from around €200,000 for a four-bedroom detached house.

When sales are slow, some developers offer inducements to buyers which may include anything from a 'free' car to a holiday including 'free' accommodation and flights. Bear in mind, however, that the cost of these 'gifts' is included in the price and you should be able to get an equivalent (or even larger) cash reduction by haggling.

It's often cheaper to buy a new home than an old property requiring modernisation or renovation, as the price is fixed, unlike the cost of renovation which can soar way beyond original estimates (as many people have discovered to their cost). If required, a new property can usually be let immediately and modern homes have good resale potential and are considered a good investment by Spanish buyers. On the other hand, new homes may be smaller than older properties, have smaller gardens and rarely come with a large plot of land. New properties are covered by a 10-year warranty against structural defects and it's against the law to sell a new home without one. In recent years, prices of new properties bought off plan in some areas have increased by up to 20 per cent before completion. Many people prefer to buy new properties that form part of a large complex, as appreciation is very high (up to 20 per cent annually), although once all phases of the complex has been finished prices stabilise quickly.

Most new properties are sold by property developers (*promotores*) or builders (*constructores*), although they're also marketed by estate agents, who generally charge 10 per cent commission on new properties. New developments usually have a sales office (*oficina de ventas*) and/or a show house or apartment (*chalet/piso piloto*). When a building is purchased off plan, payment is made in stages as building work progresses, usually over a period of up to one year, e.g. 10 per cent on signing the contract, 20 per cent for three stages and 30 per cent on completion. Note that it's important to ensure that each stage is completed satisfactorily before making payments. If you aren't able to do this yourself, you must engage an independent representative (e.g. an architectural engineer) to do it on your behalf. If you're buying a property off plan, you can usually choose your bathroom suite, kitchen, fireplace, wallpaper and paint, wall and floor tiles, and carpets in bedrooms, all of which may be included in the price. You may also be able to alter the interior room layout, although this may increase the price. Note that it's advisable to make any changes or additions to a property during the design stage, such as including a more luxurious kitchen, a chimney or an additional shower room, which will cost much more to install later.

The quality of new property in Spain is extremely variable and may be poorer than in northern European countries. Sometimes, but not always, the best (and most expensive) properties are built by northern European builders using high-quality imported materials and fittings such as doors, windows, and bathroom and kitchen suites. The quality of a building and the materials used will be reflected in the price, so when comparing prices ensure that you're comparing similar quality. Cheaper properties aren't usually the best built, although there are exceptions. If you want a permanent, rather than a holiday home, you're better off choosing high quality construction and materials. The average prices for new properties (land and building costs) per square metre (m²) has increased dramatically in recent years (prices rose by 15 per cent in 2002 alone). In early 2003 the average countrywide was €1,667 per m² and €2,500 in Madrid and Barcelona. These are average prices and in certain popular areas you can pay a lot more. The costs of land, materials and labour have increased sharply in the last few years and are still rising. In 2002-3 there was also a shortage of labour and materials in many resort areas.

The word luxury is often used very loosely in Spain and should be taken with a pinch of salt. New homes usually contain a high level of 'luxury' features which may include a full-size, fully-fitted kitchen (possibly with a microwave, hob/oven with extractor hood, dishwasher, fridge/freezer and washing machine); a utility room; large bathrooms (often *en suite* to all bedrooms) with bidets and dressing areas; a separate shower room and guest toilet; air-conditioning and central heating (possibly under-floor) in the lounge and bedrooms; double glazing and shutters (possibly electric) on all windows; cavity walls (for sound deadening and cooling); a fireplace; a wall safe; ceramic-tiled floors in the kitchen and bathrooms and marble-tiled floors in other rooms; fitted carpets in all bedrooms and dressing rooms; built-in mirror-fronted wardrobes in bedrooms; communal satellite TV; telephone outlets; 24-

hour security and resident concierge; panic call buttons and intercom to a concierge; automatic lifts; basement car parking and a lockable basement storage room.

Luxury properties that are part of a community (see page 136) also have a wide range of quality community facilities such as indoor (heated) and outdoor swimming pools, tennis courts and beautiful, landscaped gardens. Some properties have an associated golf or country club with golf, tennis and squash courts, health spa, gymnasium, sauna, Jacuzzi, snooker, indoor bowling and swimming pools, plus a restaurant and bar. Most new developments have their own sales offices (*oficinas de rentas y ventas*), usually offering a full management and rental service on behalf of non-resident owners. If you wish to furnish a property solely for letting, furniture packages are available and are usually good value for money. The complete furnishing of a holiday home costs from around €3,000 for one bedroom, €3,500 for two bedrooms and €4,000 for three bedrooms.

Note that because of the problems associated with unfinished properties in Spain in the last few decades, you must be extremely circumspect when buying off plan, i.e. a property that isn't totally complete with all the infrastructure in place (see **Avoiding Problems** on page 106). You should also use the services of a lawyer for all stages of the purchase, but especially at the beginning when you sign the contract. Contracts should be carefully checked by a professional – developers are notorious for including numerous clauses in their favour, e.g. many contracts for new properties state that **all** costs associated with buying the property are payable by the buyer, including the costs of cancelling the mortgage (around €350) if the developer has one on the apartment and you don't wish to take it on. A lawyer's services will also be useful after completion if there are any problems. According to an investigation by the National Institute of Consumers (*Instituto Nacional de Consumo*), almost half of all new properties have construction defects or deficiencies and in one-third of cases the contract conditions aren't fulfilled, particularly regarding the completion date and the quality of materials used. Note that developers are legally responsible for repairs for up to ten years after completion (finishing defects for one year, minor defects for up to three years and structural defects for ten years).

New properties are rarely completed on schedule (up to 80 per cent are delivered late) and in some cases, the property may be finished up to a year after the original estimate. You should ensure that your contract includes a clause clearly stating the date for completion as well as a penalty clause (e.g. €50 per day for late completion). Note, however, that many developers refuse to include such clauses, particularly when demand exceeds supply as is currently the case, and you may be forced to accept late completion with no compensation or look elsewhere.

# BUYING A RESALE HOME

The vast majority of homes for sale in Spain are 'resale' homes, i.e. any property which has been previously owned and occupied. There are many advantages in buying a modern resale home which may include better value for money, an established development with a range of local services and facilities in operation, more individual design and style, the eradication of 'teething troubles', furniture and other extras included in the price, a mature garden and trees, and a larger plot of land. With a resale property you can see exactly what you will get for your money (unlike when buying off plan), most problems will have been resolved, and the previous owners may have made improvements or added extras such as a swimming pool, which may not be fully reflected in the asking price.

Resale properties often represent good value for money, particularly in resort areas, where many apartments and townhouses are sold fully furnished, although the quality of furnishings varies considerably (from luxurious to junk) and may not be to your taste. Luxury properties and villas, e.g. costing upwards of around €250,000, are rarely sold furnished. Another advantage of buying a resale property is that you can see exactly what you will get for your money and will save on the cost of installing water and electricity meters and telephone lines, or the cost of extending these services to a property. When buying a resale property in a development, it's advisable to ask the neighbours about any problems, community fees, planned developments and anything else that may affect your enjoyment of the property. Most residents are usually happy to tell you, unless of course they're trying to sell you their own property!

If you want a property with abundant charm and character, a building for renovation or conversion, outbuildings, or a large plot of land, then you must usually buy an 'old' property, i.e. a property that is 50 or more years old. Note, however, that there's a relatively small market for old country homes such as farmhouses in Spain, particularly inexpensive properties requiring renovation, as the prices are usually too low to interest most agents. Most old homes purchased by foreigners are in the hinterland of the Costa del Sol and Costa Blanca, where some villages are popular, the foothills of the Pyrenees and in the Balearics. In many rural areas (including villages close to the coast) it's possible to buy old properties from as little as €10,000, although you will need to carry out major renovation and modernisation, which will usually treble the price.

Many old homes lack basic services such as electricity, a reliable water supply and sanitation. Because the purchase price is usually low, many foreign buyers are lulled into a false sense of security and believe they're getting a wonderful bargain, without fully investigating the renovation costs. If you aren't into do-it-yourself in a big way, you may be better off buying a new or recently built property. If you're planning to buy a property that needs restoration or renovation and you won't be doing the work yourself, obtain an **accurate** estimate of the costs **before** signing a contract. You should consider having a survey (see page 148) done on a resale property as major problems can even be found in properties less than five years old. Note that some old properties have no deeds (*escritura*) and ownership may be proved by a document issued by a court called an *expediente de dominio*.

Bear in mind that if you buy and restore a property with the intention of selling it for a profit, you must take into account not only the initial price and the restoration costs, but also the fees and taxes included in the purchase, plus capital gains tax if it's a second home. It's often difficult to sell an old renovated property at a higher than average market price, irrespective of its added value. The Spanish have little interest in old restored properties, which is an important point if you need to sell an old home quickly in an area that isn't popular with foreign buyers. If you're buying for investment, you're usually better off buying a new home.

Owners often advertise properties in the Spanish and expatriate press (see **Appendix B**) or by simply putting a 'for sale' (*se vende*) sign in the window. Although you can save money by buying direct from an owner, particularly when he's forced to sell, you should **always** employ a lawyer to carry out the necessary checks (see **Conveyancing** on page 190). If you're unsure of the value, you should obtain a professional valuation.

## COMMUNITY PROPERTIES

Properties in Spain with common elements (whether a building, amenities or land) shared with other properties are owned outright through a system of part-ownership, similar to owning a condominium in the USA. Community properties include apartments, townhouses, and single-family (detached) homes on a private estate with communal areas and facilities. Almost all properties that are part of a development (*urbanización*) are community properties. In general, the only properties that don't belong to a community are detached houses built on individual plots in public streets or on rural land. Owners of community properties not only own their homes, but also own a share of the common elements of a building or development, including foyers, hallways, passages, lifts, patios, gardens, roads, and leisure and sports facilities (such as swimming pools and tennis courts). When you buy a community property you automatically become a member of the community of owners (*comunidad de propietarios*), which includes some two-thirds of foreign property owners in Spain.

Many community developments are located in or near coastal resorts and offer a range of communal facilities such as a golf course, swimming pools, tennis courts, a gymnasium or fitness club, and a bar and restaurant. Golf homes are popular as no one can build in front of you and spoil your view and you can consider the golf course as your lawn and garden. They also usually include discounts on green fees or even 'free' golf membership. Most developments have landscaped gardens and some also offer high security and a full-time porter (*portero*). At the other extreme, cheaper, older developments may consist of numerous cramped, tiny studio apartments with few, if any, amenities. Note that many community developments are planned as holiday homes and aren't attractive as permanent homes.

If you're buying a holiday home that will be vacant for long periods (particularly in winter), don't buy in an apartment block where heating and/or hot water charges are shared, otherwise you will be paying towards your part-owners' bills. This is unusual in resort areas in Spain, although water and rubbish collection may be charged communally. You should also check whether there are any rules regarding short or long-term rentals or leaving a property unoccupied for long periods. Note that when buying in a large development, communal facilities may be inundated during peak periods, e.g. a large swimming pool won't look so big when 100 people are using it and getting a game of tennis can be difficult during peak periods.

To find out more about community ownership you can obtain a copy of *The Community of Owners* published by the Foundation Institute of Foreign Property Owners (see page 105).

# Advantages

The advantages of owning a community property include increased security; lower property taxes than detached homes; a range of community sports and leisure facilities; community living with lots of social contacts and the companionship of close neighbours; no garden, lawn or pool maintenance; fewer of the responsibilities of home ownership; ease of maintenance; and the opportunity to live in an area where owning a single-family home would be prohibitively expensive, e.g. a beach front or town centre.

# Disadvantages

The disadvantages of community properties may include excessively high community fees (owners may have no control over increases), restrictive rules and regulations, a confining living and social environment and possible lack of privacy, noisy neighbours (particularly if neighbouring properties are let to holiday-makers), limited living and storage space, expensive covered or secure parking (or insufficient off road parking), and acrimonious owners' meetings where management and factions may try to push through unpopular proposals. Note that unless it's prohibited under the community rules, anyone can buy up community properties and turn them into timeshares.

## Checks

Before buying a community property it's advisable to ask current owners about the community. For example:

- Do they like living there?
- What are the fees and restrictions?
- How noisy are other residents, are the recreational facilities easy to access?
- Would they buy there again (why or why not)?
- Is the community well managed?

You may also wish to check on your prospective neighbours and if you're planning to buy an apartment above the ground floor you may want to ensure that the building has a lift. Note that upper floor apartments are both colder in winter and warmer in summer and may incur extra charges for the use of lifts (they do, however, offer more security than ground floor apartments). An apartment that has other apartments above and below it will generally be more noisy than a ground or top floor apartment.

 **If you're planning to buy a community property, it's important to ensure that it's well managed and that there aren't any outstanding major problems. If there are, you could be liable to contribute towards the cost of repairs, which could run into many thousands of euros.**

## Unfinished Urbanisations

In view of the problems encountered by buyers in the past, some experts advise people not to buy a property in a community development where the infrastructure isn't complete. In many unfinished developments, owners have been required to pay a special contribution (*contribuciones especiales*) for the absent or inadequate infrastructure (which they've already paid for in the purchase price), with costs often running into thousands of euros per owner. Many developments never become fully legal and are without proper roads, lighting, mains sewage and sometimes even water. In some communities owners have been fighting (unsuccessfully in most cases) for years to get the infrastructure finished.

In an apartment block or communal development the developer divides the costs of the communal areas between the owners, who must form a community of owners. You should never buy a property in an urbanisation where there isn't a legal community of owners. To be legal, a community of apartments or townhouses must be registered in the property registry or in the registry of conservation entities if it consists of detached villas. Some communal areas (such as roads) may be cared for by the local municipality, provided it has approved the urbanisation and has included it in its general plan for the municipality. An **approved** urbanisation has the same right to public support as any other part of a municipality. Before buying a community property, it's essential to obtain a copy of both the law of horizontal division (*ley de propiedad horizontal*) and the community rules and have them explained to you. Spanish law requires that all communities have their own set of statutes (*estatutos*) which identify property that's owned privately (*cosa privativas*) and property that's owned communally (*cosa comunes*).

## Cost

Community properties vary enormously in price and quality; for example, from around €60,000 for a studio or one-bedroom apartment in an average location to tens of thousands of euros for a luxury apartment, townhouse or villa in a prime location. Garages and parking spaces must usually be purchased separately in developments, where a lock-up garage or a space in an underground car park usually costs between €8,000 and €18,000. If you're buying a resale property, check the price paid for similar properties in the same area or development in recent months, but bear in mind that the price you pay may have more to do with the seller's circumstances than the price fetched by other properties. Find out how many properties are for sale in a particular development; if there are many on offer you should investigate why, as there could be management or structural problems. If you're still keen to buy, you can use any negative points to drive a hard bargain.

## Community Fees

Owners of community properties must pay community fees (*gastos de comunidad*) for the upkeep of communal areas and for communal services. Charges are calculated according to each owner's share (*cuota de participación*) of the development or apartment building and **not** whether they're temporary or permanent residents. Shares are usually calculated according to the actual size of properties, e.g. the owners of ten properties of equal size usually each pay 10 per cent of community fees. The percentage to be paid is detailed in the property deed (*escritura*). Shares not only determine the share of fees to be paid, but also voting rights at general meetings.

Fees go towards road cleaning; green zone maintenance (including communal and possibly private gardens); cleaning, decoration and maintenance of buildings; caretaker (janitor); communal lighting in buildings and grounds; water supply (e.g. swimming pools, gardens); insurance; administration fees; urbanisation rates; maintenance of radio and television aerials and satellite TV charges. Fees are divided among owners according to the share of the utility allocated to each property. Always check the level of general and any special charges before buying a community property. Fees are usually billed monthly or bi-annually and adjusted at the end of the year when the actual expenditure is known and the annual accounts have been approved by the committee. If you're buying an apartment from a previous owner, ask to see a copy of the service charges for previous years and the minutes of the last annual general meeting, as owners may be 'economical with the truth' when stating service charges, particularly if they're high. You should obtain receipts for the previous five years (if applicable).

Community fees vary considerably depending on the communal facilities provided. For example, fees for a small studio apartment in a small, older block may be as little as €120 a year, whereas fees for a large luxury penthouse in a modern prestigious development can be over €3,000 a year. Fees for a typical two-bedroom apartment costing around €60,000 are some €300 to €450 a year, although in 'luxury' communities they can be well over €600. High fees aren't necessarily a negative point (assuming you can afford them), provided you receive value for money and the community is well managed and maintained. The value of a community property depends to a large extent on how well the development is maintained and managed. Note, however, that less than half of all communities in Spain are considered to be well run!

**Non-Payment Of Fees**

In the past, many communities have had severe debt problems because of the non-payment of fees, which in turn leads to the management failing to maintain facilities such as lifts, lighting and security systems when they break down. However, this problem has been largely eradicated with the introduction of a new community law in 1999, under which it's much easier to embargo the property of owners who don't pay their community fees and, if necessary, force a sale. The proceedings (called *procedimiento monitorio* in article 21 of the new law) now take around three months only, commencing with a demand (*demanda*) in court signed by the president and administrator of a community. After a case has been admitted, the judge will ask the debtor to deposit the amount owed within 20 days and an announcement is placed in the province's 'official bulletin' (*Boletín Oficial de la Provincia/BOP*). If he doesn't pay, an embargo is placed on the property and if the debt is still unpaid or additional debts are accrued the property can be forcibly sold at a public auction at the request of the community representatives.

Note that if you own a second home in Spain that you visit once or twice a year, it's important to ensure (double check!) that all bills are paid in your absence, otherwise you could find that your home has been sold to pay bills when you return to Spain!

## Maintenance & Repairs

If necessary, owners can be assessed an additional amount to make up any shortfall of funds for maintenance or repairs. You should check the condition of the common areas (including all amenities) in an old development and whether any major maintenance or capital expense is planned for which you could be assessed. Old run-down apartment blocks can have their community fees increased substantially to pay for new installations and repairs (such as a new water supply or sewage installations). Always enquire about any planned work and obtain a copy of the minutes of the last annual meeting where important matters are bound to have been raised. Owners' meetings can become rather heated when finances are discussed, particularly when assessments are being made to finance capital expenditure. The new law on communities introduced in 1999 requires the establishment of a maintenance reserve fund equal to a minimum of 5 per cent of the annual ordinary budget.

## Management

A community of owners or Property Community has an elected president (*presidente*) and a paid administrator (*administrador de fincas*), who may be a professional administrator from outside the community. The general running of a community is carried out by the administrator, a position that's automatically assumed by the president if an administrator isn't elected. The community of owners must be registered with the *Gobernador Civil* of the province and community books and documentation must be in Spanish, although they can be translated into other languages for owners. All owners are required to attend an annual general meeting to discuss the annual fee and to elect the president and committee members, although owners can name someone to represent and vote for them by proxy (*poder* or *autorización*).

Meetings of the community of owners are usually held in Spanish, although they can be held in another language if **everyone** is in agreement. The owners attending or voting at a meeting must hold at least 50 per cent of community property in order to pass a resolution; however, if 25 per cent of owners disagree with a resolution and consider their rights have been neglected, they can apply to a judge within one month for a decision. Changes in the Memorandum and Articles of Association require unanimity, while most other decisions require a majority of 60 per cent or a simple majority (51 per cent), the exception being the installation of communications equipment (e.g. satellite dishes), solar or electrical energy, which requires approval by just a third of owners. Note that meetings can be acrimonious, particularly when there's a mixture of nationalities and both resident and non-resident owners.

## Restrictions

Community rules allow owners to run a community in accordance with the wishes of the majority, while at the same time safeguarding the rights of the minority. Rules usually include such things as noise levels, the keeping of pets (usually permitted, although some communities prohibit all pets!), renting, exterior decoration and plants (e.g. the placement of shrubs), rubbish disposal, the use of swimming pools and other recreational facilities, the activities of children (e.g. no ball games or cycling on community grounds), parking, business or professional use, use of a communal laundry room, the installation and positioning of satellite dishes, and the hanging of laundry. Check the rules and discuss any restrictions with residents.

# RETIREMENT HOMES

Retirement homes are generally purpose-built communities (or sheltered housing) and are becoming more common, particularly on the *costas*, although they're still fairly rare. Most urbanisations are developed by foreign companies for foreigners, as the Spanish prefer to live among their family and friends in their 'twilight' years. Many sheltered housing developments attract elderly people, e.g. aged 70 plus, with limited mobility. Developments usually consist of one and two-bedroom apartments or a combination of apartments, townhouses and villas, which can be purchased freehold or leasehold, i.e. a lifetime occupancy.

Properties usually have central heating, air-conditioning, fully-fitted kitchens and satellite TV. A wide range of communal facilities and services are provided including medical and dental clinics (possibly with a resident doctor and dentist), nursing facilities, lounges, laundry, housekeeping, sauna, Jacuzzi, restaurant, bar, meal delivery, handyman, mini-supermarket, post and banking, guest apartments, free local transport, 24-hour security with closed-circuit television (CCTV), intercom service, personal emergency alarm system and a 24-hour multi-lingual reception. Sports and leisure services may include swimming pools, tennis courts, lawn bowling, gymnasium, video room, library and a social club.

Most sheltered housing developments levy monthly service charges, e.g. between €150 and €500, which may include a number of weeks' (e.g. six) nursing care per illness, per year in a residents' nursing home. Charges usually include heating and air-conditioning, hot and cold water, satellite TV, and all the other services listed above.

# TIMESHARE & PART-OWNERSHIP SCHEMES

If you're looking for a holiday home abroad, you may wish to investigate a scheme that provides sole occupancy of a property for a number of weeks each year rather than buying a property. Schemes available include part-ownership, leaseback, retirement homes, timesharing and a holiday property bond, and are described below. Don't rush into any of these schemes without fully researching the market and before you're absolutely clear what you want and what you can realistically expect to get for your money.

## Part-Ownership

Part-ownership includes schemes such as a consortium of buyers owning shares in a property-owning company and part-ownership between family, friends or even strangers. Some developers offer a turn-key deal whereby a home is sold fully furnished and equipped. Part-ownership allows you to recoup your investment in savings on holiday costs and still retain your equity in the property. A common deal is a 'four-owner' scheme (which many consider to be the optimum number of part-owners), where you buy a quarter of a property and can occupy it for up to three months a year. However, there's no reason why there cannot be as many as 12 part-owners, with a month's occupancy each per year (usually divided between high, medium and low seasons).

Part-ownership offers access to a size and quality of property that would otherwise be unimaginable, and it's even possible to have a share in a substantial *castillo*, where a number of families could live together simultaneously and hardly ever see each other if they didn't want to. Part-ownership can be a good choice for a family seeking a holiday home for a few weeks or months a year and has the added advantage that (because of the lower cost) a mortgage may be unnecessary. Note that it's cheaper to buy a property privately with friends rather than from an agent or developer who offers this sort of scheme, in which case you may pay well above the market value for a share of a property (check the market value of a property to establish whether it's good value). Part-ownership is **much** better value than a timeshare and needn't cost much more. **A water-tight contract must be drawn up by an experienced lawyer to protect the part-owners' interests.**

One of the best ways to get into part-ownership, if you can afford it, is to buy a property yourself and offer shares to others. This overcomes the problem of getting together a consortium of would-be owners and trying to agree on a purchase in advance, which is difficult unless it's just a few friends or family members. Many people form a Spanish company to buy and manage the property, which can in turn be owned by a company in the part-owners' home country, thus allowing any disputes to be dealt with under local law. Each part-owner receives a number of shares depending on how much he has paid, entitling him to so many weeks occupancy a year. Owners don't need to have equal shares and can be made direct title holders. If a part-owner wishes to sell his shares he must usually give first refusal to the other part-owners, although if they don't wish to buy them and a new part-owner cannot be found, the property will need to be sold.

## Leaseback

Leaseback or sale and leaseback schemes are designed for those seeking a holiday home for a limited number of weeks each year. Properties sold under a leaseback scheme are always located in popular resort areas, e.g. golf, ski or coastal resorts, where self-catering accommodation is in high demand. Buying a property through a leaseback scheme allows a purchaser to buy a new property at less than its true cost, e.g. 30 per cent less than the list price. In return for the discount the property must be leased back to the developer, usually for 9 to 11 years, so that he can let it as self-catering holiday accommodation. The buyer owns the freehold of the property and the full price is shown in the title deed.

The purchaser is also given the right to occupy the property for a period each year, usually six or eight weeks, spread over high, medium and low seasons. These weeks can usually be let to provide income or possibly be exchanged with accommodation in another resort (as with a timeshare scheme). The developer furnishes and manages the property and pays the maintenance and bills (e.g. for utilities) during the term of the lease, even when the owner occupies the property.

 **It's important to have a contract checked by your legal adviser to ensure that you receive vacant possession at the end of the leaseback period, without having to pay an indemnity charge, otherwise you could end up paying more than a property is worth.**

A buyer may be able to buy out of a sale and leaseback scheme after a period, e.g. two years.

# Timesharing

Timesharing (*multipropiedad*), also known as 'holiday ownership', 'vacation ownership', 'part-ownership' or 'holidays for life', is easily the most popular form of part-ownership in Spain, where there are around 450 timeshare resorts with some 500,000 owners (90 per cent non-Spanish). It's the fastest growing property market sector in Spain, which is the second-largest timeshare market in the world after the USA.

However, unlike the USA, timesharing has a dreadful reputation in Spain, where it's often associated with fraud and crime, particularly on the *costas* and in the Balearic and Canary islands. Nevertheless, there are many reputable timeshare companies operating in Spain, where the best timeshare developments are on a par with luxury hotels and offer a wide range of facilities including bars, restaurants, entertainment, shops, swimming pools, tennis courts, health clubs, and other leisure and sports facilities. If you don't wish to holiday in the same place each year, choose a timeshare development that's a member of an international organisation such as Resort Condominium International (☎ UK 0870-609 0141, 🖳 www.rci.com), Interval International (☎ UK 0870-744 4222, 🖳 www.intervalworld.com) or Marriott (🖳 www. marriott.co.uk), which allow you (usually for an additional fee) to exchange your timeshare with one in another area or country. It's also advisable to check that the timeshare development belongs to the Organisation for Timeshare in Europe (OTE) whose members must abide by a strict code of ethics.

Although timesharing has a poor reputation in Spain, things improved greatly when a new law was introduced in 1998 to protect buyers. This includes a requirement that buyers have secure occupancy rights and that their money is properly protected prior to the completion of a new property. Timeshare companies are required to disclose information about the vendor and the property, and allow prospective buyers a 10-day 'cooling off period' during which they may cancel a sales agreement they've signed without penalty. If a deposit is paid, it must go into a third party bank account or an escrow or trustee account. Timeshare purchases can now be registered with a Spanish notary and inscribed in the registry at the buyer's request (it isn't mandatory). A personal guarantee must be provided by a timeshare company that the property is as advertised and, where applicable, the contract must be in the language of the EU country where the buyer is resident or the language of the buyer's choice (you cannot sign away any of your rights irrespective of what's written in the contract). If a new contract isn't made in accordance with the new law it's null and void. However, there are disturbing reports that timeshare companies have found a way around the law by offering shares within a specially created club and other measures in order to circumvent the law such as trial packages or holiday packs (all considerably more expensive than a conventional holiday!), none of which have protection schemes for the buyer. Always seek legal advice before signing anything in connection with buying a timeshare (or anything else) in Spain!

 **If you're thinking of buying a timeshare, you should be extremely wary who you deal with. Timeshare 'muggers' are rife in most popular resorts throughout the main tourist season (or year round in the Canaries and Costa del Sol).**

Touts compete vigorously to induce tourists to attend a 'presentation' (sales pitch) by pretending to be conducting surveys, using scratch cards and other competitions (everyone's a winner – provided that you attend a sales pitch), and offering free drinks, meals, wine, cash, excursions and other baubles. Because of the adverse effects on tourism, some municipalities publish leaflets warning visitors against timeshare touts and their inducements to attend presentations (they usually target couples only). If you're tempted to attend a sales pitch (lasting up to four hours!), you should be aware that you will usually be subjected to some of the most aggressive, high-pressure sales methods employed anywhere on earth and many people are simply unable to resist (the sales staff are experts). If you decide to go to a presentation, don't take your cheque book, credit cards (or their numbers) or a lot of cash with you, so that you won't be pressured into paying a deposit without thinking it over. Credit cards are among the 'crooks' favourite methods of payment and you shouldn't rely on getting your money back from the credit card company if it turns out that you've been conned. High-pressure timeshare companies try to take as big a deposit as they can (30 per cent isn't unusual), as they know that they're unlikely to get any more. **You cannot usually be prosecuted in your home country for failing to pay for a timeshare property in Spain.** Many companies are often registered in off shore tax havens, out of the clutches of local laws and taxes.

You will often be offered inducements to sign on-the-spot such as a 'discount' (e.g. €1,200), a bonus week and no legal fees. A reputable company will allow you a cooling-off period, although you should never pay a deposit or sign a contract without giving yourself time to think it over and getting the contract checked by a lawyer. Avoid the hard-sell merchants like the plague as reputable companies don't need to resort to hard-sell tactics and **never** need to tout for business on street corners. There are so many scams associated with timeshares that it would take a dedicated book to recount them all (and it would need to updated every few months!). Suffice to say that many people bitterly regret the day they signed up for a timeshare! Complaints against timeshare companies run into tens of thousands a year and comprise 90 per cent of all property-related complaints.

It isn't difficult to understand why there are so many timeshare companies and why sales people often employ such intimidating hard-sell methods. A week's timeshare in an apartment worth around €100,000 can be sold for up to €15,000 or more, making a total income of up to €750,000 for the timeshare company if they sell 50 weeks (over six times the market value of the property!), plus management and other fees. Most experts believe that there's little or no advantage in a timeshare over a normal holiday rental and that it's simply an expensive way to pay for your holidays in advance. It doesn't make any sense to tie up your money for what amounts to a long-term reservation on an annual holiday (usually you don't actually 'own' anything). Timeshares cost up to €15,000 for one week in a one or two-bedroom apartment in a top-rated resort, to which must be added annual management fees of €200 to €500 or more for each week and other miscellaneous fees. Most financial advisers believe you're better off putting your money into a long-term investment, where you retain your capital and may even earn sufficient interest to pay for a few weeks' holiday each year. For example, €6,000 invested at just 5 per cent yields €300 a year, which when added to the saving on management fees, say €200, makes a total of €480. Sufficient to pay for a week's holiday in a self-catering apartment outside the 'high season' almost anywhere.

Often timeshares are difficult or impossible to sell at any price and 'pledges' from timeshare companies to sell them for you or buy them back at the market price are just a sales ploy, as timeshare companies aren't interested once they've made a sale. In fact some companies even persuade those wanting to sell to buy another timeshare, while offering to buy or sell their existing timeshare for well above its market value (which naturally they never do). Note that there's no real resale market for timeshares and if you need to sell you're highly unlikely to get your money back. If you want to buy a timeshare, it's best to buy a resale privately from an existing owner or a timeshare resale broker, whereby they sell for a fraction of their original cost. When buying privately you can usually drive a hard bargain and may even get a timeshare 'free' simply by assuming the current owner's maintenance contract. Further information about timesharing can be obtained from the Timeshare Council (☎ Spain 952 663 966, 💻 www.timesharecouncil.net) and the Timeshare Helpline (☎ UK 020-8296 0900, 💻 www.timeshare.freeserve. co.uk), both of which provide help and advice. The Timeshare Consumers Association (☎ 01909-591100, 💻 www.timeshare.org.uk) publishes several useful booklets as well as providing comprehensive information on the website.

# INSPECTION & SURVEYS

When you've found a property that you like, you should make a close inspection of its condition. Obviously this will depend on whether it's an old house in need of complete restoration, a property that has been partly or totally modernised, or a modern home. One of the problems with a property that has been restored is that you don't know how well the job has been done, particularly if the owner did it himself. If work has been carried out by local builders, you should ask to see the bills.

Some simple checks you can do yourself include testing the electrical system, plumbing, mains water, hot water boiler and central heating. Don't take someone's word that these are functional, but check them for yourself. If a property doesn't have electricity or mains water, check the nearest connection point and the cost of extending the service to the property, as it can be **very** expensive in remote rural areas. If a property has a well or septic tank, you should also have them tested. An old property may show visible signs of damage and decay, such as bulging or cracked walls, rising damp, missing roof slates (you can check with binoculars) and rotten woodwork. Some areas are prone to flooding, storms and subsidence, and it's advisable to check an old property after a heavy rainfall, when any leaks should come to light. If you find or suspect problems, you should have a property checked by a builder or have a full structural survey carried out by a surveyor. You may also wish to have a property checked for termites, which are found in many areas.

A Spaniard wouldn't make an offer on an old property before at least having it checked by a builder, who will also be able to tell you whether the price is too high, given any work that needs to be done. However, it's unusual to have a survey (*inspección*) on a property in Spain, particularly a property built in the last 10 or 20 years. Nevertheless, many homes built in the 1960s and 1970s are sub-standard and were built with inferior materials, and even relatively new buildings can have serious faults. It's important to check who the developer or builder was, as a major company with a good reputation is unlikely to have cut corners. Note that a property over ten years old will no longer be covered by a builder's warranty, although warranties are transferable if a property is sold during the warranty period. When buying a resale property, the vendor is obliged to pay to put right any defects that come to light during the six months following the sale, although you may have difficulty enforcing your rights.

If you're buying a detached villa, farmhouse or village house, especially one built on the side of a hill, it's **always** advisable to have a survey carried out. Common problems include rusting water pipes and leaky plumbing, inadequate sewage disposal, poor wiring, humidity and rising damp (no damp course), uneven flooring or no concrete base, collapsing façades, subsidence, and cracked internal and external walls. Some of these problems are even evident in developments less than five years old. Generally, if you would have a survey done on a similar property in your home country, then you should have one done in Spain.

You could ask the vendor to have a survey done at his expense, which, provided it gives the property a clean bill of health, will help him sell it even if you decide not to buy. You can make a satisfactory survey a condition of a contract, although this isn't usual and a vendor may refuse or insist that you carry out a survey at your expense **before** signing the contract. If a vendor refuses to allow you to do a survey before signing a contract, you should look elsewhere. Some foreign lenders require a survey before approving a loan, although this usually consists of a perfunctory valuation to ensure that a property is worth the purchase price. You can employ a foreign (e.g. British) surveyor practising in Spain, who will write a report in English. However, a Spanish surveyor (*agrimensor*) may have a more intimate knowledge of local properties and building methods. If you employ a foreign surveyor, you must ensure that he is experienced in the idiosyncrasies of Spanish properties and that he has professional indemnity insurance covering Spain (which means you can happily sue him if he does a bad job!).

Always discuss with the surveyor exactly what will be included, and most importantly, what will be excluded (you may need to pay extra to include certain checks and tests). A full structural survey should include the condition of all buildings, particularly the foundations, roofs, walls and woodwork; plumbing, electricity and heating systems and anything else you want inspected such as a swimming pool and its equipment, e.g.

filter system or heating. Note that a structural survey is usually only necessary if the building is old or suspected of being unsound. A survey can be limited to a few items or even a single system only, such as the wiring or plumbing in an old house. You should receive a written report on the structural condition of a property, including anything that could become a problem in the future. Some surveyors will allow you to accompany them and provide a video film of their findings in addition to a written report. For a property costing up to €180,000 a valuation costs around €300, a homebuyer's survey and valuation €450, and a full structural survey some €850, which is a relatively small price to pay for the peace of mind it affords.

## Land

Before buying a home on its own plot of land, you should walk the boundaries and look for any fences, driveways, roads, and the overhanging eaves of buildings that might be encroaching upon the property. If you're uncertain about the boundaries you should have the land surveyed, which is advisable in any case when buying a property with a large plot of land. When buying a rural property in Spain, you may be able to negotiate the amount of land you want included in the purchase. If a property is part of a larger plot of land owned by the vendor or the boundaries must be redrawn, you will need to hire a surveyor to measure the land and draw up a new cadastral plan (*plan catastral*). You should also have your lawyer check the local municipal plans (*plan parcial*) to find out what the land can be used for and whether there are any existing rights of way (*derechos de paso*). Rural land may be registered at the provincial 'rural fiscal property register' (*catastro rural*) and can also be registered in the general property register (*Registro de la Propiedad*).

 **Be very careful when buying a rural plot, particularly in Andalusia, where a recent law passed by the regional government severely restricts construction, or you may find that you aren't permitted to build on it. Always take professional legal advice first.**

## Inspection Checklist

Below is a list of items you should check when inspecting a property. Note, however, that this is no substitute for an inspection or survey by a professional, or for legal checks by a lawyer.

## Title

- Make sure that a property corresponds with the description in the title deeds.
- Check the number of rooms and the area of the property, terraces and the plot.

Note that if there are added rooms (e.g. an extension), terraces, a garage or a swimming pool that aren't mentioned in the property description, the owner should provide proof that planning permission was obtained. Additions or alterations to a property may require new title deeds for the entire property. If so, enquire whether the current owner will obtain the updated deeds before you buy or pay the costs if they're obtained on completion.

## Plot

This is particularly important for rural plots.

- Identify the boundaries of the plot. This may require the services of a land surveyor (*topógrafo*) on unfenced rural properties.
- Check that there are no disputes over boundaries and ensure that any additions on your plot don't encroach on to neighbouring plots.
- Check the rights of way over the plot. In rural areas, find out if your plot forms part of a hunting area.
- Check for streams and underground springs and whether any neighbours have rights to water on your land.
- If your plot isn't enclosed, check the local regulations regarding the height and type of boundary permitted.

## Orientation

- Check the orientation of the property and how much sun it receives, particularly in winter when north-facing properties are very cold and dark.

## Exterior

- Check for cracks and damp patches on walls.
- On older properties check that the walls are vertical and not bulging;

- Check that all the roof tiles are in place and that there's no sagging. Plants growing on a roof are an indication that it isn't well maintained. Note that gutters and drainpipes aren't common in Spanish properties.

## Interior

- Check for damp patches throughout a property, including inside cupboards and wardrobes.
- Check for cracks and damp patches on walls.
- Check that the flooris level and that the tiles are in good condition.
- Check the condition of doors and windows and whether they close properly.
- Check the woodwork for rot and signs of wood-boring insects, such as woodworm and termites (termites are difficult to detect unless damage is extensive).

## Furniture & Fittings

- Check what is included in the sale.
- Check that any appliances included in the sale are in good working order.

## Space

- Check that there's sufficient for your needs, particularly if you plan to live permanently in the property).
- If it's an apartment, enquire whether there's the possibility of obtaining additional storage space (usually known as a *trastero*) within the building.

## Parking

- Check that there's sufficient parking spaces for your family's needs – note that street parking is in very short supply in most towns and cities.
- Check whether there's the possibility of buying or renting a garage or parking space within a building or complex nearby.

## Utilities

- Check that the water/electricity/gas supplies are functional, particularly the hot water supply.
- Enquire about heating/cooling units in the house and the annual costs.

## Rural Properties

- Check the reliability of the electricity supply.
- If there's no electricity supply, find out whether you can connect to the mains supply or whether you can install alternative means (e.g. solar panels).
- Check the water supply. If the property's water is provided by wells, make sure that there's sufficient for your needs.
- Find out whether a property has a septic tank and have it checked.

## Garden/Land

- Check whether the garden will need extensive maintenance, and if so, how much a gardener will cost (if you cannot do it yourself). If you aren't prepared to pay for a gardener, check what it will cost to turn the garden into a low-maintenance one.
- On rural land, find out whether the trees require maintenance, e.g. olive and fruit trees, and investigate what you can do with the crops after the harvest. If land is classed as agricultural (*regadío*), check its water rights and whether they're sufficient for your needs.

## Swimming Pools

- Check the pool and equipment (especially the pump) is in good working order.
- Look for cracks on the pool structure and the condition of the paving around the pool.
- Enquire how much the pool costs to maintain a year and how much it will cost to refill it, e.g. if it's emptied in winter.
- If a property doesn't have a swimming pool, check that there's room to build one and that the terrain is suitable.

# SWIMMING POOLS

It's common for foreign buyers to install a swimming pool at a home in Spain, which, if you're letting, will greatly increase your rental prospects and the rent you can charge. Many self-catering holiday companies won't take on properties without a pool. There are many swimming pool installation companies in Spain or you can buy and install one yourself.

Above ground pools are the cheapest, but they're unsightly and are advisable only as a stop-gap or for those who really cannot afford anything better. Expect to pay around €3,000 for an 8 x 4 metre above ground pool. A better option is a liner pool which can be installed by anyone with basic DIY skills. A liner pool measuring 8 x 4 metres costs around €12,000 fully installed, around the same price as a conventional pool. A saline water option costs a bit more, but gives a better quality of water and offers lower maintenance costs. A concrete, fully-tiled pool of 8 x 4 metres costs from €15,000 to €20,000 installed, including filtration and heating, and can be almost any shape.

**You need planning permission to install a pool and should apply a few months in advance.** Pools require regular maintenance and cleaning. If you have a holiday home or let a property, you will need to employ someone to maintain your pool (you may be able to get a local family to look after it in return for being able to use it). Hot tubs, Jacuzzis, spas and whirlpools are also popular, and cost from around €4,500 to €6,000.

> **SURVIVAL TIP**
> If you have an outdoor pool, put a plank across
> it at night so that any animals (or humans) that falls in
> have a chance to get out again.

Note that if you make major improvements to a property (perhaps to a ruin), you must make a 'declaration of new work' (*declaración de obra nueva*) when it's completed, otherwise when you come to sell it you could have a huge capital gains tax bill to pay as you will be charged capital gains on it as if you had just bought it, even if the improvements were made ten years previously. See also **Buying a Resale Home** on page 135, **Inspections & Surveys** on page 148, **Water** on page 307 and **Heating & Air-Conditioning** on page 279.

# RENOVATION & RESTORATION

Many old country or village homes purchased by foreigners in Spain are in need of restoration, renovation or modernisation. Before buying a property requiring restoration or modernisation you should consider the alternatives. An extra few thousand euros spent on a purchase may represent better value for money than spending the money on building work. It's often cheaper to buy a restored or partly restored property rather than a ruin in need of total restoration, unless you're going to do most of the work yourself. The price of most restored properties doesn't reflect the cost and amount of work that went into them and many people who have restored a 'ruin' would never do it again and advise others against it.

> **SURVIVAL TIP**
> Before buying a property that needs renovation or restoration, it's vital to obtain accurate estimates of the work involved from one or more reliable local builders. You should budget for costs to be up to 100 per cent higher than quoted, as it isn't unusual for the costs to escalate wildly from original estimates.

In general, the Spanish don't care for old homes and much prefer modern apartments and villas with all mod cons, so it may be more difficult to sell an old property, even if it has been fully renovated.

## Checks

It's vital to check a property for any obvious faults, particularly an old property. Most importantly, a building must have sound walls, without which it may be cheaper to erect a new building! Almost any other problem can be fixed or overcome (at a price). A sound roof that doesn't leak is desirable, as ensuring that a building is water-proof is the most important priority if funds are scarce. Don't believe a vendor or agent who tells you that a roof or anything else can be repaired or patched up, but obtain expert advice from a local builder. Sound roof timbers are also important as they can be expensive to replace. Old buildings often need a damp-proof course, timber treatment, new windows and doors, a new roof or extensive repairs, a modern kitchen and bathroom, re-wiring and central heating. Electricity and mains water should preferably already be connected as they can be expensive to extend to a property in a remote area. If a house doesn't have electricity or mains water, it's important to check the cost of extending these services to it. Many rural properties get their water from a spring or well, which is usually fine, but you should check the reliability of the water supply – wells can and do run dry! You should also check the supply available will be adequate for your needs.

If you're seeking a waterside property, you should check the frequency of floods and, if commonplace, ensure that a building has been designed with floods in mind, e.g. with electrical installations above flood level and solid tiled floors.

## Planning Permission & Building Permits

If modernisation of an old building involves making external alterations, such as building an extension or installing larger windows or new doorways, you will need planning permission and a building licence (*licencia de obra*) from your local town hall. There are two types of building licence: one for major works (*obra major*) and another for minor works (*obra menor*), depending on the nature and size of the intended construction. If you plan to do major restoration or building work, you should ensure that a conditional clause is included in the contract stating that the purchase is dependent on obtaining planning and building permission (copies of the applications must be sent to the *notario* handling the sale). If you apply for a building permit and don't receive an answer within three months, then it's automatically approved if it's within an urbanisation or a zone already approved for such construction (however, you must apply for a certificate stating that an answer hasn't been given!). Never start any building work before you have official permission.

When erecting fences or walls, be very careful not to take even one centimetre of your neighbour's land, as Spaniards are fiercely protective of their boundaries and may make life difficult for you if you 'overstep the mark'.

## DIY or Builders?

One of the first decisions you need to make regarding restoration or modernisation is whether to do all or most of the work yourself or have it done by professional builders or local artisans. A working knowledge of Spanish is essential for DIY, especially the words associated with building materials and measurements (renovating a house in Spain will also greatly improve your ability to swear in Spanish!). Note that when restoring a period property it's important to have a sensitive approach to restoration. You shouldn't tackle jobs yourself or with friends unless you're sure you're doing them right.

In general you should aim to retain as many of a building's original features as possible and stick to local building materials such as wood, stone and tiles, reflecting the style of the property. When renovations and 'improvements' have been botched, there's often little that can be done except to start again from scratch. It's important not to over-modernise an old property, so that much of its natural rustic charm and attraction is lost. Note that even if you intend to do most of the work yourself, you will still need to hire artisans for certain jobs. Bear in mind that it can be difficult to find good artisans, who are in high demand and short supply in some areas. Artisan labour is considerably more expensive and you may find that you also have to pay their travelling expenses if your property is remote.

## Spanish Or Foreign Builders?

When it's a choice between Spanish and foreign builders, most experts recommend using local labour for a number of excellent reasons. Spanish artisans understand the materials and the traditional style of building, are familiar with local planning and building regulations, and usually do excellent work. If you employ local builders, you can virtually guarantee that the result will be authentic and it could also save you money. Bringing in foreign labour won't endear you to the local populace and may even create friction.

Nevertheless, finding a Spanish builder can be difficult (see below), finding one who will give you a quote for anything other than a major restoration project even more so (see **Quotations** below), and getting a job done within a set time next to impossible (see **Supervision** on page 158). Communication may also be a problem. There are many excellent foreign builders who have built up a good local reputation and can be relied upon to do a good job within a set period for a competitive price.

Note that you should only employ registered tradesmen and never employ 'black' labour (Spanish or foreign): apart from the fact that he won't be insured, there are stiff penalties for avoiding tax, VAT and social security contributions.

## Finding A Builder

When looking for a builder it's advisable to obtain recommendations from local people you can trust, e.g. a estate agent, surveyor, *notario*, neighbours and friends. Note, however, that estate agents or other professionals aren't always the best people to ask as they may receive commissions. Always obtain references from previous customers. It may be better to use a local building consortium or contractor than a number of independent tradesmen, particularly if you won't be around to supervise them (although it will cost you a bit more). On the other hand, if you supervise it 'yourself' using local hand-picked craftsmen, you can save money and learn a great deal into the bargain. **Always obtain references before employing a builder.**

## Supervision

If you aren't able to supervise work, you should hire a 'clerk of works' such as an architectural engineer (*aparejador*) to oversee a large job, otherwise it could drag on for months (or years) or be left half-finished. This will add around 10 per cent to the total bill, but it's usually worth it. Be extremely careful who you employ if you have work done in your absence and ensure that your instructions are accurate in every detail. Always make certain that you understand exactly what has been agreed and, if necessary, get it in writing (with drawings). It isn't unusual for foreign owners to receive huge bills for work done in their absence that shouldn't have been done at all! If you don't speak Spanish it's even more important to employ someone to oversee building works. Progressing on sign language and a few words of Spanish is a recipe for disaster!

## Quotations

Before buying a home for restoration or modernisation, it's essential to get an accurate estimate of the work and costs involved. You should obtain written estimates (*presupuestos*) from at least two builders before employing anyone. Note that for quotations to be accurate, you must detail exactly the work required, e.g. for electrical work this would include the number of lights, points and switches, and the quality of materials to be used. If you have only a vague idea of what you want, you will receive a vague and unreliable quotation. Make sure that a quotation includes everything you want done and that you fully understand it (if you don't, get it translated). You should fix a date for the start and completion of work, and if you can get a builder to agree to it, include a penalty for failing to finish on time. After signing a contract it's usual to pay a deposit, the amount of which depends on the size and cost of a job.

 **It can be difficult obtaining a detailed written quote from plumbers, electricians and small builders, as they aren't used to being asked to provide written quotations, especially on the Spanish Costas. However, their verbal quotations are usually accurate.**

## Cost

All building work such as electrical work, masonry and plumbing is priced by the square metre or metre. The cost of restoration depends on the type of work involved, the quality of materials used and the region. As a rough guide you should expect the cost of totally renovating an old 'habitable' building to be at least equal to its purchase price and possibly much more. Some estimates calculate the cost of restoring or rebuilding a large *finca* to be in the region of €430,000 to €1.4 million! How much you spend on restoring a property will depend on your purpose and the depth of your pockets. If you're restoring a property as an investment, it's easy to spend more than you could ever hope to recoup when you sell it. Always keep an eye on your budget (it's very easy to overspend) and don't be in too much of a hurry. Some people take many years to restore a holiday home, particularly when they're doing most of the work themselves. It isn't unusual for buyers to embark on a grandiose renovation scheme, only to run out of money before it's completed and be forced to sell at a huge loss.

# BUILDING YOUR OWN HOME

If you want to be far from the madding crowd, you can buy a plot of land (*parcela*) and have an individual architect-designed house built to your own design and specifications or to a standard design provided by a builder. **However, building a home in Spain isn't recommended for the timid.** Spanish red tape and the often eccentric ways of doing business can make building your own home a nightmare and it's fraught with problems. Nevertheless, there are many excellent builders who will build an individually-designed house on your plot of land or will sell you a plot and build a house chosen from a range of standard designs.

## Checks

Note that when you're looking at a particular area you should check the **medium-term** infrastructure plans for that area, both with the regional and national authorities. It's worth remembering that the road and rail infrastructure in Spain needs upgrading in many areas and many new roads and railways projects are in the pipeline. This could mean that, although a quiet rural plot may seem miles from anywhere today, there could be plans for a motorway passing along the boundaries within the next five to ten years. This is the case, for example, with the toll-motorway planned from Torremolinos to Las Pedrizas in Malaga, which will run through a large section of currently unspoilt countryside. Unfortunately many long-term plans are unavailable to the public or they may change, but information about infrastructure development for the next ten years is usually available.

You must take the same care when buying land as you would when buying a home. The most important point is to ensure that it has been approved for building (land classified as a *finca urbana* can usually be built on) and that the plot is large enough and suitable for the house you plan to build. This is done by obtaining a certificate (*certificado de situación urbanística*) from the local town hall. It may also be possible to build on agricultural land (*finca rústica*), but there are strict limits on plot and building sizes (the minimum plot that can be built on is usually 3,000m² and may be as high as 10,000m² or even 15,000m² as in the Balearics). There are also limitations on the type of building allowed in some regions. If the plot is part of an urbanisation, the contract must state that the plan has been approved and give the date and authority. You can obtain this information (*informe urbanístico*) from the local town hall.

Never assume that you will be able to build the same sort of house as your neighbours as regulations vary according to the situation and type of plot or regulations may have changed since the property was built. Some plots are unsuitable for building as they're too steep or require prohibitively expensive foundations. It's prudent to consult an architect who will be able to tell you whether the plot is suitable for construction and if you will need costly retaining walls or foundations. You should also have a land survey, which costs from €1,800 to €4,200, before you commit yourself to a purchase. A survey can also check the boundaries (rural plots commonly have more or less land than officially stated) and water rights. Also check that there aren't any restrictions such as high-tension electricity lines, water pipes or rights of way that may restrict building. It's advisable to consider the access to a plot if this isn't along a surfaced road. Rainfall in winter is often torrential and many tracks turn into impassable mud and some are even washed away.

---

## IMPORTANT NOTE

All plots, particularly those classed as 'rustic' (*rústica*), are affected by building regulations: not only those set by local councils but also those set by regional authorities, who have the final word in planning regulations. These regulations can and do change and affect whether or not you're permitted to build on the land. For example, the Junta de Andalucía introduced extensive planning regulations (*Ley de Ordenación Urbanística*) at the end of 2002, which established strict limitations on construction on land classed as 'rustic', meaning that in some cases, building is now practically impossible. The law also contemplates large fines for illegal construction. **As a result of the new regulations, some property owners have discovered that they cannot now build on the plot they purchased!**

Before you buy land, particularly in rural areas, you should take comprehensive advice from a professional (preferably a lawyer) who should thoroughly investigate the conditions and regulations affecting the land. Never believe an owner or estate agent keen to sell you a plot who says there will be 'no problem' getting planning permission. All too often, foreign buyers have found themselves the proud owners of a rustic plot they cannot build on! If possible, always make obtaining building approval a condition of the purchase of land. See also **Buying Land** on page 110.

Note also that the cost of providing services to a property in a remote rural area may be prohibitively expensive and it must have a reliable water supply. If you don't have mains water and have to rely on other sources such as wells, you should make sure that the supply will be adequate for your needs. Bear in mind that drought is common in most of southern Spain where it usually doesn't rain from the end of May to September. Always get confirmation in writing from the local town hall that land can be built on and has been approved for road access. Before buying land for building, ensure that the purchase contract is dependent on obtaining the necessary building licence (*licencia de obra*). Obtain a receipt showing that the plot is correctly presented in the local property register and check for yourself that the correct planning permission has been obtained (don't simply leave it to the builder). If planning permission is flawed you may need to pay extra to improve the local infrastructure or the property may even have to be demolished! Note also that it can take a long time to obtain planning permission.

Most builders offer package deals that include the land and the cost of building a home. However, it isn't always advisable to buy the building plot from the builder who's going to build your home and you should shop around and compare separate land and building costs. If you do decide to buy a package deal from a builder, you **must** insist on separate contracts for the land and the building and obtain the title deed for the land before signing a building contract. Note that if you're having a home built on an existing urbanisation, you must ensure that the urbanisation has been approved, as some are illegal.

## Cost

The cost of land in Spain varies considerably depending on the area, e.g. from around €50 to €300 upwards per square metre (m²), and has escalated sharply in recent years in some areas, fuelled by speculators. However, in rural areas agricultural land can be exceedingly cheap, costing as little as a few euros per square metre. Land usually represents as much as half the cost of building a home, although it's still possible in many areas to buy a plot of land and build a bigger and better home for less than the cost of a resale property. Building your own home allows you not only to design your home, but to ensure that the quality of materials and workmanship are first class. Building costs range from around €500 to €1,500 (or more) per square metre in resort areas, depending on the quality and the area. Note, however, that you should add an extra 10 to 15 per cent to the estimated price since the cost of building a house is **always** more expensive than originally planned. Note that labour costs may be considerably higher if your plot is situated in a remote area where you will also have to pay extra for transportation of materials. Value added tax (*IVA*) of 16 per cent is payable on building land (*terreno urbanizable*) and 7 per cent on building costs.

 If you want a swimming pool or a garage built, it's advisable to have it constructed at the same time as the house, when *IVA* will be 7 per cent; if they're constructed separately *IVA* is 16 per cent.

## Finding An Architect & Builder

When looking for an architect and builder it's advisable to obtain recommendations from local people you can trust, e.g. a bank manager, estate agent, lawyer, *notario*, or neighbours and friends. Note, however, that estate agents or other professionals aren't always the best people to ask, as they may receive a commission. You can also obtain valuable information from expatriates in local bars and from owners of properties in an area that you particularly like. Many Spanish architects speak English and there are also architects from other EU countries working in the main resort areas. Note that architects fees are usually calculated as a percentage of the total costs of the work, usually between 5 and 10 per cent, which doesn't encourage them to cut costs. However, there are no longer mandatory minimum fees for architects in Spain and you may be able to negotiate a good deal.

A good architect should be able to recommend a number of reliable builders, but you should also do your own research, as the most important consideration when choosing a new home is the reputation (and financial standing) of the builder. However, you should be wary of an architect with his 'own' builder (or a builder with his own architect), as it's the architect's job to ensure that the builder does his work according to the plans and specifications, so you don't want their relationship to be too cosy. Inspect other homes the builder has built and check with the owners as to what problems they've had and whether they're satisfied. Note that building standards in Spain vary considerably and you shouldn't assume that the lowest offer is the best value. Your best insurance when building a property is the reputation of the builder and his liquidity.

> **SURVIVAL TIP**
> It's important that the builder provides a 'termination' guarantee (backed by a bank or insurance company) to cover you in the event that he goes bust before completing the property and its infrastructure, which must be specified in the contract.

If you want a house built exactly to your specifications, you will need to personally supervise it every step of the way or employ an architectural engineer or technical architect (*aparejador*) to do it for you. Without close supervision it's highly likely that your instructions **won't** be followed. Around 70 per cent of an architect's fees are payable when a building is started, the balance becoming due upon completion when the 'certificate of new work' (*certificado de fin de obra nueva*), the 'licence for the first occupation' (*licencia de primera ocupación*) and *cédula de habitabilidad* (declaring the house is fit to live in) have been issued by the town hall or regional government.

## Contracts

You should obtain written quotations (*presupuestos*) from a number of builders before signing a contract. Note that one of the most important features of a home in Spain must be good insulation (against both heat and cold) and protection against humidity. The contract must include a detailed building description (*memoria de calidades*) and a list of the materials to be used (with references to the architect's plans); the exact location of the building on the plot; the building and payment schedule, which must be made in stages according to building progress (see **Buying Off Plan** on page 196); a penalty clause for late completion; the retention of a percentage (e.g. 5 to 10 per cent) of the building costs as a guarantee against defects; and how disputes will be settled. It may be difficult or impossible to get the builder to accept a penalty clause for late completion, as buildings are rarely completed on time in Spain.

Ensure that the contract includes all costs including the architect's fees (unless contracted separately); landscaping (if applicable); **all** permits and licences (including the costs of land segregation, the declaration of new building, and the horizontal division for a community property) and the connection of utilities (water, electricity, gas, etc.) to the house, not just to the building site. The only extra is usually the cost of electricity and water meters.

 Owners are also liable for a 'tax on construction, installations and work' (*impuesto sobre construcciones, instalaciones y obras*), which is levied on all work requiring a municipal licence. The tax ranges from 2 to 4 per cent of the cost of the work and may be payable when the local authorities issue the building licence.

Before accepting a quotation, it's advisable to have it checked by a building consultant to confirm that it's a fair deal. You should check whether the quotation (which must include *IVA* at 7 per cent) is an estimate or a fixed price, as sometimes the cost can escalate wildly due to contract clauses and changes made during building work. It's vital to have a contract checked by a lawyer as building contracts are often heavily biased in the builder's favour and give clients very few rights.

## Guarantees

Spanish law requires a builder to guarantee his work against structural defects for ten years (15 years if the builder failed to comply with specific conditions in the contract) and an architect is also responsible for ten years for defects due to poor supervision, incorrect instructions given to the builder, or problems caused by poor foundations, e.g. subsidence. Note that it isn't uncommon to have problems during construction, particularly regarding material defects. If you experience problems you must usually be extremely patient and persistent in order to obtain satisfaction. You should have a completed building checked by a structural surveyor for defects and a report drawn up, and if there are any defects, he should determine exactly who was responsible for them.

A useful booklet entitled *Building A House in Spain* is published by the Foundation Institute of Foreign Property Owners (see page 105).

## SELLING YOUR HOME

Although this book is primarily concerned with buying a home in Spain, you may wish to sell your home at some time in the future (or you may wish to sell a home in order to buy another). Before offering your Spanish home for sale it's advisable to investigate the state of the property market. For example, unless you're forced to sell, it definitely isn't advisable during a property slump when prices are depressed. It may be wiser to let your home long-term and wait until the market has recovered. It's also unwise to sell in the early years after purchase, when you will probably make a loss unless it was an absolute bargain. Having decided to sell, your first decision will be whether to sell it yourself (or try) or use the services of an estate agent. Although the majority of properties are sold through estate agents, a large number of people also sell their own homes. If you need to sell a property before buying a new one, this must be included as a conditional clause (see page 198) in the contract for a new home.

# Price

It's important to bear in mind that (like everything) property has a market price and the best way of ensuring a quick sale (or any sale) is to ask a realistic price. In the early 1990s when prices plummeted and buyers dried up, many properties remained on the market for years largely because owners asked absurd prices. As in most countries, it's easier to sell a cheaper property, say one priced below €150,000, than an expensive property. However, there's also a strong and constant demand for exceptional villas priced from around €250,000 upwards, particularly if they're especially attractive and in a popular area or a superb location.

If your home's fairly standard for the area, you can find out its value by comparing the prices of other homes on the market or those that have recently been sold. Most agents will provide a free appraisal of a home's value in the hope that you will sell it through them. However, don't believe everything they tell you as they may over-price it simply to encourage you. You can also hire a professional valuer (*tasador*) to determine the market value. You should be prepared to drop the price slightly (e.g. 5 or 10 per cent) and should set it accordingly, but shouldn't grossly over-price a home as it will deter buyers. Don't reject an offer out of hand unless it's ridiculously low, as you may be able to get a prospective buyer to raise his offer.

When selling a second home in Spain, you may wish to include the furnishings (plus major appliances) in the sale, which is a common practice in resort areas when selling a relatively inexpensive second home with modest furnishings. In this case you should add an appropriate amount to the price to cover the value of the furnishings. If you don't wish to include them you can use them as an inducement to a prospective buyer at a later stage, although this isn't normal practice.

# Presentation

The secret to selling a home quickly lies in its presentation (assuming that it's well priced). First impressions (both exteriors and interiors) are vital when marketing a property and it's important to present it in its best light and make it as attractive as possible to potential buyers. It may pay to invest in new interior decoration, new carpets, exterior paint and landscaping. A few plants and flowers can do wonders. Note that when decorating a home for resale, it's important to be conservative and not to do anything radical (such as install a red or black bathroom suite, or paint the walls purple). White is a good neutral colour for walls, woodwork and porcelain.

It may also pay you to do some modernisation such as installing a new kitchen or bathroom, as these are of vital importance (particularly kitchens) when selling a home. Note, however, that although modernisation may be necessary to sell an old home, you shouldn't overdo it, as it's easy to spend more than you could ever hope to recoup on the sale price. If you're using an agent, you can ask him what you should do (or need to do) to help sell your home. If a home's in poor repair this must be reflected in the asking price and if major work is needed that you cannot afford, you should obtain a quotation (or two) and offer to knock this off the price. Note that you have a duty under Spanish law to inform a prospective buyer of any defects that aren't readily apparent and which materially affect the value of a property.

## Selling Your Home Yourself

While certainly not for everyone, selling your own home is a viable option for many people and is particularly recommended when you're selling an attractive home at a **realistic** price in a favourable market. It may allow you to offer it at a more appealing price, which could be an important factor if you're seeking a quick sale. Even if you aren't in a hurry, selling your own home saves you an agent's fees, which can be up to 25 per cent in Spain.

How you market your home will depend on the type of property, the price, and the country or area from where you expect your buyer to come. For example, if your property isn't of a type and style or in an area that's desirable to local inhabitants, it's usually a waste of time advertising it in the local Spanish press.

### Marketing

Marketing is the key to selling your home. The first step is to get a professional looking 'for sale' sign made (showing your telephone number) and erect it in the garden or place it in a window. Do some research into the best newspapers and magazines for advertising your property (see **Appendix B**), and place an advertisement in those that look most promising. It's also a good idea to add the words 'no agents' at the end of your advertisement, otherwise most of the calls you receive will be from agents keen to sell your home! You could also have a leaflet printed (with pictures) extolling the virtues of the property, which you could drop into local letter boxes or have distributed with a local newspaper (many people buy a new home in the immediate vicinity of their present one). You may also need a 'fact sheet' printed (if your home's vital statistics aren't included in the leaflet mentioned above) and could offer a finder's fee, e.g. €500, to anyone who finds you a buyer. Don't omit to market your home around local companies, schools and organisations, particularly if they have many itinerant employees. Finally, it may help to provide information about local financing sources for potential buyers. Unless you're in a hurry to sell, set yourself a realistic time limit for success, after which you can try an agent. When selling a home yourself, you will need to provide a contract or engage a lawyer to do this for you.

# Using An Agent

Most owners usually prefer to use the services of one or more estate agents, either in Spain or in their home country, e.g. when selling a second home in Spain.

If you purchased the property through an agent, it's often advisable to use the same agent when selling, as he will already be familiar with it and may still have the details on file. You should take particular care when selecting an agent as they vary considerably in their professionalism, expertise and experience (the best way to investigate agents is by posing as a buyer). Note that many agents cover a relatively small area, so you should take care to choose one who regularly sells properties in your area and price range. If you own a property in an area popular with foreign buyers, it may be worthwhile using an overseas agent or advertising in foreign newspapers and magazines, such as the English-language publications listed in **Appendix B**.

### Agents' Contracts

Before he can offer a property for sale, an estate agent must have a signed authorisation from the owner in the form of an exclusive or non-exclusive contract. An exclusive contract (*exclusiva*) gives a single agent the exclusive right to sell a property, while a non-exclusive contract allows you to deal with any number of agents and to negotiate directly with private individuals. Most people find that it's better to place a property with a number of agents under non-exclusive contracts. Exclusive contracts are rare and are for a limited period (*plazo*) only, e.g.

three to six months, and state the agent's commission and what it includes. Choose an agent who regularly sells properties in your price range and enquire how the property will be marketed and who will pay the costs.

**Agents' Fees**

When selling a property in Spain, the agent's commission is usually paid by the vendor and included in the purchase price. Fees normally vary from around 5 to 10 per cent, depending on the price of a property, although they can be as high as 25 per cent in some rural areas. Fees are higher with an exclusive contract than with a non-exclusive contract. Shop around and negotiate for the best deal, as there's fierce competition among agents to sell good properties (many agents 'tout' for properties to sell by advertising in the expatriate press).

If you sign a contract without reserving the right to find your own buyer, you must pay the agent's commission even if you sell your home yourself! Make sure that you don't sign two or more exclusive contracts to sell your home – check the contract (exclusive contracts tend to be binding) and make sure you understand what you're signing. Contracts state the agent's commission, what it includes, and most importantly, who must pay it. Generally, you shouldn't pay any fees unless you require extra services and you should never pay the agent's commission before a sale is completed and you've been paid.

# Capital Gains Tax (CGT)

Anyone selling a second home must pay CGT (see page 240), depending on when it was purchased and how long it has been owned. When a non-resident sells a property, 5 per cent of the price (called the *retención*) **must** be retained by the buyer (the notary will ensure that this is done) and be paid to the local tax authorities as a deposit on any tax due.

---

**SURVIVAL TIP**

If you're a resident in Spain and are selling your principal home and buying another in Spain, you must sell your home first before buying another in order to benefit from the CGT concession for residents.

---

If you need to buy a home before you've sold your current home, one solution is to buy it on a private contract and not register it until after you've sold your present home (obtain legal advice).

## IMPORTANT NOTE

As when buying a home in Spain, you must be very, very careful who you deal with when selling a home. Make sure that you're paid with a certified banker's draft before signing over your property to a buyer, as once the deed of sale (*escritura*) has been signed the property belongs to the buyer, whether you've been paid or not. Be extremely careful if you plan to use an intermediary, as it isn't uncommon for a 'middle man' to disappear with the proceeds! Never agree to accept part of the sale price 'under the table', as if the buyer refuses to pay the extra money there's nothing you can do about it (at least legally). Although rare, sellers occasionally end up with no property **and** no money! All sales should be conducted through a lawyer. See also **Estate Agents** on page 116 and **Capital Gains Tax** on page 240.

# 4.

# MONEY MATTERS

One of the most important aspects of buying a home in Spain and living there (even for relatively brief periods) is finance, which includes everything from transferring and changing money to mortgages and taxes (see **Chapter 7**). If you're planning to invest in a property or a business in Spain financed with imported funds, it's important to consider both the present and possible future exchange rates (even a small change in the exchange rate can increase the price of a home dramatically). On the other hand, if you live and work in Spain and are paid in euros this may affect your financial commitments abroad.

 **If your income is received in a currency other than euros it can be exposed to risks beyond your control when you live in Spain, particularly regarding inflation and exchange rate fluctuations.**

Although the Spanish generally prefer to pay cash (*dinero en efectivo/dinero contante*) rather than use credit or charge cards, it's wise to have at least one credit card when visiting or living in Spain (Visa is the most widely accepted). Even if you don't like credit cards and shun any form of credit, they do have their uses; for example, no-deposit car rentals; no pre-paying hotel bills (plus guaranteed bookings); obtaining cash 24-hours a day; the convenience of shopping by phone or via the Internet; greater safety and security than cash and above all, convenience. Note, however, that not all Spanish businesses accept credit cards.

---

**SURVIVAL TIP**

**If you plan to live in Spain for long periods, you must ensure that your income is (and will remain) sufficient to live on, bearing in mind devaluations, rises in the cost of living, and unforeseen expenses such as medical bills or anything else that may reduce your income.**

---

Foreigners, particularly retirees, shouldn't under-estimate the cost of living (see page 26), which has increased significantly in the last decade.

In the early 1990s many pensioners with a fixed income paid in a foreign currency saw it fall dramatically as exchange rates worsened and the cost of living rose, although in the last few years some have made gains on the exchange rate. The cost of living in Spain is still lower than in most other EU countries and inflation was 4 per cent in 2002. If you're planning to live there permanently, it's wise to seek expert financial advice as it may provide the opportunity to reduce your taxes.

This chapter includes information about Spanish currency, importing and exporting money, banking and mortgages.

# SPANISH CURRENCY

On 1st January 1999 the euro (€) was introduced in Spain (plus Austria, Belgium, Finland, France, Germany, Greece, Ireland, Italy, Luxembourg, the Netherlands and Portugal) and is now the country's currency. Euro notes and coins became legal tender on 1st January 2002 replacing the peseta. The euro (€) is divided into 100 cents (*céntimo*) and coins are minted in values of 1, 2, 5, 10, 20, 50 cents, €1 and €2. The 1, 2 and 5 cent coins are copper-coloured, the 10, 20 and 50 cent brass-coloured. The €1 coin is silver-coloured in the centre with a brass-coloured rim, and the €2 coin has a brass-coloured centre and silver-coloured rim. The reverse ('tail' showing the value) of euro coins is the same in all euro-zone countries, but the obverse ('head') is different in each country. Spanish coins carry three designs (e.g. the king's head on the €1 and €2 coins, Cervantes on the 10, 20 and 50 cent coins, and the cathedral in Santiago de Compostela on the 1, 2 and 5 cent coins), the word '*España*' and the date of minting. All euro coins can, of course, be used in all euro-zone countries (although minute differences in weight occasionally cause problems in cash machines, e.g. at motorway tolls!).

Euro banknotes (*billets*) are identical throughout the euro-zone and depict a map of Europe and stylised designs of buildings. Notes are printed in denominations of €5, €10, €20, €50, €100, €200 and €500 (worth over £300), with the size increasing with their value. Euro notes have been produced using all the latest anti-counterfeiting devices; nevertheless, you should be especially wary of €200 and €500 notes. The euro symbol may appear before the amount (as in this book), after it (commonly used by the Spanish, e.g. 24,50€) or even between the euros and cents, e.g. 16€50. When writing figures (for example on cheques), a full stop/period (.) is used to separate units of millions, thousands and hundreds, and a comma to denote fractions.

If possible, it's wise to obtain some euro coins and banknotes before arriving in Spain and to familiarise yourself with them. Bringing some euros with you (e.g. €50 to €100 in small notes) will save you having to change money on arrival. It's sensible not to carry a lot of cash and ideally you should avoid high value notes (above €50), which aren't widely accepted, particularly for small purchases or on public transport.

# IMPORTING & EXPORTING MONEY

Exchange controls were abolished in Spain on 1st February 1992 and there are no restrictions on the import or export of funds. A Spanish resident is permitted to open a bank account in any country and to import (or export) unlimited funds in any currency. However, when a resident opens an overseas account his Spanish bank must routinely inform the Bank of Spain within 30 days of any account movements over €3,000.

## Declaration

Cash, notes and bearer-cheques in any currency, plus gold coins and bars up to the value of €6,000 may be freely imported or exported from Spain by residents and non-residents without approval or declaration. However, if you intend to re-export funds you should declare them, as this will certify that the foreign currency was imported legally and will allow a non-EU person to convert euros back into a foreign currency. Residents receiving funds from non-residents or making payments to them of over €6,000 (or the equivalent in foreign currency) in cash or bearer cheques must declare them within 30 days. A form must be completed (B-3) giving the name, address and *NIE* of the resident, the name and address of the non-resident, and the reason for the payment.

Sums of €6,000 to €30,000 (per person and journey) must be declared to the customs authorities (on form B-1) when entering or leaving Spain. For sums above €30,000, prior authorisation was previously required from the Dirección General de Transacciones Exteriores (DGTE) by completing form B-2 at your bank. However, although sums above €6,000 must be declared, the European Union ruled that the demand for prior authorisation was illegal under EU laws relating to the free transfer of capital between member states and it now applies to non-EU nationals only. These regulations are designed to curb criminal activities, particularly drug-trafficking, and also apply to transit travellers stopping in Spain for less than 24 hours. **Note that if you don't declare funds, they're subject to confiscation.**

## International Bank Transfers

When transferring money to Spain, shop around for the best exchange rate and the lowest costs. Banks are often willing to negotiate on fees and exchange rates when you're transferring a large amount of cash.

 **Don't be too optimistic about the exchange rate, which can change at short notice and can cost you tens of thousands of euros more than you planned.**

For example, if you're buying a home in Spain costing □300,000 and are paying in pounds sterling, this would be equal to £193,548 at an exchange rate of £1 = □1.55. However, if the £/□ exchange rate 'falls' to □1.45, it will cost you £206,896 – an increase of £13,348!

When transferring or sending money to (or from) Spain, you should be aware of the alternatives and shop around for the best deal. A bank-to-bank transfer can be made by a normal transfer or by a SWIFT electronic transfer. A normal transfer is supposed to take three to seven days, but in reality takes longer (particularly when sent by post), whereas a SWIFT telex transfer **should** be completed in as little as two hours (although SWIFT transfers aren't always reliable to and from Spain). It's usually quicker and cheaper to transfer funds between branches of the same bank or affiliated banks than between non-affiliated banks.

If you intend to send a large amount of money abroad for a business transaction such as buying a property, you should ensure that you receive the commercial rate of exchange rather than the tourist rate. Shop around and compare your bank's rate with that of at least one foreign exchange broker who specialises in sending money abroad (particularly large sums). The leading companies include Foreign Currency Direct (☎ UK 0800-328 5884/+44-1494-725353, 🖳 www.currencies.co.uk), Halewood (☎ UK 01753-859159, 🖳 www.hifx.co.uk) and Moneycorp (☎ UK 020-7808 0500, 🖳 www.moneycorp.com).

Some banks levy high charges (as much as 4 per cent) on the transfer of funds to Spain to buy a home, which is the subject of numerous complaints, while others charge nothing if the transfer is made in euros. Always check charges and rates in advance and agree them with your bank (you can often negotiate a lower charge or a better exchange rate when transferring a large sum of money). The cost of transfers vary considerably, not only the commission and exchange rates, but also the transfer charges (such as the telex charge for a SWIFT transfer). Shop around a number of banks. Many Spanish banks deduct commission, whether a transfer is made in euros or a foreign currency. An EU directive limits banks in EU countries to being able to pass on to customers the costs incurred by sender banks only and money has to be deposited in customers' accounts within five working days.

Spanish banks (along with Portuguese) are reportedly the slowest in Europe to process bank transfers. It isn't unusual for transfers to and from Spain to get stuck in the pipeline (usually somewhere in Madrid), which allows the Spanish bank to use your money for a period interest-free. For example, transfers between British and Spanish banks occasionally take weeks and money can 'disappear' for months or even completely! (Except for the fastest and most expensive methods, cash transfers between international banks are a joke in the age of electronic banking when powerful financiers can switch funds almost instantaneously.)

# Telegraphic Transfers

One of the quickest (it takes around ten minutes) and safest methods of transferring cash is via a telegraphic transfer, e.g. Moneygram (☎ UK 0800-666 3947, 🖳 www.moneygram.com) or Western Union (☎ Spain 902 010 701, 🖳 www.westernunion.com), but it's also one of the most expensive, e.g. commission of 7 to 10 per cent of the amount sent! Western Union services are also available at post offices (☎ 902 197 197, 🖳 www.correos.es) in Spain under the agreement known as 'Dinero en minutos' (Money in Minutes) There are special rates and deals for certain countries such as Equador, Russia and the Ukraine. Money can be sent via overseas American Express offices by Amex card holders (using Amex's Moneygram service) to American Express offices in Spain in just 15 minutes.

# Bank Drafts & Personal Cheques

Another way to transfer money is via a bank draft (*giro bancario*), which should be sent by registered post. Note, however, that in the event that it's lost or stolen, it's impossible to stop payment and you must wait six months before a new draft can be issued. Bank drafts aren't treated as cash in Spain and must be cleared like personal cheques. It's also possible to send a creditor a cheque drawn on a personal account, although they can take a long time to clear (usually a matter of weeks) and fees are high. Some people prefer to receive a cheque direct (by post) from their overseas banks, which they then pay into their Spanish bank (although you must usually wait for it to clear). **The main problem with sending anything by post to or from Spain is that it leaves you at the mercy of the notoriously unreliable Spanish post office.**

It's possible to pay cheques drawn on a foreign account into a Spanish bank account, however, they can take weeks to clear as they must usually be cleared with the paying bank (although some Spanish banks credit funds to accounts immediately or within a few days).

# Postcheques & Eurogiro

Giro postcheques (*Eurogiros*) issued by European post offices can be cashed (with a postcheque guarantee card) at main post offices in Spain where there's usually a special counter marked *reintegros*. Note, however, that the hours of service for this counter may be restricted. The maximum value per cheque depends on the country where issued, e.g. €250 if issued in the UK. There's a standard charge for each cheque of €3.80 plus 0.70 per cent of the amount. You can also send money to Spain via the Girobank Eurogiro system from post offices in 15 European countries and the USA to some Spanish banks.

# Obtaining Cash

One of the quickest methods of obtaining of cash in Spain is to draw cash on debit, credit or charge cards (but there's usually a daily limit). Many foreigners living in Spain (particularly retirees) keep the bulk of their money in a foreign account (perhaps in an offshore bank) and draw on it with a cash or credit card. This is an ideal solution for holidaymakers and holiday homeowners (although homeowners will still need a Spanish bank account to pay their bills).

Most banks in major cities have foreign exchange windows where you can buy and sell foreign currencies, buy and cash traveller's cheques, and obtain a cash advance on credit and charge cards.

Most banks charge around 1 per cent commission with a minimum charge of between €3 to €6, so it's expensive to change small amounts. However, some banks charge a flat fee of €3 and no commission, irrespective of the amount, especially if you're a client of the bank. There are numerous private *bureaux de change* in Spain, many of which are open long hours. They can be found at most travel agencies and even in some stores (such as El Corte Inglés department stores). **Note that banks at airports and railway stations often offer the worst exchange rates and charge the highest fees.** There are automatic change machines at airports and in tourist areas in major cities accepting up to 15 currencies including US$, £Sterling and Swiss francs.

Most *bureaux de change* offer competitive exchange rates and charge no commission (but always check) and are also usually easier to deal with than banks. If you're changing a lot of money you may be able to negotiate a better exchange rate. However, although commercial *bureaux de change* charge less commission than banks, they don't usually offer the best exchange rates and you're usually better off going to a bank. The posted exchange rates may apply only when changing high amounts, so ask before changing any money. **Note that no commission often equals a poor exchange rate.** The euro exchange rate (*cambio*) for most major international currencies is listed in banks and daily newspapers and announced on Spanish and expatriate radio and TV. **Always shop around for the best exchange rate and the lowest commission**.

# Traveller's Cheques

If you're visiting Spain, it's safer to carry traveller's cheques (*cheques de viaje*) than large amounts of cash, although they aren't as easy to cash as in some other countries. They aren't usually accepted as cash by businesses, except perhaps in some major hotels, restaurants and shops, which usually offer a poor exchange rate. You may wish to buy traveller's cheques in euros in order to take advantage of a favourable exchange rate and in order to avoid commission charges; most banks charge a commission of 1 per cent when cashing foreign currency traveller's cheques with a minimum fee of between €3 and €6 (so you should avoid changing small amounts). Note that you must show your passport when changing traveller's cheques. Banks offer a better exchange rate for traveller's cheques than for banknotes.

Always keep a separate record of traveller's cheque numbers and note where and when they were cashed. Most cheque issuers offer a replacement service for lost or stolen cheques, although the time taken to replace them varies significantly. American Express claims a free, three-hour replacement service at any of their offices world-wide, provided you know the serial numbers of the lost cheques. Without the serial numbers, replacement can take three days or longer. Note that for Europeans travelling within Europe, postcheques are a useful alternative to traveller's cheques.

**Footnote:** There isn't a lot of difference in the cost between buying euros using cash, buying traveller's cheques or using a credit card to obtain cash in Spain. However, many people simply take cash when visiting Spain, which is asking for trouble, particularly if you have no way of obtaining more cash there, e.g. with a credit card.

> **SURVIVAL TIP**
> One thing to bear in mind when travelling anywhere is not to rely only on one source of funds!

# BANKS

Banking in Spain has changed out of all recognition in the last few decades, during which period the number of banks and branches has increased considerably (some have also gone bust). There are two main types of banks in Spain: clearing banks and savings banks (*cajas de ahorros*). The Spanish clearing banks with the largest branch networks are the two giants, Banco Santander-Central Hispano (BSCH) and Banco Bilbao Vizcaya-Argentaria (BBVA), and the smaller ones are Banco Atlántico, Banco Popular and Banesto. All banks in Spain are listed in the yellow pages under *Bancos*.

Many banks went broke in the 1970s and 1980s, but they've since emerged from the dark ages and are now much more efficient. Banking has become highly automated in recent years, although many Spanish banks remain frustratingly slow and inefficient compared with banks in many other EU countries. Where human involvement is concerned, Spanish banks remain Neanderthal, although with regard to electronic banking they compare favourably with other European countries and their ATMs (cash dispensers) are among the world's most advanced (how many other countries' ATMs 'talk' to you in a number of languages?). There are no drive-in banks in Spain.

Most banks also offer home banking services via telephone and/or the Internet, and there are several Internet/telephone-only banks such as ING Direct (☎ 901 020 901, 💻 www.ingdirect.es) owned by ING Nationale-Nedenlanden, Patagon (☎ 902 365 366, 💻 www.patagon.es) owned by BSCH, Evolvebank (☎ 902 157 213, 💻 www.evolvebank.com), part of the Lloyds TSB group and Uno-e (☎ 901 111 113, 💻 www.uno-e.es) owned by BBVA and Telefónica. All four Internet banks offer (relatively) high interest current accounts with immediate access to your money, plus the usual banking services.

In addition to clearing banks, Spain also has around 50 savings banks (*cajas de ahorros*), which were originally charitable organisations granting loans for public interest and agricultural policies. There are also some 100 co-operative savings banks (*cooperativas de crédito*), whose members are agricultural co-operatives, although they play only a small part in Spain's banking system and hold just a few per cent of total bank assets. Savings banks are similar to building societies in the UK and savings and loans in the USA, and hold around 45 per cent of deposits and make some 25 per cent of personal loans. The two largest Spanish savings banks are La Caixa (some 3,600 branches) and Caja de Madrid (almost 1,900 branches). In general, savings banks offer a more personal friendly service than clearing banks and are excellent for local business (many have limited regional branch networks). However, although they provide the same basic services as clearing banks, they aren't always best for international business. A strange idiosyncrasy of some Spanish banks is that in addition to financial services they also sell goods (household appliances, bicycles, computers, etc.) and services (holidays and household insurance), which is rare in other countries.

There are also around 50 foreign banks operating in Spain, although there are fewer (with an overall smaller market share) than in most other European countries. However, competition from foreign banks is set to increase as EU regulations allow any bank trading legitimately in one EU country to trade in any other EU country. Most major foreign banks are present in Madrid and Barcelona, but branches are rare in other cities. Among foreigners in Spain, the British are best served by their national banks, both in the major cities and resort areas. The most prominent

British banks in Spain are, in order of the number of branches, Natwest, represented by Solbank (some 65), Barclays (28 branches) and Lloyds TSB (around 10). These banks are full members of the Spanish clearing and payment system and can provide cheque accounts, cash and credit cards, and direct debit/standing order services. The Royal Bank of Scotland also operates at some BSCH branches. Note, however, that foreign banks in Spain operate in exactly the same way as Spanish banks, so you shouldn't expect, for example, a branch of Barclays in Spain to behave like a branch in the UK or any other country. Surprisingly, considering the size and spending power of foreign residents and tourists in Spain, most Spanish banks make few concessions to foreign clients, e.g. by providing general information and statements in foreign languages and having staff who speak foreign languages.

If you have a complaint regarding a bank, don't expect to receive a quick resolution or any resolution. A complaint should be addressed to the ombudsman (*defensor del cliente*, although the title may vary) of your bank. If a *defensor* doesn't exist or you don't receive a reply within two months, you should contact the Bank of Spain (Banco de España, Servicio de Reclamaciones, Alcalá, 50, 28014 Madrid, ☎ 913 385 068/851).

# Opening Hours

Normal bank opening hours in Spain are from between 8.15 and 9am until around 1.30pm, Mondays to Fridays, and from between 8.30 and 9.30am until 1pm on Saturdays in winter (banks are closed on Saturdays from around 1st June to 30th September). Savings banks open all day on Thursdays (until 7pm) but are closed on Saturdays. Some branches in major cities remain open continually from the morning until 4 or 4.30pm from autumn to spring, although they may close earlier on Fridays. Some banks are experimenting with longer hours at certain branches and opening from, for example, 8.15am until 8.30pm (or they may open from around 8.15am to 2pm and again from around 4.30 until 7.45pm). Banks in shopping centres may also open all day until late in the evening (some are open the same hours as hypermarkets, e.g. from 10am until 10pm). One of the drawbacks to longer opening hours is resistance from trade unions to their members working longer or irregular hours.

At major international airports and railway stations in major cities, there are also banks with extended opening hours, although they often have long queues. Banks are closed on public holidays, including local holidays (when banks in neighbouring towns often close on different days), and they may also close early during local *fiestas*. Note that many *bureaux de change* have long opening hours and some are even open 24 hours in summer in some resort areas.

# Opening an Account

You can open a bank account in Spain whether you're a resident or a non-resident. It's best to open a Spanish bank account in person, rather than by correspondence from abroad. Ask your friends, neighbours or colleagues for their recommendations and just go along to the bank of your choice and introduce yourself. You must be aged at least 18 and provide proof of identity (e.g. a passport), your address in Spain and your passport number or *NIE* (see page 223). If you wish to open an account with a Spanish bank while you're abroad, you must first obtain an application form, available from foreign branches of Spanish banks or direct from a Spanish bank in Spain. You need to select a branch from the list provided, which should preferably be close to where you will be living in Spain. If you open an account by correspondence, you need to provide a reference from your current bank.

**Non-Residents:** Since Spain became a full member of the EU on 1st January 1993, banking regulations for both resident and non-resident EU citizens have been identical. However, if you're a non-resident you're entitled to open a non-resident euro account (*cuenta de euros de no residente*) or a foreign currency account only. An important point for non-resident, non-EU citizens to note is that when importing funds for the purchase of a property (or any other major transaction) in Spain, the transfer of funds must be verified by a certificate from your bank (*certificado de cambio de divisas*). This allows you to re-export the funds if (or when) you sell the property later. This is unnecessary for EU nationals. Although it's possible for non-resident homeowners to do most of their banking via a foreign account using debit and credit cards, you will need a Spanish bank account to pay your Spanish utility and tax bills (which are best paid by direct debit). If you own a holiday home in Spain, you can have your correspondence (e.g. cheque books, statements, payment advices, etc.) sent to an address abroad.

**Residents:** You're considered to be a resident of Spain if you have your main centre of interest there, i.e. you live and work there almost permanently. To open a resident's account you must usually have a residence permit (*residencia*) or evidence that you have a job in Spain. It isn't advisable to close your bank accounts abroad, unless you're sure you won't need them in the future. Even when you're resident in Spain, it's cheaper to keep money in local currency in an account in a country you visit regularly, rather than pay commission charges to change money. Many foreigners living in Spain maintain at least two cheque (current) accounts, a foreign account for international transactions and a local account with a Spanish bank for day-to-day business.

# Offshore Banking

If you have a sum of money to invest or wish to protect your inheritance from the tax man, it may be worthwhile looking into the accounts and services (such as pensions and trusts) provided by offshore banking centres in tax havens (*paraísos fiscales*) such as the Channel Islands (Guernsey and Jersey), Gibraltar and the Isle of Man (around 50 locations world-wide are officially classified as tax havens). The big attraction of offshore banking is that money can be deposited in a wide range of currencies, customers are usually guaranteed complete anonymity, there are no double-taxation agreements, no withholding tax is payable, and interest is paid tax-free. Many offshore banks also offer telephone banking (usually seven days a week).

A large number of American, British and other European banks and financial institutions provide offshore banking facilities in one or more locations. Most institutions offer high-interest deposit accounts for long-term savings and investment portfolios in which funds can be deposited in any major currency. Many people living abroad keep a local account for everyday business and maintain an offshore account for international transactions and investment purposes.

> **SURVIVAL TIP**
> Most financial experts advise investors never to rush into the expatriate life and invest their life savings in an offshore tax haven until they know what their long-term plans are.

Accounts have minimum deposit levels that usually range from the equivalent of around €750 to €15,000 (e.g. £500 to £10,000), with some as high as €150,000 (£100,000). In addition to large minimum balances, accounts may also have stringent terms and conditions, such as restrictions on withdrawals or high early withdrawal penalties. You can deposit funds on call (instant access) or for a fixed period, e.g. from 90 days to one year (usually for larger sums). Interest is usually paid monthly or annually; monthly interest payments are slightly lower than annual payments, although they have the advantage of providing a regular income. There are usually no charges provided a specified minimum balance is maintained. Many accounts offer a cash card or a credit card (e.g. Mastercard or Visa) which can be used to obtain cash from ATMs throughout the world.

When selecting a financial institution and offshore banking centre, your first priority should be for the safety of your money. In some offshore banking centres, a percentage of bank deposits up to a maximum sum is guaranteed under a deposit protection scheme in the event of a financial institution going bust (the Isle of Man, Guernsey and Jersey all have such schemes). Unless you're planning to bank with a major international bank, you should check the credit rating of a financial institution before depositing any money, particularly if it doesn't provide deposit insurance. All banks have a credit rating (the highest is 'AAA') and a bank with a high rating will be happy to tell you (but get it in writing). You can also check the rating of an international bank or financial organisation with Moody's Investor Service. You should be wary of institutions offering higher than average interest rates, as if it looks too good to be true it probably will be – like the Bank of International Commerce and Credit (BICC) which went bust in 1992.

# MORTGAGES

Mortgages or home loans (*hipotecas*) are available from most Spanish banks (both for residents and non-residents), foreign banks in Spain, and overseas and offshore banks. In recent years, both Spanish and foreign lenders have tightened their lending criteria due to the repayment problems experienced by many borrowers in the early 1990s, although in 2002 there were a record number of mortgages in Spain with the average amount around €100,000.

The amount you can borrow will depend on various factors such as your income, trade or profession, whether you're an employee or self-employed, and whether your married, and if so, whether your partner works. Lenders may also have a maximum lending limit based on a percentage of your income, but this isn't required by law.

Most banks offer mortgages of up to 80 per cent, although non-residents can usually borrow a maximum of 60 per cent only. To obtain a mortgage from a Spanish bank, you must usually provide proof of your monthly income and major outgoings (e.g. loans or commitments). There are no self-assessment mortgages such as in the UK and mortgages without proof of income (although advertised in the expatriate press) are difficult to find and virtually non-existent. If you want a Spanish mortgage to buy a property for commercial purposes, you will need to provide a detailed business plan in Spanish. Note that a mortgage can be assumed by the new owner (called *subrogación*) when a property is sold, which is a common practice in Spain.

Some foreign lenders apply stricter rules than Spanish lenders regarding income, employment and the type of property on which they will lend. Foreign lenders, e.g. offshore banks, may also have strict rules

regarding the nationality and domicile of borrowers (some won't lend to Spanish residents), and the percentage they will lend. They may levy astronomical charges if you get into arrears. If you raise a mortgage outside Spain for a Spanish property, you should be aware of any impact this may have on **all** your tax liabilities or allowances.

Spanish mortgages have been among the most competitive in Europe and in early 2003 variable interest rates were around 4.5 per cent. Around 90 per cent of home loans in Spain have a variable (*interés variable*) instead of a fixed interest (*interés fijo*) rate and they've traditionally been set at 1 to 2 per cent above the base rate (European inter-bank rate or EURIBOR). A low interest rate may be more than offset by increased commission charges. Shop around and ask for the effective rate (*Tasa Anual Equivalente/TAE*) including commissions and fees.

It's customary for a property to be held as security for a home loan, i.e. the lender takes a first charge on the property, which is recorded at the property registry. If a loan is obtained using a Spanish property as security, additional fees and registration costs are payable to the notary (*notario*) for registering the charge against the property.

Spanish banks also often insist that you take out home insurance with them together with the mortgage, although you aren't legally required to do so. **Their rates are invariably higher than other insurers so it's wise to shop around.**

Mortgages are granted on a percentage of the valuation, which itself is usually below the market value. The maximum mortgage in Spain is usually 80 per cent of the purchase price for a principal home (*vivienda habitual*) and 50 to 60 per cent for a second home (*segunda residencia*). The normal term is 10 to 15 years, although mortgages can be repaid over 10 to 35 years. The repayment period may be shorter for second homes. Repayment mortgages are the most common, although endowment and pension-linked mortgages are also available. Payments can usually be made monthly or quarterly.

Note that you must add expenses and fees totalling around 10 per cent of the purchase price, to the cost of a property. For example, if you're buying a property for €150,000 and obtain a 60 per cent mortgage, you must pay a 40 per cent deposit (€60,000) plus around 10 per cent fees (€15,000), making a total of €75,000. There are various fees associated with mortgages, e.g. most lenders levy an 'arrangement' fee (*comisión de apertura*) of 0.5 to 2.5 per cent. Although it's unusual to have a full survey carried out in Spain, most lenders will insist on a 'valuation' (this usually costs between €150 to €300) before they will grant a loan. Mortgages also usually have a cancellation fee of around 1 per cent.

# Remortgaging

If you have equity in an existing property, either in Spain or abroad, then it may be more cost effective to remortgage (or take out a second mortgage) on that property, rather than take out a new mortgage for a second home in Spain. It involves less paperwork, and therefore lower legal fees, and a plan can be tailored to meet your individual requirements. Depending on your equity in your existing property and the cost of your Spanish property, this may enable you to pay cash for a second home. Note, however, that when a mortgage is taken out on a Spanish property it's based on that property and not the individual, which could be important if you get into repayment difficulties.

# Foreign Currency Loans

It's also possible to obtain a foreign currency mortgage, other than in euros (either in Spain or abroad), e.g. pounds sterling, Swiss francs or US dollars. In previous years, high Spanish interest rates meant that a foreign currency mortgage was a good bet for many foreigners. However, you should be extremely wary about taking out a foreign currency mortgage, as interest rate gains can be wiped out overnight by currency swings and devaluations. It's generally recognised that you should take out a mortgage in the currency in which you're paid or in the currency of the country where a property is situated.

In this case, if the foreign currency in which you have your mortgage is heavily devalued, you will have the consolation of knowing that the value of your Spanish property will ('theoretically') have increased by the same percentage when converted back into euros. When choosing between a euro and a foreign currency loan, take into account all costs, fees, interest rates and possible currency fluctuations. Regardless of how you finance your purchase, you should always obtain professional advice. If you have a foreign currency mortgage, you must usually pay commission charges each time you transfer foreign currency into euros or remit money to Spain. If you let a second home, you may be able to offset the interest (pro rata) on your mortgage against letting income. For example, if you let a property for three months of the year, you can offset a quarter of your annual mortgage interest against your letting income.

> **SURVIVAL TIP**
> If you need to obtain a mortgage to buy a home in Spain, shop around and compare interest rates, terms and fees from a number of banks and financial institutions – not just in Spain but also your home country.

Bear in mind that mortgages in Spain are generally for a shorter period than in the UK and USA, and therefore your repayments may be much higher than you expect.

# Payment Problems & Changing Lenders

If you're unable to meet your mortgage payments, lenders are usually willing to re-schedule your mortgage so that it extends over a longer period, thus allowing you to make lower payments. Note that you should contact your lender as soon as you have payment problems, as lenders are quick to embargo a property and could eventually repossess it and sell it at auction, which can take just a few months.

Because banks were reluctant to allow existing lenders to transfer to other lenders, the government passed new legislation in 1994 that made it much easier for borrowers with fixed rate mortgages to change lenders or re-negotiate a mortgage with their existing lender. New regulations require lenders to issue a list of conditions and interest rates (*hojas vinculantes*) that are binding on the lender for ten days. This enables applicants to compare rates and allows existing mortgage holders to transfer their mortgage if their present lender cannot meet the terms offered by another lender.

The new law established two ways of improving existing mortgage terms: by 'compulsory substitution' (*subrogación forzosa*), whereby the lender offering more favourable terms/interest rates takes over the existing mortgage, and by 'variation' (*novación modificativa*), whereby the existing lender offers a reduced interest rate or changes the repayment period. Some lenders offer to pay all the associated expenses if you switch your mortgage to them. In 1996 the government and the banks agreed that banks would charge a maximum of 2.5 per cent when a lender wished to cancel a mortgage with fixed interest and make one with a variable interest (a common event when interest rates are falling).

> **SURVIVAL TIP**
> If you're a Spanish taxpayer
> you can claim a deduction for your Spanish mortgage
> against your tax liabilities.

# 5.

# THE PURCHASE PROCEDURE

This chapter details the purchase procedure for buying a home in Spain. It's advisable to employ a lawyer before paying any money and, if necessary, have him check anything you're concerned about regarding a property you're planning to buy. See also **Avoiding Problems** on page 106.

# CONVEYANCING

Conveyancing (or more correctly conveyance) is the legal term for processing the paperwork involved in buying and selling a property and transferring the deeds of ownership. In Spain, some aspects of conveyancing such as drawing up the deeds and witnessing the signatures, can be performed only by a public notary (*notario*). A *notario* represents the Spanish government and one of his main tasks is to ensure that state taxes are paid on the completion of a sale.

 **Note that a *notario* doesn't verify or guarantee the accuracy of statements made in a contract or protect you against fraud!**

It's therefore vital to employ a lawyer to carry out the following checks:

- verifying that a property belongs to the vendor or that he has legal authority to sell it (shown in the *escritura pública* in the property register). If a property has no *escritura* you should be extremely wary;

- making sure that there are no tenants. If there are, you must ensure that you will obtain vacant possession, as the law protects long-term tenants in Spain and getting them out can be a problem;

- checking that there are no pre-emption rights over a property and that there are no plans to construct anything that would adversely affect the value, enjoyment or use of the property such as roads, railway lines, airports, shops, factories or any other developments;

- checking that the boundaries and measurements in the *escritura* are accurate. For some strange reason, Spain has two property registries: the property registry office (*Registro de la Propiedad*) which is concerned mainly with the ownership of property and the regional property register (*Catastro*) that's concerned with the physical description of a property and its boundaries. Obtain a *certificado catastral* from the *Catastro*, which contains an accurate physical description of the property and maps;

- ensuring that building permits and planning permissions are in order (e.g. building licence, water and electricity supply, sewage connection) and are genuine, and that a property was built in accordance with the plans. This can be done by checking the *plan parcial*, which must be registered with the local urban development office (*urbanismo*). You can obtain an *informe urbanístico* from the local town hall verifying that a property has been built legally.

  If a building is located on a beach-front, you should also check that it was approved by the coastal authorities (*Jefatura de Costas*). Note that beach-front properties are subject to special building licences and it can be difficult to restore or rebuild the original building.

  A newly completed building must have a 'certificate of new work' (*certificado de fin de obra nueva*) certifying the completion of work in accordance with the building plans and a 'licence for the first occupation' (*licencia de primera ocupación*). The latter is necessary in order to get an electricity meter installed. Building certificates are issued by the town hall for most services such as electricity and water (*boletín de instalaciones eléctricas/de agua*).

 **Make sure than any extensions or major structures, such as a swimming pool, have planning permission. It isn't unusual for alterations to be made illegally without planning permission in Spain, which can result in them having to be demolished or the owner incurring huge fines.**

- checking that there are no encumbrances or liens, e.g. mortgages or loans, against a property or any outstanding debts such as local taxes (rates), community charges, water, electricity or telephone bills. This includes:

  - obtaining the registration number (*referencia catastral*) of the property and an extract of the property register (*nota simple*), which will cost you around €6. This will tell you if the vendor is the owner, the size of the property and whether there are any charges or encumbrances registered against it (e.g. mortgages or debts);

  - where a property is part of a community development (see page 136), checking that there are no outstanding community charges for the last five years. The law now requires that a vendor presents a certificate from the community stating that payments are up to date, which must be presented to the *notario* when the deeds are signed.

- enquiring at the town hall whether there are any unpaid taxes such as property tax or *IBI* (see page 236) or other charges outstanding against a property. Note that many town council now refuse to provide such information to anyone other than the owner so you should ask to see a certificate of no debts issued by the council. Some notaries are now asking to see this when the title deeds are signed;

- checking that all bills for electricity, water, telephone and gas have been paid for the last few years. Receipts should be provided by the vendor for all taxes and services.

● ensuring that a proper title is obtained and arranging the necessary registration of ownership.

Note that if you buy a property on which there's an outstanding loan or taxes, the lender or local authority has first claim on the property and has the right to take possession and sell it to repay the debt. All unpaid debts on a property in Spain are inherited by the buyer.

 **You *must* ensure that any debts against a property are cleared before you sign the deed of sale (*escritura*) and your lawyer must obtain another *nota simple* immediately prior to completion to make sure that no debts have been added since the previous check.**

Many estate agents will carry out the above checks for you and pass the information to your lawyer. However, it's still advisable to have your lawyer double check.

**SURVIVAL TIP**
If an estate agent tells you that vacant land surrounding or adjacent to a property are 'green belt' and cannot be built on, check with the planning office of the town hall that this so. Even if it is, green belt is often built on, so if it's crucial for you not to live next to a future building site, avoid buying a property with vacant land adjacent to it.

The cost of conveyancing for a property in Spain depends on whether you employ a foreign or Spanish lawyer or both. If you employ a foreign-based lawyer, you should expect to pay €150 or more an hour for his services plus additional fees for the work of his Spanish partners or associates. The fees may be stated as a percentage of the purchase price, e.g. 1 to 1.5 per cent, with a minimum fee of €600 to €1,200. Before hiring a lawyer, compare the fees charged by a number of practices and obtain quotations in writing. Always check what's included in the fee and whether it's 'full and binding' or just an estimate (a low basic rate may be supplemented by much more expensive 'extras'). You should also employ a lawyer to check the contract (see below) before signing it to ensure that it's correct and includes everything necessary, particularly regarding any necessary conditional clauses.

## Notary's Duties

Since 1993, a notary has been required to make a check of the property registry (such as the name of the title holder, description and whether there are any charges or encumbrances against the property) not longer than four days prior to the signing of the *escritura*. This information **must** be included in the title deed. However, some notaries try to release themselves from their obligations by adding an escape clause to the *escritura* stating that the buyer agrees that the notary isn't responsible if charges are found against a property after the purchase. Naturally, this isn't explained to a buyer and could be construed as fraud on the part of the notary, because if he took the trouble to explain it to the buyer he wouldn't sign it.

**You should refuse to sign a title deed when such as clause is included** (yet another good reason to have a lawyer check a contract).

In Spain, the sales contract (*escritura pública de compraventa*, commonly referred to simply as the *escritura*) is prepared by a public notary (*notario*), who's responsible for ensuring that it's drawn up correctly and that the purchase price is paid to the vendor.

The notary also certifies the identity of the parties, witnesses the signing of the deed, arranges for its registration (in the name of the new owner) in the local property register and collects any fees or taxes that are due.

 **A *notario* represents the state and doesn't protect the interests of the buyer or the seller and will rarely point out possible pitfalls in a contract, proffer advice or volunteer any information (as, for example, an estate agent often will).**

You shouldn't expect a *notario* to speak English or any language other than Spanish (although there are some that do) or to explain any of the intricacies of Spanish property law.

Your lawyer should check that the notary is doing his job correctly, thus providing an extra safeguard. It isn't advisable to use the same lawyer as the vendor, even if it would save you money, as he is primarily concerned with protecting the interests of the vendor and not the buyer.

Note that it isn't always necessary to use a lawyer to do the conveyancing and you can save yourself a considerable sum by employing a 'conveyancer' in Spain, who usually charges a flat fee irrespective of the price of a property.

For further information, see **Legal Advice** on page 106 and **Avoiding Problems** on page 106.

## CONTRACTS

The first stage in buying a property in Spain is usually the signing of a 'private contract' (*contrato privado de compraventa*), although it's possible to go to a notary and have him draw up the *escritura* without having a prior contract. However, when you're paying a deposit, which is usual, it's necessary to have a contract drawn up. It's also possible to sign a reservation contract, where you pay a small 'godwill deposit', e.g. €1,000 to €5,000, which usually secures a property for a period, e.g. 30 days.

 **Some estate agents may pressurise you to pay a goodwill deposit in order to take the property off the market while you make a decision. Although this is common practice, you shouldn't pay a deposit unless you're absolutely certain you wish to buy the property; otherwise, if you withdraw from the sale for any reason, the deposit will be forfeited.**

If you pay a deposit, you should ensure that it's deposited in a separate bonded account and that the receipt states that if there are any problems with the property (legal or otherwise) the deposit will be returned.

You can also sign an option 'contract' (*contrato de opción de compra*) that isn't a binding purchase contract. Note, however, that a 10 per cent deposit must usually be paid, which is forfeited if you decide not to buy within the time limit specified in the contract. Should the vendor not sell within the time limit, then he usually has to return the deposit plus the same amount again, resulting in a return of double the deposit.

When you sign the contract (*contrato privado de compraventa*) for a new or resale property or a plot of land you must pay a deposit (see below). If you're buying a resale or a new completed property (i.e. not off plan), you usually pay a deposit of 10 per cent when signing the contract (the actual amount may be negotiable), with the balance being paid at the completion when the deed of sale is signed. **Before you sign a contract, it's important to have it checked by your lawyer.** One of the main reasons is to safeguard your interests by including any necessary conditional clauses (see below) in the contract.

# Buying Off Plan

When buying an uncompleted property off plan, i.e. a property still to be built or which is partly built only, payment is made in stages. Stage payments vary considerably and may consist of a 20 per cent deposit; 20 per cent on completion of the roof; 20 per cent on tiling the bathroom and kitchen (or when the doors and window frames are installed); 20 per cent when the building is complete; 10 per cent when the exterior work is completed (such as the patio, pool and landscaping); and the remaining 10 per cent withheld for six or 12 months as an insurance against defects. Other common stage schemes are the payment of a fixed amount every few months (three to six) regardless of how much of the property has been completed. If a property is already partly built, the builder may ask for a higher initial payment, depending on its stage of completion.

The contract contains the timetable for the property's completion; stage payment dates; the completion date and penalties for non-completion; guarantees for building work; details of the builder's insurance policy (against non-completion); and a copy of the plans and drawings. The floor plan and technical specifications are signed by both parties to ensure that the standard and size of construction is adhered to. The contract should also contain a clause allowing you to withhold up to 10 per cent of the purchase price for 6 to 12 months as a guarantee against the builder not correcting any faults in the property. The completion of each stage should be certified in writing by your own architect or lawyer before payments are made. Note that it's important to ensure that payments are made on time, otherwise you could lose all previous payments and the property could be sold to another buyer. See also **Avoiding Problems** on page 106, which particularly applies to buying off plan or when buying unfinished properties.

> **SURVIVAL TIP**
> It's important that the builder or developer has an insurance policy (or 'termination' guarantee) to protect your investment in the event that he goes bust before completing the property and its infrastructure. If he doesn't then you shouldn't buy from him!

Your money should be deposited in a special 'client' bank account and should be returned with interest if the building isn't completed by the date listed in the contract, or the official certificate declaring that it's fit to live in isn't obtained.

## Deposits

There are various kinds of deposits when buying property in Spain. Deposits are refundable under strict conditions only, notably relating to any conditional clauses such as failure to obtain a mortgage, although a deposit can also be forfeited if you don't complete the transaction within the period (e.g. 60 or 90 days) specified in the contract. If you withdraw from a sale after all the conditions have been met, you won't only lose your deposit, but may also be required to pay the estate agent's commission. If a deposit is paid in the form of an *arras*, the contract can be cancelled by either party, with the buyer forfeiting his deposit or the vendor paying the buyer double the deposit, but neither party can demand that the other party goes through with the sale. However, in some cases, if one of the parties wishes to withdraw from the sale/purchase, the other party can demand that he goes through with it or that he receives compensation for damages. **Always make sure that you know exactly what the conditions are regarding the return or forfeiture of a deposit.**

Note that many estate agents don't have the legal authority to hold money on behalf of their clients and that deposits should be deposited only in a separate, bonded account.

It isn't advisable to make out cheques for deposits in the name of an estate agent, as there have been cases where an estate agent has disappeared with the money! Never pay a deposit to anyone acting as a go-between, however well-meaning they may appear.

In general, a deposit should always be paid to the vendor under the supervision of your lawyer.

## Conditional Clauses

All contracts, whether for new or resale properties, usually contain a number of conditional clauses (*cláusulas abrogatorias*) that must be met to ensure the validity of the contract. Conditions usually apply to events out of control of either the vendor or buyer, although almost anything the buyer agrees with the vendor can be included in a contract. If any of the conditions aren't met, the contract can be suspended or declared null and void, and the deposit returned. However, if you fail to go through with a purchase and aren't covered by a clause in the contract, you will forfeit your deposit or could even be compelled to go through with a purchase. Note that if you're buying anything from the vendor such as carpets, curtains or furniture that are included in the purchase price, you should have them listed and attached as an addendum to the contract. Any fixtures and fittings present in a property when you view it (and agree to buy it) should still be there when you take possession, unless otherwise stated in the contract (see also **Completion** on page 200).

There are many possible conditional clauses concerning a range of subjects, including the following:

- being able to obtain a mortgage (although it's common in Spain to have a mortgage approved before signing a contract);
- obtaining planning permission and building permits;
- plans to construct anything (e.g. roads, railways, etc.) that would adversely affect your enjoyment or use of a property;
- confirmation of the land area being purchased with a property;
- pre-emption rights or restrictive covenants over a property such as rights of way – look for the words 'affected by servitudes' (*afecta a servidumbres*) in an extract of the property register (*nota simple*);
- dependence on the sale of another property;
- subject to a satisfactory building survey or inspection.

You should discuss whether conditional clauses are necessary with your lawyer. Note that the vendor remains responsible for any major hidden defects in a property for six months from the date of signing the deed of sale (although this is no consolation if you cannot find him).

## Inheritance & Capital Gains Tax

Property can be registered in a single name; both names of a couple or joint buyers' names; the name or names of children, giving the parents sole use during their lifetime; or in the name of a Spanish or foreign company (see below).

> **SURVIVAL TIP**
> Before registering the title deed of a home, carefully consider the tax and inheritance consequences for those in whose name the deed will be registered.

See also **Capital Gains Tax** on page 240 and **Inheritance & Gift Tax** on page 243.

## Buying Through A Company

It's possible to avoid Spanish capital gains, inheritance tax and transfer tax on a sale by registering a property through a limited company (which in turn could be owned by an offshore company).

> **SURVIVAL TIP**
> Before buying a property through a company, it's essential to obtain expert legal advice and carefully consider theadvantages and disadvantages.

Buying through a company may be worthwhile when a large sum is being invested (e.g. €500,000 or more) or when the buyer has a complicated family or inheritance situation, e.g. an elderly person who's planning to leave a property to a non-relative.

Since January 1992, the beneficial owners of such properties have been required to register their ownership with the authorities or pay an annual tax of 3 per cent of the rated value (*valor catastral*). It's possible to obtain an exemption from this tax if a property is owned by a company in a country with a double taxation treaty with Spain.

The Foundation Institute of Foreign Property Owners (see page 105) will vet contracts for members for a small fee to ensure that they're legal and fair.

 **However you decide to buy a property, it should be done at the time of purchase as it will be more expensive (or even impossible) to change it later. Discuss the matter with your lawyer before signing a contract.**

For further information, see **Avoiding Problems** on page 106 and **Conveyancing** on page 190.

# COMPLETION

Completion (or closing) is the name for the signing of the final deed (*escritura de compraventa*), the date of which is usually one to three months after signing the contract, as stated in the contract (although it may be 'moveable' if both parties agree). Completion involves the signing of the deed of sale, transferring legal ownership of a property and the payment of the balance of the purchase price, plus other payments such as the *notario's* fees, taxes and duties (although these may be paid at a later date). When all the necessary documents relating to a purchase have been returned to the *notario*, he will contact you and request the balance of the purchase price less the deposit and, if applicable, the amount of a mortgage. He will also send you a bill for his fees and taxes, which must usually be paid within 30 days of completion (check in advance). At the same time the *notario* should also provide a draft deed of sale (if he doesn't, you should request one). This should be complete and shouldn't contain any blank spaces to be completed later. If you don't understand the deed of sale, you should have it checked by your lawyer or, alternatively, have him prepare it on your behalf. Note that if you've contracted the services of a lawyer, all of the above will be organised by him.

## Final Checks

When you sign the final deed, you agree to accept the property in the condition that it's in at that time. Therefore, it's important to check that the property hasn't fallen down or been damaged in any way, e.g. by a storm, vandals or the previous owner, since you signed the initial contract. If you've employed a lawyer or are buying through an agent, he should accompany you on this visit. You should also do a final inventory immediately prior to completion (the previous owner should have already vacated the property) to ensure that the vendor hasn't absconded with anything that was included in the price.

You should have an inventory of the fixtures and fittings and anything that was included in the contract or purchased separately, e.g. carpets, light fittings, curtains or kitchen appliances, and check that they're present and in good working order. This is particularly important if furniture and furnishings (and major appliances) were included in the price. You should also ensure that expensive items (such as kitchen apparatus) haven't been substituted by inferior (possibly second-hand) items. Any fixtures and fittings (and garden plants and shrubs) present in a property when you viewed it should still be there when you take possession, unless otherwise stated in the contract.

If you find anything is missing, damaged or isn't in working order you should make a note and insist on immediate restitution, such as an appropriate reduction in the amount to be paid. In such cases it's normal for the *notario* to delay the signing of the deed until the matter is settled, although an appropriate amount could be withheld from the vendor's proceeds to pay for repairs or replacements.

> **SURVIVAL TIP**
> You should refuse to go through with the purchase
> if you aren't completely satisfied, as it will be difficult or
> impossible to obtain redress later.

If it isn't possible to complete the sale, you should consult your lawyer about your rights and the return of your deposit and any other funds already paid.

# Signing

The final act of the sale is the signing of the deed of sale (*escritura de compraventa*), which takes place in the *notario's* office. Before the deed of sale is signed, the *notario* checks that the conditions contained in the contract have been fulfilled. It's normal for all parties to be present when the deed of sale is read, signed and witnessed by the *notario*, although either party can give someone a power of attorney (*poder especial*) to represent them. This is quite common among foreign buyers and sellers and can be arranged by your *notario* (costing from €40 to €100). If a couple buys a property in both their names, the wife can give the husband power of attorney (or vice versa). Note that if a power of attorney isn't completed in Spain, it must be signed and authenticated with an official stamp (*apostille*) before a public notary abroad, which is much more expensive than doing it in Spain.

Bear in mind, however, that a power of attorney can be a dangerous document to sign, and in most cases is unnecessary. For example, you can have someone represent you in Spain as a 'verbal representative' (*representante verbal*), where you ratify the representation afterwards at a Spanish Consulate in your home country or at the notary's office on your next visit to Spain, although the ratification should be done shortly after the purchase. A non-resident requires a 'certificate of non-residence' (*certificado de no residencia*), confirming that he is a non-resident in Spain (available from foreigners' offices in provincial capitals). This must be presented at the signing of the deed or within 30 days. The *notario* reads through the *escritura* and both the vendor and buyer must sign it, indicating that they've understood and accept the terms of the document. If you don't understand sufficient Spanish you should take along an interpreter, although if you have a lawyer he will usually translate for you.

## Payment

The balance of the price (after the deposit and any mortgages are subtracted) must be paid by banker's draft or bank transfer. For most people the most convenient way is by banker's draft, which also means that you will have the payment in your possession (a bank cannot lose it!) and the *notario* can confirm it immediately. It also allows you to withhold payment if there's a last minute problem that cannot be resolved. Note that when the vendor and buyer are of the same foreign nationality, they can agree that the balance is paid in any currency, and payment can also be made abroad, although signing of the title deeds may be held up until confirmation of payment is received. However, the deed of sale must state the sale price in euros and Spanish taxes must be paid on this price. At the time of signing, both the vendor and buyer declare that payment has been made in the agreed foreign currency. In this case the payment should be held by an independent lawyer or solicitor in the vendor's and buyer's home country.

Non-resident purchasers no longer need a certificate from a Spanish bank stating that the amount to be paid has been exchanged or converted from a foreign currency, although it must be reported to the Bank of Spain (see page 173). If the vendor is a non-resident, the buyer must withhold 5 per cent of the purchase price (as security against a non-resident's possible tax liability) and pay it to the Spanish Ministry of Finance within 30 days of the transaction (see page 242). After paying the money and receiving a receipt, the *notario* will give you an unsigned copy (*copia simple*) of the *escritura* showing that you're the new owner of the property. You will also receive the keys! The fees and taxes associated with the purchase must be paid within around 30 days of completion (there are penalties for late payment).

## Registration

After the deed is signed, the original (*primera copia*) is lodged at the property registry office (*Registro de la Propiedad*) and the new owner's name(s) is/are entered on the registry deed. It's important to send the signed escritura to the property registry as soon as possible, preferably the same day it has been signed. The notary will usually do this within 30 days of it being signed and many fax a copy on the day of signing. You can also take it yourself or get your lawyer to take it for you or fax a copy to the registry, which is advisable.

 **Registering ownership of a property is the most important act of buying property, because, until the property is registered in your name, even after you've signed the contract in the presence of a notary, charges can be registered against it without your knowledge.**

Only when the *escritura* has been registered and becomes an *escritura pública* are you the legal owner of the property. Following registration, the original deeds are returned to the notary's office or your lawyer, usually after two to three months.

# 6.

# MOVING HOUSE

This chapter contains information about moving house, immigration and customs. It also contains checklists of tasks to be completed before or soon after arrival in Spain and when moving house, plus suggestions for finding local help and information.

# SHIPPING YOUR BELONGINGS

After finding a home in Spain it usually takes only a few weeks to have your belongings shipped from within continental Europe. From anywhere else it varies considerably, e.g. around four weeks from the east coast of America, six weeks from the US west coast and the Far East, and around eight weeks from Australasia. Customs clearance is no longer necessary when shipping your household effects between European Union (EU) countries. However, when shipping your effects from a non-EU country to Spain, you should enquire about customs formalities in advance. If you fail to follow the correct procedure you can encounter problems and delays, and may be erroneously charged duty or fined. The relevant forms to be completed by non-EU citizens depend on whether your Spanish home will be your main residence or a second home. Removal companies usually take care of the paperwork and ensure that the correct documents are provided and properly completed (see **Customs** on page 210).

It's advisable to use a major shipping company with a good reputation. For international moves it's best to use a company that's a member of the International Federation of Furniture Removers (FIDI) or the Overseas Moving Network International (OMNI), with experience in Spain. Members of FIDI and OMNI usually subscribe to an advance payment scheme providing a guarantee, whereby, if a member company fails to fulfil its commitments to a client, the removal is completed at the agreed cost by another company or your money is refunded. Some removal companies have subsidiaries or affiliates in Spain, which may be more convenient if you encounter problems or need to make an insurance claim. If you engage a shipping company in Spain, it's wise to avoid small unregistered companies ('man and van') as some have been known to disappear with their client's worldly possessions (on the other hand, some are extremely reliable). A Spanish shipping company should have a Spanish business address, a registered licence number, a VAT (*IVA*) number and must be licensed to do removals in Spain. For information about Spanish removal companies contact the Federación Española de Empresas de Mudanzas (FEDEM), López de Hoyos 322, 28043 Madrid (☎ 917 444 703, 🖳 www.fedem.es).

You should obtain at least three written quotations before choosing a company, as rates vary considerably. Removal companies should send a representative to provide a detailed quotation. Most companies will pack your belongings and provide packing cases and special containers, although this is naturally more expensive than packing them yourself. Ask a company how they pack fragile and valuable items, and whether the cost of packing cases, materials and insurance (see below) are included in a quotation.

If you're doing your own packing, most companies will provide packing crates and boxes. You should make a simple floor plan of your new home with rooms numbered and mark corresponding numbers on furniture and boxes as they're packed, so that the removal company will know where everything is to go and you can leave them to it. Shipments are charged by volume, e.g. the square metre in Europe and the square foot in the USA. You should expect to pay from €3,000 to €6,000 to move the contents of a three to four-bedroom house within western Europe, e.g. from London to the south of Spain. If you're flexible about the delivery date, shipping companies will usually quote a lower fee based on a 'part load', where the cost is shared with other deliveries. This can result in savings of 50 per cent or more compared with a 'special' delivery.

> **SURVIVAL TIP**
> **Whether you have an individual or shared delivery,**
> **obtain the maximum transit period in writing, otherwise**
> **you may have to wait months for delivery!**

Be sure to fully insure your belongings during removal with a well established insurance company. Don't insure with a shipping company that carries its own insurance as they will usually fight every euro of a claim. Insurance premiums are usually 1 to 2 per cent of the declared value of your goods, depending on the type of cover chosen. It's prudent to make a photographic or video record of valuables for insurance purposes. Most insurance policies cover for 'all-risks' on a replacement value basis. Note, however, that china, glass and other breakables can usually be included in an 'all-risks' policy only when they're packed by the removal company. Insurance usually covers total loss or loss of a particular crate only, rather than individual items (unless they were packed by the shipping company).

If there are any breakages or damaged items, they must be noted and listed before you sign the delivery bill (although it's obviously impossible to check everything on delivery). If you need to make a claim be sure to read the small print, as some companies require clients to make a claim within a few days, although seven is usual. Send a claim by registered post. Some insurance companies apply an 'excess' of around 1 per cent of the total shipment value when assessing claims.

This means that if your shipment is valued at €25,000 and you make a claim for less than €250, you won't receive anything.

If you're unable to ship your belongings directly to Spain, most shipping companies will put them into storage and some offer a limited free storage period prior to shipment, e.g. 14 days.

---

**SURVIVAL TIP**
**If you need to put your household effects into storage,**
**it's advisable to have them fully insured as**
**warehouses have been known to burn down!**

---

Make a complete list of everything to be moved and give a copy to the removal company. Don't include anything illegal (e.g. guns, bombs, drugs or pornography) with your belongings as customs checks can be rigorous and penalties severe. Give the shipping company **detailed** instructions how to find your Spanish address from the nearest *autopista* (or main road) and a telephone number where you can be contacted.

After considering the shipping costs, you may decide to ship only selected items of furniture and personal effects, and buy new furniture in Spain. If you're importing household goods from another European country, it's possible to rent a self-drive van or truck, although if you rent a vehicle outside Spain you usually need to return it to the country where it was hired. If you plan to transport your belongings to Spain personally, check the customs requirements in the countries you must pass through. Most people find it isn't advisable to do their own move unless it's a simple job, e.g. a few items of furniture and personal effects only. It's no fun heaving beds and wardrobes up stairs and squeezing them into impossible spaces! If you're taking pets with you, you may need to get your vet to tranquillise them, as many pets are frightened (even more than people) by the chaos and stress of moving house.

If you're moving permanently to Spain, take the opportunity to sell, give away or throw out at least half of your possessions. It will cut down your removal bill, clear your mind, and make life simpler, plus you will have the fun of buying new furniture that really suits your new house.

Bear in mind when moving home that everything that can go wrong often does, so allow plenty of time and try not to arrange your move to your new home on the same day as the previous owner is moving out.

Note that if large items of furniture need to be taken in through an upstairs window or balcony, you may need to pay extra. See also **Customs** on page 210 and the **Checklists** on page 215.

Last but not least, if your Spanish home has poor or impossible access for a large truck you must inform the shipping company (the ground must also be firm enough to support a heavy vehicle).

# PRE-DEPARTURE HEALTH CHECK

If you're planning to take up residence in Spain, even for part of the year only, it's wise to have a health check (medical or screening, eyes, teeth, etc.) before your arrival, particularly if you have a record of poor health or are elderly. If you're already taking regular medication, you should note that the brand names of drugs and medicines vary from country to country, and should ask your doctor for the generic name. If you wish to match medication prescribed abroad, you will need a current prescription with the medication's trade name, the manufacturer's name, the chemical name and the dosage. Most drugs have an equivalent in other countries, although particular brands may be difficult or impossible to obtain in Spain.

It's possible to have medication sent from abroad, when no import duty or value added tax is usually payable. If you're visiting a holiday home in Spain for a limited period, you should take sufficient medication to cover your stay. In an emergency a local doctor will write a prescription that can be filled at a local pharmacy or a hospital may refill a prescription from its own pharmacy. It's also advisable to take some of your favourite non-prescription drugs (e.g. aspirins, cold and flu remedies, lotions, etc.) with you, as they may be difficult or impossible to obtain in Spain or may be much more expensive. If applicable, take a spare pair of spectacles, contact lenses, dentures or a hearing aid with you. See also **Health** on page 34.

# IMMIGRATION

On arrival in Spain, your first task will be to negotiate immigration and customs. Fortunately this presents few problems for most people, particularly European Union (EU) nationals since the establishment of 'open' EU borders on 1st January 1993. Note, however, that non-EEA (European Economic Area) or Swiss nationals coming to Spain for any purpose other than as a visitor usually require a visa (see page 28). Spain is a signatory to the Schengen agreement (named after a Luxembourg village on the Moselle River) which came into effect in 1994 and was intended to introduce an open-border policy between member countries. Other Schengen members include Austria, Belgium, France, Germany, Greece, Iceland, Italy, Luxembourg, the Netherlands, Portugal and Sweden. Under the agreement, immigration checks and passport controls take place when you first arrive in a member country, after which you can travel freely between member countries without further checks.

When you arrive in Spain from a country that's a signatory to the Schengen agreement (see above), there are usually no immigration checks or passport controls, which take place when you first arrive in a Schengen member country. Officially, Spanish immigration officials should check the passports of EU arrivals from non-Schengen countries (such as the UK and Ireland), although this doesn't usually happen except at airports. If you're a non-EU national and arrive in Spain by air or sea from outside the EU, you must go through immigration (*imigración*) for non-EU citizens. Non-EU citizens are required to complete an immigration registration card, which are provided on aircraft, ships, trains and at land border crossings. If you have a single-entry visa it will be cancelled by the immigration official. **If you require a visa to enter Spain and attempt to enter without one, you will be refused entry.**

Some people may wish to get a stamp in their passport as confirmation of their date of entry into Spain.

If you're a non-EU national coming to Spain to work, study or live, you may be asked to show documentary evidence. Immigration officials may also ask non-EU visitors to produce a return ticket and proof of accommodation, health insurance and financial resources, e.g. cash, travellers' cheques and credit cards. Spanish regulations require visitors to have a minimum of €100 per day on entry to Spain or a total of €700, although this doesn't apply to visitors on pre-paid package holidays (this rule was brought in mainly to deter illegal immigrants from Morocco). The onus is on visitors to show that they're genuine and that they don't intend to breach Spanish immigration laws. Immigration officials aren't required to prove that you will breach the immigration laws and can refuse you entry on the grounds of suspicion only.

## CUSTOMS

The Single European Act, which came into effect on 1st January 1993, created a single trading market and changed the rules regarding customs (*aduanas*) for EU nationals. The shipment of personal (household) effects to Spain from another EU country is no longer subject to customs formalities. EU nationals planning to take up permanent or temporary residence in Spain are permitted to import their furniture and personal effects free of duty or taxes, provided they were purchased tax-paid within the EU or have been owned for at least six-months. A detailed inventory is advisable (although it's unlikely that anyone will check your belongings) and the shipping company should have a photocopy of the owner's passport legalised by a Spanish consulate. There are no restrictions on the import or export of Spanish or foreign banknotes or securities, although if you enter or leave Spain with €6,000 or more in cash or negotiable instruments (see page 174), you must make a declaration to Spanish customs.

If you require general information about Spanish customs regulations, or have specific questions, contact the Dirección General de Aduanas, Ministerio de Economía y Hacienda, Guzman el Bueno, 137, 28071 Madrid (☎ 915 543 200, 🖳 www.aeat.es/aduanas). Information about duty-free allowances can be found on page 289 and pets on page 36.

# Visitors

Visitors' belongings aren't subject to duty or VAT when they're visiting Spain for up to six months (182 days). This applies to the import of private cars, camping vehicles (including trailers or caravans), motorcycles, aircraft, boats and personal effects. Goods may be imported without formality, provided their nature and quantity doesn't imply any commercial aim. All means of transport and personal effects imported duty-free mustn't be sold or given away in Spain and must be exported when a visitor leaves Spain. If you cross into Spain by road you may drive slowly through the border post without stopping (unless requested to do so). However, any goods and pets that you're carrying mustn't be subject to any prohibitions or restrictions (see page 213). Customs officials can still stop anyone for a spot check, e.g. to check for drugs or illegal immigrants.

If you arrive at a seaport by private boat, there are no particular customs formalities, although you must show the boat's registration papers on request. A vessel registered outside the EU may remain in Spain for a maximum of six months in any calendar year, after which it must be exported or imported (when duty and tax must be paid). However, you can ask the local customs authorities to seal (*precintar*) a foreign-registered boat while you're absent and unseal it when you wish to use it, thus allowing you to keep it in Spain year round (although you can use it for six months of the year only). Foreign-registered vehicles and boats mustn't be lent or rented to anyone while in Spain.

# Non-EU Nationals

Non-EU nationals planning to take up permanent or temporary residence in Spain are permitted to import their furniture and personal effects free of duty or taxes, provided they've owned them for at least six months. An application form for primary (*cambio de residencia*) or secondary (*vivienda secundaria*) residence must be completed (available from Spanish consulates), plus a detailed inventory of the items to be imported showing their estimated value in euros. All items to be imported should be included on the list, even if some are to be imported at a later date. You should the make and serial numbers of all electrical appliances on the inventory. These documents must be signed and presented to a Spanish consulate with the owner's passport. If the owner won't be present when the effects are cleared by customs in Spain, a photocopy of the principal pages of his passport are required, which must be legalised by the local Spanish embassy.

**Permanent Residence:** Non-EU nationals importing personal effects for a permanent residence must present their residence permit (*residencia*) to the consulate, or if the permit hasn't yet been granted, evidence that an application has been made. Permanent residents must provide Spanish customs with a bank guarantee (of up to 60 per cent of the value of their belongings) until the residence permit is granted in the following 12 months. The deposit 'exempts' the holder from customs duties and is returned when a residence permit has been obtained.

 **You have one year in which to obtain a residence permit and request the return of your deposit. If you take longer than one year without obtaining an extension, you may lose your deposit!**

**Secondary Residence:** Non-EU applicants importing personal effects for a secondary residence (*vivienda secundaria*) must present the title deed (*escritura*) of a property that they own in Spain or a rental contract (lease) for a minimum period of two years. They must provide a two-year bank guarantee (see above) issued by a bank in Spain to ensure that the goods will remain in the same dwelling, that the property won't be sub-let by the foreign owner or lessee, and that it will be reserved for his family's exclusive use. The deposit must be paid into a Spanish bank, which issues a certificate for the customs office stating the funds have been received. The deposit is supposed to be returned after two years. When the two-year period has expired you must obtain a certificate from your local town hall verifying that the goods are still in your possession. When customs receive the certificate they will issue you with a document authorising your bank to release your funds. Note that it can take some time to get your deposit returned and many people simply give up trying after numerous unsuccessful attempts.

An application must be made within three months of your entry into Spain and goods should be imported within one year of taking up residence. They may be imported in one or a number of consignments, although it's best to have one consignment only. If there's more than one consignment, subsequent consignments should be cleared through the same customs office. Note that items subject to special customs requirements such as electrical appliances, carpets and works of art should be packed at the container door to facilitate customs inspection. Goods imported duty-free mustn't be sold in Spain within two years of their importation and if you leave Spain within two years, everything imported duty-free must be exported or the duty paid.

If you use a shipping company to transport your belongings, they will usually provide the necessary forms and take care of the paperwork. Always keep a copy of forms and communications with customs officials, both with Spanish customs officials and customs officials in your previous country of residence. Note that if the paperwork isn't in order, your belongings may end up incarcerated in a Spanish customs storage depot for a number of months. If you personally import your belongings, you may need to employ a customs agent (*agente de aduanas*) at the point of entry to clear them. You should have an official record of the export of valuables from any country, in case you wish to re-import them later.

Because of the restrictions and the deposit payable by non-EU homebuyers in Spain, you may wish to consider buying a property that's already furnished or buy furniture and furnishings locally.

## Prohibited & Restricted Goods

Certain goods are subject to special regulations in Spain and in some cases their import and export is prohibited or restricted. This particularly applies to the following goods:

- animal products; plants (see below);
- wild fauna and flora and products derived from them;
- live animals;
- medicines and medical products (except for prescribed drugs and medicines);
- firearms and ammunition (see below);
- certain goods and technologies with a dual civil/military purpose;
- works of art and collectors' items.

If you're unsure whether any goods you're importing fall into the above categories, you should check with Spanish customs. If you're planning to import sports guns into Spain you must obtain a certificate from a Spanish consulate abroad, which is issued on production of a valid firearms licence. The consular certificate must be presented to the customs authorities upon entry and can be used to exchange a foreign firearms licence for a Spanish licence when taking up residence.

To import certain types of plants, you must obtain a health certificate. There's usually a limit on the number of plants that can be imported, although when they're included in your personal effects they aren't usually subject to any special controls. Visitors arriving in Spain from 'exotic' regions, e.g. Africa, South America, and the Middle and Far East, may find themselves under close scrutiny from customs and security officials looking for illegal drugs.

# EMBASSY REGISTRATION

Nationals of some countries are recommended to register with their local embassy or consulate after taking up residence in Spain. Registration isn't usually compulsory, although most embassies like to keep a record of their country's citizens resident in Spain.

# FINDING HELP

One of the major problems facing new arrivals in Spain is how and where to obtain help with day-to-day problems, for example, banking, insurance, utilities and so on. **This book and its sister publication 'Living and Working in Spain' were written in response to this need.** However, in addition to the comprehensive information provided in these books, you will also need detailed **local** information. How successful you are at finding local help depends on your employer, the town or area where you live (e.g. residents of resort areas are far better served than those living in rural areas), your nationality, Spanish language proficiency and your sex (women are usually better catered for than men through women's clubs).

There's an abundance of information available in Spanish, but little in English and other foreign languages. An additional problem is that much of the available information isn't intended for foreigners and their particular needs. You may find that your friends and colleagues can help as they can often offer advice based on their own experiences and mistakes. **But take care!** Although they mean well, you're likely to receive as much false and conflicting information as accurate (it may not necessarily be wrong, but often won't apply to your particular situation).

Your local town hall (*ayuntamiento*) may be a good source of information, but you usually need to speak Spanish to benefit and may still be sent on a wild goose chase from department to department. However, some town halls in areas where there are many foreign residents have a foreigners' department (*departamento de extranjeros*) where staff speak English and other foreign languages such as Danish, Dutch, Finnish, French, German and Swedish (an advantage of living somewhere where there are many other foreigners). Apart from assisting with routine everyday matters, a foreigner's department can be helpful when applying for a residence permit, social security membership or a Spanish driving licence (and other formal applications), and they may save you the expense of employing a *gestor* (see page 107) to make these applications on your behalf.

A wealth of useful information is available in major cities and resort towns, where foreigners are well-served by English-speaking clubs and expatriate organisations. Contacts can also be found through many expatriate publications (see **Appendix B**). Most consulates provide their nationals with local information including details of lawyers, translators, doctors, dentists, schools, and social and expatriate organisations.

Finally, you may wish to buy a copy of *Living and Working in Spain* written by your author David Hampshire, which contains essential information about everyday life in Spain for both visitors and residents.

# CHECKLISTS

When moving permanently to Spain there are many things to be considered and a 'million' people to inform. Even if you plan to spend just a few months a year in Spain, it may still be necessary to inform a number of people and companies in your home country. The checklists below are designed to make the task easier and help prevent an ulcer or a nervous breakdown (provided of course you don't leave everything to the last minute). Note that not all points are applicable to non-residents or those who spend only a few weeks or months each year in Spain.

## Before Arrival

The following are tasks that should be completed (if possible) before your arrival in Spain:

- Check that your family's passports are valid;
- Obtain a visa, if necessary, for all your family members (see page 28). Obviously this **must** be done before arrival in Spain;
- It's advisable to arrange health, dental and optical check-ups for your family before leaving your home country. Obtain a copy of health records and a statement from your private health insurance company stating your present level of cover;
- Arrange health and travel insurance for your family (see pages 251 and 260). This is essential if you aren't already covered by an international health insurance policy and won't be covered by Spanish social security;
- Arrange inoculations and shipment for any pets that you're taking with you (see page 36);

- Visit Spain before your move to compare schools and to arranging schooling for your children (if applicable);
- Open a bank account in Spain (see page 181) and transfer funds. Give the details to any companies that you plan to pay by direct debit or standing order (e.g. utility and property management companies).
- If you don't already have one, it's advisable to obtain an international credit card or two, which will prove particularly useful in Spain;
- If you live in rented accommodation you will need to give your landlord notice (check your contract);
- Arrange shipment of your furniture and belongings by booking a shipping company well in advance (see page 206);
- Arrange to sell or dispose of anything you aren't taking with you (e.g. house, car and furniture). If you're selling a home or business, you should obtain expert legal advice as you may be able to save tax by establishing a trust or other legal vehicle. Note that if you own more than one property, you may need to pay capital gains tax (see page 240) on any profits from the sale of second and subsequent homes;
- If you are planning to export a car to Spain, you need to complete relevant paperwork in your home country before you do this;
- Check whether you need an international driving licence or a translation of your foreign driving licence(s). Note that some foreigners are required to take a driving test before they can buy and register a car in Spain;
- Check whether you're entitled to a rebate on your road tax, car and other insurance. Obtain a letter from your motor insurance company stating your no-claims' discount;
- You may qualify for a rebate on your tax and social security contributions. If you're leaving a country permanently and have been a member of a company or state pension scheme, you may be entitled to a refund or may be able to continue payments to qualify for a full (or larger) pension when you retire. Contact your company personnel office, local tax office or pension company for information;
- Terminate any outstanding loan, lease or hire purchase contracts and pay all bills (allow plenty of time as some companies are slow to respond);
- Return any library books or anything borrowed;
- Obtain as many credit references as possible, for example from banks, mortgage companies, credit card companies, credit agencies, companies with which you've had accounts, and references from

professionals such as lawyers and accountants. These will help you establish a credit rating in Spain;

- Take any documents that are necessary to obtain a residence permit plus certified copies, official translations and numerous passport-size photographs (students should take at least a dozen);
- Take all your family's official documents with you. These may include:
  - birth certificates;
  - driving licences;
  - marriage certificate, divorce papers or death certificate (if a widow or widower);
  - educational diplomas and professional certificates;
  - employment references and curriculum vitaes;
  - school records and student ID cards;
  - medical and dental records;
  - bank account and credit card details;
  - insurance policies (plus records of no claims' allowances);
  - receipts for any valuables.
- Inform the following:
  - Your employers (e.g. give notice or arrange leave of absence) or clients if self-employed;
  - Your local town hall or municipality. You may be entitled to a refund of your local property or income taxes;
  - If it was necessary to register with the police in your home country (or present country of residence), you should inform them that you're moving abroad;
  - Your electricity, gas, water and telephone companies. Contact companies well in advance, particularly if you need to get a deposit refunded;
  - Your insurance companies (for example health, car, home contents and private pension); banks, post office (if you have a post office account), stockbroker and other financial institutions; credit card, charge card and hire purchase companies; lawyer and accountant; and local businesses where you have accounts;
  - Your family doctor, dentist and other health practitioners. Health records should be transferred to your new doctor and dentist in Spain, if applicable;

- Your children's schools. Try to give a term's notice and obtain a copy of any relevant school reports or records from your children's current schools;

- All regular correspondents, subscriptions, social and sports clubs, professional and trade journals, and friends and relatives. Give them your new address and telephone number and arrange to have your post redirected by the post office or a friend. Give close friends, relatives and business associates a telephone number where you can be contacted in Spain;

- If you have a driving licence or car you will need to give the local vehicle registration office your new address in Spain and, in some countries, return your car's registration plates;

● If you will be living in Spain for an extended period (but not permanently), you may wish to give someone 'power of attorney' over your financial affairs in your home country so that they can act for you in your absence. This can be for a fixed period or open-ended and can be for a specific purpose only.

**SURVIVAL TIP**
You should take expert legal advice before
giving someone 'power of attorney' over
any of your financial affairs!

● Obtain some euros, as this will save you time on arrival and you may receive a better exchange rate;

● Finally, allow plenty of time to get to the airport, register your luggage, and clear security and immigration.

## After Arrival

The following tasks should be completed after arrival in Spain (if not done before):

● Have your visa cancelled and your passport stamped, as applicable;

● If you took your car to Spain, you will need to have it re-registered in Spain;

● If you haven't brought a vehicle with you, rent one or buy one locally. Note that it's practically impossible to get around in rural areas without a car.

- Arrange whatever insurance is necessary such as health, car, household and third party liability;

- Contact offices and organisations to obtain local information (see page 214);

- Make courtesy calls on your neighbours and the local mayor within a few weeks of your arrival. This is particularly important in small villages and rural areas if you want to be accepted and become part of the local community.

- Apply for a residence permit at your local town hall within 15 days of your arrival unless you're an EU, EEA or Swiss national with full-time employment (including self-employment) or in full-time study in Spain;

- Apply for a social security card from your local social security office;

- Apply for a Spanish driving licence (if necessary);

- Find a local doctor and dentist;

- Arrange schooling for your children (if applicable).

# 7.

# TAXATION

An important consideration when buying a home in Spain is taxation, even for non-residents, which includes property tax, wealth tax, income tax (if you earn an income from a home), capital gains tax and inheritance tax. You will also have to pay Spanish income tax on all your earnings if you live permanently in Spain.

Spain is no longer the tax haven it was in the 1960s and 1970s, when taxes were low and tax evasion was a way of life and almost encouraged! Spain's taxes have increased dramatically during the last few decades, particularly income tax; nevertheless, income tax and social security contributions in Spain remain among the lowest in the European Union. The current government has reduced income tax rates over the last three years, but increased indirect taxes (e.g. on petrol).

Today, it's much more difficult to avoid paying taxes in Spain and penalties are severe. However, despite the efforts of the authorities to curb tax dodgers, tax evasion is still widespread. Many non-resident home-owners and foreign residents think they should be exempt from Spanish taxes and are among the worst offenders. Some inhabit a twilight world as 'eternal tourists', not officially resident in any country, and some even have the effrontery to boast about not paying taxes. It has been estimated that around 20 per cent of foreign property owners in Spain live there permanently, which means there could be as many as 250,000 foreign residents not paying income tax in Spain. A common dodge for casual employees in Spain is to get paid 'cash in hand', thus avoiding paying value added tax (*IVA*) and income tax. (Cash is preferred by many Spaniards to payment by cheque or credit card, even when large sums are involved.) Since 1986, when VAT was introduced, many Spaniards have been salting their money away from the prying eyes of the tax authorities.

Needless to say, evading Spanish taxes is a criminal offence, although there are ways of legally avoiding taxes in both your home country and Spain.

**SURVIVAL TIP**
**Before you decide to settle in Spain permanently, you should obtain expert advice regarding Spanish taxes. This will (hopefully) ensure that you take maximum advantage of your current tax status and that you don't make any mistakes that you will regret later.**

As you would expect in a country with millions of bureaucrats, the Spanish tax system is inordinately complicated and most Spaniards don't understand it. In fact even the experts have difficulty agreeing with the tax authorities (Agencia Estatal de Administración Tributaria, previously known as *hacienda*) and tax advisers often give different advice. It's difficult to obtain accurate information from the tax authorities and, just when you think you have it cracked, (ho! ho!) the authorities change the rules or hit you with a new tax.

It isn't so much the level of taxes in Spain that's burdensome, but the number of different taxes for which individuals are liable. Taxes are levied by three tiers of government in Spain: central government, autonomous regional governments and local municipalities. Government taxes are administered by the Ministry of Economy and Taxation (*Ministerio de Económica y Hacienda*), which has its headquarters in Madrid and assessment and tax collection centres in provincial capitals. At the last count there were around 15 taxes, including those associated with buying and selling property and motoring.

Most taxes in Spain are based on self-assessment, meaning that individual taxpayers are liable to report and calculate any tax due within the time limits established by law. Tax forms must be purchased by taxpayers and are obtainable from a tobacconist's (*estanco*), although some are available only from tax offices (*agencia tributaria*). Late payment of any tax bill usually incurs a surcharge of 20 per cent. Note that here's a five-year statute of limitations (*prescripción*) on the collection of back taxes in Spain, i.e. if no action has been taken during this period to collect unpaid tax, it cannot be collected.

If you own a holiday home in Spain you can employ a local accountant or tax adviser as your fiscal representative to look after your financial affairs there and declare and pay your local taxes (see below).

# FISCAL IDENTIFICATION NUMBER

All residents and non-resident foreigners with financial affairs in Spain must have a foreigner's identification number called a *Número de Identificación de Extranjero* (*NIE*). This is similar to the fiscal number (*Numero de Identificación Fiscal/NIF*) all Spaniards have, which is the same as their identity card and passport numbers. An *NIE* works as both an identity card and a social security number. Without an *NIE*, you won't be able to open a bank account, arrange credit terms or use temporary employment agencies.

Your *NIE* must be used in all dealings with the Spanish tax authorities, when paying property taxes and in various other transactions. Anyone placing money or assets in deposits or other forms or receiving credits or loans in Spain must give his foreigner's number to the bank within 30 days of the operation. A bank cannot issue a cheque against a deposit without reporting the fiscal number of the client and must report any activities where a fiscal number hasn't been provided.

Banks and individuals can be heavily fined for non-compliance with the law regarding fiscal numbers.

You can apply for an *NIE* at any national police station (*comisaría*) with a foreigners' department or obtain the necessary forms via a Spanish lawyer or from the website of the regional government of Spain in the area you intend to move to. If you have an employment contract or a letter from a Spanish employer or business stating why it requires you to have an *NIE*, you can obtain a number in around a week. Otherwise, you may have to wait up to three months.

# FISCAL REPRESENTATION

The term fiscal representation (as used here) refers to anyone who provides tax and other financial services, including a fiscal representative (*representante fiscal*), accountant (*contable*) or tax adviser (*asesor fiscal*). Since 1994, it hasn't been necessary for non-resident owners of a single dwelling in Spain to have a fiscal representative, provided it's used as the address for communications from the tax authorities. If you have more than one asset in Spain, e.g. separate title deeds for a property and a garage or garden, or you own a commercial property, you must still appoint a fiscal representative. A foreign company owning a property in Spain must have a fiscal representative, and a foreigner receiving income from a business in Spain may need one. If you fail to appoint a fiscal representative when you're required to have one, you can be fined up to €6,000. All accountants and tax advisers in Spain act as fiscal representatives for their clients.

If you're a non-resident, you should have someone in Spain to look after your financial affairs and declare and pay your taxes. This person is normally your fiscal representative, to whom communications will automatically be sent by the Spanish tax authorities. You can also have your fiscal representative receive your bank statements, ensure that your bank is paying your regular bills (such as electricity, water and telephone) by standing order, and that you have sufficient funds in your account to pay them. Your fiscal representative can also apply for a fiscal number (*Número de Identificación de Entranjero/NIE*) on your behalf (see page 223).

A fiscal representative can be a Spaniard or a foreign resident in Spain, an individual or a company (such as a bank). The local provincial office of the Ministry of Finance must be notified of the appointment of a fiscal representative within two months by letter and the representative must expressly communicate his acceptance of the appointment at the office where your taxes are to be paid. Before employing a fiscal representative, you should obtain recommendations from friends, colleagues and acquaintances. However, bear in mind that, if you consult a number of 'experts', you're liable to receive conflicting advice.

 **Note that some fiscal representatives fail to pay tax bills on time (or at all), thereby incurring their clients a fine equal to 20 per cent of the amount due.**

You should check with the town hall and tax authorities that your bills have actually been paid!

Fiscal representation usually costs from €150 per year for a single person and □300 for a couple, depending on the services provide, although many representatives charge only 50 per cent more for a couple than for a single person. There may be additional charges for tax administration and completing tax returns, the cost depending on the complexity of your tax affairs. For the relatively small cost involved, most people (both residents and non-residents) are usually better off employing a fiscal representative to handle their Spanish tax and other financial affairs than doing it themselves, particularly as the regulations change frequently.

# INCOME TAX

Income tax (*impuesto sobre la renta de las personas físicas/IRPF*) in Spain is below the EU average and isn't supplemented by crippling social security rates as in some other EU countries (e.g. France). Major tax reforms have been introduced in recent years and income tax rates for the 2003 fiscal year have fallen by around 11 per cent, although government critics claim the reforms favour higher taxpayers. The reforms are designed to make taxation simpler for both the taxpayer and taxman, and to reduce tax fraud, which is still wide-spread. Paying Spanish income tax can be advantageous, as there are more allowances than there are in some other countries. If you're able to choose the country where you're taxed, you should obtain advice from an international tax expert.

Employees' income tax (*retenciones*) is deducted at source by employers, i.e. pay-as-you-earn, and individuals aren't responsible for paying their own income tax, although they must still make a tax declaration. Self-employed people pay their income tax quarterly (*pago fraccionado*). Non-residents who receive an income from a Spanish source and non-resident property owners (see page 229) should instruct their fiscal representative to file an income tax declaration on their behalf (or do it themselves).

Moving to Spain (or another country) often provides opportunities for legal 'favourable tax planning'. To make the most of your situation, it's advisable to obtain income tax advice before moving to Spain, as there are usually a number of things you can do in advance to reduce your tax liability, both in Spain and abroad. Be sure to consult a tax adviser who's familiar with both the Spanish tax system and that of your present country of residence. For example, you may be able to avoid paying tax on a business abroad if you establish both residence and domicile in Spain before you sell it. On the other hand, if you sell a foreign home after establishing your principal residence in Spain, it becomes a second home and you may then be liable to capital gains tax abroad (this is a complicated subject and you should obtain expert advice). You should notify the tax authorities in your former country of residence that you're going to live permanently in Spain.

Tax evasion is illegal and a criminal offence in Spain, and offenders can be heavily fined or even imprisoned. Although Spanish tax inspectors make a relatively small number of inspections, they target them at those among whom tax fraud is most prevalent, such as the self-employed.

 **Note that new legislation is being introduced to tackle fraud and it's expected that 'fiscal nomads' will find it more difficult to avoid Spanish taxation in the future.**

On the other hand, tax avoidance (i.e. legally paying as little tax as possible, if necessary by finding and exploiting loopholes in the tax laws) is highly recommended! Residents have a number of opportunities to legally reduce their taxes, while non-residents have very few or none at all.

You can obtain free tax advice from the information section (*servicio de información* or *oficina de información al contribuyente*) at your local provincial tax office in Spain, where staff will answer queries and assist you in completing your tax declaration (but they won't complete it for you) via their PADRE computer system. Some offices, particularly those located in resort areas, have staff who speak English and other foreign languages. The tax office provides a central telephone information service from 9am to 7pm Mondays to Fridays (☎ 901 335 533). Note that during May and June the line is open from 9am to 9pm Mondays to Fridays and from 9am to 2pm on Saturdays.

If you require information about income tax and VAT refunds or need to order tax labels, the tax office runs an automatic telephone service which is open 24 hours a day, seven days a week (☎ 901 121 224). There's also a useful website (🖥 www.aeat.es), although your Spanish needs to be fluent to understand most of it and there are few pages in English. Tax clearance permits aren't required by those leaving Spain to live abroad.

# Liability

Your liability for income tax in Spain depends on whether you're officially resident there. Under Spanish law you become a fiscal resident in Spain if you spend 183 days there during a calendar year or your main centre of economic interest, e.g. investments or business, is in Spain. Temporary absences are included in the calculation of the period spent in Spain (or Spanish territories) unless residence is shown to have been in another country for 183 days in a calendar year. If your spouse and dependent minor children normally reside in Spain and have residence permits, and you aren't legally separated, you're also considered to be a tax resident in Spain (unless you can prove otherwise). Note that the 183-day rule also applies to other EU countries, and the UK limits visits by non-residents to 182 days in any one year or an average of 91 days per tax year over a four-year period.

If you're tax resident in two countries simultaneously, your 'tax home' may be resolved under the rules applied under international treaties. Under such treaties you're considered to be resident in the country where you have a permanent home; if you have a permanent home in both countries, you're deemed to be resident in the country where your personal and economic ties are closer. If your residence cannot be determined under this rule, you're deemed to be resident in the country where you have a habitual abode. If you have a habitual abode in both or in neither country, you're deemed to be resident in the country of which you're a citizen. Finally, if you're a citizen of both or neither country, the authorities of the countries concerned will decide your tax residence between them!

If you plan to live permanently in Spain, you should notify the tax authorities in your previous country of residence. You may be entitled to a tax refund (*devolución*) if you depart during the tax year, which usually requires the completion of a tax return. The authorities may require evidence that you're leaving the country, e.g. proof that you have a job in Spain or have bought or rented a property there. If you move to Spain to take up a job or start a business, you must register with the local tax authorities soon after your arrival.

**Double Taxation:** Spanish residents are taxed on their world-wide income, whereas non-residents are taxed in Spain only on income arising in Spain, which is exempt from tax in their home countries. Spain has double taxation treaties with around 45 countries, including Argentina, Australia, Austria, Belgium, Bolivia, Brazil, Bulgaria, Canada, China, Cuba, the Czech Republic, Denmark, Ecuador, Finland, France, Germany, Hungary, India, Indonesia, Ireland, Israel, Italy, Japan, Luxembourg,

Mexico, Morocco, the Netherlands, Norway, the Philippines, Poland, Portugal, Romania, Russia, Slovakia, South Korea, Sweden, Switzerland, Thailand, Tunisia, the United Kingdom and the USA. Treaties are designed to ensure that income that has already been taxed in one treaty country isn't taxed again in another treaty country. Treaties establish a tax credit or exemption on certain kinds of income, either in your country of residence or the country where the income was earned. Where applicable, a double taxation treaty prevails over domestic law.

The USA is the only country that taxes its non-resident citizens on income earned abroad (US citizens can obtain a copy of a brochure, Tax Guide for Americans Abroad, from American consulates). Citizens of most countries are exempt from paying taxes in their home country when they spend a minimum period abroad, e.g. a year.

However, even if there's no double taxation agreement between Spain and another country, you can still obtain relief from double taxation through a direct deduction of any foreign tax paid or through a 'foreign compensation' (*compensación extranjera*) formula. Note that, if your tax liability in another country is lower than that in Spain, you must pay the Spanish tax authorities the difference. If you're in doubt about your tax liability in your home country, contact your nearest embassy or consulate in Spain.

**Leaving Spain:** Before leaving Spain, foreigners should pay any tax due for the previous year and the year of departure by applying for a tax clearance. A tax return should be filed prior to departure and includes your income and deductions from 1st January of the departure year up to the date of departure. Your local tax office will calculate the tax due and provide a written statement. When departure is made before 31st December, the previous year's taxes are applied. If this results in overpayment, a claim must be made for a refund.

If you're a pensioner and your earned, world-wide annual income (i.e. income from pensions plus a maximum of €1,600 from investments) is less than €8,000, you aren't required to make a tax declaration or pay Spanish income tax. If your earned annual income from work in Spain is less than €22,000, you're exempt from making a tax declaration, as your salary will have been correctly taxed at source. If you're entitled to deductions for pension plans or housing, you must make a tax declaration irrespective of your earnings. Taxpayers entitled to double taxation relief must also declare.

# Taxable Income

Income tax is payable on both earned and unearned income. Taxable income includes salaries, pensions, capital gains, property and investment income (dividends and interest), and income from professional, artistic, business or agricultural activities. If you're a non-resident or own more than one property in Spain, your 'income' also includes 2 per cent of its fiscal value (*valor catastral*). For example, if your Spanish property is officially valued at €150,000, then €3,000 must be added to your income. Principal residences are exempt from this.

## Taxation of Property Income

**Residents:** Property income earned by residents is included in their annual income tax declaration and tax is payable at the standard income tax rate (see above). You're eligible for deductions such as repairs and maintenance, security, cleaning costs, mortgage interest (Spanish loans only), management and letting expenses (e.g. advertising), local taxes, and insurance, plus an amortisation deduction of 3 per cent per year of the value of the property. You should seek professional advice to ensure that you're claiming everything to which you're entitled.

**Non-Residents:** Non-resident property owners in Spain are liable for income tax at a flat rate of 25 per cent on any income arising in Spain, including income from letting a property. For short-term letting, owners should obtain a form from the tourist authorities to apply for registration of their property (although few do so). Income must be declared on form 210 (*Impuestos Sobre la Renta de las Personas Físicas y Sobre Sociedades*) and paid quarterly to the tax authorities by your fiscal representative. There's a 10 per cent surcharge for late payment. For the part of the year when you don't have rental income, e.g. the winter, you must declare and pay tax using form 214 (see below).

From 1994, non-residents owning a single property in Spain have been able to declare their income and wealth tax (see pages 225 and 234) together on a single form at any time during the year, e.g. the declaration for 2003 could be made any time up to 31st December 2004. This is done on form 214 (*Impuesto sobre el Patrimonio y sobre la Renta de No Residente*), which is obtainable only from a tax office (*agencia tributaria*) and not from a tobacconist's (*estanco*). Note that if you own two or more properties in Spain, you cannot use form 214 and must make separate declarations for income and wealth tax (forms 714 and 210) between 1st May and 20th June (and you must appoint a fiscal representative in Spain).

Form 214 is a simple form and most homeowners should be able to complete it themselves (instructions are printed on the reverse). When a husband and wife own a property jointly, they should complete separate forms, although it's possible for a couple to make their declaration on one form (check with your fiscal representative). When a property is used partly for letting and partly for habitation, an apportionment is made between the amount of time used for each purpose. You're supposed to be able to pay your tax at a bank, although most banks are unwilling to accept the tax forms and payment, in which case you must pay in cash or by a certified bank cheque at a tax office. This tax may be offset against taxes paid in other countries.

**Income Tax On Deemed Letting Income:** The tax that causes most confusion (and resentment), particularly among non-resident property owners, is the income tax on deemed or notional 'letting income' (*rendimientos del capital inmobiliario*, usually referred to simply as *renta*). All non-resident property owners or residents owning more than one property in Spain are deemed to receive an income of 2 per cent of the fiscal value (*valor catastral*) of their property (1.1 per cent if the fiscal value has been revised since 1st January 1994). Non-residents pay a flat rate tax of 25 per cent on this income. For example, if you own a property valued at €100,000, 2 per cent of this is €2,000, on which the 25 per cent 'income' tax is €500. There are no deductions. In the case of residents, the deemed letting income is added to other income for income tax purposes.

## Allowances & Deductions

Before you're liable for income tax, you can deduct social security payments and certain costs from your gross income (allowances) and from the sum due after establishing your tax base (deductions). For details, see *Living and Working in Spain* (Survival Books).

## Taxation of Pensions

The taxation of pensioners changed in 1992, and since then pensions have been taxed according to the source of the income, as detailed below.

> **SURVIVAL TIP**
> The taxation of investment capital and insurance-based pensions can be very complicated and you should obtain expert professional advice from an accountant or tax adviser before deciding where and how to receive your pension.

**Employment-based pensions** are taxed in the same way as salary income (see above). You're entitled to the same allowances and deductions, and the same tax rates apply. However, the situation isn't as straightforward if your pension is paid from a savings scheme such as a pension fund established through an employment relationship with tax advantages in your home country.

**Investment capital pensions**, whereby you pay a sum of money or transfer assets such as property to another party in return for annuity payments (or a monthly income) for a fixed period or until death. This may give rise to capital gains and interest income, each of which is taxed differently in Spain.

**Insurance-based pensions** are schemes that permit you to choose between taking the whole amount accrued under the policy in a lump sum and having it paid in the form of annuities. This income is taxed either as a capital gain (see page 240) or as ordinary income (see above).

**Civil service pensions** are usually tax-free in Spain and don't need to be declared to the Spanish authorities if they're your only source of income, although this depends on the country paying your pension and whether it has a double taxation treaty with Spain (see page 227). However, you may need to provide the tax office with proof that your pension is taxed at source. Civil service pensions don't include United Nations pensions, as the UN cannot tax its former employees (unlike individual countries). Note, however, that if you have other income that's taxable in Spain, your civil service pension is usually taken into account when calculating your Spanish tax rate and it must usually be declared. If you pay tax in error on a pension that wasn't in fact taxable, you can claim a refund only for the previous five years, which is Spain's statute of limitations (if they aren't collected, taxes also usually lapse after five years).

**Non-resident pensions** received from a Spanish source are subject to special tax rates depending on the amount, as follows:

| Amount (€) | Tax Rate (%) | Cumulative Tax (€) |
| --- | --- | --- |
| Up to 9,616.19 | 8 | 769.30 |
| 9,616.19 to 15,025.30 | 30 | 2,392.03 |
| Over 15,025.30 | 40 | |

# Calculation

The tax year in Spain is the same as the calendar year: from 1st January to 31st December. There are no longer different tax rates for couples who choose to be taxed individually or jointly. Income tax rates for individuals (*personas físicas*) start at 15 per cent on income up to €4,000 and rise to 45 per cent on income above €45,000. Tax is divided between the Spanish state (85 per cent) and the autonomous regions (15 per cent), although some autonomous regions (e.g. the Basque Country, Catalonia and La Rioja) offer deductions from tax due. You must add the two rates to obtain the total tax payable, which is as follows:

| Taxable Income (€) | Tax Rate (%) | Cumulative Tax (€) |
|---|---|---|
| 0 to 4,000 | 15 | 600 |
| 4,000 to 13,800 | 24 | 2,952 |
| 13,800 to 25,800 | 28 | 6,312 |
| 25,800 to 45,000 | 37 | 13,416 |
| Over 45,000 | 45 | |

# Tax Return

An annual income tax declaration (*declaración sobre la renta de personas físicas*) must be lodged between 1st May and 20th June by both residents and non-residents with income in Spain (other than income from property letting). If you're entitled to a refund (*devolución*), the deadline is extended until 30th June. The above deadlines also apply to declarations for property tax and wealth tax for residents. Income tax is paid a year in arrears, e.g. the declaration filed in the year 2004 is for the 2003 tax year.

If your earned personal income is below €8,000 for an individual declaration, it isn't necessary to complete an income tax declaration. Note that if you're a Spanish resident, these limits apply to your world-wide family income wherever it arises, but don't include income taxed in another country. If you're resident in Spain, the authorities will ask to see your income tax declaration when you renew your residence permit (*residencia*). Rather than try to explain that your income is below the tax threshold (and therefore possibly below the income necessary to obtain a *residencia*!), it's advisable to make a 'negative' tax declaration.

Tax returns aren't sent out by the tax office each year and must be purchased from a tobacconist's (estanco) for around €0.30 each (they come with a set of instruction booklets). It you're unable to obtain a tax return from a tobacconist's, you can obtain one from a tax adviser or your local tax office (*agencia tributaria*).

There are three kinds of tax declaration form in Spain: an abbreviated declaration (*declaración abreviada*), a simple declaration (*declaración simplificada*) and an ordinary declaration (*declaración ordinaria*).

**Abbreviated Declaration:** The *declaración abreviada* (form 103) was introduced in 1996 and consists of two pages. It's used by an estimated 7 million taxpayers whose income derives entirely from earnings or from pensions and investments that have already been subject to Spanish withholding tax. Note that, if your income consists of a pension that has had some deductions made in another country and which you intend to subtract from your Spanish declaration, you cannot use this form.

**Simple Declaration:** The *declaración simplificada* (form 101) consists of five pages and is for those with the same sources of income (usually below €600,000) as for the abbreviated declaration (see above), plus income from letting, certain business and agricultural income, and capital gains from the sale of a permanent home where the total gain will be invested in a new home in Spain. Form 101 is used for refunds and the declaration and payment of the first stage of income tax, while form 102 is used for the second payment.

**Ordinary Declaration:** The *declaración ordinaria* (form 100) consists of 13 pages and is for incomes from all sources other than those mentioned above, e.g. business or professional activities and capital gains.

An instruction booklet is provided with returns, and the tax office publishes a booklet, *Manual Práctico – Renta* (costing €0.75), containing examples of how to complete tax forms and an interpretation of the current Finance Act.

If you can use the (*declaración abreviada*), you should be able to complete your own tax form, perhaps with a little help from the tax office. However, most people require professional help to complete the *simplificada* and *ordinaria* tax forms. (Until the introduction of the *declaración abreviada*, only some 15 per cent of Spain's 14 million taxpayers made their own tax declarations.) If you need any assistance, you can contact the information section (*servicio de información*) of your local tax office, which may have multi-lingual staff. Note, however, that tax offices won't help you complete an *ordinaria* tax form and you must make an appointment (☎ 901 223 344). When you go to the tax office, you should take along the following:

- your end-of-year bank statements (*estado de cuenta*) showing any interest received and your average balance (*saldo medio*);

- any papers relating to stocks, shares, bonds, deposit certificates or any other property owned, either in Spain or abroad;

- declarations and receipts for any taxes paid in another country (if you're seeking to offset payment against your Spanish taxes);

- your passport, residence permit and *NIE*.

Income tax in Spain is self-assessed (*auto-liquidación*) and is paid at the same time as the tax declaration is made. You can pay either the whole amount when the form is filed or 60 per cent with your declaration and the balance by the following 5th November. Tax returns should be submitted to the district tax office where you're resident for tax purposes or they can be filed (and payment made) at designated banks in the province. Note that payment must be made in cash and personal cheques aren't accepted, although if you're filing at a bank where you hold an account, they will make a transfer to the tax authorities. If no payment is due on a return, it must be filed at the tax office. If you delay filing your tax return by even a day, you must pay a surcharge on the tax due, although it's possible to request a payment deferral.

Late payment of any tax bill usually incurs a surcharge of 20 per cent. Large fines can be imposed for breaches of tax law and in certain cases forfeiture of the right to tax benefits or subsidies for a period of up to five years. The fraudulent evasion of €30,000 or more in tax is punishable by fines of up to six times the amount defrauded and/or imprisonment, although it's rare for someone to be prosecuted for tax evasion in Spain and fines have been reduced in recent years. You should retain copies of your tax returns for at least five years, which is the maximum period that returns are liable for audit by the Spanish tax authorities.

Unless your tax affairs are simple, it's advisable to employ an accountant or tax adviser (*asesor fiscal*) to complete your tax return and ensure that you're correctly assessed. There are 'foreign' tax assessors (*asesores de extranjero*) who specialise in filing returns for foreigners, particularly non-residents. The fees charged for filing tax returns vary and for residents are around €35 for a simple return and €60 for an ordinary return. The fee for filing a tax return for a non-resident is usually around €35. **Make sure that you have your tax return stamped as proof of payment by your advisor.**

# WEALTH TAX

Spain levies a wealth tax (*impuesto extraordinario sobre el patrimonio*, commonly referred to simply as *patrimonio*), on both residents and non-residents (unlike most other countries, which exempt non-residents). Your wealth is calculated by totalling your assets and deducting your liabilities. When calculating your liability to wealth tax, you must include the value of all your assets, including property, vehicles, boats, aircraft, business ownership, cash (e.g. in bank accounts), life insurance, gold bars, jewellery, stocks, shares and bonds. The value of property is whichever is the highest among the purchase price, its fiscal value (*valor catastral*) and its value as assessed by the authorities (e.g. in the case of a house which has not yet been built or a property in an area where there are no property taxes). If you fail to declare your total assets, you can be fined.

Bank balances should be declared by producing your end-of-year bank statement (*estado de cuenta*) showing any interest you've received and your average balance (*saldo medio*). However, if you're a non-resident and your country of residence has a double taxation treaty with

Spain (see page 227), bank balances and interest are taxable only in your country of residence, not in Spain.

Certain assets are exempt from wealth tax, including objets d'art and antiques (provided their value doesn't exceed certain limits), the vested rights of participants in pension plans and funds, copyrights (provided they remain part of your net worth), and assets forming part of Spain's historical heritage. Deductions are made for mortgages (for both residents and non-residents), business and other debts, and any 'wealth' tax paid in another country.

## Tax Rates

There's a general allowance against wealth tax of €108,182.18 per person for all assets except a principal residence, for which there's an additional allowance of €150,253 per person. Therefore, if your principal residence is in Spain, you qualify for a wealth tax allowance of €258,435.18. If a property is registered in the names of both spouses (or a number of unrelated people), they should make separate declarations and are each entitled to claim the exemption. If you've bought a property with a loan or mortgage, there are deductions from your wealth tax liability. If you make an income tax declaration and your world-wide assets are below the relevant limit, you're exempt from making a wealth tax declaration.

**There's no allowance for non-residents**, who must pay wealth tax on all their assets in Spain, which for most non-resident property owners consists only of their home.

In 2002, assets were taxed on a sliding scale as follows:

| Asset Value above Allowance (€) | Tax Rate (%) | Cumulative Tax (€) |
| --- | --- | --- |
| Up to 167,129 | 0.2 | 338 |
| 167,130 to 334,253 | 0.3 | 839 |
| 334,254 to 716,581 | 0.5 | 2,751 |
| 716,582 to 1,337,000 | 0.9 | 8,335 |
| 1,337,001 to 2,673,999 | 1.3 | 25,716 |
| 2,674,000 to 5,347,998 | 1.7 | 71,174 |
| 5,347,999 to 10,695,996 | 2.1 | 183,482 |
| Over 10,695,996 | 2.5 | |

In the above table, the cumulative tax is the tax payable for each band of asset value, e.g. €2,751 is payable on assets of €716,581. If your assets are valued at €500,000, you pay 0.2 per cent on the first €167,129 (€338),

0.3 per cent on the next €167,124 (€501) and 0.5 per cent on the balance of €165,747 (€829), making a total wealth tax bill of €1,668.

## Declaration

Residents in Spain must make a declaration for wealth tax at the same time as they make their income tax declaration, i.e. between 1st May and 20th June. The declaration is made on form 714 (*Impuesto sobre el Patrimonio*), which is available from tobacconists' and tax offices. The form must be presented with payment to your regional tax office or participating banks. When a husband and wife own a property in Spain jointly, each of them should complete a form, although it's possible for a couple to make their declaration on just one form (check with your fiscal representative).

Non-residents owning a single property in Spain can make their tax on deemed letting income (see page 230) and wealth tax declarations together on a single form at any time during the year, e.g. the declaration for 2003 can be made any time until 31st December 2004. This is done on form 214 (*Impuesto sobre el Patrimonio y sobre la Renta de No Residente*). Non-residents can have their fiscal representative in Spain make the declaration and arrange for payment on their behalf.

**Note that it's no longer necessary for most people to declare their average bank balance (*saldo medio*) in Spain for wealth tax.**

## PROPERTY TAX

Property tax or rates (*impuesto sobre bienes inmuebles urbana/rústica/IBI*) are payable by both resident and non-resident property owners in Spain. Property taxes go towards local council administration, education, sanitary services (e.g. street and beach cleaning), social assistance, community substructure, and cultural and sports amenities. Before buying a property, check with the local town hall that there aren't any outstanding local taxes for previous years (you should go back at least five years). As with all property-related taxes and debts, if the previous year's taxes are unpaid, the new owner becomes liable (you can, however, reclaim the tax from the previous owner – if you can find him!). A town hall has five years in which to either bill you or take legal action to recover unpaid taxes. Note, however, that it's now obligatory for the vendor to produce his last *IBI* receipt when completing a sale in front of a notary.

When you buy a property in Spain, you must register your ownership with the local town hall (take along your *escritura*). Registration must be done within two months of signing the deeds and there are fines ranging from €6 to €1,000 for non-registration. At one time there were literally millions (3 million were discovered in the last decade or so) of undeclared and untaxed properties in Spain, although most have now been registered, as local authorities have clamped down. However, there remain tens of thousands of properties in Spain that aren't registered with the local council for local taxes.

## Assessment

IBI is based on the fiscal or rateable value (*valor catastral*) of a property, which has traditionally been around 70 per cent of a property's market value. However, due to the sorry state of many municipalities' financial affairs (many are bankrupt), there have been huge increases in fiscal values in many areas in recent years (it may be worth checking the level of local government debt before buying a property!). Due to the collapse of property values in recent years, this has resulted in the fiscal value being above the market value in some cases. Therefore, it's advisable to check the *valor catastral* (see below) of a property before buying it; if it has been over-valued, it will result in increased taxes. A table of values (*ponencia de valores*) is used by local municipalities to assess the fiscal value of a property.

If the fiscal value of your property increases greatly, check that it has been correctly calculated. Property values are calculated according to a variety of measurements and evaluations, including the area (in square metres) of the property (the built, terraced and land areas), building and zoning restrictions in the area, the quality of the building (e.g. whether it's classified as luxury, normal or simple), the date of construction, and the proximity to services and roads. To check that a property is correctly specified, go to the town hall or the *urbanismo* office and ask to see its dossier (*expediente*) and obtain a *certificación catastral*, which is a physical description of a property used to determine the *valor catastral*. The dossier contains official papers relating to a property and may also contain plans and photographs. Check that the data recorded is correct, as errors are fairly common.

If an error is made in your assessment, it can take years to have it corrected, although it's important to persevere. You can appeal against the valuation of your property or an increase in valuation if you believe it's too high, particularly if it's higher than that of similar properties in the same area, although you have only 15 days in which to lodge an appeal (yet another good reason for non-residents to have a local fiscal representative).

It's important that the fiscal value of your property is correct, as a number of taxes are linked to this value (in addition to property tax), including deemed 'letting' income tax and wealth tax.

## Tax Rates

The *IBI* rate depends on both the population of the municipality and the level of public services provided and can vary considerably for similar properties in different areas. Rates tend to be higher in resort and coastal areas than in inland areas. Some municipalities have invested huge sums in recent years improving civic amenities, e.g. building indoor sports complexes (with swimming pools, gymnasiums, etc.) and cultural centres, and have increased property taxes to pay for them. General revisions are permitted once every eight years, but they can be adjusted annually in accordance with coefficients set annually by the state government in its budget.

The basic *IBI* rate is 0.3 per cent for agricultural properties (*rústicas*) and 0.5 per cent for urban properties (*urbana*). However, provincial capitals, towns with over 5,000 inhabitants and towns providing 'special services' can increase the rate to up to 1.7 per cent. To calculate your property tax, simply multiply the fiscal value by the tax rate, e.g. if the fiscal value of your property is €100,000 and the tax rate is 1 per cent, your *IBI* bill will be €1,000.

Note that in an attempt to open up the rental market and encourage owners to rent empty properties rather than leave them vacant, some cities (e.g. Seville) will charge double the usual rates for empty properties from 2003.

## Payment

Payment dates of property taxes vary with the municipality, e.g. between 1st September and 31st October. **Note that many town halls don't send out bills and it's your responsibility to find out how much you have to pay and when.**

Payment can usually be made in cash or by guaranteed bank cheque at the tax collection office or by postal giro at certain banks, and some municipalities accept payment by credit card such as MasterCard and Visa. Non-resident property owners should pay their *IBI* (and other local taxes) by direct debit from a Spanish bank account.

If the tax isn't paid on time, a surcharge (*recargo*) of 10 to 20 per cent is levied in addition to interest (plus possible collection costs), depending on how late payment is made. Note that some municipalities conveniently 'forget' to send non-residents' bills to their fiscal representatives so that they can levy surcharges for late payment. If you're unable to pay your property tax, you should talk to your local tax office. They will be pleased that you haven't absconded and will usually be willing to agree a payment schedule.

Some town halls have instituted a system of discounts to encourage residents to pay their bills early and thus spread the municipality's income throughout the year. For example, Mijas (Malaga province) offers a discount of 9 per cent for payments received in the first quarter, 6 per cent for payment in the second quarter and 3 per cent for payment in the third quarter. There's no discount for payments made between October 1st and 20th November and a surcharge of 20 per cent for payment after 20th November.

## Non-Payment

In the past, many people have been able to avoid paying property taxes. Incredibly, many municipalities with a high proportion of foreign residents and non-resident property owners collect only 50 to 75 per cent of property and other local taxes (over 90 per cent of property tax debts in Spain are owed by foreigners). In the past, some municipalities even considered they were doing well if around 65 per cent of taxes were collected! This laissez-faire attitude toward tax collection goes a long way towards explaining why most councils are so deeply in debt. Only some 70 per cent of taxes are paid voluntarily and authorities must take administrative steps to obtain payment for around a third of bills.

However, in recent years local municipal tax authorities have made strenuous efforts to collect unpaid property taxes. If you owe back taxes and refuse to pay them, your property can be seized and sold at auction, perhaps for as little as 10 per cent of its value. There have been many cases of foreigners arriving in Spain after a long absence to find that their homes had been sold to pay taxes. Using the threat of embargoes and the forced sale of properties, many town halls have collected hundreds of thousands of euros in back taxes. Local authorities also have the power to seize vehicles and place garnishment orders on bank accounts.

 **There's little sympathy with those who blatantly avoid paying property taxes in Spain, which means that other owners must bear the burden (through increased taxes) or municipalities are forced to cut services.**

If you don't pay your local taxes, your name will be listed in your province's 'official bulletin' (*Boletín Oficial de la Provincia/BOP*), the official publication in which changes in provincial regulations are promulgated and where embargoes against properties are listed. If you're a non-resident owner, it's essential that you know when an embargo has been placed on your property. The names of foreigners listed in the *boletines oficiales* in the ten Spanish provinces with the most foreign property owners (Alicante, Almería, Baleares, Gerona, Granada, Las Palmas de Gran Canaria, Málaga, Murcia, Santa Cruz de Tenerife and Valencia) are published by the Foundation Institute of Foreign Property Owners (see page 105) in its monthly newsletter.

Note that local authorities also levy fees (*tasas*) for services such as rubbish collection, street and beach cleaning, issuing documents, local parking restrictions and fire-fighting services.

# CAPITAL GAINS TAX

Capital gains tax (*impuesto sobre incremento de patrimonio de la venta de un bien inmueble*) is payable on the profit from the sale of certain assets in Spain, including antiques, art and jewellery, stocks and shares, property and businesses. Capital gains revealed as a result of the death of a taxpayer, gifts to government entities and donations of certain assets in lieu of tax payments are exempt from capital gains tax (CGT). Spain's taxation system combines capital gains (*incremento de patrimonio*) and capital losses (*disminución de patrimonio*). Capital losses can be offset against capital gains, but not against ordinary income. Capital losses in excess of gains can be carried forward to offset against future gains for a five-year period.

## Property

A capital gain is based on the difference between the purchase price (as declared in the *escritura*) and the sale price of a property, less buying and selling costs (and the cost of improvements). In the past it has been common practice to under-declare the purchase price of a property, thus allowing the vendor to reduce his CGT liability. However, if you agree to this, when you sell the property and the actual price is declared, you will pay increased CGT.

A capital gain on property must be declared within three months. Note that the period of ownership (for CGT purposes) starts from the day a property is registered or after a declaration of new work (*declaración de obra nueva*) if you make major improvements, so it's important to ensure that it's correctly registered. If you have a *declaración de obra nueva* in addition to your purchase *escritura*, you must make separate CGT calculations for the land and the house.

Residents aged over 65 are exempt from CGT on the profit made from the sale of their principal home, irrespective of how long they've owned it. Residents aged below 65 are also exempt from CGT on their principal home, provided they've lived there for at least three years and plan to buy another home in Spain within three years of the sale (from the date on the *escritura*), when they're taxed only on the amount that isn't re-invested. It is, however, important not to buy a new home until you've sold the old one, or you may not be entitled to this concession.

## Tax Rates

Non-residents are taxed at a flat rate of 35 per cent. Capital gains made by residents are treated as income and taxed in the year in which the gain was made. Prior to 8th June 1996, capital gains were taxed at your maximum income tax rate; however, since 8th June 1996, CGT for residents has been limited to a maximum of 18 per cent (less if your maximum rate of income tax is below 18 per cent).

**Assets Purchased Before 8th June 1996:** Capital gains on assets purchased before 8th June 1996 are taxed on a sliding scale according to how long they've been owned. After the first two years of ownership (when CGT is applied to 100 per cent of the value), there's an annual deduction of 25 per cent for quoted shares, 14.28 per cent for 'general' assets (other than shares and real estate) and 11.11 per cent for property. This means that gains on these assets are free of tax after five, eight and ten years respectively, as shown in the table below:

| Years Held | Taxable Value (%) | | |
| --- | --- | --- | --- |
| | Shares | General | Property |
| 1 | 100.00 | 100.00 | 100.00 |
| 2 | 100.00 | 100.00 | 100.00 |
| 3 | 75.00 | 85.72 | 88.89 |
| 4 | 50.00 | 71.44 | 77.78 |
| 5 | 55.00 | 57.16 | 66.67 |
| 6 | 00.00 | 42.88 | 55.56 |
| 7 | | 28.60 | 44.45 |
| 8 | | 14.32 | 33.33 |
| 9 | | 00.00 | 22.23 |
| 10 | | | 11.12 |
| 11 | | | 00.00 |

Using the above table, it's easy to calculate your CGT. For example, if you're a non-resident and you purchased a second home in Spain in 1994 and sell it in 2003 (i.e. you've held it for nine years), the gain is reduced to 22.23 per cent before tax is applied. Therefore, if you made a profit of €100,000, your CGT liability is 22.32 per cent of €100,000 (€22,320), which is taxed at 35 per cent, making a CGT bill of €7,812.

**Assets Purchased After 8th June 1996:** For gains arising from assets (including property) purchased after 8th June 1996, the above table doesn't apply. Instead, a coefficient or inflation index (*coeficiente de actualización*) is applied when you sell to allow for inflation and the loss of value of the amount originally invested. This means that owners who purchase (or purchased) a property after 8th June 1996 will always have a CGT liability. The coefficients for the years up to 2002 are shown below – new figures are published annually.

| Purchase Date | 2003 Sale |
|---|---|
| 1997 | 1.1016 |
| 1998 | 1.0802 |
| 1999 | 1.0608 |
| 2000 | 1.0404 |
| 2001 | 1.0200 |
| 2002 | 1.0000 |

The difference between the purchase price (as declared in the *escritura*) and the sale price, after the application of the coefficient, is the capital gain. For example, if you paid €120,000 for a home in 1997 and sold it in 2002, you would have multiplied the cost price by the inflation figure for 1997 of 1.1016, which comes to €132,192. If you sold your home for €175,000, you would have paid capital gains on €175,000 minus €132,192, which equals €42,808. If you're a non-resident, your CGT bill would therefore have been €14,983.

# Buying From A Non-Resident

Anyone buying from a non-resident is required to subtract 5 per cent from the purchase price and pay it to the Spanish Ministry of Finance within 30 days of the transaction. A declaration must be made on form 211 (*Impuestos Sobre La Renta De Las Personas Físicas Y Sobre Sociedades*). The payment is a 'guarantee' against a vendor trying to avoid paying capital gains and other taxes (as many did before this was introduced).

The 5 per cent deduction must be made only when the vendor is a non-resident, irrespective of whether the buyer is a resident or not.

Provided the buyer deducts 5 per cent from the purchase price and pays this to the tax authorities within 30 days, he cannot be pursued for additional CGT if the seller's liability was greater than the 5 per cent deducted (and he fails to pay it).

 **If the buyer fails to subtract and pay the 5 per cent, he's liable to pay any CGT due on the sale and could also be heavily fined.**

After paying the 5 per cent to the tax office, the buyer must give the vendor a copy of form 211. The vendor must then apply (on form 212) for a return of the difference between his 5 per cent deposit and his CGT liability within three months of the payment. If he doesn't, the tax office will keep the money (if the buyer is responsible for the delay, he will be responsible for the vendor's loss). If a representative or agent obtains the refund for you, you should request copies of the above forms and a statement showing the tax paid and the agent's fees.

Where applicable, the 5 per cent deposit is supposed to be repaid within six months of the documentation being completed, although it often takes vendors up to a year to get their money back. Note also that, when a non-resident sells a property in Spain, he may be asked for proof that he has paid his wealth and income tax for the previous five years before the deposit is repaid.

# INHERITANCE & GIFT TAX

As in most countries, dying doesn't free you (or more correctly your beneficiaries) from the clutches of the tax man. Spain imposes an inheritance and gift tax (*impuesto sobre sucesiones y donaciones*), which is called estate tax or death duty in some countries, on assets or money received as an inheritance or gift. The estates of both residents and non-residents are subject to Spanish inheritance tax if they own property or have other assets in Spain. Inheritance tax is paid by the beneficiaries, e.g. a surviving spouse, and not by the deceased's estate (as in some other countries). The country where the beneficiaries pay inheritance tax is usually decided by their domicile (see **Liability** on page 227). If you're domiciled in Spain, Spanish inheritance tax is payable on an inheritance, whether the inheritance is located (or received) in Spain or abroad.

Tax is payable by beneficiaries within six months of a death if the deceased died in Spain, although it's possible to obtain a six-month extension, or within 30 days following the transfer of a lifetime gift. If the deceased died abroad, the inheritance tax declaration and the payment of inheritance tax duties must be made within 16 months.

Tax is assessed on the net amount received and accrues from the date of death or the date of the transfer of a gift. Some people have managed to avoid inheritance tax by failing to inform the Spanish authorities of a death, although this is illegal (after five years and six months the tax can no longer be collected). However, if this is done, all other taxes must still be paid during this five-year period.

Since 8th June 1996, those who have been Spanish residents for at least three years have received an exemption of 95 per cent of inheritance tax when their principal residence or family business (in Spain) is bequeathed to a spouse, parent or child who have been living with them for at least two years prior to their death. The principal residence must be valued at less than €120,000 (there's no limit for a business) or the inheritance mustn't exceed €120,000 per heir, above which normal inheritance tax rates apply.

For example, if the residence is worth €150,000, you pay tax at only 5 per cent on the first €120,000 and tax at the full rate on the balance of €30,000. The inheritor must retain ownership of the property for a minimum of ten years, although if he dies within the ten-year period no further tax is payable. However, if the property or business is sold during this period, tax may be levied at the discretion of the relevant authorities, e.g. the regional government.

## Liability

Inheritance and gift tax liability depends on your relationship to the donor, the amount inherited and your wealth before receipt of the gift or inheritance.

**Relationship:** Direct descendants and close relatives of the deceased receive an allowance before they become liable for inheritance tax, as shown below.

| Group | Includes | Allowance |
|---|---|---|
| 1 | direct descendants under 21 years | €15,956.87 plus €3,990.72 for each year under 21 up to a maximum allowance of €48,000 |
| 2 | direct descendants over 21 years, direct ascendants (parents and up), spouse | €15,956.87 |
| 3 | relatives to third degree (and ascendants by affinity) including brother, sister, uncle, aunt, niece or nephew | €7,993.46 |

| 4 | unrelated people and more remote relatives (including common-law spouses*) | None |
|---|---|---|

* Note that some regions (e.g. Madrid) now recognise common-law spouses as spouses for inheritance tax exemption purposes if they're registered as such in the region.

**Amount Inherited:** Your inheritance tax liability is calculated as a percentage of the amount inherited (in excess of any allowance), as shown below:

| Net Value of Transfer (€) | Tax Rate (%) | Cumulative Tax Liability (€) |
|---|---|---|
| Up to 7,993 | 7.65 | 611.46 |
| 7,994 to 15,980 | 8.50 | 1,290 |
| 15,981 to 23,968 | 9.35 | 2,037 |
| 23,969 to 31,955 | 10.20 | 2,852 |
| 31,956 to 39,943 | 11.05 | 3,735 |
| 39,944 to 47,930 | 11.90 | 4,685 |
| 47,931 to 55,918 | 12.75 | 5,703 |
| 55,919 to 63,905 | 13.60 | 6,790 |
| 63,906 to 71,893 | 14.45 | 7,944 |
| 71,894 to 79,880 | 15.30 | 9,166 |
| 79,881 to 119,757 | 16.15 | 15,606 |
| 119,758 to 159,634 | 18.70 | 23,063 |
| 159,635 to 239,389 | 21.25 | 40,011 |
| 239,390 to 398,777 | 25.50 | 80,655 |
| 398,778 to 797,555 | 29.75 | 199,291 |
| Over 797,555 | 34.00 | |

Note that the regions of Catalonia, Madrid and Valencia each have different inheritance tax scales to the one above.

**Current Wealth:** Your current wealth is the value of all your assets **before** the inheritance transfer.

# Calculation

Once you've worked out your relationship group and calculated your inheritance tax liability, use the table below to calculate the inheritance tax payable based on your current wealth by multiplying your inheritance tax liability (shown in the above table) by the figure shown under the relevant relationship group.

| Current Wealth (€) | Relationship Group | | |
|---|---|---|---|
| | 1/2 | 3 | 4 |
| Up to 402,678 | 1.00 | 1.5882 | 2.0 |
| 402,678 to 2,007,380 | 1.05 | 1.6676 | 2.1 |
| 2,007,380 to 4,020,770 | 1.10 | 1.7471 | 2.2 |
| Over 4,020,770 | 1.20 | 1.9059 | 2.4 |

For example, if you're in relationship group 3 and you've inherited €71,893 (giving you a tax liability of €7,944) and you earn between €402,678 and €2,007,380 (lucky you!), you must pay 1.6676 times €7,944 in tax, which equals €13,247.41.

## Avoiding Inheritance & Gift Tax

It's important for both residents and non-residents with property in Spain to decide in advance how they wish to dispose of their Spanish property. Ideally this should be decided even before buying a home in Spain. Property can be registered in a single name, both names of a couple or joint buyers' names, the names of children, giving the parents sole use during their lifetime, or in the name of a Spanish or foreign company or trust. You should obtain professional advice regarding the registration of a Spanish property. It's advisable for a couple not only to register joint ownership of a property but to share their other assets and have separate bank accounts, which will help to reduce their dependants' liability for inheritance tax. In most regions, Spanish law doesn't recognise the rights to inheritance of a non-married partner, although there are a number of solutions to this problem, e.g. a life insurance policy.

One way of reducing your liability to inheritance tax is to transfer legal ownership of property to a relative as a gift during your lifetime. However, this is treated as a sale (at the current market price) and incurs fees of around 10 per cent plus CGT (see page 240), which need to be compared with your inheritance tax liability. Whether you should will or 'sell' a property to someone depends on the value of the property and your relationship, and it may be cheaper for a beneficiary to be taxed under the inheritance laws. Take, for example, a couple jointly owning a property in Spain who wish to leave it to a child. When one of the parents dies, the child inherits half the property and pays inheritance tax on that amount. Inheritance tax on the other half of the property is paid when the other parent dies. In this way little tax is paid on a property with a low value. If you're elderly, it may pay you to make the title deed (*escritura*) directly in the names of your children.

Spanish inheritance law is a complicated subject and professional advice should be sought from an experienced lawyer who understands both Spanish inheritance law and the law of any other countries involved. Your will (see below) is also a vital component in reducing Spanish inheritance and gift tax to the minimum or deferring its payment.

*The Spanish Inheritance* is an information file published by the Foundation Institute of Foreign Property Owners (see page 105) in various languages, including Dutch, English, German, Norwegian and Swedish.

# 8.

# INSURANCE

An important aspect of owning a home in Spain is insurance, not only for your home and its contents, but also health insurance for your family when visiting Spain. If you live in Spain permanently you will require additional insurance. It's unnecessary to spend half your income insuring yourself against every eventuality, from the common cold to being sued for your last euro, although it's important to insure against any event that could precipitate a major financial disaster, such as a serious accident or your house being demolished by a storm. The cost of being uninsured or under-insured can be astronomical.

 **It's vital to ensure that you have sufficient insurance when visiting your home abroad, which includes travel insurance, building and contents insurance and health insurance (covered in this chapter) as well as continental car insurance (including breakdown insurance) and third party liability insurance.**

As with anything connected with finance, it's important to shop around when buying insurance. Collecting a few brochures from insurance agents or making a few calls can save you a lot of money.

> **SURVIVAL TIP**
> Not all insurance companies are equally reliable or
> have the same financial stability and it may be better to
> insure with a large international company with a good
> reputation rather than with a small (e.g. Spanish) company,
> even if this means paying higher premiums.

Read insurance contracts carefully and make sure that you understand the terms and the cover provided before signing them. Some insurance companies will do almost anything to avoid paying claims and will use any available legal loophole, therefore it pays to deal with reputable companies only (not that this provides a foolproof guarantee). Note that Spanish insurance companies can compel you to renew your insurance for a further year if you don't give adequate written notice (e.g. up to three months) of your intention to terminate it, although most companies allow policyholders to cancel on renewal. Check in advance.

In matters regarding insurance, you're responsible for ensuring that you and your family are legally insured in Spain. Regrettably you cannot insure yourself against being uninsured or sue your insurance agent for giving you bad advice! Bear in mind that if you wish to make a claim on an insurance policy, you may be required to report an incident to the police within 24 hours (this may also be a legal requirement). The law in

Spain may differ considerably from that in your home country or your previous country of residence and you should **never** assume that it's the same. If you're uncertain of your rights, you're advised to obtain legal advice for anything other than a minor claim. Under EU rules, an insurance company registered in an EU member country can sell its policies in any other EU country.

# HEALTH INSURANCE

If you're visiting, living or working in Spain, it's extremely risky not to have health insurance for your family, as if you're uninsured or under-insured you could be faced with some very high bills. When deciding on the type and extent of health insurance, make sure that it covers **all** your family's present and future health requirements **before** you receive a large bill. A policy should cover you for **all** essential health care whatever the reason, including accidents (e.g. sports accidents) and injuries, whether they occur in your home, at your place of work or while travelling. Don't take anything for granted, but check in advance.

 **Spanish health insurance doesn't cover car accidents, which are automatically covered by Spanish car insurance. Therefore, if you have Spanish health insurance and your car is insured by a foreign insurance policy, you may not be covered for car accidents.**

If you're planning to take up residence in Spain and will be contributing to social security there, you and your family will be entitled to subsidised or free medical and dental treatment. However, most Spaniards and foreign residents who can afford it take out private health insurance, which offers a wider choice of medical practitioners and hospitals, and more importantly, frees them from public health waiting lists. If you aren't covered by Spanish social security, it's important that you have private health insurance (unless you have a **very** large bank balance). The policies offered by Spanish and foreign companies generally differ considerably in the extent of cover, limitations and restrictions, premiums, and the choice of doctors, specialists and hospitals.

Proof of health insurance must usually be provided when applying for a visa or residence permit (*residencia*). Note that some foreign insurance companies don't provide sufficient cover to satisfy Spanish regulations and therefore you should check the minimum cover necessary with a Spanish consulate in your country of residence. Long-stay visitors should have travel or long-stay health insurance or an international health policy (see **Health Insurance for Visitors** on page 252). If your stay in Spain is limited, you may be covered by a reciprocal agreement between your home country and Spain (see page 255). When travelling you should always have proof of your health insurance with you.

# Visitors

Visitors spending short periods in Spain (e.g. up to a month) should have travel health insurance (see page 260), particularly if they aren't covered by an international policy. If you plan to spend up to six months in Spain you should take out either a travel, special long-stay or international health policy, which should cover you in your home country and when travelling in other countries. Premiums vary greatly, so shop around. Most international health policies include repatriation or evacuation (although it may be optional), which may also include shipment by air of the body of a person who dies abroad to his home country for burial. Note that an international policy also allows you to choose to have non-urgent medical treatment in the country of your choice.

Most international insurance companies offer health policies for different areas, e.g. Europe, world-wide excluding North America, and world-wide including North America. Most companies also offer different levels of cover, for example basic, standard, comprehensive and prestige levels of cover. There's always an annual limit on the total annual medical costs, which should be at least €300,000 (although many provide cover of up to €1.2 million), and some companies also limit the charges for specific treatment or care such as specialists' fees, operations and hospital accommodation. A medical examination isn't usually required for international health policies, although pre-existing health problems are excluded for a period, e.g. one or two years.

Claims are usually settled in major currencies and large claims are usually settled directly by insurance companies (although your choice of hospitals may be limited). Always check whether an insurance company will settle large medical bills directly – if you're required to pay bills and claim reimbursement it can take several months before you receive your money (some companies are slow to pay). It isn't usually necessary to translate bills into English or another language, although you should check a company's policy. Most international health insurance companies provide emergency telephone assistance.

The cost of international health insurance varies greatly depending on your age and the extent of cover. With most international insurance policies, you must enrol before you reach a certain age, e.g. between 60 and 80 depending on the company, to be guaranteed continuous cover in your old age. Premiums can sometimes be paid monthly, quarterly or annually, although some companies insist on payment annually in advance. When comparing policies, carefully check the extent of cover and exactly what's included and excluded (often indicated only in the **very** small print), in addition to premiums and excess charges.

In some countries, premium increases are limited by law, although this may apply only to residents of the country where a company is registered and not to overseas policyholders. Although there may be significant differences in premiums, generally you get what you pay for and can tailor premiums to your requirements. The most important questions to ask yourself are: does the policy provide the cover required and is it good value for money? If you're in good health and are able to pay for your own out-patient treatment, such as visits to a family doctor and prescriptions, then the best value is usually a policy covering specialist and hospital treatment only.

# Residents

If you contribute to Spanish social security, you and your family are entitled to free or subsidised medical and dental treatment. Benefits include general and specialist care, hospitalisation, laboratory services, discounted drugs and medicines, basic dental care, maternity care, appliances and transportation. Over 95 per cent of the population are covered by the Instituto Nacional de la Salud (INSALUD), Spain's public health scheme, including retired EEA residents (with a residence permit) receiving a state pension. Note that some autonomous regions have their own health schemes, such as Andalusia where the Andalusian Health Services (Servicio Andaluz de Salud/SAS) operates, although INSALUD remains the central power. If you aren't entitled to public health benefits through payment of Spanish social security or being in receipt of a state pension from another EEA country, you must usually have private health insurance and must present proof of your insurance when applying for your residence permit. If you're an EEA national of retirement age, who **isn't** in receipt of a pension, you may be entitled to public health benefits if you can show that you cannot afford private health insurance.

Anyone who has paid regular social security contributions in another EU country for two full years prior to coming to Spain is entitled to public health cover for a limited period from the date of their last contribution. Social security form E106 must be obtained from the social security authorities in your home country and be presented to the local provincial office of the Instituto Nacional de la Seguridad Social (INSS) in Spain. Similarly, pensioners and those in receipt of invalidity benefits must obtain form E-121 from their home country's social security administration. Retirees living in Spain and receiving a state pension from another EU country are entitled to free state health benefits.

You will be registered as a member of INSALUD and will be given a social security card (*tarjeta sanitaria*), a list of local medical practitioners and hospitals, and general information about services and charges. If you're receiving an invalidity pension or other social security benefits on the grounds of ill-health, you should establish exactly how living in Spain will affect those benefits. In some countries there are reciprocal agreements regarding invalidity rights, but you must confirm that they apply to you. Citizens of EEA countries can make payments in their home country entitling them to use public health services in Spain and other EEA countries.

INSALUD places the emphasis on cure rather than prevention and treats sickness rather than promote good health. There's little preventive medicine in Spain such as regular health checks and a comprehensive immunisation programme for children (preventable diseases such as TB, tetanus, diphtheria and typhoid haven't yet been totally eradicated in Spain). The public health service has limited resources for out-patient treatment, nursing and post-operative care, geriatric assistance, terminal illnesses and psychiatric treatment. Perfunctory treatment due to staff shortages, long waiting lists as a result of a shortage of hospital facilities, and a general dehumanisation of patients are frequent complaints made against Spain's social security health system. Many problems are related to crippling bureaucracy, bad management and general disorganisation. However, attempts at reform have had some success and there are several public hospitals in Spain run as successful profit-making enterprises. Eventually, the health service intends to make all hospitals and general practises, self-administrating.

When you receive your social security card, you will usually be assigned a general doctor (*médico de cabecera*) at a health centre (*centro de salud*) in the area where you live. You can switch to another doctor in the same area, depending on availability and a doctor's number of patients. No payment is made when visiting a public health service doctor, where you're simply required to produce your social security card.

## Private Health Insurance

If you aren't covered by Spanish social security you should take out private health insurance. It's advantageous to be insured with a company that will pay large medical bills directly. Most private health insurance policies don't pay family doctors' fees or pay for medication that isn't provided in a hospital or there's an 'excess', e.g. you must pay the first €60 of a claim, which often exceeds the cost of treatment. Most will, however, pay for 100 per cent of specialist fees and hospital treatment in the best Spanish hospitals.

Annual premiums for comprehensive private insurance with a Spanish company range from around €2,000 for a family of four (two adults aged 40 years and two children aged under 16) or from €450 for a man under 60 (policies for women under 60 are up to twice as expensive). There may be an annual surcharge for those aged over 60, which increases with age, and supplements for certain services such as basic dental treatment or for a pregnant woman. Generally, the higher the premium, the more choice you have regarding doctors, specialists and hospitals. Note that Spanish insurance companies can cancel a policy at the end of the insurance period if you have a serious illness with continuous high expenses, and some companies automatically cancel a policy when you reach the age of 65. You should avoid such companies, because to take out a new policy at the age of 65 at a reasonable premium is difficult or impossible. If you already have private health insurance in another country, you may be able to extend it to cover you in Spain.

# Changing Employers or Insurance Companies

When changing employers or leaving Spain, you should ensure that you have continuous health insurance. If you and your family are covered by a company health plan, your insurance will probably cease after your last official day of employment. If you're planning to change your health insurance company, you should ensure that important benefits aren't lost, e.g. existing medical conditions won't usually be covered by a new insurer. When changing health insurance companies, it's advisable to inform your old company if you have any outstanding bills for which they're liable.

# Reciprocal Health Agreements

If you're entitled to social security health benefits in another EU country or in a country with a reciprocal health agreement with Spain, you will receive free or reduced cost medical treatment in Spain. If you're an EU resident, you should apply for a certificate of entitlement to treatment (form E111) from your local social security office (or a post office in the UK) at least three weeks before you plan to travel to Spain. An E111 is open-ended and valid for life. However, you must continue to make social security contributions in the country where it was issued and if you become a resident in another country (e.g. in Spain) it becomes invalid. It covers emergency hospital treatment but doesn't include prescribed medicines, special examinations, X-rays, laboratory tests, physiotherapy and dental treatment. If you use the E111 in Spain, you must apply for reimbursement to Spanish social security (instructions are provided with the form), which can take months. Note, however, that you can still receive a large bill from a Spanish hospital, as your local health authority assumes only a percentage of the cost!

Participating countries include all EU and EEA member states plus Switzerland, Australia, Canada and the USA as well as several South-American countries. If your country doesn't have an agreement with Spain and you aren't covered by Spanish social security, you **must** have private health insurance. British visitors and those planning to live in Spain can obtain information about reciprocal health treatment from the Department of Social Security, Pensions and Overseas Benefits Directorate, Newcastle-upon-Tyne, NE98 1BA, UK (☎ 0191-218 7777, 🖳 www.dwp.gov.uk).

# HOUSEHOLD INSURANCE

Household insurance (*seguro de hogar*) in Spain generally includes the building, its contents and third party liability, all of which are contained in a multi-risk household insurance policy. Policies are offered by both Spanish and foreign insurance companies and premiums are similar, although foreign companies may provide more comprehensive cover.

## Building

Although not compulsory, it's wise to take out property insurance that covers damage to a building (*continente*) due to fire, smoke, lightning, water, explosion, storm, freezing, snow, theft, vandalism, malicious damage, acts of terrorism, impact, broken windows and natural catastrophes (such as falling trees). Insurance should include glass, external buildings, aerials and satellite dishes, gardens and garden ornaments. Note that if a claim is the result of a defect in building or design, e.g. the roof is too heavy and collapses, the insurance company won't pay up (yet another reason to have a survey before buying!).

Property insurance is based on the cost of rebuilding your home and should be increased each year in line with inflation. Make sure that you insure your property for the true cost of rebuilding. It's particularly important to have insurance for storm damage in Spain, which can be severe in some areas. If floods are one of your concerns, make sure you're covered for water coming in from ground level, not just for water seeping in through the roof. **Always read the small print of contracts.** Note that if you own a home in an area that has been hit by a succession of natural disasters (such as floods), your household insurance may possibly be cancelled.

# Contents

Contents (*contiendo*) are usually insured for the same risks as a building (see above) and are insured for their replacement value (new for old), with a reduction for wear and tear for clothes and linen. Valuable objects are covered for their actual declared (and authenticated) value. Most policies include automatic indexation of the insured sum in line with inflation. Contents insurance may include accidental damage to sanitary installations, theft, money, replacement of locks following damage or loss of keys, frozen food, alternative accommodation cover, and property belonging to third parties stored in your home. Some items are usually optional, e.g. credit cards, frozen foods, emergency assistance (plumber, glazier, electrician, etc.), redecoration, garaged cars, replacement pipes, loss of rent, and the cost of travel to Spain for holiday homeowners. Many policies include personal third party liability, e.g. up to €300,000, although this may be an option.

Items of high value must usually be itemised and photographs and documentation (e.g. a valuation) provided. Some companies even recommend or insist on a video film of belongings. When claiming for contents, you should produce the original bills if possible (always keep bills for expensive items) and bear in mind that replacing imported items in Spain may be more expensive than buying them abroad. Contents' policies contain security clauses and if you don't adhere to them a claim won't be considered. If you're planning to let a property, you may be required to inform your insurer. Note that a building must be secure with iron bars (*rejas*) on ground-floor windows and patio doors, shutters and secure locks. Most companies give a discount if properties have steel reinforced doors, high security locks and alarms (particularly alarms connected to a monitoring station). An insurance company may send someone to inspect your home and advise on security measures. Policies pay out for theft only when there are signs of forcible entry, and you aren't covered for thefts by a tenant (but may be covered for thefts by domestic staff). All-risks policies offering a world-wide extension to a household policy covering jewellery, cameras and other items aren't usually available from Spanish insurance companies, but are available from a number of foreign companies.

# Community Properties

If you own a property that's part of a community development (see page 136), the building will usually be insured by the community (although you should ensure that it's comprehensively insured). You must, however, be insured for third party risks (*riesgo a terceros*) in the event that you cause damage to neighbouring properties, e.g. through flood or fire. Household insurance policies in Spain usually includes third party liability up to a maximum amount, e.g. €300,000.

## Holiday Homes

Premiums are generally higher for holiday homes, due to their high vulnerability, particularly to burglaries. Premiums are usually based on the number of days a year a property is inhabited and the interval between periods of occupancy. Cover for theft, storm, flood and malicious damage may be suspended when a property is left empty for an extended period. Note that you're required to turn off the water supply at the mains when vacating a building for more than 72 hours. It's possible to negotiate cover for periods of absence for a hefty surcharge, although valuable items are usually excluded (unless you have a safe). If you're absent from your property for long periods, e.g. longer than 30 days a year, you may be required to pay an excess on a claim arising from an occurrence that takes place during your absence (and theft may be excluded). Where applicable, it's important to ensure that a policy specifies a holiday home and **not** a principal home. In areas with a high risk of theft (e.g. major cities and most resort areas), an insurance company may insist on extra security measures. It's unwise to leave valuable or irreplaceable items in a holiday home or a property that will be vacant for long periods. Note that some insurance companies will do their utmost to find a loophole that makes you negligent and relieves them of liability. You should ensure that the details listed on a policy are correct, otherwise your policy could be void.

## Insuring Abroad

It's possible and legal to take out building and contents insurance in another country for a property in Spain (some foreign insurance companies offer special policies for holiday homeowners), although you must ensure that a policy is valid under Spanish law. The advantage is that you will have a policy you can understand and you will be able to handle claims in your own language. This may seem like a good option for a holiday home in Spain, although it can be more expensive than insuring with a Spanish company and can lead to conflicts if, for example, the building is insured with a Spanish-registered company and the contents with a foreign based company. Most experts advise that you insure a Spanish home and its contents (*continente y contenido*) with a Spanish insurance company through a local agent.

# Rented Property

Your landlord will usually insist that you have third party liability insurance. A lease requires you to insure against 'tenant's risks', including damage you may cause to the rental property and to other properties if you live in an apartment, e.g. due to a flood, fire or explosion. You can choose your own insurance company and aren't required to use one recommended by your landlord.

# Premiums

Premiums are usually calculated on the size (constructed area in square metres) of a property, its age, the value of the contents and security protection, e.g. window protection at ground level, the number of entrance doors and their construction. As a rough guide, building insurance costs around €10 a year per €5,000 of value insured, e.g. a property valued at €60,000 will cost €120 a year to insure. Contents insurance costs from around €15 a year per €5,000 of value insured (e.g. a premium of €30 for contents valued at €10,000) and may be higher for a detached villa than an apartment, e.g. up to €20 per €5,000 insured. Detached, older and more remote properties often cost more to insure than apartments and new properties (especially if located in towns), due to the higher risk of theft. Premiums are higher in certain high-risk areas.

# Claims

If you wish to make a claim, you must usually inform your insurance company in writing (by registered letter) within two to seven days of an incident or 24 hours in the case of theft. Thefts should also be reported to the local police within 24 hours, as the police report (*denuncia*), of which you receive a copy for your insurance company, constitutes irrefutable evidence of your claim. Check whether you're covered for damage or thefts that occur while you're away from your property and are therefore unable to inform the insurance company immediately.

Take care that you don't under-insure your house contents and that you periodically reassess their value and adjust your insurance premium accordingly. You can arrange to have your insurance cover automatically increased annually by a fixed percentage or amount. If you make a claim and the assessor discovers that you're under-insured, the amount due will be reduced by the percentage by which you're under-insured (e.g. if you're insured for €5,000 and you're found to be under-insured by 50 per cent, your claim for €1,500 will be reduced by 50 per cent to €750).

# HOLIDAY & TRAVEL INSURANCE

Holiday and travel insurance (*seguro de viajes*) is recommended for all who don't wish to risk having their holiday or travel ruined by financial problems or to arrive home broke. As you probably know, anything can and often does go wrong with a holiday, sometimes before you even get started (particularly when you **don't** have insurance). The following information applies equally to both residents and non-residents, whether you're travelling to or from Spain or within Spain. Nobody should visit Spain without travel (and health) insurance!

Travel insurance is available from many sources, including travel agents, insurance companies and agents, banks, automobile clubs and transport companies (airline, rail and bus). Package holiday companies and tour operators also offer insurance policies, some of which are compulsory, too expensive and don't usually provide adequate cover. You can also buy 24-hour accident and flight insurance at major airports, although it's expensive and doesn't offer the best cover. Before taking out travel insurance, carefully consider the range and level of cover you require and compare policies. Short-term holiday and travel insurance policies should include cover for holiday cancellation or interruption; missed flights; departure delay at both the start **and** end of a holiday (a common occurrence); delayed, lost or damaged baggage; personal effects and money; medical expenses and accidents (including evacuation home); flight insurance; personal liability and legal expenses; and default or bankruptcy insurance, e.g. against a tour operator or airline going bust.

## Health Cover

Medical expenses are an important aspect of travel insurance and you shouldn't rely on insurance provided by reciprocal health arrangements (see page 255), charge and credit card companies, household policies or private medical insurance (unless it's an international policy), none of which usually provide adequate cover (although you should take advantage of what they offer). The minimum medical insurance recommended by experts is €300,000 in Spain and the rest of Europe, and €1.2 million for the rest of the world (many policies have limits of between €1.8 million to €2.4 million). If applicable, check whether pregnancy related claims are covered and whether there are any restrictions for those over a certain age, e.g. 65 or 70, as travel insurance is becoming increasingly more expensive for those aged over 65.

Always check any exclusion clauses in contracts by obtaining a copy of the full policy document, as not all the relevant information is included in an insurance leaflet. High-risk sports and pursuits should be

(© Living Spain)

▲ *Villa, Costa Cálida* (© *Parador Properties*)

*Denia, Costa Blanca* ▶
(© *Parador Properties*)

▼ *Apartment complex,*
*Costa Blanca*
(© *Parador Properties*)

▼ *Villa, Costa Blanca* (© *Parador Properties*)

(© Living Spain)

▲ Mazarron, Costa Calida
   (© Parador Properties)

▶ Denia, Costa Blanca
   (© Parador Properties)

▼ Altea, Costa Blanca
   (© Parador Properties)

▲ Villa, Costa Blanc
   (© Parador Properties

▲ Villa, Costa Brava
*(© Parador Properties)*

▲ Altea, Costa Blanca
*(© Parador Properties)*

◀ Finestrat, Costa Blanca
*(© Parador Properties)*

▼ Finca, Mallorca
*(© Living Spain)*

▲ Blanes, Costa Brava
*(© Parador Properties)*

▲ *Peníscola, Costa del Azahar*
  *(© Parador Properties)*

▼ *Townhouses, Costa Brava*
  *(© Parador Properties)*

▲ *Marbella, Costa del Sol*
  *(© Living Spain)*

◀ *Villa on golf course, Costa Blanca*
  *(© Parador Properties)*

▲ *Alicante, Costa Blanca*
  *(© Parador Properties)*

specifically covered and **listed** in a policy (there's usually an additional premium). Special winter sports policies are available and are more expensive than normal holiday insurance ('dangerous' sports are excluded from most standard policies). Third-party liability cover should be €2.4 million in North America and €1.2 million in the rest of the world. Note that this doesn't cover you when you're using a car or other mechanically propelled vehicle.

# Cost

The cost of travel insurance varies considerably, depending on where you buy it, how long you intend to stay in Spain and your age. Generally, the longer the period covered, the cheaper the daily cost, although the maximum period covered is usually limited, e.g. six months. With some policies an excess must be paid for each claim. As a rough guide, travel insurance for Spain (and most other European countries) costs from around €35 for one week, €60 for two weeks and €100 for a month for a family of four (two adults and two children under 16). Premiums may be higher for those aged over 65 or 70.

# Annual Policies

For people who travel abroad frequently, whether on business or pleasure, an annual travel policy usually provides the best value, but carefully check exactly what it includes. Many insurance companies offer annual travel policies for a premium of around €150 for an individual (the equivalent of around two months insurance with a standard travel insurance policy), which are excellent value for frequent travellers. Some insurance companies also offer an 'emergency travel policy' for holiday homeowners who need to travel abroad at short notice to inspect a property, e.g. after a severe storm. The cost of an annual policy may depend on the area covered, e.g. Europe, world-wide (excluding North America) and world-wide (including North America), although it doesn't usually cover travel within your country of residence. There's also a limit on the number of trips a year and the duration of each trip, e.g. 90 or 120 days. An annual policy is usually a good choice for owners of a holiday home in Spain who travel there frequently for relatively short periods. However, carefully check exactly what's covered (or omitted) as an annual policy may not provide adequate cover.

# 9.

# LETTING

Many people planning to buy a holiday home are interested in owning a property that will provide them with an income, e.g. from letting, to cover the running costs and help with the mortgage payments. Letting a home for a few weeks or months in the summer can more than recoup your running costs (see page 127) and pay for holidays. Note that it's difficult to make a living providing holiday accommodation in most areas, as the season is too short and there's often too much competition.

 **If you're planning to let a property, it's important not to overestimate the income, particularly if you're relying on letting income to help pay the mortgage and running costs.**

The letting season varies with the region, e.g. 12 to 16 weeks on the Costa Brava, 20 to 24 weeks in the Balearics, 24 to 30 weeks on the Costa Blanca and the Costa del Sol, and year-round in the Canary Islands. However, you're unlikely to achieve this many weeks' occupancy and you should budget for around half these figures, even when letting full time. Apartments and townhouses tend to have year-round letting potential, whereby villas (especially large ones) are in demand from Easter to late autumn plus Christmas.

 **You may be unable to meet all your mortgage payments and running costs from rental income, even if a property is available to let year-round. Most experts recommend that you don't purchase a home in Spain if you need to rely on rental income to pay for it.**

Buyers who over-stretch their financial resources often find themselves on the rental treadmill, constantly struggling to earn enough money to cover their running costs and mortgage payments.

In the early 1990s many foreigners lost their Spanish homes after they defaulted on their mortgage payments, often because the rental income failed to meet expectations.

See also **Buying For Investment** on page 18.

# RULES & REGULATIONS

If you let a property in Spain, you're required by law to pay tax on your rental income in Spain and not in the country where the income is received (e.g. in the UK). However, the authorities do have a problem getting foreign, non-resident owners to comply with these regulations and many simply turn a blind eye, although there are fines of up to €6,000 for offenders.

See also **Taxation Of Property Income** on page 229.

If you provide bed and breakfast or something similar in a rural property, you must obtain a permit from the local tourist board and have the property inspected.

From July 1995, all legal short-term 'tourist' letting in the Canaries has been conducted by registered letting agencies, thus ensuring that income tax is paid on earnings. In the Balearics you may be liable for the ecological tax (the so-called *'eco-tasa'*) levied on all holiday accommodation. Check the latest regulation with the local authorities. Note that if you're planning to buy a community property (see page 136), you must check whether there are any rules that prohibit or restrict short-term letting. You may also be required to notify your insurance company.

## Contracts

Most people who do holiday letting just have a simple agreement form that includes a property description, the names of the clients, and the dates of arrival and departure. However, if you do regular letting you may wish to check with a lawyer that your agreement is legal and contains all the necessary safeguards. If you plan to let to non-English speaking clients, you must have a letting agreement in Spanish or other languages. If you use an agent, they will provide a standard contract.

However, if you do longer lets, you need to ensure that you or your agent uses the correct contract. In Spain, 'long-term' lets usually refer to lets of one year or more, for which contracts (*arriendos de viviendas*) are for a minimum of five years (after an initial period). The contract for short-term lets, usually of one year's duration or less, in called an *arriendo de temporada*. These contracts are available from tobacconists (*estancos*), but they don't apply to holiday letting. Because of the dangers of a tenant refusing to leave after the rental period expires, some foreign landlords are wary of letting to Spaniards.

> **SURVIVAL TIP**
> If you receive rent and accept a lessee without protest, you're deemed under Spanish law to have entered into a contractual relationship, even if there's no written contract.

# LOCATION

If income from a Spanish home has a high priority, then the location (see also page 73) must be one of the main considerations when buying.

When considering the location for a property you plan to let, you should bear in mind certain factors.

## Climate

Properties in areas with a pleasant year-round climate such as the Costa Blanca, Costa del Sol, and the Canaries have a greater rental potential, particularly outside high season. This is also important should you wish to use the property yourself outside the high season; for example you could let a property over the summer months when rental income is at its highest, and use it yourself in May or October and still enjoy fine weather.

## Proximity To An Airport

A property should be situated within easy reach of a major airport, as most holidaymakers won't consider travelling more than 30 to 45 minutes to their destination after arriving at an airport. Choose an airport with frequent flights from your home country and one with a range of scheduled and charter flights. It isn't wise to rely on an airport served only by budget airlines, as they may alter or cancel routes at short notice.

## Public Transport & Access

It's an advantage if a property is served by public transport or is situated in a town where a car is unnecessary. If a property is located in a town or urbanisation within a maze of streets, you should provide a detailed map. However, if it's in the country where signposts are all but non-existent, you'll need to provide not only a detailed map with plenty of landmarks, but you may also need to erect signs. Holidaymakers who spend hours driving around trying to find a place are unlikely to return or recommend it! Maps are also helpful for taxi drivers, who may not know the area.

## Attractions

The property should be close to attractions and/or a good beach, depending on the sort of clientele you wish to attract. If you want to let to families, then a property should be within easy distance of leisure activities such as theme parks, water parks, sports activities and night-life. If you're planning to let a property in a rural area, it should be somewhere with good hiking possibilities, preferably near one of Spain's many natural parks. Proximity to one or more golf courses is also an advantage to many holidaymakers and is an added attraction outside the high season, particularly on the Costa del Sol.

# SWIMMING POOL

If you're planning to let your property, a swimming pool is obligatory in most areas, as properties with pools are much easier to let than those without, unless a property is situated on a beach, lake or river. It's usually necessary to have a private one with a single-family home (e.g. a detached villa), although a shared pool is adequate for an apartment or townhouse. If you plan to let mainly to families, it's advisable to choose an apartment or townhouse with a 'child-friendly' communal pool, e.g. with a separate paddling pool or a pool with a shallow area. Country properties should have a private pool (some private letting agencies won't handle properties without a pool). You can charge a higher rent for a property with a private pool and it may be possible to extend the letting season even further by installing a heated or indoor pool, although the cost of heating a pool may be higher than the rental return. Note that there are strict regulations regarding pool safety (including private pools) in Spain and you should check that your pool complies with them.

**SURVIVAL TIP**
**You should have third party insurance covering accidents and injury for guests (or anyone) using your pool (and your property in general).**

# LETTING RATES

Rates vary greatly depending on the season, the region, and the size and quality of a property. An average apartment or townhouse sleeping four to six in an average area can be let for between €150 to €600 per week, depending on the season, location and quality. At the other extreme, a luxury villa in a popular area with a pool and accommodation for 8 to 12 can be let for €1,500 to €3,000 (or more) a week in the high season.

Most people who let year-round have low, medium and high season rates. The high season usually includes the months of July and August and possibly the first two weeks of September. Mid-season usually comprises June, late September and October, plus the Easter and Christmas/New Year periods, when rents are around 25 per cent lower than the high season. The rest of the year is classed as the low season. During the low season, which may extend from October to May, rates are usually up to 50 per cent lower than the high season. In winter rents may drop to as low as €500 or €600 per month for a two-bedroom apartment on the *costas*.

Note that rates usually include linen, gas and electricity, although electricity and heating (e.g. gas bottles) are usually charged separately for long lets in winter.

# FURNISHINGS

If you let a property, it isn't advisable not to fill it with expensive furnishings or valuable personal belongings. While theft is rare, items will get damaged or broken over a period of time. When furnishing a property that you plan to let, you should choose hard-wearing, dark-coloured carpets or rugs which won't show stains (although most properties have tiled or marble floors rather than carpets) and buy durable furniture and furnishings. Simple inexpensive furniture is best in a modest home, as it will need to stand up to hard wear. Small, two-bedroom properties usually have a sofa bed in the living room. Properties should be well equipped with cooking utensils, crockery and cutlery (including a kitchen knife that cuts!), and it's also usual to provide bed linen and towels (some agents provide a linen hire service). Make sure the bed linen and towels are of good quality and replace them often before they wear out. You can buy good quality, inexpensive household linen at most hypermarkets in Spain and during the Corte Inglés sales in January and July. You may also need a cot and/or high chair. Electricity is usually included in the rent, with the possible exception of long winter lets.

Appliances should include a washing machine and microwave, and possibly a dishwasher and tumbledryer. Depending on the rent and quality of a property, your guests may also expect central heating, air-conditioning, covered parking, a barbecue and garden furniture (including loungers). Heating is essential if you want winter lets, while air-conditioning is an advantage when letting property in summer, although it's only considered mandatory when letting a luxury villa. Some owners provide bicycles, and badminton and table tennis equipment. It isn't usual to have a telephone, although you could install a credit card telephone or one that just receives incoming calls.

# KEYS

You will need several sets of spare keys (plus spare remote controls for electric gates, etc.), which will probably get lost at some time. If you employ a management company, their address should be on the key fob and not the address of the house. If you lose keys or they can easily be copied, you should change the lock barrels regularly (at least annually). You don't need to provide guests with keys to all the external doors, only the front door (the others can be left in your home). If you arrange your own lets, you can send keys to guests in your home country or they can be collected in Spain. It's also possible to install a security key-pad entry system, the code of which can be changed after each let.

## CLEANING

A property should always be spotlessly clean when holidaymakers arrive and you should provide basic cleaning equipment. You will need to arrange for cleaning in between lets and also at regular intervals, e.g. weekly or twice-weekly, for lets of more than one week. If you use a local agent, they will usually arrange cleaning at your expense, currently around €8 an hour in coastal resorts. If applicable, you will also need to arrange pool cleaning and a gardener.

## USING AN AGENT

If you're letting a second home, the most important decision is whether to let it yourself or use a letting agent (or agents). If you don't have much spare time, then you're better off using an agent, who will take care of everything and save you the time and expense of advertising and finding clients. Agents usually charge commission of between 20 and 30 per cent of the gross rental income, although some of this can be recouped through higher rents. If you want your property to appear in an agent's catalogue or website, you must usually contact him the summer before you wish to let it (the deadline for catalogues is usually September). Note that although self-catering holiday companies may fall over themselves to take on a luxury villa in Majorca or Ibiza, the top letting agents turn down many properties.

There are numerous self-catering holiday companies operating in Spain and many Spanish estate agents also act as agents for holiday and long-term lets.

 **Take care when selecting an agent, as it isn't uncommon for them to go bust or simply disappear owing their clients thousands of euros.**

If possible, make sure that your income is kept in an escrow account and paid regularly, or even better choose an agent with a bonding scheme who pays you the rent **before** the arrival of guests (some do). It's absolutely essential to employ a reliable and honest (preferably long-established) company. Note that anyone can set up a holiday letting agency and there are many 'cowboy' operators. Always ask a management company to substantiate rental income claims and occupancy rates by showing you examples of actual income received from other properties. Ask for the names of satisfied customers and contact them.

Other things to ask a letting agent include:

- when the letting income is paid;
- what extras are levied and what for;
- whether he provides detailed accounts of income and expenses (ask to see samples);
- who he lets to (e.g. what nationalities and whether families, children or singles, etc.);
- how he markets properties;
- whether you're expected to contribute towards marketing costs;
- whether you're free to let the property yourself and use it when you wish. (Many agents don't permit owners to use a property during the months of July and August.)

The larger companies market homes via newspapers, magazines, the Internet, overseas agents and coloured brochures, and have representatives in a number of countries. Management contracts usually run for a year and should include arranging emergency repairs; routine maintenance of house and garden, including lawn cutting and pool cleaning; arranging cleaning and linen changes between lets; advising guests on the use of equipment if necessary and providing guests with information and assistance (24-hours a day in the case of emergencies).

Agents may also provide someone to meet and greet guests, hand over the keys and check that everything is in order. The actual services provided usually depend on whether a property is a budget apartment or a villa costing €1,500 or more per week. A letting agent's representative should also make periodic checks when a property is empty to ensure that it's secure and everything is in order. You may wish to check whether a property is actually let when the agent tells you it's empty, as it isn't unknown for some agents to let a property and pocket the rent (you can get a local friend or neighbour to call round).

## DOING YOUR OWN LETTING

Some owners prefer to let a property to family, friends, colleagues and acquaintances, which allows them more control – and **hopefully** the property will also be better looked after. In fact, the best way to get a high volume of lets is usually to do it yourself, although many owners use a letting agency in addition to doing their own marketing in their home country. You will need to decide whether you want to let to smokers or accept pets and young children – some people won't let to families with children under five years of age due to the risk of bed-wetting. Some owners also prefer not to let to young, single groups. Note, however, that this reduces your letting prospects.

## Rental Rates & Deposits

To get an idea of the rent you can charge (see **Letting Rates** on page 267), simply ring a few letting agencies and ask them what it would cost to rent a property such as yours at the time of year you plan to let it. They're likely to quote the highest possible rent you can charge. You should also check advertisements. Set a realistic rent as there's lots of competition. Add a returnable deposit (e.g. €150 to €500 depending on the rent) as security against loss (e.g. of keys) and breakages. This is returnable less any deductions. A booking deposit is usually refundable up to six weeks before the booking, after which it's forfeited. Many people have a minimum two-week rental period in July and August.

## Advertising

If you wish to let a property yourself, there's a wide range of Spanish and foreign newspapers and magazines in which you can advertise, e.g. *Dalton's Weekly* (☎ UK 020-8329 0100, 🖳 www.daltons.co.uk) and newspapers such as the *Sunday Times* in the UK. Many of the English-language newspapers and magazines listed in **Appendix B** also include advertisements from property owners. You will need to experiment to find the best publications and days of the week or months to advertise. Note, however, that most owners find it's prohibitively expensive to advertise a single property in a national newspaper or magazine.

A cheaper and better method is to advertise in property directories such as *Private Villas* (☎ UK 020-8329 0170, 🖳 www.privatevillas.co.uk) or on websites such as Owners Direct (☎ UK 01372-722708, 🖳 www.ownersdirect.co.uk) and Holiday Rentals (☎ UK 020-8743 5577, 🖳 www.holiday-rentals.co.uk), where you pay for the advertisement and handle the bookings yourself. Another option is to let through a company such as Brittany Ferries Holidays (☎ UK 0870-9000 259, ✉ holidayhomes@brittany-ferries.com), who provide a bond and include a discount on ferries. **These need to be arranged the previous year.**

For rural properties it's best to advertise within Spain targeting Spanish residents or long-term visitors who make up the majority of guests. Spanish regional tourist agencies can put you in touch with letting agents. There are many rural tourism websites where you can advertise. Typical arrangements include posting your property's details (in up to four languages), photos and prices, and links from major search engines. Some companies will even provide you with your own website. Rates for such services start at around €120 plus VAT per year. Among the best Spanish websites are ▦ www.toprural.com and ▦ www.azrural.com.

You can also advertise among friends and colleagues, in company and club magazines (which may even be free), and on notice boards in companies, stores and public places. The more marketing you do, the more income you're likely to earn, although you should also ensure that you provide a quick and efficient response to any enquiries. It also pays to work with local people in the same business and send surplus guests to competitors (they will usually reciprocate). In addition to advertising locally and in your home country, you can also extend your marketing abroad (or advertise via the Internet). Note that it's usually necessary to have a answer machine and preferably also a fax machine.

**Internet**

Advertising on the Internet is an increasingly popular option for property owners, particularly as a personalised website is an excellent advertisement and can include photographs, booking forms and maps, as well as comprehensive information about your property. You can also provide information about flights, ferries, car rental, local attractions, sports facilities and links to other website. A good website should be easy to navigate (avoid complicated page links or indexes) and must include contact details, ideally e-mail. It's wise to subscribe to a company that will submit your website to the main search engines, such as Altavista, Google and Yahoo. You can also exchange links with other websites.

# Brochures & Leaflets

If you don't have a website containing photographs and information, you should ideally produce a coloured brochure or leaflet. This should contain external and internal pictures, comprehensive details, the exact location, local attractions and details of how to get there (with a map included). You should enclose a stamped addressed envelope when sending out details and follow up within a week if you don't hear anything. It's necessary to make a home look as attractive as possible in a brochure or leaflet without distorting the facts – advertise honestly and don't over-sell the property.

# Handling Enquiries

If you plan to let a home yourself, you will need to decide how to handle enquiries about flights and car rentals. It's easier to let clients do it themselves, but you should be able to offer advice and put them in touch with airlines, ferry companies, travel agents and car rental companies.

# INFORMATION PACKS

## Pre-Arrival

After accepting a booking, you should provide guests with a pre-arrival information pack containing the following:

- a map of the local area and instructions how to find the property;
- information about local attractions and the local area (available free from tourist offices);
- emergency contact numbers in your home country (e.g. the UK) and Spain if guests have any problems or plan to arrive late;
- the keys or instructions on where to collect them on arrival.

It's ideal if someone can welcome your guests when they arrive, explain how things work, and deal with any special requests or problems.

## Post-Arrival

You should also provide an information pack in your home for guests explaining the following:

- how things work such as kitchen appliances, TV/video, heating and air-conditioning;
- security measures (see page 275);
- what not to do and possible dangers (for example, if you allow young children and pets, you should make a point of emphasising dangers such as falling into the pool);
- local emergency numbers and health services such as a doctor, dentist and hospital/clinic;
- emergency assistance such as a general repairman, plumber, electrician and pool maintenance (you may prefer to leave the telephone number of a local caretaker who can handle any problems);
- recommended shops, restaurants and attractions.

Many people provide a visitors' book for guests to write comments and suggestions, and some send out questionnaires. If you want to impress your guests, you can arrange for fresh flowers, fruit, a bottle of wine and a grocery pack to greet them on their arrival. It's personal touches that ensure repeat business and recommendations; you may even find after the first year or two that you rarely need to advertise. Many people return to the same property year after year. Simply do an annual mail-shot to previous clients. **Word-of-mouth advertising is the cheapest and always the best.**

# MAINTENANCE

If you do your own letting, you will need to arrange for cleaning and maintenance, including pool cleaning and a gardener if applicable. Ideally you should have someone on call seven days a week.

## Caretaker

If you own a second home in Spain, you will find it beneficial or even essential to employ a local caretaker, irrespective of whether you let it. You can have your caretaker prepare the house for your family and guests, as well as looking after it when it isn't in use. If it's a holiday home, have your caretaker check it periodically (e.g. weekly) and allow him to authorise minor repairs. If you let a property yourself, your caretaker can arrange for (or do) cleaning, linen changes, maintenance, repairs and gardening and pay bills. If you employ a caretaker, you should expect to pay at least the minimum Spanish hourly wage.

## Closing A Property For The Winter

Before closing a property for the winter, you should turn off the water at the mains (required by insurance companies), remove fuses (except ones for a dehumidifier or air-conditioner if you leave them on), empty food cupboards and the fridge/freezer, disconnect gas cylinders and turn off mains gas, and empty bins. You should leave interior doors and a few small windows (with grilles or secure shutters), as well as wardrobes, open to provide ventilation. Lock main doors, windows and shutters, and ecure anything of value or leave it with a neighbour or friend. Check whether any work needs to be done before you leave and if necessary arrange for it to be done in your absence. Most importantly, leave a set of keys with a neighbour or friend and arrange for them (or a caretaker) to check your property periodically.

# SECURITY

Most people aren't security conscious when on holiday and you should therefore provide detailed instructions for guests regarding security measures and emphasise the need to secure the property when they're out. It's also important for them to be security conscious when in the property, particularly when having a party or in the garden, as it isn't unusual for valuables to be stolen while guests are outside.

When leaving a property unattended, it's important to employ all the security measures available, including:

- storing valuables in a safe (if applicable) – hiding them is not a good idea, as thieves know **ALL** the hiding places;
- closing and locking all doors and windows;
- locking grilles on patio and other doors;
- closing shutters and securing any bolts or locks;
- setting the alarm (if applicable) and notifying the alarm company when absent for an extended period;
- making it appear as if a property is occupied by the use of timers and leaving lights and a TV/radio on;

**Bear in mind that prevention is always better than cure, as stolen possessions are rarely recovered.** If you have a robbery, you should report it to your local police station, where you must make a statement. You will receive a copy, which is required by your insurance company if you make a claim. See also **Home Security** on page 282.

# INCREASING RENTAL INCOME

Rental income can be increased outside high season by offering special interest or package holidays – which can be organised in conjunction with local businesses or tour operators – to broaden the appeal and cater for larger parties. These may include:

- activity holidays, such as golf, tennis, cycling or hiking;
- cooking, gastronomy and wine tours/tasting;
- arts and crafts such as painting, sculpture, photography and writing courses.

You don't need to be an expert or conduct courses yourself, but can employ someone to do it for you.

# 10.

# MISCELLANEOUS MATTERS

This chapter contains miscellaneous – but nevertheless important – information for homeowners in Spain, including crime, heating & air-conditioning, postal services, security, shopping, telephone, television and radio, and utilities.

# CRIME

Spain's crime rate is among the lowest in Europe, although it has increased dramatically in the last decade (petty crime increased by a dramatic 11 per cent in 2001 alone). The Spanish generally have a lot of respect for law and order, although 'petty' laws are often ignored. In villages away from the tourist areas, crime is almost unknown and windows and doors are usually left unlocked. Major cities have the highest crime rates and Alicante, Barcelona, Madrid, Seville and Valencia are among the worst. Many cities are notorious for 'petty' crime such as handbag snatching, pickpockets and thefts of and from vehicles. Stealing from cars, particularly those with foreign registrations, is endemic throughout Spain.

The most common crime in Spain is theft, which embraces a multitude of forms. One of the most common is the ride-by bag snatcher on a motorbike or moped. Known as the 'pull' (*tirón*), it involves grabbing a hand or shoulder bag (or a camera) and riding off with it, sometimes with the owner still attached (occasionally causing serious injuries). Motorcycle thieves also smash car windows at traffic lights to steal articles left on seats, so stow bags on the floor or behind seats. Tourists and travellers are the targets of some of Spain's most enterprising criminals, including highwaymen, who pose as accident or breakdown victims and rob motorists who stop to help them.

Foreigners are often victims of burglary, particularly holiday home owners, which is rife in resort areas, especially in the province of Alicante where housebreaking crimes rose dramatically during 2001 and 2002. In some areas it isn't unusual for owners to return from abroad to find their homes ransacked. Many developments and urbanisations are patrolled by security guards, although they usually have little influence on crime rates and may instil a false sense of security. It's advisable to arrange for someone to frequently check your property when it's left unoccupied. Petty theft by gypsies, who wander into homes when the doors are left open, is common in some parts of Spain.

Violent crime is still relatively rare in Spain, although armed robbery has increased considerably. Muggings at gun or knife-point are also rare in most towns, although they're becoming increasingly common in some areas. The most common source of violent crime in Spain comes from

Euskadi ta Azkatasuna (ETA), meaning 'Basque homeland and liberty', the Basque terrorist organisation, which has been waging a struggle for independence since 1959. ETA's campaign of violence has claimed over 1,000 lives in the last 30 years (after a brief truce in 1999) and it continues to murder members of the police and security forces (and random other victims). It isn't, however, a threat to most foreigners in Spain and its activities are largely confined to Madrid and the north of Spain.

The Costa del Sol has earned an unsavoury reputation as a refuge for criminals and fugitives from justice, hence its nickname the 'Costa del Crime', although in recent years the Costa Blanca and Costa Brava have also attracted the wrong sort of tourists. Spain previously had no extradition treaty with most other European countries, although this changed with Spain's entry into the EU. Much organised crime (particularly money laundering and drug trafficking) on the Costa del Sol is centred on Marbella.

One of the biggest dangers to most foreigners in Spain isn't from the Spanish, but from their own countrymen and other foreigners. It's common for expatriate 'businessmen' to run up huge debts, either through dishonesty or incompetence, and cut and run owing their clients and suppliers thousands of euros. In resort areas, confidence tricksters, swindlers, cheats and fraudsters lie in wait around every corner. Fraud of every conceivable kind is a fine art in Spain and is commonly perpetrated by foreigners on their fellow countrymen.

See also **Household Insurance** on page 256, **Security** on page 275 and **Home Security** on page 282.

# HEATING & AIR-CONDITIONING

Central heating (*calefacción*) is essential in winter in northern and central Spain and is useful in some other areas. If you like a warm house in winter, you will almost certainly miss central heating, even on the Costa del Sol. Central heating systems in Spain may be powered by oil, gas, electricity, solid fuel (usually wood) or even solar power. Oil-fired central heating isn't common due to the high cost of heating oil and the problems associated with storage and deliveries. In rural areas, many houses have open, wood-burning fireplaces and stoves, which may be combined with a central heating system. Whatever form of heating you use, it's important to have good insulation, without which up to 60 per cent of the heat generated is lost through the walls and roof. Many homes, particularly older and cheaper properties, don't have good insulation and even with new homes builders don't always adhere to current regulations.

In cities, apartment blocks may have a communal central heating system providing heating for all apartments, the cost of which is divided among the tenants. If you're a non-resident or absent for long periods, you should choose an apartment with a separate heating system, otherwise you will be contributing towards your neighbours' heating bills.

# Heating

### Electric

Electric heating isn't particularly common, as it's too expensive and requires good insulation and a permanent system of ventilation. It's advisable to avoid totally electric apartments in regions with a cold winter, such as Madrid, as the bills can be astronomical. However, a system of night-storage heaters operating on night tariff can be economical. Some stand-alone electric heaters are expensive to run and are best suited to holiday homes. If you rely on electricity for your heating, you should expect to pay between €50 and €125 a month during the coldest months, i.e. November to February. An air-conditioning system with a heat pump provides cooling in summer and economical heating in winter. Note that if you have electric central heating or air-conditioning, you may need to upgrade your power supply.

### Gas

Stand-alone gas heaters using standard gas bottles cost from €60 to €150 and are an economical way of providing heating in areas that experience mild winters (such as the Costa del Sol). Note that gas heaters must be used only in rooms with adequate ventilation, inspected and approved by Repsol Butano, and it can be dangerous to have too large a difference between indoor and outdoor temperatures. Gas poisoning due to faulty ventilation ducts for gas heaters (e.g. in bathrooms) isn't uncommon in Spain. It's possible to install a central heating system operating from standard gas bottles, which costs around €2,000 for a small home. The Spanish oil providers Cepsa and Repsol offer good deals on gas central heating including low-cost financing of the installation. Primus of Sweden is the leading foreign manufacturer. Mains gas central heating is popular in cities and is the cheapest to run.

### Solar Energy

The use of solar energy to provide hot water and heating is surprisingly rare in Spain, where the amount of energy provided by the sun each year per square metre is equivalent to eleven gas bottles. A solar power system can be used to supply all your energy needs, although it's usually combined with an electric or gas heating system as it cannot usually be relied upon for year round heating and hot water. If you own a home on Spain's Mediterranean coast (or on the islands), solar energy is a viable option and the authorities (both regional and national governments) offer grants and interest-free finance to encourage homeowners to install solar-energy systems.

The main drawback is the high cost of installation, which varies considerably depending on the region and how much energy you require. A 400-litre hot-water system costs around €2,500 and must be installed by an expert. The advantages are no running costs, silent, maintenance-free operation, and no (or very small) electricity bills. A system should last 30 years (it's usually guaranteed for ten years) and can be upgraded to provide additional power in the future. Solar power can also be used to heat a swimming pool. A solar power system can also be used to provide electricity in a remote rural home, where the cost of extending mains electricity is prohibitive.

# Air-Conditioning

In some regions, summer temperatures can reach over 40°C (104°F) and although properties are built to withstand the heat, you may wish to install air-conditioning (*aire acondicionado*). Note, however, that there can be negative effects if you suffer from asthma or respiratory problems. Air-conditioning units cost from around €600 (plus installation) for a unit (2,000 frigorías) that's sufficient to cool an average sized room. Some air-conditioners are noisy, so check the noise level before buying one. An air-conditioning system with a heat pump provides cooling in summer and economical heating in winter – a system with an outside compressor providing radiant heating and cooling costs around €1,200 per room. Many people fit ceiling fans for extra cooling in the summer (costing from around €65), which are standard fixtures in some new homes.

### Humidifiers & De-Humidifiers

Note that central heating dries the air considerably and may cause your family to develop coughs and other ailments. Those who find dry air unpleasant can install humidifiers which will add moisture to the air. These range from simple water containers hung from radiators to electrical or battery-operated devices. Humidifiers that don't generate steam should be disinfected occasionally with a special liquid available from chemists.

On the other hand, if you're going to be using a holiday home only occasionally, it's worthwhile installing de-humidifiers, especially in the bedrooms, to prevent clothes and linen going mouldy.

# HOME SECURITY

Security is of paramount importance when buying a home in Spain, particularly if it will be left empty for long periods. Obtain advice from local security companies and neighbours.

 **Bear in mind, however, that no matter how good your security, a property is rarely impregnable, so you should never leave valuables in an unattended home unless they're kept in a safe.**

When moving into a new home it's often wise to replace the locks (or lock barrels) as soon as possible, as you have no idea how many keys are in circulation for the existing locks. This is true even for new homes. In any case, it's advisable to change the external lock barrels regularly, e.g. annually, particularly if you let a home. If they aren't already fitted, it's advisable to fit high security (double cylinder or dead bolt) locks. Most modern apartments are fitted with an armoured door (*puerta blindada*) with individually numbered, high security locks with three sets of levers.

Note, however, that the door should be armoured with steel (costing around €1,000) otherwise thieves will be able to force it open easily. In areas with a high risk of theft, your insurance company may insist on extra security measures such as two locks on external doors, internal locking shutters, and security bars or metal grilles (*rejas*) on windows and patio doors on ground and lower floors, e.g. the first and second floors of high and low-rise buildings. A policy may specify that all forms of protection on doors must be employed when a property is unoccupied and that all other forms (e.g. shutters) must also be used after 10pm and when a property is left empty for two or more days.

You may wish to have a security alarm fitted, which is a good way to deter thieves and may also reduce your insurance (see page 256). It should include all external doors and windows, internal infra-red security beams, and may also include a coded entry keypad (which can be frequently changed and is useful for clients if you let) and 24-hour monitoring (with some systems it's possible to monitor properties remotely via a computer from another country). With a monitored system, when a sensor (e.g. smoke or forced entry) detects an emergency or a panic button is pushed, a signal is sent automatically to a 24-hour monitoring station. The person on duty will telephone to check whether it's a genuine alarm (a password must be given) and if he cannot contact you someone will be sent to investigate. Some developments and urbanisations have security gates and are patrolled 24-hours a day by security guards, although they often have little influence on crime rates and may instil a false sense of security.

You can deter thieves by ensuring that your house is well lit at night and not conspicuously unoccupied. External security 'motion detector' lights (that switch on automatically when someone approaches); random timed switches for internal lights, radios and televisions; dummy security cameras; and tapes that play barking dogs (etc.) triggered by a light or heat detector may all help deter burglars. In rural areas it's common for owners to fit two or three locks on external doors, alarm systems, grilles on doors and windows, window locks, security shutters and a safe for valuables. Note, however, that security grilles must be heavy duty, as the bars on cheap grilles can be prised apart with a car jack.

Many people also wrap a chain around their patio security grille and secure it with a padlock when a property is unoccupied (although it might not withstand bolt-cutters). You can fit UPVC (toughened clear plastic) security windows and doors, which can survive an attack with a sledge-hammer without damage, and external steel security blinds (which can be electrically operated), although these are expensive. A dog can be useful to deter intruders, although it should be kept inside where it cannot be given poisoned food. Irrespective of whether you actually have a dog, a warning sign showing an image of a fierce dog may act as a deterrent. You should have the front door of an apartment fitted with a spy-hole and chain so that you can check the identity of visitors before opening the door. **Remember, prevention is better than cure, as stolen possessions are rarely recovered.**

Holiday homes are particularly vulnerable to thieves, especially in rural areas, and are often ransacked. In isolated areas, thieves can strip a house bare at their leisure and an unmonitored alarm won't be a deterrent if there's no-one around to hear it. If you have a holiday home in Spain, it inadvisable to leave anything of real value (monetary or sentimental) there and to have full insurance for your belongings (see page 256). One 'foolproof' way to protect a home when you're away is to employ a house-sitter to look after it. This can be done for short periods or for six months (e.g. during the winter) or longer if you have a holiday home in Spain. It isn't usually necessary to pay someone to house-sit for a period of six months or more, when you can usually find someone to do it in return for free accommodation. However, take care who you engage and obtain references.

An important aspect of home security is ensuring you have early warning of a fire, which is easily accomplished by installing smoke detectors. Battery-operated smoke detectors can be purchased for around €6 and should be tested periodically to ensure that the batteries aren't exhausted. You can also fit an electric-powered gas detector that activates an alarm when a gas leak is detected. When closing up a property for an extended period, e.g. over the winter, you should ensure that everything is switched off and that it's secure. If you vacate your home for an extended period, you may also be obliged to notify a caretaker, landlord or insurance company, and to leave a key with a caretaker or landlord in case of emergencies. If you have a robbery, you should report it immediately to your local police station where you must make a statement (*denuncia*). You will receive a copy, which is required by your insurance company if you make a claim.

There are many specialist home security companies who will inspect your home and offer free advice on security, although you should always shop around and obtain at least two quotations before having any work done.

# POSTAL SERVICES

There's a post office (*oficina de correos*) in most towns, main railway stations, major airports and ports in Spain. In addition to postal services, a limited range of other services are provided, including banking and savings accounts. Telephones aren't available in most Spanish post offices. The Spanish post office produces few leaflets and brochures, and you may even have difficulty obtaining a tariff. You shouldn't expect post office staff to speak English or other foreign languages, although main post offices in major cities may have an information desk with multi-lingual staff.

The Spanish postal (*correo*) service has a reputation of being one of the slowest and most unreliable in Europe. It's advisable to send international post by airmail (*por correo aéreo*). There's a cheaper surface post (*por barco* or *correo ordinario*) service outside Europe, but it takes eons, e.g. six weeks or more to North America. Delivery times in Europe vary considerably depending on the countries concerned and where letters are posted (possibly even the post box used), and letters may arrive quicker when posted at a main post office.

Never rely on any important European post being delivered in under ten days, as instances of letters taking many weeks to arrive at a European destination are fairly commonplace. Even sending letters by express (*urgente*) post isn't the answer, as there's no guarantee at all that they will arrive earlier than ordinary post. The only way to ensure express delivery within Spain or from Spain to another country is to use a courier or to send letters by fax or e-mail.

# SHOPPING

Spain isn't one of Europe's great shopping countries, either for quality or bargains, although the variety and quality of goods on offer has improved considerably since Spain joined the European Union. Prices of many consumer goods such as TVs and stereo systems, computers, cameras, electrical apparatus and household appliances have fallen dramatically in recent years and are now similar to most other EU countries. Furthermore, if you're fortunate enough to get paid in a currency that has increased in value against the euro, you may be pleasantly surprised how far your money will stretch. However, Spain is no longer an inexpensive country and the cost of living (see page 26) has risen considerably in the last decade.

Small family-run stores (*tiendas*) still constitute the bulk of Spanish retailers, although the shopping scene has been transformed in the last few decades with the opening of numerous shopping centres (many beautifully designed) and hypermarkets. Following the trend in most European countries, there has been a drift away from town centres by retailers to out-of-town shopping centres (malls) and hypermarket complexes, which has left some 'high streets' run down and abandoned. The biggest drawback to shopping in cities and towns is parking, which can be a nightmare.

The best time to have a shopping spree is during the winter and summer sales (*rebajas*) in January-February and July-August respectively, when prices are often slashed by 50 per cent or more. If you're looking for bargains (*gangas*), you may also wish to try the cut-price shops which sell everything for €1, €2 or €5 (*todo desde 1€, 2€ ó 5€*), much of it bankrupt stock.

Among the best buys in Spain are the diverse handicrafts which include antiques, cultured pearls, shawls, pottery, ceramics, damascene, embroidery, fans, glassware, hats, ironwork, jewellery, knives, lace, suède and leather, paintings, porcelain, rugs, trinkets and carvings.

In major cities and tourist areas you should be wary of pickpockets and bag-snatchers, particularly in markets and other crowded places. The Spanish generally pay cash when shopping, although credit and debit cards are widely accepted. However, personal cheques (even local ones) aren't usually accepted.

## Opening Hours

Opening hours in Spain vary depending on the region, city or town and the type of shop. There are no statutory closing days or hours for retail outlets, except in Catalonia where shops must close by 9pm.

Most small shops open from between 8.30 and 9.30am (or earlier for food shops) until between 1 and 2pm and from around 5pm until between 7.30 and 9pm, Mondays to Fridays, and from 9.30am until 2pm on Saturdays. Department stores, hypermarkets and many supermarkets are open continually (without a break for a *siesta*) from around 9.30 or 10am, until between 8 and 10pm from Mondays to Saturdays. Department stores and hypermarkets may also open on Sundays (e.g. 10am to 3pm or noon to 8pm) and public holidays (e.g. 10am to 10pm). During the summer, shops in resort areas (particularly food shops and tobacconist's) often remain open until 10 or 11pm (except in Catalonia). Shops in resort areas may also remain open longer on Saturdays and open on Sunday mornings in the summer. In major cities such as Madrid and Barcelona and some resort towns there are 24-hour, American-style, drugstores comprising a supermarket, cafeteria, tobacconist's and restaurant.

A big surprise for many foreigners is the long afternoon *siesta*, when most small shops close from 1.30 or 2pm until around 5pm. Apart from department stores and many large supermarkets, there's no such thing as afternoon shopping in Spain. The *siesta* makes good sense in the summer when it's often too hot to do anything in the afternoon, but it isn't so practical in winter when evening shopping must be done in the dark.

In general, shops close for one whole day and one half day each week, usually on Saturday afternoon and Sunday (some shops also close on Mondays or Monday mornings). In Madrid and other cities some shops close for the whole of August, when most people are on holiday.

# Furniture & Furnishings

The kind of furniture (*muebles*) you buy for your Spanish home will depend on a number of factors, including its style and size, whether it's a permanent or holiday home, your budget, the local climate, and not least, your personal taste. Holiday homes are often sold furnished, particularly apartments, although furniture may be of poor quality and not to your taste. However, buying a furnished property can represent a bargain as the cost of the furnishings often isn't reflected in the price. If you're buying a new property as an investment for letting, some developers or agents will arrange to furnish it for you.

If you plan to furnish a holiday home with antiques or expensive modern furniture, bear in mind that you will need adequate security and insurance. If you own a holiday home in Spain, it's usually worthwhile shipping surplus items of furniture you have in your home abroad. If you intend to live permanently in Spain in the future and already have a house full of good furniture abroad, there's little point in buying expensive furniture in Spain. However, many foreigners who decide to live permanently in Spain find that it's better to sell their furniture abroad rather than bring it to Spain, as foreign furniture often isn't suitable for Spain's climate and house styles.

A wide range of modern and traditional furniture is available in Spain at reasonable prices. Modern furniture is popular and is often sold in huge stores in commercial centres and reasonably priced furniture can also be purchased from large hypermarkets. Pine and cane furniture is inexpensive and widely available. If you're looking for classic modern furniture, you may wish to try Roche Bobois. Department stores such as El Corte Inglés also sell a wide range of (mostly up-market) furniture.

If you're buying a large quantity of furniture, don't be reluctant to ask for a reduction as most stores will give you a discount. The best time to buy furniture and furnishings is during sales (particularly in winter), when prices of many items are slashed. Most furniture stores also offer special deals on complete furniture packages, e.g. from around €3,000 to totally furnish a two-bedroom apartment. It's possible for residents to pay for furniture and large household appliances over 12 months interest-free or over five years (with interest).

If you're looking for antique furniture at affordable prices, you may find a few bargains at antique and flea markets in rural areas. However, you must drive a hard bargain as the asking prices are often ridiculous, particularly in tourist areas during the summer. There's a reasonable market for second-hand furniture in Spain and many sellers and dealers advertise in the expatriate press. There are do-it-yourself hypermarkets (such as Akí and Leroy Merlin) in most areas, selling everything for the home including DIY, furniture, bathrooms, kitchens, decorating and lighting, plus services such as tool rental and wood cutting.

## Household Goods

Household goods in Spain are generally of high quality and although the choice isn't as wide as in some other European countries, it has improved considerably in recent years. Electrical items have traditionally been more expensive in Spain, although the gap has narrowed and prices are now comparable (particularly in hypermarkets). Note, however, that Spanish-made appliances, electrical apparatus and consumer goods aren't always the most reliable and they're sometimes of eccentric design, although a wide range of imported brands are also available.

Bear in mind when importing household goods that aren't sold in Spain, that it may be difficult or impossible to get them repaired or serviced locally (however, should you need to get something repaired, there are strict rules to protect consumers). If you import appliances, don't forget to bring a supply of spares and consumables such as bulbs for a refrigerator or sewing machine, and spare bags for a vacuum cleaner. Note that the standard size of kitchen appliances and cupboard units in Spain **isn't** the same as in other countries and it may be difficult to fit an imported dishwasher or washing machine into a Spanish kitchen. Check the size **and** the latest Spanish safety regulations before shipping these items to Spain or buying them abroad, as they may need expensive modifications.

 **Spanish washing machines take in cold water ONLY and heat it in the machine, which makes machines that take in hot water (such as those sold in the USA) obsolete in Spain.**

If you already own small household appliances it's worthwhile bringing them to Spain, as usually all that's required is a change of plug. However, if you're coming from a country with a 110/115V electricity supply such as the USA, you will need a lot of expensive transformers (see page 303) and it's usually better to buy new appliances in Spain. Don't bring a TV or video recorder without checking its compatibility first, as TVs made for other countries often don't work in Spain without modification. If your need is only temporary, many electrical and other household items (such as TVs, beds, cots/highchairs, electric fans, refrigerators, heaters and air conditioners), can be rented by the day, week or month. Tools and do-it-yourself equipment can also be rented in most towns. There are DIY hypermarkets such as Akí and Leroy Merlin in most areas, although DIY equipment and supplies are generally more expensive than in many other EU countries (many items are imported).

If you need kitchen measuring equipment and cannot cope with decimal measures, you will need to bring your own measuring scales, jugs, cups and thermometers. Foreign pillow sizes (e.g. American and British) aren't the same as in Spain, although various sizes can be purchased in stores such as El Corte Inglés.

# Shopping Abroad

Shopping 'abroad' includes day trips to Andorra, France, Portugal, Morocco and Gibraltar, as well as shopping excursions further afield. A day trip to a neighbouring country makes an interesting day out and can save you money. Don't forget your passports or identity cards, car papers, children, dog's vaccination papers and foreign currency. From 1st January 1993 there have been no cross-border shopping restrictions within the European Union for goods purchased duty and tax paid, provided goods are for personal consumption or use and not for resale.

Although there are no restrictions, there are 'indicative levels' for items such as spirits, wine, beer and tobacco products, above which goods may be classified as commercial quantities.

**Gibraltar:** Considerable savings can be made on cigarettes, petrol, foodstuffs, luxury goods (e.g. perfumes) and various consumer goods in Gibraltar. You can also buy British drugs and medicines that are unavailable in Spain. Note that Gibraltar uses its own currency, Gibraltar pounds, although British currency is also accepted. Spanish residents are permitted to import goods up to the value of €175 (€90 for under 14s), exclusive of duty-free items (see below). There are often long delays for vehicles at the border crossing into Spain, so it may be advisable to park on the Spanish side of the border and get a bus or taxi (or walk) into Gibraltar. **Make sure that you lock and secure your car against theft**, as cars are sometimes stolen while their owners are shopping in Gibraltar!

Opening hours are usually from 9am until 7pm Mondays to Fridays and 9am to 1pm on Saturdays (most shops close on Sundays).

**Andorra:** Europe's biggest duty-free 'shop'. Considerable savings can be made on almost everything, including alcohol, tobacco products, cheese and other foodstuffs, clocks and watches, cameras, film, electrical goods, perfume and luxury goods, and petrol.

# Duty-Free Allowances

Duty-free (*libre de impuestos*) shopping within the EU ended on 30th June 1999. If you travel to or from Spain to or from another EU country you're entitled to import goods of an unlimited value as long as they're for personal use plus cigarettes and alcohol as listed below. Note the list is issued as a guide line only and if you import more than the amounts shown below, you must be able to show that the goods are for your personal use. If you cannot, they may be confiscated by customs officials. Note, also that guide lines are subject to change and you should check with an official source before you import large amounts:

- 800 cigarettes;
- 400 cigarillos;
- 20 cigars;
- 1kg smoking tobacco;
- 90 litres wine (of which no more than 60 should be sparkling);
- 10 litres spirits;
- 20 litres fortified wine;
- 110 litres beer.

From 1st January 1993, for each journey to a non-EU country travellers aged 17 or over (unless otherwise stated) are entitled to import the following goods purchased duty-free:

- one litre of spirits (over 22 degrees proof) **or** two litres of fortified wine, sparkling wine or other liqueurs (under 22 degrees proof);
- two litres of still table wine;
- 200 cigarettes **or** 100 cigarillos **or** 50 cigars **or** 250g of tobacco;
- 60cc/ml of perfume;
- 250cc/ml of toilet water;
- other goods, including gifts and souvenirs to the value of €175 (€90 for under 14s).

Duty-free allowances apply on both outward and return journeys, even if both are made on the same day, and the combined total (i.e. double the above limits) can be imported into your 'home' country. It's rarely worthwhile buying duty-free alcohol when travelling to Spain, as it's much cheaper in Spanish supermarkets and off-licences.

Special rules apply when shopping in duty-free areas such as Andorra and Gibraltar. In Andorra the duty-free limits for those aged over 17 are:

- 1.5 litres of alcohol over 22 degrees proof or three litres of alcohol under 22 degrees proof;
- five litres of still table wine;
- 300 cigarettes OR 150 cigarillos OR 75 cigars OR 400g of pipe tobacco;
- 75g of perfume and 375ml of toilet water;
- up to €175 worth of other 'agricultural' goods, although there are limits for some products such as milk (six litres), butter (1kg), cheese (4kg), sugar (5kg), coffee (1kg) and tea (200g);
- up to €525 worth of manufactured goods.

Duty-free allowances for Gibraltar include 200 cigarettes, one bottle of spirits and 200 litres of petrol, plus other purchases to the value of €175 (€90 for under 14s).

If you reside outside the EU, you can reclaim value added tax (*IVA*) on single purchases over €90. An export sales invoice is provided by retailers listing purchases, which must be validated by a customs officer when leaving Spain, so don't pack purchases in your checked baggage. Your refund will be posted to you later or paid to a credit card account.

With certain purchases, particularly large items, it's better to have them sent directly abroad, when *IVA* won't be added. Large department stores such as El Corte Inglés have a special counter where non-EU shoppers can arrange for the shipment of goods.

# TELEPHONE SERVICES

Although Spanish technology isn't highly rated, its communications services (both domestic and international) have improved considerably in the last decade.

The Spanish telephone service is operated by one company, Telefónica, offering a complete service, including the installation of telephone lines, and numerous others which currently only provide call services, but this is likely to change. Telefónica was fully privatised in 1997 and its monopoly ended in 1998, when other companies were allowed to offer provincial, inter-provincial and international calls.

In 2002, liberalisation was extended to local calls. Many companies have entered the market, but some have experienced serious financial problems, having discovered that the market is less lucrative than expected mainly because many consumers continue to use Telefónica exclusively in spite of the competitive prices offered by other companies.

In early 2003 the main telecommunication providers for private phone use were Âlo (USA Communications), Auna (previously Retevisión and owned largely by Endesa and Telecom Italia), Jazztel (Nortel) and Tele2 (Netcom). Other smaller companies include BT (British Telecom), Sinple (Interoute), TeleConnect (ITS Networks), SpanTel (Spantel Comms Inc) and Uni2 (owned mainly by France Télécom and Santander Bank). Competition in the market has resulted in a sharp reduction in the cost of calls, which have fallen dramatically since 1999, although Spain still has some of the highest telephone charges in the EU.

## Installation & Registration

When moving into a new home in Spain with a telephone line, you must have the account transferred to your name. If you're planning to move into a property without an existing telephone line, you may want to get one installed, which costs €77.53. To have a telephone installed or reconnected, you can visit your local Telefónica office (the only company permitted to install telephone lines). Take along your passport or residence permit (*residencia*), proof of your address such as a recent electricity bill, and a copy of your property deed (*escritura*) or rental contract. Alternatively, you can phone Telefónica (☎ 1004) or fill in a form online (💻 www.telefonica.es). If you're renting and don't have a residence permit (*residencia*), you must pay a deposit of €200. Note that staff don't usually speak English.

> **SURVIVAL TIP**
> If a property doesn't have a telephone line, ensure that you will be able to get one installed within a reasonable time if it's important to you. You may also wish to check whether it's possible to have an ADSL connection installed (see page 297).

If you're taking over a property from the previous occupants, you should arrange for the telephone account to be transferred to your name from the day you take possession. Before buying or renting a property, check that all the previous bills have been paid, otherwise you may find yourself liable for them.

# Using the Telephone

There are no town codes as such in Spain, where each province has its own area code (*prefijo* or *códigos territoriales*). All numbers now have nine digits and include the area code, which must be dialled whether you're making a local call or calling Spain from abroad. The codes are listed in telephone directories.

To make an international call from Spain, you need to first dial 00 to obtain an international line, then dial the country code, e.g. 44 for the UK, the area code **without** the first zero and the subscriber's number. Note that if you're using a service other than Telefónica, you need to dial the company's prefix, e.g. 1050 for Auna and 1073 for Tele2, before making a call. So to call Madrid 912 345 678 with Auna, you would dial 1050-912 345 678.

# Costs

Line rental and call charges in Spain are among the highest in Europe, although they've been reduced in recent years.

If you have a private line (*línea individual*), the monthly line rental or service charge (*cuota de abono*) is about €13 (levied monthly). Handicapped people and those aged 65 or over with an income below the Spanish minimum pension pay a reduced tariff and receive a number of free calls. A reduction is also granted on the monthly standing charge and on the installation fee. Telephone charges from other companies include general call charges and may include a fixed monthly fee. To save money you should shop around for the lowest rates and choose the company with the lowest rate depending on the type of call you wish to make.

 **Rates for calls may not be consistently low in the same company and that some companies have aggressive marketing campaigns with cheap offers which often expire once the client has signed up.**

For information on services and tariffs, contact Âlo (☎ 902 107 701 🖳 www.alo.es), Auna (☎ 015, 🖳 www.auna.es), Jazztel (☎ 1567 🖳 www.jazz tel.es), Spantel (☎ 900 181 718, 🖳 www.span-tel.com), Tele2 (☎ 800 760 772, 🖳 www.tele2.es), TeleConnect (☎ 900 902 122, 🖳 www.telecon nect.es) Telefónica (☎1004, 🖳 www.telefonica.es) and Uni2 (☎ 902 011 414, 🖳 www.uni2.es).

# International Calls

It's possible to make direct IDD (International Direct Dialling) calls from Spain to most countries, from both private and public telephones. A full list of country codes is shown in the information pages (*páginas informativas*) of your local white pages. To make an international call you must first dial 00 to obtain an international line. Then dial the country code (e.g. 44 for the UK), the area code without the first zero (e.g. 207 for central London) and the subscriber's number. For example to call the central London number 020-7123 4567 from Spain you would dial 00-44-20-7123 4567. To make a call to a country without IDD you must dial 9198 for European countries plus Algeria, Lebanon, Syria and Tunisia, and 9191 for all other countries. Calls to Gibraltar are charged at the domestic rate for interprovincial calls. There's a high surcharge for operator connected international calls.

Spain subscribes to a Home Direct (*servicio directo país*) service that enables you to call a number giving you direct and free access to an operator in the country you're calling, e.g. for the UK dial 0-800-890034 (BT) or 0-800-559 3145 (C&W). The operator will connect you to the number required and will also accept credit card calls. Countries with a home direct service include most European countries, Canada, the USA, Australia, New Zealand and South Africa. Note, however, that this service can be expensive, particularly when making reverse charge calls. Information about Home Direct services is provided in the 'international communications' (*comunicaciones internacionales*) section of telephone directories, on the Telefónica website (🖳 www.telefonica.es) under *España Directo* or by calling 11825.

To obtain an operator from one of the four major US telephone companies, call 1-800-247 7246 (AT&T), 1-800-937 7262 (MCI) or 1-800-676 4003 (Sprint), 1-800-746 5020 (Worldcom). You're connected directly with a US operator and you can place calls with a domestic USA telephone card or make a collect (reverse charge) call. International calls can also be made from Telefónica telephone offices (*locutorios públicos*) in major towns and cities (see **Public Telephones** on page 295), where you can pay for calls costing over €3 with a credit card. There are also numerous private telephone offices in resort towns.

An increasing number of expatriates (and Spaniards) make use of a 'callback' service, such as those provided by ITS Europe (☎ 902 103 906, 🖳 www.itseurope.es) and Telegroup Global Access (☎ 966 922 285, ✉ spain@affinitytele.com). It's no longer necessary to wait for a call back. Subscribers simply dial a local freephone number or possibly a prefix.

# Bills

Bills (*facturas*) are sent at varying intervals depending on the company although it's usually monthly and you're given 20 days to pay. Value added tax (*IVA*) at 16 per cent is levied on all charges. Itemised bills (*factura detallada*) are provided listing all numbers called with the date and time, duration and the charge. Bills can be paid in cash at most banks, via a bank account or in cash at a Telefónica office. You can also have your telephone bill paid by direct debit (*domiciliación bancaria*) from a bank account, which is advisable for holiday-home owners as it ensures that you aren't disconnected for non-payment. If your bill isn't paid within 20 days, your line may be cut without further warning, although a new system has been introduced whereby lines with unpaid bills are reduced for ten days to incoming calls only, prior to cutting the service completely. If your line is cut, there's a reconnection fee, which depends on the amount owing and the elapsed period, after which it should be reconnected within two working days. Note that all companies offer the possibility of checking your bills and telephone usage online.

# Emergency Numbers

Emergency numbers (*servicios de urgencia*) are listed at the front of all telephone directories (white and yellow pages). Note that there are few national emergency numbers in Spain, although a new all-purpose emergency number 112 was introduced in 2002 and 061 for the ambulance service, 062 for the *guardia civil*, 080 for the fire service, 091 for national police and 092 for the local police are valid throughout Spain.

Calls to emergency numbers cost €0.09 from private telephones. You need to insert at least €0.10 or a telephone card when using a public telephone, although your money is returned when the emergency service answers. Calls to 112 are free. There are free SOS telephones on motorways and main highways. For gas, electricity and water emergency numbers, look in your local directory under *Otros servicios de interés*. Dial 1002 to report telephone breakdowns or line problems.

## Fax

If you're planning to take a fax machine to Spain, check that it will work there or that it can be modified. Most fax machines made for other European countries will operate in Spain, although getting them repaired locally may be impossible unless the same machine is sold there.

Faxes can be purchased from Telefónica and purchased or rented from telephone and business equipment retailers.

Public fax services (*Burofax*) are provided by main post offices in most towns.

## Public Telephones

Public telephones (*cabinas telefónicas* or *teléfonos públicos*) are widely available. However, they aren't found in post offices with the exception of a few main post offices in major cities. All payphones allow International Direct Dialling (IDD) and international calls can also be made via the operator.

Public telephones in Spain accept coins and/or telephone cards (credit cards aren't accepted in public telephones). Telephone cards (*tarjetas telefónicas*) costing €5, €10 or €15 are available from post offices, newsagents, tobacconists and some other retailers. Telephones accept €2, €1, 50, 20, 10, 5 and 2 cent coins. You must insert at least €0.20 for a local call, €0.40 for a national call (to another province) and €1 a long-distance, international call or a call to a mobile phone. If you don't insert enough money you will be unable to make your call. If you're using a telephone card (*tarjeta Telefónica*), simply insert it in the card slot and dial the number you want.

**Telefónica Booths:** You can also make telephone calls from Telefónica phone booths in towns and resort areas. In small towns, Telefónica cabins (*locutorios públicos*) are franchised businesses, where you pay a 35 per cent surcharge on all calls. Telephone cards and most credit cards are accepted in payment for calls costing over €3. Reverse charge calls can also be made. You can make a number of calls in succession and receive an itemised receipt which includes the surcharge and *IVA*.

**Private Booths:** In cities and resort towns there are booths (*centro telefónicos* or *cabinas*) which are leased from Telefónica by private companies. They charge a high commission on calls and don't handle reverse charge (collect) calls as they don't make any money on them.

# Mobile Phones

Mobile telephones (*telefonía móvil*) were relatively slow to take off in Spain but in the last few years prices have fallen dramatically and sales have rocketed. All the major population areas are covered by both analogue and digital networks, although sparsely populated areas aren't served or reception is difficult. Spain has both analogue (Moviline) and digital (Amena, Movistar and Vodafone) networks, although the analogue Moviline network is due to shut down in 2007. All networks cover around 90 per cent of the country and 98 per cent of the population. Note that all mobile telephone numbers in Spain start with the number 6.

Tariffs have fallen dramatically due to the price war that has been raging between the three service providers in the last few years.

Recently in Spain numerous mobile phone scams have come to light including many which leave you a message asking you to phone a number urgently for important news regarding your family or a prize. The number you have to ring is invariably a high charge number (e.g. 906) and you're deliberately kept on the line by an answering machine or telephonists for as long as possible, resulting in a very expensive phone call. Needless to say, the important news or prize doesn't exist.You should also be aware that mobile phones are highly prized by petty thieves and mobile phone theft is big business in Spain.

# Internet

The Internet in Spain got off to a slow start but now around 23 per cent of households are online, a huge increase from a mere 0.7 per cent in 1996. High connection and monthly charges for ADSL mean only around 3 per cent of households have broadband technology, although this figure is increasing. Competition for clients is fierce and there has been a prolific growth in servers (*servidores*). There are also many other companies who charge an annual amount for Internet and e-mail services.

The cost of connecting to the Internet is the same as for local calls, although most companies offer discount services, which generally allow you to purchase a fixed number of Internet access hours per month at a discount, which depends on the number of hours. For example, Telefónica's *Bononet* offers either 10 or 50 hours a month for use during peak daytime hours (8am to 8pm Mon-Fri) or night (10pm to

8am Mon-Fri and at weekends). The 50-hour, daytime *bono* costs €45.98 per month (10 hours €12.62), a large saving on normal call rates, and the 50-hour night-time *bono* €18.03 per month (10 hours €5.11). Telefónica also offers the possibility of combining local and Internet call charges under the *Bono Ciudad Plus* service where you purchase 600-minutes a month for €8.41.

### Broadband

Broadband Internet (ADSL) is now available in most of Spain's urban areas. Rural areas are less well-served and some more remote areas don't have ADSL facilities at all. Competition for ADSL clients is also fierce, although the initial charge and monthly rates vary little from one company to another. For example, Telefónica currently charges €76.90 for a USB Modem and €126.90 for a Router (allowing more than one computer to connect to the ADSL line). Initial connection charges are €38.10 and there's a monthly fee of €39.07.

# TELEVISION & RADIO

Spanish television isn't renowned for its quality, although it has improved considerably in recent years. In addition to terrestrial TV, satellite TV reception is excellent in most areas of Spain and is particularly popular among the expatriate community. Cable TV isn't common, only some 5 per cent of households have it. Spanish radio (including many expatriate stations) is generally excellent.
   **There's no TV or radio licence in Spain.**

## TV Standards

The standards for TV reception in Spain **aren't the same as in some other countries**. Due to the differences in transmission standards, TVs and video recorders operating on the British (PAL-I), French (SECAM) or North American (NTSC) systems won't function in Spain, which, along with most other continental European countries, uses the PAL B/G standard. It's possible to buy a multi-standard European TV (and VCR) containing automatic circuitry that switches between different systems. Some multi-standard TVs also include the North American NTSC standard and have an NTSC-in jack plug connection allowing you to play back American videos. A standard British, French or US TV won't work in Spain, although they can be modified. The same applies to 'foreign' video recorders, which won't operate with a Spanish TV unless they're dual-standard.

If you decide to buy a television in Spain, you will find it advantageous to buy one with teletext, which, apart from allowing you to display programme schedules, also provides a wealth of useful and interesting information.

Most furnished rental property comes equipped with a television.

# Satellite TV

Spain is well served by satellite TV and there are a number of satellites positioned over Europe carrying over 200 stations broadcasting in a variety of languages.

## BBC

The BBC's commercial subsidiary, BBC Worldwide Television, broadcasts two 24-hour channels: BBC Prime (general entertainment) and BBC World (24-hour news and information). BBC World is free-to-air and is transmitted via the Eutelsat Hot Bird satellite, while BBC Prime is encrypted and requires a D2-MAC decoder and a smartcard, available on subscription from BBC Prime, PO Box 5054, London W12 0ZY, UK (☎ 020-8433 2221, ✉ bbcprime@bbc.co.uk). For more information and a programming guide contact BBC Worldwide Television, Woodlands, 80 Wood Lane, London W12 0TT, UK (☎ 020-8576 2555). A programme guide is also available on the Internet (🖥 www.bbc.co.uk/schedules) and both BBC World and BBC Prime have websites (🖥 www. bbcworld.com and 🖥 www.bbcprime.com).

## Satellite Dishes

To receive programmes from any satellite, there must be no obstacles between the satellite and your dish, i.e. no trees, buildings or mountains must obstruct the signal, so check before renting or buying a home. Before buying or erecting a satellite dish, you must check whether you need permission from your landlord or the local authorities. Some towns and buildings (such as apartment blocks) have strict laws regarding the positioning of antennae, although generally owners can mount a dish almost anywhere without receiving complaints. Dishes can be usually be mounted in a variety of unobtrusive positions and can also be painted. All new community properties must include a collective antenna to receive television, radio and telephone services, and this also applies to existing communities when one-third of the owners agree.

**If you're unable to install your own antenna, you may be unable to receive the TV stations that you wish.**

## Community Properties

Note that when an apartment or townhouse is advertised as having satellite TV, it often means that it has a communal system and not its own satellite dish. Satellite stations are received via a communal satellite dish (or a number) and transmitted via cable to all properties in an urbanisation. Only a limited number of programmes are usually available and no scrambled programmes may be included. Only two English-language stations are currently unscrambled on BSkyB: Sky News and Eurosport, although some communities pay to receive more.

# Video & DVD

Video and DVD films are popular in Spain and there are video and DVD rental shops in all towns. Video and DVD films are expensive to buy in Spain and there's little available in English. However, there are English-language rental shops in the major cities and resort areas, where films can be rented from around €3 per day for the latest films or three films for three days for €6 ('classic' films) or three for €8 (standard films). DVD format films can also be hired for €3 per day. If you aren't a permanent resident with proof of your address, you usually need to pay a deposit, e.g. €60 and show your passport. Rental costs can sometimes be reduced by paying a monthly membership fee or a lump sum in advance. If you have a large collection of SECAM or NTSC video tapes, you can buy a multi-standard TV and VCR, or buy a separate TV and video to play back your favourite videos.

# Radio

The Spanish are a nation of inveterate radio listeners and spend more time listening to the radio than watching TV. There are numerous high-quality local, regional and national radio stations. There are also English and other foreign-language commercial stations in major cities and resort areas (e.g. Central FM, Coastline Radio, ONDA Cero International, Global Radio and Spectrum on the Costa del Sol). Some English-language radio programmes are listed in the local expatriate press.

## BBC

The BBC World Service is broadcast on short wave on several frequencies (e.g. 12095, 9760, 9410, 7325, 6195, 5975 and 3955 Khz) simultaneously and you can usually receive a good signal on one of them. The signal strength varies depending on where you live in Spain, the time of day and year, the power and positioning of your receiver, and atmospheric conditions. All BBC radio stations, including the World Service, are also available via the Astra satellites. The BBC publishes a monthly magazine, *BBC On Air*, containing comprehensive information about BBC world service radio and television programmes. It's available on subscription from the BBC (On Air Magazine, Room 207 NW, Bush House, Strand, London WC2B 4PH, UK, ☎ 020-7240 4899, ✉ on.air. magazine@bbc.co.uk) and from some newsagents in Spain.

**Satellite Radio**

If you have satellite TV you can also receive many radio stations via your satellite receiver. For example, BBC Radio 1, 2, 3, 4 and 5, BBC World Service, Sky Radio, Virgin 1215 and many foreign (i.e. non-English) stations are broadcast via the Astra satellites. Satellite radio stations are listed in British satellite TV magazines such as the *Satellite Times*. For radio stations from further afield, the *World Radio TV Handbook* (Billboard) will be of interest.

# UTILITIES

Electricity, gas and water connections and supplies are covered in this section. See also **Heating & Air-Conditioning** on page 279 and **Sewerage** on page 312

Immediately after buying or renting a property (unless utilities are included in the rent), you should arrange for meter (if applicable) to be read, the contract (e.g. electricity, gas or water) to be registered in your name and the service switched on (e.g. mains gas).

 **Always check in advance that all bills have been paid by the previous owner, otherwise you will be liable for any debts outstanding.**

This usually entails a visit to the company's office, although many companies offer the possibility of registering online or by telephone. Note that in order to register for electricity via the Internet or telephone you will need your identification as well as the reference number for the electricity supply (usually found on the top left-hand corner of an electricity bill under *Contrato de Suministro No*).

If you go to the utility company's office, you must take with you some identification (passport or residence permit) and the contract and bills paid by the previous owner. **Note that the registration procedure for water connection is sometimes via the local town hall.** If you've purchased a home in Spain, the estate agent may arrange for the utilities to be transferred to your name or go with you to the offices (no charge should be made for this service).

If you're a non-resident owner, you should also give your foreign address in case there are any problems requiring your attention, such as a bank failing to pay the bills. You may need to pay a deposit.

# Electricity

Spain's main electricity companies include Grupo Endesa (the largest), Iberdrola, Union Fenosa and Hidrocantábrico. In January 2003 the energy market was completely liberalised and clients can now choose which company provides their electricity. Note, however, that in many areas there's still only one company providing electricity and unless you live in a large city, as yet you have no choice! Endesa (🖳 www. endesaonline.com) provides electricity under the following names: Fecsa in Catalonia; Gesa in the Baleares; Sevillana Endesa in Andalusia; and Unelco in the Canaries. Iberdrola (☎ 901 202 020, 🖳 www.iberdrola.es) provides electricity in Asturias, the Basque country, Cantabria, Catalonia, Comunidad Valenciana (including the Costa Brava), Galicia and Madrid.

## Power Supply

The electricity supply in most of Spain is 220 volts AC with a frequency of 50 hertz (cycles). However, some areas still they have a 110-volt supply and it's even possible to find dual voltage 110 and 220-volt systems in the same house or the same room! All new buildings have a 220-volt supply and the authorities have mounted a campaign to encourage homeowners with 110-volt systems to switch to 220 volts. Note that not appliances, e.g. televisions made for 240 volts, will function with a power supply of 220 volts. Spain is committed to introducing the international standard (adopted in 1983) of 230 volts AC by the end of 2003.

Power cuts are frequent in many areas. When it rains heavily the electricity supply can become unstable, with frequent power cuts lasting from a few micro seconds (just long enough to crash a computer) to a few hours (or days). If you use a computer it's wise to fit an uninterrupted power supply (UPS) with a battery backup (costing around €150), which allows you time to shut down your computer and save your work after a power failure. If you live in an area where cuts are frequent and rely on electricity for your livelihood, e.g. for operating a computer, fax machine and other equipment, you may need to install a back up generator.

---

**SURVIVAL TIP**
Even more important than a battery backup
is a power surge protector for appliances such as TVs,
computers and fax machines, without which you risk
having equipment damaged or destroyed.

---

In remote areas you **must** install a generator if you want electricity as there's no mains electricity, although some people make do with gas and oil lamps (and without television and other modern conveniences). Note that in many urbanisations, water is provided by electric pump and, therefore, if your electricity supply is cut off, so is your water supply.

If the power keeps tripping off when you attempt to use a number of high-power appliances simultaneously, e.g. an electric kettle and a heater, it means that the power rating (*potencia*) of your property is too low. This is a common problem in Spain. If this is the case, you may need to contact your electricity company and ask them to upgrade the power supply in your property (it can also be downgraded if the power supply is more than you require). The power supply increases by increments of 1.1kW, e.g. 2.2kW, 3.3kW, 4.4kW, 5.5kW, etc. The power supply rating is usually shown on your meter. Your standing charge (see page 304) depends on the power rating of your supply, which is why owners tend to keep it as low as possible and most holiday homes have a power rating of just 3.3kW.

**Wiring Standards**

Most modern properties (e.g. less than 20 years old) have good electrical installations. However, if you buy an old home you may be required to obtain a certificate (*boletin*) from a qualified electrician stating that your electricity installation meets the required safety standards, even when the previous owner already had an electricity contract. You should ensure that the electricity installations are in a good condition well in advance of moving, as it can take some time to get a new meter installed or to be reconnected. If you buy a rural property (*finca rústica*), there are usually public guarantees of services such as electricity (plus water, sewage, roads, telephone, etc.) and you aren't obliged to pay for the installation of electricity lines or transformers, only the connection to your property.

**Plugs, Fuses & Bulbs**

Depending on the country you've come from, you will need new plugs (*enchufes*) and/or a lot of adapters. Plug adapters for most foreign electrical apparatus can be purchased in Spain, although it's wise to bring some adapters with you, plus extension leads and multi-plug extensions that can be fitted with Spanish plugs. There's often a shortage of electric points in Spanish homes, with perhaps just one per room (including the kitchen), so multi-plug adapters may be essential. Most Spanish plugs have two round pins, possibly with an earth built into the plug, although most sockets aren't fitted with earth contacts. Sockets in modern properties may also accept three-pin plugs (with a third earth pin), although few appliances are fitted with three-pin plugs.

Small low-wattage electrical appliances such as table lamps, small TVs and computers, don't require an earth. However, plugs with an earth must always be used for high-wattage appliances such as fires, kettles, washing machines and refrigerators. These plugs must be used with earthed sockets, although they also fit non-earthed, two-pin sockets. Electrical appliances that are earthed have a three-core wire and must never be used with a two-pin plug without an earth socket. **Always make sure that a plug is correctly and securely wired, as bad wiring can be fatal.**

In modern properties, fuses (*fusibles*) are of the earth trip type. When there's a short circuit or the system has been overloaded, a circuit breaker is tripped and the power supply is cut. If your electricity fails, you should suspect a fuse of tripping off, particularly if you've just switched on an electrical appliance.

Electric light bulbs in Spain are of the Edison type with a screw fitting. If you have lamps requiring bayonet bulbs you should bring some with you, as they cannot be easily purchased in Spain. You can, however, buy adapters to convert from bayonet to screw fitting (or vice versa). Bulbs for non-standard electrical appliances (i.e. appliances that aren't made for the Spanish market) such as refrigerators and sewing machines may not be available in Spain.

### Converters & Transformers

Assuming that you have a 220-volt power supply, if you have electrical equipment rated at 110 volts AC (for example, from the USA) you will require a converter or a step-down transformer to convert it to 220 volts. If you have a 110-volt supply, you can buy converters or step-up transformers to convert appliances rated at 220 volts to 110 volts. However, some electrical appliances are fitted with a 110/220-volt switch. Check for the switch, which may be inside the casing, and make sure it's switched to 220 volts **before** connecting it to the power supply. Converters can be used for heating appliances, but transformers are required for motorised appliances. Total the wattage of the devices you intend to connect to a transformer and make sure that its power rating **exceeds** this sum.

Generally, small, high-wattage, electrical appliances, such as kettles, toasters, heaters, and irons need large transformers. Motors in large appliances such as cookers, refrigerators, washing machines, dryers and dishwashers, will need replacing or fitting with a large transformer. In most cases it's simpler to buy new appliances

An additional problem with some electrical equipment is the frequency rating, which, in some countries, e.g. the USA, is designed to run at 60Hertz (Hz) and not Europe's 50Hz. Electrical equipment **without** a motor is generally unaffected by the drop in frequency to 50Hz (except televisions). Equipment with a motor may run okay with a 20 per cent drop in speed, however, automatic washing machines, cookers, electric clocks, record players and tape recorders must be converted from the US 60Hz cycle to Spain's 50Hz cycle. To find out, look at the label on the back of the equipment. If it says 50/60Hz it should be okay; if it says 60Hz you can try it, **but first ensure that the voltage is correct as outlined above.** Bear in mind that the transformers and motors of electrical devices designed to run at 60Hz will run hotter at 50Hz, so make sure that apparatus has sufficient space around it to allow for cooling.

### Connection & Registration

The cost of electricity connection (*acometida*) and the installation of a meter is usually between €100 to €300, although it varies considerably depending on the region, power supply and the type of meter installed.

 **When you buy a community property, the cost of connection to utility services is included in the price of the property and it's illegal for developers to charge buyers extra for this.**

### Tariffs

Electricity is generally cheap in Spain and the cost has remained stable since 1995, although in 2003 prices were set to rise for the first time in 8 years by 1.5 per cent. The actual charges will depend on your local electricity company (the rates shown in the example below are those charged by Sevillana Endesa in Andalusia). The tariff depends on your power rating (*potencia*), which for domestic users with a power rating of up to 15kW is 2.0 (above 15kW it's 3.0). This tariff is used to calculate your bi-monthly standing charge. For example, if your power rating is 3.3kW this is multiplied by the tariff of 2.0 and then multiplied by the standing charge rate per kW (e.g. €1.39), i.e. 3.3 x 2.0 x €1.39, making a total of €9.17. The standing charge is payable irrespective of whether you use any electricity during the billing period.

The actual consumption is charged per kW, e.g. €0.08 in Andalusia. To save on electricity costs, you can switch to night tariff (*tarifa nocturna, 2.0N*) and run high-consumption appliances overnight, e.g. storage heaters, water heater, dishwasher and washing machine, which can be operated by a timer. If you use a lot of water, it's better to have a large water heater (e.g. 150 litres) and heat water overnight. If you use electricity for your heating, you can install night-storage heaters that run on the cheaper night tariff. The night tariff rate consists of paying 2.7 per cent more than the normal tariff during the day and evening (from 7am to 11pm), but provides a reduction of 53.3 per cent for electricity used overnight (between 11pm and 7am). In the summer night hours start at midnight and run until 8am. Value added tax at 16 per cent must be added to charges.

**Cuota Fija:** Some electricity companies allow their customers to pay a set amount (*cuota fija*) monthly regardless of consumption. At the end of the year the actual consumption is calculated and the customer either pays the outstanding amount to the electricity company or has money returned to them.

## Meters

In an old apartment block there may be a common meter, with the bill being shared among the apartment owners according to the size of their apartments. It's obviously better to have your own meter, particularly if you own a holiday home that's occupied for a few months of the year only. Meters for an apartment block or community properties may be installed in a basement in a special room or be housed in a meter 'cupboard' in a stair well or outside a group of properties. You should have free access to your meter and should be able read it.

## Bills

Electricity is billed every two months, usually after meters have been read. However, companies are permitted to make an estimate of your consumption every second period without reading the meter. You should learn to read your electricity bill and check your consumption.

Paying your bills by direct debit (*transferencia*) from a Spanish bank account is advisable if you own a holiday home in Spain. Bills should then be paid automatically on presentation to your bank, although some banks cannot be relied on 100 per cent. Both the electricity company and your bank should notify you when they've sent or paid a bill. Alternatively, you can pay bills at a post office, local banks (listed on the bill) or at the electricity company's office (in cash).

Electricity companies aren't permitted to cut your electricity supply without authorisation from the proper authorities, e.g. the Ministry of Industry and Energy, and without notifying the owner of a property. If you're late paying a bill, you should be sent a registered letter demanding payment and stating that the power will be cut on a certain date if you don't pay. If you disagree with a bill, you should notify the *Servicio Territorial de Ministerio de Industria y Energía* in writing, who will refuse your electricity company permission to cut your supply if your complaint is founded. If your supply is cut off, you must usually pay to have it reconnected (*enganche*).

## Gas

Mains gas is available only in major cities in Spain, although with the recent piping of gas from North Africa (Algeria and Libya) it may soon be more widely available.

As with electricity, you're billed every two months and bills include VAT (*IVA*) at 16 per cent. Like all utility bills, gas bills can be paid by direct debit (*transferencia*) from a Spanish bank account. In rural areas, bottled gas is used and costs less than half that of mains gas in most northern European countries. Many people use as many gas appliances as possible, including cooking, hot-water and heating. You can have a combined gas hot-water and heating system (providing background heat) installed, which is relatively inexpensive to install and cheap to run.

In most areas of Spain, gas bottles (*bombonas*) are delivered to homes by Repsol Butano, for which a contract is required. You must pay a deposit of around €25 and an exchange 12.5kg bottle costs around €8.50 (the price fluctuates frequently) when delivered to your home or less if purchased directly from a Butano depot. A contract is drawn up only after a safety inspection has been made of the property where the gas appliance is to be used. In some areas you must exchange your bottles at a local supplier. A bottle used just for cooking will last an average family around six to eight weeks. If a gas boiler is installed outside, e.g. on a balcony, it must be protected from the wind, otherwise you will continually be re-lighting the pilot light.

You must have your gas appliances serviced and inspected at least every five years. If you have a contract with Repsol Butano, they will do this for you or it will be done by your local authorised distributor. Some distributors will try to sell you a package which includes third party insurance and free parts should they be required, although it isn't necessary to have this insurance and is a waste of money. Beware of 'bogus' gas company representatives calling unannounced to inspect gas appliances. Most are usually legitimate companies, but their charges are extortionate and they will give you a large bill for changing tubing and regulators (which usually don't need changing at all), and demand payment in cash on the spot. If you wish you can let them make an inspection and give you an estimate (*presupuesto*) for any work that needs doing, but don't let them do any work or pay any money before checking with your local Repsol Butano distributor. Incidentally, plastic tubes have an expiry date printed on them and you can buy them from a hardware store (*ferretería*) and change them yourself.

# Water

Water, or rather the lack of it, is a major concern in Spain and the price paid for all those sunny days. Like some other countries that experience regional water shortages, Spain as a whole has sufficient water, but it isn't distributed evenly. There's (usually) surplus rainfall in the north-west and centre and a deficiency along most of the Mediterranean coast and in the Balearic and Canary islands. In the Canaries there's a permanent water shortage and most drinking water is provided by desalination plants, while in the Balearics 20,000 wells are employed to pump water to the surface (there are also desalination plants in Majorca and Ibiza). In 1997, a desalination plant was built on the Costa del Sol (although it has yet to be paid for or used!) and plants are in use in Almería and Murcia where two more are currently under construction.

On the Costa del Sol, purification plants recycle waste water from urban areas for crop irrigation and watering golf courses. Shortages are exacerbated in resort areas, where the local population swells five to tenfold during the summer tourist season, the hottest and driest period of the year. The government has drawn up a national hydrological plan (*plan hidrológico nacional*) to solve water shortages and pipe water from northern Spain to eastern and southern coastal areas, although it has yet to be passed through parliament and is highly controversial.

In summer 1995, the reservoirs in southern and eastern Spain were almost empty after four years of severe drought (the worst this century), during which millions of people had to endure water rationing. At the time of writing, many parts of the south were again facing serious drought, particularly Alicante and Murcia. Water shortages are exacerbated by poor infrastructure and wastage due to poor irrigation methods. There's also surprisingly little emphasis on water conservation in Spain, particularly considering the frequent droughts. For example, the Costa del Sol uses double the national average per person (500 litres a day) for its numerous swimming pools, lawns, gardens and golf courses, and people in towns and cities consume some 300 litres of water per person, per day, one of the highest figures in Europe. At the same time, hundreds of rural towns and villages have water on tap for just a few hours a day during the summer months and farmers regularly face ruin due to the lack of water for irrigation. However, domestic consumption has reduced in many regions with the sharp increase in water costs in recent years, and people have learnt to use less water during the prolonged drought.

## Quality

Water is supposedly safe to drink in all urban areas, although it can be of poor quality (possibly brown or rust coloured), full of chemicals and taste awful. Many residents prefer to drink bottled water, of which over 3,000 million litres are consumed each year. In rural areas, water may be extracted from mountain springs and taste excellent, although the quality standards applied in cities are usually absent and it may be of poor quality. Water in rural areas may also be contaminated by the fertilisers and nitrates used in farming, and by salt water in some coastal areas. If you're in any doubt about the quality of your water you should have it analysed. **Note that although boiling water will kill any bacteria, it won't remove any toxic substances contained in it.** You can install filtering, cleansing and softening equipment to improve its quality or a water purification unit (costing around €1,300) to provide drinking water. Note, however, that purification systems operating on the reverse osmosis system waste three times as much water as they produce. Obtain expert advice before installing a system as not all equipment is effective.

Many areas of Spain have hard water containing high concentrations of calcium and magnesium. Water is very hard (*muy dura*) in the east, hard (*dura*) in the north and most of the south, and soft in the north-west (e.g. Galicia), and central and western regions. You can install a water softener that prevents the build-up of scale in water heaters and water pipes which increases heating costs and damages electric heaters and other appliances. Costs vary considerably and can be hundreds of euros for a sophisticated system, which also consumes large quantities of water for regeneration. Note that it's necessary to have a separate drinking water supply if you have a water softener installed in your home.

## Restrictions

During water shortages, local municipalities may restrict the water consumption or cut off supplies altogether for days at a time.

Restrictions can be severe and householders may be limited to as little as three cubic metres (m3) per month, which is sufficient for around 10 baths or 20 showers. You can forget about watering the garden or washing your car unless you have a private water supply. If a water company needs to cut your supply, e.g. to carry out maintenance work on pipes and other installations, they will usually notify you in advance so that you can store water for cooking. In some areas, water shortages can create low water pressure, resulting in insufficient water to take a bath or shower. Note that in many developments, water is provided by electric pump and therefore if your electricity is cut off, so is your water supply. In urbanisations, the tap to turn water on or off is usually located outside properties and therefore if your water goes off suddenly you should check that someone hasn't switched it off by mistake. In the hotter parts of Spain, where water shortages are common, water tankers deliver to homes. Some properties don't have a mains supply at all, but a storage tank (*depósito*) that's filled from a tanker. If you have a storage tank, water will be pumped into it and you will be charged by the litre plus a delivery charge.

## Supply

One of the most important tasks before renting or buying a home in Spain is to investigate the reliability of the local water supply (over a number of years) and the cost. Ask your prospective neighbours and other local residents for information. In most towns and cities, supplies are adequate, although there may be cuts in summer. It's inadvisable to buy a property where the water supply is controlled by the developer, some of whom charge owners many times the actual cost or charge for a minimum quantity, even when they're non-residents. In rural areas there are often severe shortages in summer unless you have your own well.

 **A well containing water in winter may be bone dry in summer and you may have no rights to extract water from a water channel (*acequia*) running alongside your land.**

Dowsing (finding water by holding a piece of forked wood) is as accurate as anything devised by modern science (it has an 80 per cent success rate) and a good dowser can also estimate the water's yield and purity to within a 10 or 20 per cent accuracy. Before buying land without a water supply, engage an experienced dowser with a successful track record to check it. Although rare, some people in remote areas have spent a fortune (e.g. €50,000 or more) ensuring a reliable, year-round water supply, which may need to be piped from many kilometres away.

## Storage Tanks

If you have a detached house or villa, you can reduce your water costs by collecting and storing rainwater and by having a storage tank (*depósito*) installed. Tanks can be both roof-mounted or installed underground, which are cheaper and can be any size, but require an electric pump. Check whether a property has a water storage tank or whether you can install one. Most modern properties have storage tanks which are usually large enough to last a family of four for around a week or even longer with careful use. It's also possible to use recycled water from baths, showers, kitchens and apparatus such as washing machines and dish washers, to flush toilets or water a garden. In recent years it has become common to have a storage tank installed that refills itself automatically when the water supply is restored after having been cut off.

## Hot Water

Water heating in apartments may be provided by a central heating source for the whole building or apartments may have their own water heaters. If you install your own water heater, it should have a capacity of at least 75 litres. Many holiday homes have quite small water boilers, which are often inadequate for more than two people. If you need to install a water heater (or fit a larger one), you should consider the merits of both electric and bottled gas heaters. An electric water boiler with a capacity of 75 litres (sufficient for two people) costs from €130 to €250 and usually takes between 60 and 90 minutes to heat water to 40 degrees in winter.

A gas flow-through water heater is more expensive to purchase and install than an electric water boiler, but you get unlimited hot water immediately whenever you want it with no standing charges. Make sure that a gas heater has a capacity of 10 to 16 litres per minute if you want it for a shower. A gas heater costs from €150 to €275 (although there's little difference in quality between the cheaper and more expensive heaters), plus installation costs. **A gas water heater with a permanent flame may use up to 50 per cent more gas than one without one.** A resident family with a constant consumption is better off with an electric heater operating on the night-tariff (see page 305), while non-residents using a property for short periods will find a self-igniting gas heater more economical. Solar energy can also be used to provide hot water (see page 280).

## Costs

Water is a local matter in Spain and is usually controlled by local municipalities, many of which have their own wells. In some municipalities, water distribution is the responsibility of a private company. The cost of connection to the local water supply for a new home varies considerably from around €75 up to €500 (when a private company controls the distribution), or even €1,500 in an isolated area. In most municipalities there's a standing quarterly charge or a monthly charge for a minimum consumption (*canon de consumo*), e.g. 14 cubic metres a month or €10 a month plus *IVA* at 7 per cent, even if you don't use any water during the billing period. Water shortages don't stop municipalities from levying high standing charges for a water supply that's sometimes non-existent.

The cost of water has risen dramatically in recent years (as a result of drought) and in some towns, water bills have increased by over 300 per cent or more. The cost of water varies considerably from an average of around €1 per cubic metre (m3) on the mainland to between €28 and €3 per m3 in the Canaries and some parts of the Balearics, where drinking water is often provided by desalination plants and is very expensive. In some areas, tariffs start with a low basic charge, but become prohibitively expensive above a certain consumption. Many municipalities levy a standing charge, which is usually for a minimum amount of water per quarter or month, e.g. 45m3 a quarter or 15m3 a month, whether any water is used or not (which hits non-residents hardest).

Some municipalities levy a quarterly surcharge (*canón de servicio*) and regional governments may also levy a charge for water purification. Sometimes a higher water rate is charged for holiday homeowners or owners in community developments, where the water supply isn't controlled by the local municipality, while in others the cost of water is included in community fees (see page 139). Water bills usually include sewerage and may also include rubbish collection, e.g. when a city provides all services, in which case the cost of rubbish collection may be calculated on how much water you use. There's also a rental charge for the water meter, e.g. around €4 per quarter. Always check your water bill carefully as overcharging on bills is rife. Sometimes water company meters show a huge disparity (increase!) in consumption compared with a privately installed meter and when confronted with the evidence water companies often refuse to reply! Some municipalities arbitrarily levy higher tariffs on certain urbanisations, although this is illegal.

To reduce your water costs, you can buy a 'water saver' that mixes air with water, thus reducing the amount of water used. The cost of fitting an apartment with water savers is only around €40, which can reportedly be recouped in six months through lower water bills. Water savers can be purchased from El Corte Inglés and Hipercor stores, hypermarkets and DIY stores.

## Bills

Bills are generally sent out quarterly. If you don't pay your water bill on time you should receive an 'enforced collection' (*recaudación ejecutiva*) letter demanding payment of your bill (plus a surcharge). If you don't pay your bill your water supply can be cut off, although this doesn't usually happen until customers are around a year in arrears. If your supply is cut, you must pay a reconnection fee, e.g. €40, plus any outstanding bills.

# Sewerage

Surprisingly for a western industrialised country, around a third of the population isn't connected to a sewage treatment system, with untreated waste water going straight into the ground, rivers or the sea. In some areas there are no sewage plants and sewage is drained into cesspools (*pozos negros*) or septic tanks (*fosas sépticas*) which are emptied by tankers. Septic tanks can cause problems in summer in some buildings, for example when holiday homes are fully occupied and the septic tank isn't emptied frequently. If you have a septic tank, you should use enzyme bio-digesters and employ bleach and drain unblockers sparingly, as they kill the friendly bacteria that prevent nasty smells. Note that cesspools are illegal in many areas and properties must be connected to mains drainage.

Most sewage treatment deficiencies are found in central Spain and along the northern Atlantic coast, although raw sewage is dumped into the sea throughout the country. A special tax (*canon*) is levied in many areas to pay for the installation of sewage treatment plants. Most towns with over 2,000 inhabitants should have one by the year 2006.

# APPENDICES

---

## Appendix A: Useful Addresses

### Embassies & Consulates

Embassies are located in the capital Madrid; many countries also have consulates in other cities (British provincial consulates are listed on page 319). Embassies and consulates are listed in the yellow pages under *Embajadas*. Note that some countries have more than one office in Madrid and, before writing or calling in person, you should telephone to confirm that you have the correct office.

**Algeria:** C/General Oraá, 12, 28006 Madrid (☎ 915 629 705).

**Angola:** C/Serrano, 64, 28001 Madrid (☎ 914 356 166).

**Argentina:** C/Pedro de Valdivia, 21, 28006 Madrid (☎ 915 622 800, 💻 www.portalargentino.net).

**Australia:** Pza Descubridor Diego Ordás, 3, 28003 Madrid (☎ 914 416 025, 💻 www.spain.embassy.gov.au).

**Austria:** Paseo de la Castellana, 91, 28046 Madrid (☎ 915 565 315).

**Belgium:** Paseo de la Castellana, 18, 28046 Madrid (☎ 915 776 300).

**Bolivia:** C/Velázquez, 26, 28001 Madrid (☎ 915 780 835).

**Brazil:** C/de Fernando el Santo, 6, 28010 Madrid (☎ 917 004 650).

**Bulgaria:** C/Travesia de Santa Maria Magdalena, 15, 28016 Madrid (☎ 913 455 761).

**Cameroon:** C/Rosario Pino, 3, 28020 Madrid (☎ 915 711 160).

**Canada:** C/Núñez de Balboa, 35, 28001 Madrid (☎ 914 233 250, 💻 www.canada-es.org).

**Chile:** C/Lagasca, 88, 28001 Madrid (☎ 914 319 160).

**China:** C/Arturo Soria, 113, 28043 Madrid (☎ 915 194 242, 💻 www.embajadachina.es).

**Colombia:** C/General Martinez Campos, 48, 28010 Madrid (☎ 917 004 770).

**Costa Rica:** Paseo de la Castellana, 164, 28046 Madrid (☎ 913 459 622).

**Croatia:** C/Claudio Coello, 78, 28001 Madrid (☎ 915 776 881).

**Cyprus:** C/Serrano, 23, 28001 Madrid (☎ 915 783 114).

**Czech Republic:** Avda. Pío XII, 22-24, 28016 Madrid (☎ 913 531 880, ✉ madrid@embassy.mzv.cz).

**Cuba:** Paseo de la Habana, 194, 28036 Madrid (☎ 913 592 500).

**Denmark:** C/Claudio Coello, 91, 28006 Madrid (☎ 914 318 445).

**Dominica:** C/Castello, 25, 28001 Madrid (☎ 914 315 321).

**Ecuador:** C/Velázquez, 114, 28006 Madrid (☎ 915 627 215/627 216).

**Egypt:** C/Velázquez, 69, 28006 Madrid (☎ 915 776 308).

**El Salvador:** C/Serrano, 114, 28006 Madrid (☎ 915 628 002).

**Estonia:** C/Claudio Coello, 91, 28006 Madrid (☎ 914 261 671, 💻 www. estemb.es).

**Finland:** Paseo de la Castellana, 15, 28046 Madrid (☎ 913 196 172, 💻 www. finlandia.org).

**France:** C/Salustiano Olózaga, 9, 28001 Madrid (☎ 914 238 900, 💻 www. ambafrance.es).

**Gabon:** C/Angel Diego Roldán, 14, 28016 Madrid (☎ 914 138 211).

**Germany:** C/Fortuny, 8, 28010 Madrid (☎ 915 579 000, 💻 www.embajada-alemania.es).

**Greece:** Avda. Doctor Arce, 24, 28002 Madrid (☎ 915 644 653).

**Guatemala:** C/Rafael Salgado, 3, 28036 Madrid (☎ 913 440 347).

**Haiti:** C/Marqués del Duero, 3, 28001 Madrid (☎ 915 752 624).

**Honduras:** C/Rosario Pino, 6, 28020 Madrid (☎ 915 793 149/790 251).

**Hungary:** C/Angel de Diego Roldán, 21, 28016 Madrid (☎ 914 137 011, 💻 www.embajada-hungria.es).

**India:** Avda. Pío XII, 30-32, 28016 Madrid (☎ 902 901 010, 💻 www. embajadaindia.com).

**Indonesia:** C/Agastia, 65, 28043 Madrid (☎ 914 130 294/130 394).

**Iran:** C/Jerez, 5, 28016 Madrid (☎ 913 450 112).

**Iraq:** C/Ronda de Sobradiel, 67, 28043 Madrid (☎ 917 591 282).

**Ireland:** Paseo de la Castellana, 46, 28046 Madrid (☎ 914 364 093).

**Israel:** C/Velázquez, 150, 28002 Madrid (☎ 917 829 500, 💻 www. embajada-israel.es).

**Italy:** C/Lagasca, 98, 28006 Madrid (☎ 914 233 300).

**Ivory Coast:** C/Serrano, 154, 28006 Madrid (☎ 915 626 916).

**Japan:** C/Serrano, 109, 28006 Madrid (☎ 915 907 600).

**Jordan:** Paseo General Martinez Campos, 41, 28010 Madrid (☎ 913 191 100).

**Korea:** C/González Amigó, 15, 28033 Madrid (☎ 913 532 000).

**Kuwait:** Paseo de la Castellana, 141, 28046 Madrid (☎ 915 792 467).

**Latvia:** C/Alfonso XII, 52, 28014 Madrid (☎ 913 691 362).

**Lebanon:** Paseo de la Castellana, 178, 28046 Madrid (☎ 913 451 368).

**Libya:** C/Pisuerga, 12, 28002 Madrid (☎ 915 635 753).

**Lithuania:** C/Fortuny, 19, 28010 Madrid (☎ 913 102 075, 💻 www.emb lituania.es).

**Luxembourg:** C/Claudio Coello, 78, 28001 Madrid (☎ 914 359 164).

**Malaysia:** Paseo de la Castellana, 91, 28046 Madrid (☎ 915 550 684).

**Malta:** Paseo de la Castellana, 45, 28046 Madrid (☎ 913 913 061).

**Mauritania:** C/Velázquez, 90, 28006 Madrid (☎ 915 757 007).

**Mexico:** Carrera de San Jerónimo, 46, 28014 Madrid (☎ 913 692 814, 💻 www.sre.gob.mx/españa).

**Monaco:** C/Villanueva, 12, 28001 Madrid (☎ 915 782 048).

**Morocco:** C/Serrano, 179, 28002 Madrid (☎ 915 631 090, 💻 www. embajadamarruecos.org).

**The Netherlands:** Avda. del Comandante Franco, 32, 28016 Madrid (☎ 913 537 500, 💻 www.embajadapaisesbajos.es).

**New Zealand:** Plza. de la Lealtad, 2, 28014 Madrid (☎ 915 230 226).

**Nicaragua:** Paseo de la Castellana, 127, 28046 Madrid (☎ 915 555 510).

**Nigeria:** C/Segre, 23, 28002 Madrid (☎ 915 630 911).

**Norway:** Paseo de la Castellana, 31, 28046 Madrid (☎ 913 103 116, 💻 www.emb-noruega.es).

**Pakistan:** Avda. Pío XII, 11, 28016 Madrid (☎ 913 458 986).

**Panama:** C/Claudio Coello, 86, 28006 Madrid (☎ 915 765 001).

**Paraguay:** C/Eduardo Dato, 21, 28010 Madrid (☎ 913 082 746).

**Peru:** C/Príncipe de Vergara, 36, 28001 Madrid (☎ 914 314 242).

**Philippines:** C/Eresma, 2, 28002 Madrid (☎ 917 823 830).

**Poland:** C/Guisando, 23 bis, 28035 Madrid (☎ 913 736 605, 💻 www. embajada-polonia.org).

**Portugal:** C/Pinar, 1, 28006 Madrid (☎ 917 824 960, 💻 www.embajada portugal-madrid.org).

**Romania:** Avda. Alfonso XIII, 157, 28016 Madrid (☎ 913 504 436).

**Russia:** C/Joaquín Costa, 33, 28002 Madrid (☎ 914 112 957, 💻 http:// visados.narod.ru).

**Saudi Arabia:** C/Doctor Alvarez Sierra, 3, 28033 Madrid (☎ 913 834 300).

**Slovakia:** C/Pinar, 20, 28006 Madrid (☎ 915 903 861).

**Slovenia:** C/Hermanos Bécquer, 7, 28006 Madrid (☎ 914 116 893).

**South Africa:** C/Claudio Coello, 91, 28006 Madrid (☎ 914 363 780, 🖳 www.sudafrica.com).

**Sweden:** C/Caracas, 25, 28010 Madrid (☎ 917 022 000, 🖳 www.embajada suecia.es).

**Switzerland:** C/Núñez de Balboa, 35, 28001 Madrid (☎ 914 363 960, 🖳 www.eda.admin.ch/madrid_emb).

**Syria:** Pza. Platerías Martínez, 1, 28014 Madrid (☎ 914 203 946).

**Thailand:** C/Joaquín Costa, 29, 28002 Madrid (☎ 915 632 903).

**Tunisia:** Pza. de Alonso Martinez, 3, 28004 Madrid (☎ 914 473 508).

**Turkey:** C/Rafael Calvo, 18, 28010 Madrid (☎ 913 198 064, 🖳 www.tc madridbe.org).

**United Arab Emirates:** C/Capitán Haya, 40, 28020 Madrid (☎ 915 701 001).

**United Kingdom:** C/de Fernando el Santo, 16, 28010 Madrid (☎ 913 190 200, 🖳 www.ukinspain.com).

**United States of America:** C/Serrano, 75, 28006 Madrid (☎ 915 872 200, 🖳 www.embusa.es).

**Uruguay:** Paseo Pintor Rosales, 32, 28008 Madrid (☎ 917 580 475).

**Venezuela:** C/Capitán Haya, 1, 28020 Madrid (☎ 915 981 200).

**Yugoslavia:** C/Velázquez, 162, 28002 Madrid (☎ 915 635 045, 🖳 www. embajada-yugoslavia.es).

# British Provincial Consulates in Spain

**Alicante:** British Consulate, Plaza Calvo Sotelo, 1/2, 03001 Alicante (☎ 965 216 190, ✉enquiries.alicante@fco.gov.uk).

**Barcelona:** British Consulate-General, Edif. Torre de Barcelona, Avda. Diagonal, 477-130, 08036 Barcelona (☎ 934 199 044, ✉ bcon@ cyberbcn.com).

**Bilbao:** British Consulate-General, Alamada de Urquijo, 2-8, 48008 Bilbao (☎ 944 157 600, ✉ bcgbilbao@readysoft.es).

**Granada:** British Consulate, Carmen de San Cristóbal, Ctra de Murcia s/n, 18010 Granada (☎ 958 274 724).

**Ibiza:** British Vice-Consulate, Avenida de Isidoro Macabich, 45, 07800 Ibiza (☎ 971 301 818, ✉ ibizacons@worldonline.es).

**Madrid:** British Consulate-General, Centro Colón, Marqués de la Ensenada, 16, 28004 Madrid (☎ 913 085 201).

**Malaga:** British Consulate, Edif. Eurocom, C/Mauricio Moro Pareto, 2-2°, 29006 Malaga (☎ 952 352 300, ✉ malaga@fco.gov.uk).

**Palma de Mallorca:** British Consulate, Plaza Mayor, 3D, 07002 Palma de Mallorca (☎ 971 712 445, ✉ consulate@palma.mail.fco.gov.uk).

**Menorca:** Honorary British Vice-Consulate, Sa Casa Nova, Cami de Biniatap, 30, Es Castell, 07720 Menorca (☎ 971 363 373, ✉ deborah@infotelecom.es).

**Las Palmas:** British Consulate, Edif. Cataluña, Luis Morote, 6-3, 35007 Las Palmas (☎ 928 262 508, ✉ laspalmasconsulate@ukinspain.com).

**Santa Cruz de Tenerife:** British Consulate, Plaza Weyler, 8-1, 38003 Santa Cruz de Tenerife (☎ 922 286 863, ✉ tenerifeconsulate@ukinspain.com).

**Santander:** Honorary British Consulate, Paseo de Pereda, 27, 39004 Santander (☎ 942 220 000, ✉ mpineiro@nexo.es).

**Seville:** The British Consulate is temporarily closed.

**Vigo:** British Consulate, Plaza Compostela, 23-6, 36201 Vigo (☎ 986 437 133, ✉ vigoconsulate@ukinspain.com).

Note that the British Consulate in Benidorm has closed and enquiries should be directed to the British Consulate in Alicante.

## Major Property Exhibitions

Property Exhibitions are common in the UK and Ireland, and are popular with prospective property buyers who can get a good idea of what's available in a particular area and make contact with estate agents and developers. Below is a list of the main exhibition organisers in the UK and Ireland. Note that you may be charged a small admission fee.

**Homes Overseas** (☎ UK 020-7939 9852, ⌨ www.blendoncommunications.co.uk). Homes Overseas are the largest organisers of international property exhibitions and stage a number of exhibitions each year at a range of venues in both the UK and Ireland.

**Incredible Homes** (☎ UK 0800-652 2992, Spain 952-924 645, ⌨ www.incredible-homes.com). Incredible Homes are based on the Costa del Sol and organise several large exhibitions a year in both the UK and Ireland.

**International Property Show** (☎ UK 01962-736712, ⌨ www.international-propertyshow.com). The International Property Show is held several times a year in London and Manchester.

**Spain on Show** (☎ UK 0500-780878, 🖥 www.spainonshow.com). Spain on Show organises several annual property exhibitions at venues around the UK.

**Town & Country** (☎ UK 0845-230 6000, 🖥 www.spanishproperty. uk.com). This large estate agency organises small Spanish property exhibitions at venues around the UK twice monthly.

**World Class Homes** (☎ UK 0800-731 4713, 🖥 www.worldclass homes.co.uk). Exhibitions organised by World Class Homes are held in small venues around the UK and mainly include only UK property developers.

**World of Property** (☎ UK 01323-726040, 🖥 www.outboundpublishing. com). The *World of Property* magazine publishers (see **Appendix B**) organise three large property exhibitions a year, two in the south of the UK and one in the north.

## APPENDIX B: FURTHER READING

## English-Language Newspapers & Magazines

Unless otherwise stated, addresses and telephone numbers are in Spain.

**Absolute Marbella**, Office 602, Edif. King Edward Ramón Gómez de la Serna, 22, 29660 Marbella, Malaga (☎ 952 820 065, 💻 www.absolute-marbella.com).

**Barcelona Metropolitan**, (☎ 934-514 486, 💻 www.barcelona-metro politan.com). Free monthly magazine.

**The Broadsheet**, (☎ 911-310 180, ✉ frontdesk@thebroadsheet.com). Free monthly magazine.

**Costa Blanca News**, Apartado, 95, 03500 Benidorm, Alicante (☎ 966 812 841, 💻 www.costablanca-news.com). Weekly newspaper published on Fridays.

**Costa del Sol News**, CC Las Moriscas Local 10, Avda Juan Lusi Peralta, 29629 Benalmádena Pueblo, Malaga (☎ 952 448 730, 💻 www.costadelsol news.es). Weekly newspaper published on Fridays.

**Costa Española International**, ATCF Publicaciones, SL, Apartado de Correos 116, C/Ronda Sur, 6 bis, 03730 Jávea, Alicante (☎ 966 461 102, 💻 www.costaespinmo. com). Bi-monthly magazine.

**The Entertainer**, Avda de la Constitución, Edificio Fiesta, Locales 32 & 33, Arroyo de la Miel, 29630 Benalmadena, Malaga (☎ 952-561 245, 💻 www. theentertainer.net). Weekly free newspaper.

**Essential Marbella**, (☎ 952-766 344, 💻 www.essentialmagazine.com). Free monthly magazine.

**Homes Overseas**, Blendon Communications, 46 Oxford Street, London W1N 9FJ, UK (☎ 0207-636 6050, 💻 www.homesoverseas.co.uk). Bi-monthly property magazine.

**The Ibiza Sun** (💻 www.ibiza-spotlight.com). Free weekly newspaper.

**Island Connections**, (☎ 922-750 609, 💻 www.ic-web.com). Fortnightly newspaper published in the Canary Islands.

**Lookout**, Lookout Publications SA, Urb. Molino de Viento, C/Rio Darro, Portal 1, 29650 Mijas Costa, Malaga (☎ 952 473 090, ✉ lookout@jet.es). Monthly lifestyle magazine.

**The Mallorca Daily Bulletin**, San Feliu, 25, Palma de Mallorca, Mallorca, Balearics.

**Property News**, Jarales de Alhamar, Calahonda, 29647 Mijas-Costa, Malaga (☎ 952-931 603, 💻 www.property-spain.com). Free monthly newspaper.

**Property World**, C/España, 1, Edif. Buendia, 1oA, 29640 Fuengirola, Malaga (☎ 952 666 234, 🖳 www.propertyworldmagazine.com). Free monthly magazine.

**The Reporter**, Avda. Alcalde Clemente Diaz Ruiz, 37, Pueblo López, 29640 Fuengirola, Malaga (☎ 952 468 545, 🖳 www.spanishreporter.com). Free monthly news magazine (also sold on news kiosks).

**Spanish Country Homes**, Pérez Galdós 36, 08012 Barcelona (☎ 902 392 396).

**Sur in English**, Diario Sur, Avda. Doctor Marañón, 48, 29009 Malaga (☎ 952 649 600, 🖳 www.surinenglish.com). Free weekly newspaper.

**Tenerife News**, (🖳 www.tennews.com). Free fortnightly newspaper.

**Valencia Life**, (☎ 639-600 911, 🖳 www.valencialife.net). Quarterly magazine.

**Villas & . . .**, SKR Española, SL, Apartado de Correos 453, 29670 San Pedro Alcántara, Malaga (☎ 952 884 994, 🖳 www.villas.com). Monthly property magazine with articles in English, French, German and Spanish.

**World of Property**, 1 Commercial Road, Eastbourne, East Sussex BN21 3XQ, UK (☎ 01323-726040, ✉ outbounduk@aol.com). Quarterly property magazine.

# Books

The books listed below are just a selection of the hundreds written about Spain. For example, in addition to the general tourist guides listed, there are numerous guides covering individual cities and regions of Spain. The publication title is followed by the author's name and the publisher's name (in brackets). Note that some titles may be out of print but may still be obtainable from book shops or libraries. Books prefixed with an asterisk are recommended by the author.

## Living & Working in Spain

**\*\*The Best Places to Buy a Home in Spain**, Joanna Styles (Survival Books)

**Choose Spain**, John Howells & Bettie Magee (Gateway)

**Introducing Spain**, B.A. McCullagh & S. Wood (Harrap)

**Life in a Spanish Town**, M. Newton (Harrap)

**\*\*Living and Working in Spain**, David Hampshire (Survival Books)

**\*Madrid Inside Out**, Artur Howard & Victoria Montero (Frank)

**Simple Etiquette in Spain**, Victoria Miranda McGuiness (Simple Books)

**Spain: Business & Finance** (Euromoney Books)

**Traditional Houses of Rural Spain**, Bill Laws (Collins & Browns)

**You and the Law in Spain**, David Searl (Santana)

## General Tourist Guides

**AA Essential Explorer Spain** (AA)

**Andalucía Handbook**, Rowland Mead (Footprint)

***Andalucía: The Rough Guide** (Rough Guides)

***Baedeker's Spain** (Baedeker)

**Berlitz Blueprint: Spain** (Berlitz)

**Berlitz Discover Spain**, Ken Bernstein & Paul Murphy (Berlitz)

***Blue Guide to Spain: The Mainland**, Ian Robertson (Ernest Benn)

***Cadogan Guides: Spain**, Dana Facaros & Michael Pauls (Cadogan)

**Collins Independent Travellers Guide Spain**, Harry Debelius (Collins)

**Daytrips Spain & Portugal**, Norman Renouf (Hastings House Pub)

**Excursions in Eastern Spain**, Nick Inman & Clara Villanueva (Santana)

**Excursions in Southern Spain**, David Baird (Santana)

***Eyewitness Travel Guide: Spain**, Deni Bown (Dorling Kindersly)

**Fielding's Paradors in Spain & Portugal**, A. Hobbs (Fielding Worldwide)

***Fodor's Spain** (Fodor's)

***Fodor's Exploring Spain** (Fodor's Travel Publications)

***Frommer's Spain's Best-Loved Driving Tours**, Mona King (IDG Books)

**Guide to the Best of Spain** (Turespaña)

***Inside Andalusia**, David Baird (Santana)

**The Insider's Guide to Spain**, John de St. Jorre (Moorland)

***Insight Guides: Spain** (APA Publications)

**Lazy Days Out in Andalucía**, Jeremy Wayne (Cadogan)

***Let's Go Spain & Portugal** (Macmillan)

***Lonely Planet Spain** (Lonely Planet)

***Madrid**, Michael Jacobs (George Philip)

**Madrid: A Traveller's Companion**, Hugh Thomas (Constable)

***Michelin Green Guide Spain** (Michelin)

***Michelin Red Guide to Spain and Portugal** (Michelin)

**Off the Beaten Track: Spain**, Barbara Mandell & Roger Penn (Moorland)

*Paupers' Barcelona, Miles Turner (Pan)

Rick Steves' Spain & Portugal, Rick Steves (John Muir Pubns)

*Rough Guide to Andalucía, Mark Ellingham & John Fisher (Rough Guides)

The Shell Guide to Spain, David Mitchell (Simon & Schuster)

Spain: A Phaidon Cultural Guide (Phaidon)

Spain at its Best, Robert Kane (Passport)

Spain: Everything Under the Sun, Tom Burns (Harrap Columbus)

Spain on Backroads (Duncan Petersen)

*Spain: The Rough Guide, Mark Ellingham & John Fisher (Rough Guides)

Special Places to Stay in Spain, Alistair Sawday (ASP)

Time Off in Spain and Portugal, Teresa Tinsley (Horizon)

*Time Out Madrid Guide (Penguin)

Travellers in Spain: An Illustrated Anthology, David Mitchell (Cassell)

Welcome to Spain, RAN Dixon (Collins)

*Which? Guide to Spain (Consumers' Association and Hodder & Stoughton)

## Travel Literature

*As I Walked Out One Midsummer Morning, Laurie Lee (Penguin)

*Between Hopes and Memories: A Spanish Journey, Michael Jacobs (Picador)

*The Bible in Spain, George Borrow (Century Travellers Series)

*Cider With Rosie, Laurie Lee (Penguin)

Gatherings in Spain, Richard Ford (Dent Everyman)

*Handbook for Travellers in Spain, Richard Ford (Centaur Press)

Iberia, James A. Michener (Fawcett)

*Jogging Round Majorca, Gordon West (Black Swan)

In Search of Andalucía, Christopher Wawn & David Wood (Pentland Press)

*In Spain, Ted Walker (Corgi)

*A Rose for Winter, Laurie Lee (Penguin)

*Spanish Journeys: A Portrait of Spain, Adam Hopkins (Penguin)

*South from Granada, Gerald Brenan (Penguin)

*A Stranger in Spain, H.V. Morton (Methuen)

Two Middle-Aged Ladies in Adalusia, Penelope Chetwode (Murray)

*A Winter in Majorca, George Sands

## Food & Wine

\*AA Essential Food and Drink Spain (AA)
\*The Best of Spanish Cooking, Janet Mendel (Santana)
The Complete Spanish Cookbook, Jacki Passmore (Little Brown)
\*Cooking in Spain, Janet Mendel (Santana)
Delicioso: The Regional Cooking of Spain, Penelope Casas (Knoff)
A Flavour of Andalucía, Pepita Aris (Chartwell)
\*Floyd on Spain, Keith Floyd (Penguin)
The Food and Wine of Spain, Penelope Casas
404 Spanish Wines, Frank Snell (Santana)
Great Dishes of Spain, Robert Carrier (Boxtree)
\*The 'La Ina' Book of Tapas, Elisabeth Luard (Schuster)
Mediterranean Seafood, Alan Davidson (Penguin)
\*\*Rioja and its Wines, Ron Scarborough (Survival Books)
Shopping for Food and Wine in Spain (Santana)
\*Spanish Cooking, Pepita Aris (Apple Press)
\*The Spanish Kitchen, Pepita Aris (Wardlock)
The Spanish Table, Marimar Torres (Ebury Press)
\*Spanish Wines, Jan Read (Mitchell Beazley)
The Spanishwoman's Kitchen, Pepita Aris (Cassell)
The Tapas Book, Adrian Linssen & Sara Cleary (Apple Press)
Tapas, Silvano Franco (Lorenz)
\*The Wine and Food of Spain, Jan Read & Maite Manjón (Wedenfeld & Nicolson)
The Wine Roads of Spain, M&K Millon (Santana)

## Miscellaneous

The Art of Flamenco, DE Pohren (Musical News Services Ltd.)
\*Blood Sport: A History of Spanish Bullfighting, Timothy Mitchell
Cities of Spain, David Gilmour (Pimlico)
Dali: A Biography, Meredith Etheringon-Smith (Sinclair-Stevenson)
\*A Day in the Life of Spain (Collins)
\*Death in the Afternoon, Ernest Hemingway (Grafton)

**Gardening in Spain**, Marcelle Pitt (Santana)

**The Gardens of Spain**, Consuela M Correcher (Abrams)

***In Search of the Firedance**, James Woodall (Sinclair-Stevenson)

**The King**, Jose Luis de Vilallonga (Weidenfeld)

***Nord Riley's Spain**, Nord Riley (Santana)

***On Foot Through Europe: A Trail Guide to Spain and Portugal**, Craig Evans (Quill)

***Or I'll Dress You in Mourning**, Larry Collins & Dominique Lapierre (Simon & Schuster)

**La Pasionaria**, Robert Low (Hutchinson)

**Spain: A Literary Companion**, Jimmy Burns (John Murray)

**Spain's Wildlife**, Eric Robins (Santana)

**Trekking in Spain**, Marc S. Dubin (Lonely Planet)

***Walking Through Spain**, Robin Nellands

***Wild Spain**, Frederic Grunfeld & Teresa Farino (Ebury)

***Xenophobe's Guide to the Spanish** (Ravette)

# APPENDIX C: USEFUL WEBSITES

The following list contains some of the many websites dedicated to Spain as well as websites containing information about a number of countries. Websites about particular aspects of life and work in Spain are mentioned in the relevant chapters.

## Spanish Websites

**About Spain** (🖳 www.aboutspain.net): information about specific regions in Spain.

**All About Spain** (🖳 www.red2000.com): general tourist information about Spain.

**Andalucia** (🖳 www.andalucia.com): comprehensive information about the region of Andalusia in English.

**Barcelona** (🖳 www.xbarcelona.com): information including job opportunities and useful tips for foreigners living in Barcelona.

**Escape to Spain** (🖳 www.escapetospain.co.uk): general information and a property guide to the Costa Blanca, Costa Brava and Costa del Sol.

**Ideal Spain** (🖳 www.idealspain.com): information about many aspects of living in Spain.

**Madrid Man** (🖳 www.madridman.com): a wealth of useful and continually updated information about living and working in Madrid including an 'ask the expert' facility.

**Spain Alive** (🖳 www.spainalive.com): information about specific areas of Spain as well as general information.

**Spain Expat** (🖳 www.spainexpat.com): information about living in Spain, including an 'ask the legal expert' facility. The site has particularly good links.

**Spain For Visitors** (🖳 http://spainforvisitors.com): good general information about visiting Spain.

**Spanish Forum** (🖳 www.spanishforum.org): a wealth of useful and continually updated information about all aspects of living and working in Spain, including a free monthly 'e-newsletter'.

**Survival Books** (🖳 www.survivalbooks.net): Survival Books are the publishers of this book and *Buying a Home in Spain, The Best Places to Buy a Home in Spain*, and *The Wines of Spain*. The website includes useful tips for anyone planning to buy a home, live, work, retire or do business in Spain.

**TurEspaña (Spanish National Tourist Office)** (🖳 www.tourspain.co.uk or 🖳 www.spain.info).

**Travelling in Spain** (🖥 http://travelinginspain.com): information about Spanish cities with particular emphasis on Madrid.

**TuSpain** (🖥 www.tuspain.com): general information about Spain with the emphasis on buying property and residential matters.

**Typically Spanish** (🖥 www.typicallyspanish.com): information about a wide range of Spanish topics.

# General Websites

**Australia Shop** (🖥 www.australia.shop.com): Expatriate shopping for homesick Australians.

**British Expatriates** (🖥 www.britishexpat.com and www.ukworldwide. com): Two sites designed to keep British expatriates in touch with events in and information about the UK.

**Direct Moving** (🖥 www.directmoving.com): General expatriate information, tips and advice, and numerous links.

**Escape Artist** (🖥 www.escapeartist.com): One of the most comprehensive expatriate sites, including resources, links and directories covering most expatriate destinations. You can also subscribe to the free monthly online expatriate magazine, *Escape from America*.

**ExpatAccess** (🖥 www.expataccess.com): Aimed at those planning to move abroad, with free moving guides.

**ExpatBoards** (🖥 www.expatboards.com): A comprehensive site for expatriates, with popular discussion boards and special areas for Britons and Americans.

**Expat Exchange** (🖥 www.expatexchange.com): Reportedly the largest online 'community' for English-speaking expatriates, including articles on relocation and a question and answer facility.

**Expat Forum** (🖥 www.expatforum.com): Provides cost of living comparisons as well as over 20 country-specific forums.

**Expat Mums** (🖥 www.expat-moms.com): Information for expatriate mothers.

**Expat Network** (🖥 www.expatnetwork.com): The UK's leading expatriate website, which is essentially an employment network for expatriates, although it also includes numerous support services and a monthly online magazine, *Nexus*.

**Expat Shopping** (🖥 www.expatshopping.com): Order your favourite foods from home.

**Expat World** (🖥 www.expatworld.net): Information for American and British expatriates, including a subscription newsletter.

**Expatriate Experts** (💻 www.expatexpert.com): Run by expatriate expert Robin Pascoe, providing advice and support.

**Global People** (💻 www.peoplegoingglobal.com): Includes country-specific information with a particular emphasis on social and political issues.

**Living Abroad** (💻 www.livingabroad.com): Includes an extensive list of country profiles, which are available only on payment.

**Outpost Information Centre** (💻 www.outpostexpat.nl): Contains extensive country-specific information and links operated by the Shell Petroleum Company for its expatriate workers, but available to everyone.

**Real Post Reports** (💻 www.realpostreports.com): Includes relocation services, recommended reading lists and 'real-life' stories written by expatriates in cities throughout the world.

**SaveWealth Travel** (💻 www.savewealth.com/travel/warnings): Travel information and warnings.

**Trade Partners** (💻 www.tradepartners.gov.uk): A UK government-sponsored site providing trade and investment (and general) information about most countries, including the USA.

**The Travel Doctor** (💻 www.tmvc.com.au/info10.html): Includes a country by country vaccination guide.

**Travelfinder** (💻 www.travelfinder.com/twarn/travel_warnings.html): Travel information with warnings about danger areas.

**World Health Organization** (💻 www.who.int): Health information.

**The World Press** (💻 www.theworldpress.com): Links to media sites in practically every country in the world's media.

**World Travel Guide** (💻 www.wtgonline.com): A general website for world travellers and expatriates.

**Yankee Doodle** (💻 www.yankeedoodleiow.com): Import American products.

## Websites for British Expatriates

**British Expatriates** (💻 www.britishexpat.com and www.ukworldwide.com): These websites keep British expatriates in touch with events and information in the United Kingdom.

**Trade Partners** (💻 www.tradepartners.gov.uk): A government-sponsored website whose main aim is to provide trade and investment information for most countries. Even if you aren't intending to do business, the information is comprehensive and up to date.

# Websites for Women

**Career Women** (💻 www.womenconnect.com): Contains career opportunities for women abroad plus a wealth of other useful information.

**Expatriate Mothers** (💻 http://expatmoms.tripod.com): Help and advice on how to survive as a mother on relocation.

**Spouse Abroad** (💻 www.expatspouse.com): Information about careers and working abroad. You need to register and subscribe.

**Third Culture Kids** (💻 www.tckworld.com): Designed for expatriate children.

**Women Abroad** (💻 www.womanabroad.com): Advice on careers, expatriate skills and the family abroad. Opportunity to subscribe to a monthly magazine of the same name.

**Worldwise Directory** (💻 www.suzylamplugh.org/worldwise): Run by the Suzy Lamplugh charity for personal safety, the site provides practical information about a number of countries with special emphasis on safety, particularly for women.

## Appendix D: WEIGHTS & MEASURES

Spain uses the metric system of measurement. Those who are more familiar with the imperial system of measurement will find the tables on the following pages useful. Some comparisons shown are only approximate, but are close enough for most everyday uses. In addition to the variety of measurement systems used, clothes sizes often vary considerably with the manufacturer (as we all know only too well). Try all clothes on before buying and don't be afraid to return something if, when you try it on at home, you decide it doesn't fit (most shops will exchange goods or give a refund).

### Women's Clothes

| | | | | | | | | | | |
|---|---|---|---|---|---|---|---|---|---|---|
| Continental | 34 | 36 | 38 | 40 | 42 | 44 | 46 | 48 | 50 | 52 |
| UK | 8 | 10 | 12 | 14 | 16 | 18 | 20 | 22 | 24 | 26 |
| USA | 6 | 8 | 10 | 12 | 14 | 16 | 18 | 20 | 22 | 24 |

### Pullovers

| Pullovers | Women's | Men's |
|---|---|---|
| Continental | 40 42 44 46 48 50 | 44 46 48 50 52 54 |
| UK | 34 36 38 40 42 44 | 34 36 38 40 42 44 |
| USA | 34 36 38 40 42 44 | sm  med  lar  xl |

### Men's Shirts

| | |
|---|---|
| Continental | 36 37 38 39 40 41 42 43 44 46 |
| UK/USA | 14 14 15 15 16 16 17 17 18 - |

### Men's Underwear

| Continental | 5 | 6 | 7 | 8 | 9 | 10 |
|---|---|---|---|---|---|---|
| UK | 34 | 36 | 38 | 40 | 42 | 44 |
| USA | sm | med | | lar | xl | |

**Note:** sm = small, med = medium, lar = large, xl = extra large

### Children's Clothes

| Continental | 92 | 104 | 116 | 128 | 140 | 152 |
|---|---|---|---|---|---|---|
| UK | 16/18 | 20/22 | 24/26 | 28/30 | 32/34 | 36/38 |
| USA | 2 | 4 | 6 | 8 | 10 | 12 |

## Children's Shoes

| Continental | 18 | 19 | 20 | 21 | 22 | 23 | 24 | 25 | 26 | 27 | 28 | 29 | 30 | 31 | 32 |
|---|---|---|---|---|---|---|---|---|---|---|---|---|---|---|---|
| UK/USA | 2 | 3 | 4 | 4 | 5 | 6 | 7 | 7 | 8 | 9 | 10 | 11 | 11 | 12 | 13 |

| Continental | 33 | 34 | 35 | 36 | 37 | 38 |
|---|---|---|---|---|---|---|
| UK/USA | 1 | 2 | 2 | 3 | 4 | 5 |

## Shoes (Women's and Men's)

| Continental | 35 | 36 | 37 | 37 | 38 | 39 | 40 | 41 | 42 | 42 | 43 | 44 |
|---|---|---|---|---|---|---|---|---|---|---|---|---|
| UK | 2 | 3 | 3 | 4 | 4 | 5 | 6 | 7 | 7 | 8 | 9 | 9 |
| USA | 4 | 5 | 5 | 6 | 6 | 7 | 8 | 9 | 9 | 10 | 10 | 11 |

## Weight

| Avoirdupois | Metric | Metric | Avoirdupois |
|---|---|---|---|
| 1oz | 28.35g | 1g | 0.035oz |
| 1lb* | 454g | 100g | 3.5oz |
| 1cwt | 50.8kg | 250g | 9oz |
| 1 ton | 1,016kg | 500g | 18oz |
| 2,205lb | 1 tonne | 1kg | 2.2lb |

## Length

| British/US | Metric | Metric | British/US |
|---|---|---|---|
| 1in | 2.54cm | 1cm | 0.39in |
| 1ft | 30.48cm | 1m | 3ft 3.25in |
| 1yd | 91.44cm | 1km | 0.62mi |
| 1mi | 1.6km | 8km | 5mi |

## Capacity

| Imperial | Metric | Metric | Imperial |
|---|---|---|---|
| 1 UK pint | 0.57 litre | 1 litre | 1.75 UK pints |
| 1 US pint | 0.47 litre | 1 litre | 2.13 US pints |
| 1 UK gallon | 4.54 litres | 1 litre | 0.22 UK gallon |
| 1 US gallon | 3.78 litres | 1 litre | 0.26 US gallon |

**Note:** An American 'cup' = around 250ml or 0.25 litre.

## Area

| British/US | Metric | Metric | British/US |
|---|---|---|---|
| 1 sq. in | 0.45 sq. cm | 1 sq. cm | 0.15 sq. in |
| 1 sq. ft | 0.09 sq. m | 1 sq. m | 10.76 sq. ft |
| 1 sq. yd | 0.84 sq. m | 1 sq. m | 1.2 sq. yds |
| 1 acre | 0.4 hectares | 1 hectare | 2.47 acres |
| 1 sq. mile | 2.56 sq. km | 1 sq. km | 0.39 sq. mile |

## Temperature

| °Celsius | °Fahrenheit | |
|---|---|---|
| 0 | 32 | (freezing point of water) |
| 5 | 41 | |
| 10 | 50 | |
| 15 | 59 | |
| 20 | 68 | |
| 25 | 77 | |
| 30 | 86 | |
| 35 | 95 | |
| 40 | 104 | |
| 50 | 122 | |

**Notes:** The boiling point of water is 100°C / 212°F.

Normal body temperature (if you're alive and well) is 37°C / 98.4°F.

## Temperature Conversion

Celsius to Fahrenheit: multiply by 9, divide by 5 and add 32. (For a quick and approximate conversion, double the Celsius temperature and add 30.)

Fahrenheit to Celsius: subtract 32, multiply by 5 and divide by 9. (For a quick and approximate conversion, subtract 30 from the Fahrenheit temperature and divide by 2.)

## Oven Temperatures

| Gas | Electric | |
|---|---|---|
| | °F | °C |
| - | 225–250 | 110–120 |
| 1 | 275 | 140 |
| 2 | 300 | 150 |
| 3 | 325 | 160 |
| 4 | 350 | 180 |
| 5 | 375 | 190 |
| 6 | 400 | 200 |
| 7 | 425 | 220 |
| 8 | 450 | 230 |
| 9 | 475 | 240 |

## Air Pressure

| PSI | Bar |
|---|---|
| 10 | 0.5 |
| 20 | 1.4 |
| 30 | 2 |
| 40 | 2.8 |

# APPENDIX E: MAPS

The map opposite shows the 17 autonomous regions and 50 provinces of Spain (listed below). The maps on the following pages show airports with scheduled services from the UK and Ireland (see **Appendix F**), high speed train (AVE) routes, and motorways and other major roads.

**Galicia**
1. Coruña
2. Lugo
3. Pontevedra
4. Orense
**Asturias**
5. Asturias
**Castilla y León**
6. León
7. Palencia
8. Burgos
9. Zamora
10. Valladolid
11. Soria
12. Salamanca
13. Avila
14. Segovia
**Cantabria**
15. Cantabria
**La Rioja**
16. La Rioja
**País Vasco**
17. Vizcaya
18. Guipúzcoa
19. Alava
**Navarra**
20. Navarra
**Aragón**
21. Huesca
22. Zaragossa
23. Teruel
**Cataluña**
24. Lérida (Lleida)
25. Gerona (Girona)

26. Barcelona
27. Tarragona
**Extremadura**
28. Cáceres
29. Badajoz
**Castilla La Mancha**
30. Guadalajara
31. Toledo
32. Cuenca
33. Ciudad Real
34. Albacete
**Madrid**
35. Madrid
**Communidad Valenciana**
36. Castellón
37. Valencia
38. Alicante
**Andalucía**
39. Huelva
40. Seville
41. Córdoba
42. Jaén
43. Cadiz
44. Málaga
45. Granada
46. Almeria
47. Murcia
**Baleares**
48. Baleares
**Canarias**
49. Santa Cruz de Tenerife
50. Las Palmas de Gran Canaria

# REGIONS & PROVINCES

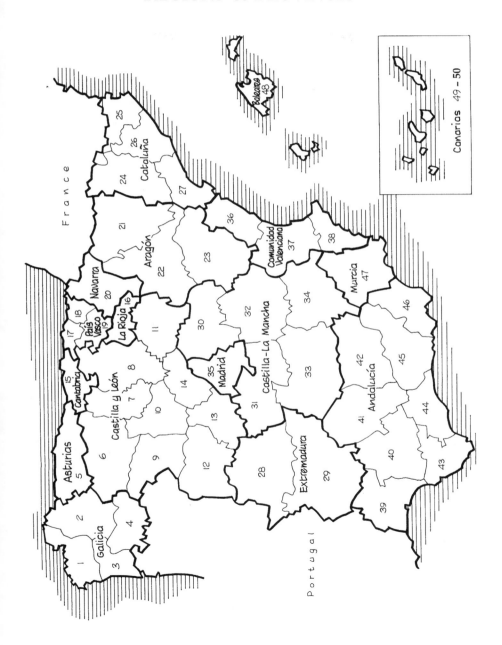

# AIRPORTS

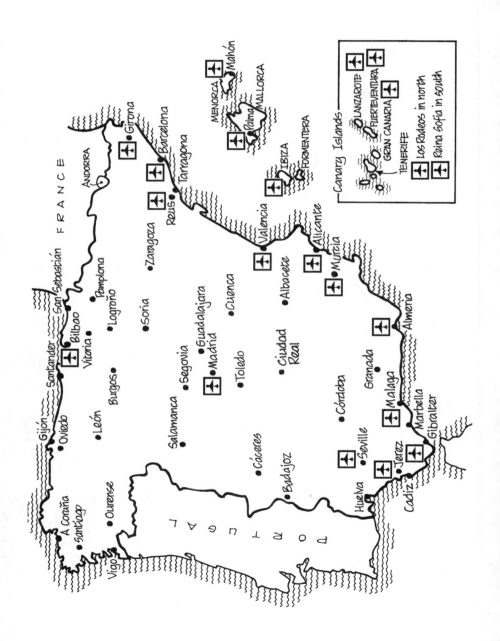

# AVE Network

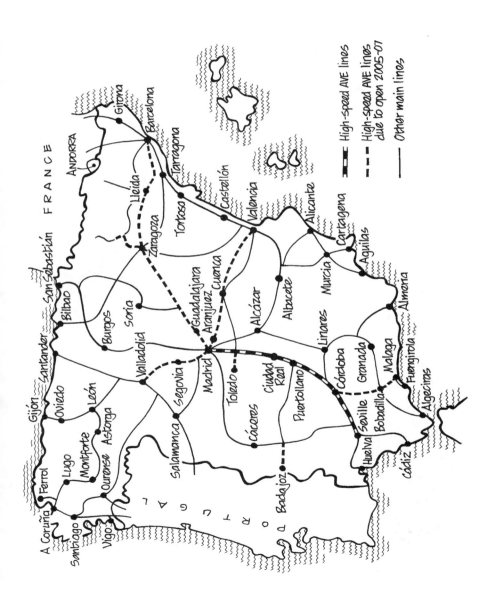

# Motorways & Major Roads

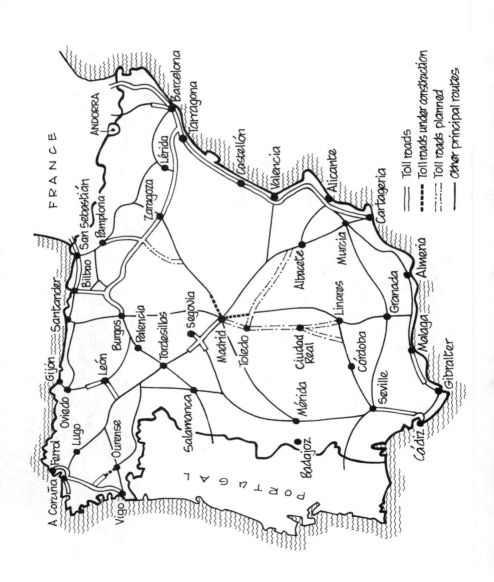

# APPENDIX F: AIRLINE SERVICES

The tables on the following pages indicate scheduled flights from UK and Irish airports to Spain. Details were current in April 2003. Airlines are coded as shown below (note that these aren't all official airline codes). Telephone numbers in italics are Irish numbers; those in plain type are UK numbers.

| Code | Airline | Telephone | Website |
|------|---------|-----------|---------|
| AE | Air Europa | 0870-240 1501 | www.aireuropa.com |
| AL | Aer Lingus | *0813-365 000* | www.aerlingus.com |
| BA | British Airways | 0845-773 3377 | www.britishairways.com |
| BI | BMIbaby (British Midland) | 0870-264 2229 | www.bmibaby.com |
| BM | British Midland | 0870-607 0555 | www.flybmi.com |
| BR | Britannia* | 0800-000747 | www.britanniadirect.com |
| CJ | City Jet | *01-844 5566* | www.cityjet.com |
| EJ | EasyJet | 0870-600 0000 | www.easyjet.com |
| FS | Flyglobe Spain | 0870-556 1522 | www.flyglobespan.com |
| GB | GB Airways (British Airways) | 0845-773 3377 | www.gbairways.com |
| IB | Iberia | 0845-601 2854 | www.iberia.com |
| J2 | Jet 2 | 0870-737 8282 | www.jet2.com |
| ML | MyTravelLite (Airtours) | 0870-156 4564 | www.mytravellite.com |
| MO | Monarch | 0870-040 5040 | www.monarch-airlines.com |
| RA | Ryanair | 0871-246 0000 | www.ryanair.com |

* Note that many Britannia flights to and from smaller airports in the UK and Spain don't operate outside high season.

| | Aberdeen (01224-722331) | Belfast City (028-9093 9093) | Birmingham (0870-733 5511) | Bristol (0870-121 2747) | Cardiff (01446-711111) | Dublin (01-814 1111) | East Midlands (01332-852852) | Edinburgh (0131-333 1000) | Exeter (01392-367433) | Glasgow Prestwick (01292-511000) | Humberside (01652-688456) |
|---|---|---|---|---|---|---|---|---|---|---|---|
| Alicante | | BM | BR<br>ML | BR<br>EJ | BI<br>BR | AL | BI<br>BR<br>EJ | BI<br>BR | | BM<br>BR | BR |
| Almeria | | | BR | | | | | | | | |
| Barcelona | | | BA<br>ML | EJ | | AL<br>IB | BI<br>EJ | FS | | BA | |
| Fuerteventura | | | BR | BR | | | BR | | | BR | |
| Girona | | | BR | | BR | | BR | | | BR | |
| Ibiza | | BR | BR | BR | BR | | BR | BR | BR | BR | BR |
| Lanzarote | | | BR | BR | BR | | | | | BR | |
| Las Palmas | | | BR | BR | BR | | | | BR | BR | |
| Madrid | | BM | BA | | | AL<br>IB | | BM | | AE<br>BA<br>BM | |
| Mahon | | BR | BR | BR | | | BR | | | BR | |
| Malaga | | BR | BR<br>ML | BR<br>EJ | BI<br>BR | AL<br>CJ | BI<br>EJ | BR<br>FS | | BR<br>EJ | BR |
| Murcia | | | ML | | | | BI | | | | |
| Palma | BR | BM<br>BR | BR<br>ML | BR<br>EJ | BI<br>BR | | BI<br>BR | BM<br>BR<br>FS | BR | BI<br>BR<br>EJ<br>FS | BR |
| Reus | | BR | | BR | BR | | BR | | | | |
| Tenerife | BR | BR | BR | BR | BR | | BR | BR | BR | BR | BR |

| | Leeds/Bradford (0113-250 9696) | Liverpool (0151-288 4000) | London Gatwick (0870-0002 468) | London Heathrow (0870-000 0123) | London Luton (01582-405100) | London Stansted (0870-000 0303) | Manchester (0161-489 3000) | Newcastle (0191-286 0966) | Teesside (01325-332811) |
|---|---|---|---|---|---|---|---|---|---|
| Alicante | BM BR J2 | BR EJ | BA BR EJ IB MO | BM | BR EJ MO | BR EJ | BM BR MO EJ | BR EJ | BM BR |
| Almeria | | | BA BR | | | RA | BR | | |
| Barcelona | J2 | EJ | BA EJ | BA IB | EJ | EJ | | EJ | |
| Fuerteventura | | | BR | | BR | BR | BR | | |
| Gibraltar | | | GB | | MO | | | | |
| Girona | | | BR GB | | BR | BR RA | BR | BR | |
| Ibiza | BR | BR | BR | | BR | BR EJ | BR | BR | BR |
| Jerez | | | BR | | | RA | | | |
| Lanzarote | | | BR GB | | BR | BR | BR | BR | |
| Las Palmas | | BR | BR GB | | BR | BR | BR | BR | |
| Madrid | | EJ | AE BA | BA BM IB | EJ | | BA BM | | BM |
| Mahon | BR | BR | BR GB | | BR MO | BR | BR | BR | BR |
| Malaga | BR J2 | BR EJ | BR GB MO | BA IB | BR EJ MO | BR EJ | BI BR MO | BR | |
| Murcia | | | | | | RA | BI | | |
| Palma | BM BR J2 | BR EJ | AE BR GB | BM | BR EJ | BR EJ | BI BR MO | BR | BR |
| Reus | BR | | BR | | BR | BR | BR | BR | |
| Seville | | | GB | IB | | | | | |
| Tenerife | BR | BR | BR GB | | BR | BR | BR | BR | BR |
| Valencia | | | GB | IB | | | | | |

# Appendix G: GLOSSARY

**Abogado**: Lawyer or solicitor.

**Acequia:** Water channel/ditch.

**Acometida:** Connection, e.g. of electricity or water.

**Administrador:** Administrator, e.g. of a community of property owners in a community development.

**Adosado:** Semi-detached, but usually refers to terraced townhouses.

**Agencia estatal de administración tributaria:** The tax office, usually shortened to *Agencia Tributaria*, previously called *hacienda* (and still used by most people).

**Agente de Propiedad Inmobiliaria (API):** Qualified and registered real estate agent.

**Aire acondicionado:** Air-conditioning.

**Albañil:** Builder such as a bricklayer or stone mason.

**Alcalde:** Mayor.

**Alcantarillado:** Sewage system.

**Aljibe:** Water cistern.

**(Se) Alquila:** For rent.

**Alquiler:** Rent.

**Amortización:** Amortisation. The gradual process of systematically reducing debt in equal payments (as in a mortgage) comprising both principal and interest, until the debt is paid in full.

**Amueblada:** Furnished. Unfurnished is *sin muebles* or *sin amueblar*.

**Aparcamiento:** Parking, usually refers to private off-road parking.

**Aparcamiento opcional:** Optional parking, i.e. the option to buy a private garage or parking space.

**Aparejador:** Architectural engineer (the person who usually supervises the building of a property) or quantity surveyor.

**Apartamento:** Apartment.

**Apartamento dúplex:** Apartment on two floors.

**Apartamento independiente:** Separate apartment, e.g. with a villa.

**Apartamento de vacaciones sin servicio de comida:** Self-catering apartment.

**API:** See *Agente de Propiedad Inmobiliaria*.

**Apliques:** Light fittings.

**Apostilla:** An official stamp on a document that certifies the signature of the official who signed it, his capacity or office, and the identity of the seal or stamp which the document bears.

**Arboles:** Trees.

**Armario empotrado:** Fitted (built-in) wardrobe.

**Aseo:** Toilet, but often refers to a separate toilet room, possibly with a shower (*aseo con ducha*).

**Ascensor:** Lift, elevator.

**Asesor fiscal:** Financial or tax consultant.

**Aspiradora:** Vacuum cleaner.

**Arquitecto:** Architect.

**Arras:** A deposit paid on a *contrato de opción de compra* (option contract) where the contract can be cancelled by either party, with the buyer forfeiting his deposit or the vendor paying the buyer double the deposit.

**Atico:** Attic.

**Atico de lujo:** Penthouse.

**Avenida:** Avenue, usually abbreviated *Avda*.

**Ayuntamiento:** City or town hall.

**Azotea:** Flat roof.

**Baja de residencia:** Certificate of non-residence or proof that you no longer reside at a certain address.

**Balcón:** Balcony.

**Baño:** Bath/bathroom.

**Barbacoa:** Barbecue.

**Barrio:** City quarter or neighbourhood.

**Basura:** Rubbish/Garbage.

**Basura y Alcantarillado:** Rubbish collection and mains drainage, for which a charge is made by the local municipal council.

**Bodega:** Wine cellar or vat room.

**Boletín:** Certificate.

**Boletín de instalaciones eléctricas:** Certificate from an electrician stating that a property has been wired according to the regulations (necessary to obtain a contract with the local electricity company).

**Boletín oficial:** Official bulletin for legal documents, e.g. a provincial, regional (e.g. *Boletín Oficial de la Junta de Andalucía (BOJA)* in Andalusia) or national (*Boletín Oficial del Estado/BOE* for all of Spain) listing of people who have had their properties embargoed or which are to be auctioned for non payment of debts such as mortgages or property taxes. Official bulletins are usually published weekly.

**Bombona:** Gas bottle.

**Bricolaje:** Do-it-yourself (DIY) supplies.

**(En) Buen estado:** In good condition.

**Calefacción:** Heating.

**Calefacción central:** Central heating.

**Calidad:** Quality.

**Calle:** Street, often written as C./ in addresses.

**Cambio:** Exchange, but also the currency exchange rate.

**Campo:** In the country.

**Cargos:** Costs or charges.

**Carpintería:** Carpentry, woodwork.

**Casa:** House.

**Casa adosada:** Terraced house.

**Casa de huéspedes:** Guest house.

**Casa de pueblo:** Village house.

**Caserío:** Country house or chalet.

**Castillo:** Castle.

**Cédula de habitabilidad:** A certificate certifying that a property can be lived in, which is issued when a building conforms with the building standards and codes. It must be issued before the electricity can be connected or a gas contract signed.

**Censo electoral:** Electoral roll.

**Certificado:** Certificate.

**Certificado de empadronamiento:** Certificate certifying that a person resides or owns property in a certain town.

**Certificado de fin de obra:** Certificate provided by an architect or building engineer certifying completion of work in accordance with the building plans.

**Certificado de No Residencia:** Certificate confirming that you're a non-resident in Spain, required by non-resident homebuyers in Spain.

**Césped:** Lawn.

**Chalet:** Detached villa.

**Chalet piloto:** Show house.

**Chalet sencillo:** A simple or basic villa.

**Cheque de viaje:** Traveller's cheque.

**Chimenea:** Fireplace, chimney.

**Ciudad:** Town or city.

**Cláusula adicional:** Additional clause.

**Cláusula abrogatoria:** Annulling clause.

**Cocina:** Kitchen (also stove, cooker).

**Cocina americana:** American (fitted) kitchen.

**Cocina-comedor:** Eat-in kitchen.

**Código postal:** Postal code.

**Colegio:** College or professional association (also a school).

**Comedor:** Dining room.

**Comisaría:** National police station where a *Número de Identificación de Entranjero* (*NIE*) can be obtained.

**Comisión de apertura:** Opening or arrangement fee, e.g. for a mortgage.

**Complejo:** Complex, e.g. a community development.

**Comunidad:** Community.

**Comunidad de propietarios:** Community of owners in a community development such as apartments or townhouses.

**Comunidades autónomas:** Autonomous regions.

**(Al) Contado:** Cash.

**Compra:** Purchase.

**Comprar al contrado:** To buy or pay in cash.

**Comprador:** Purchaser, buyer.

**Comprar sobre plano:** To buy 'off-plan', ie. before the building has been built or finished.

**Compraventa:** The purchase of a property.

**Concejales:** Councillors.

**Congelador:** Freezer.

**Constructor:** Builder.

**Construidos:** Constructed area (usually listed in property advertisements).

**Contable:** Accountant.

**Contador:** Meter (electricity, gas, water).

**Contenedor de la basura:** Dustbin/garbage can.

**Contrato:** Contract.

**Contrato de arrendamiento:** Rental contract.

**Contrato de arrendamiento (de finca urbana amueblada) por temporada:** A short term rental contract, e.g. for a holiday apartment.

**Contrato de arrendamiento de vivienda:** A rental contract.

**Contrato de compraventa:** Sales contract.

**Contrato exclusivo:** An exclusive contract between a vendor and an estate agent to sell a property.

**Contrato de opción de compra:** An option to purchase contract.

**Contraventanas:** Shutters.

**Contribución rústica o territorial:** Formerly property or real estate tax on agricultural property, now replaced by *Impuesto Sobre Bienes Inmuebles Rústicos*.

**Contribución territorial urbana:** Formerly property or real estate tax on urban property, now replaced by *Impuesto Sobre Bienes Inmuebles Urbana*.

**Contribuciones especiales:** Special levies or taxes, e.g. to improve the infrastructure of an urbanisation.

**Copia autorizada:** Authorised or certified copy, e.g. of a contract.

**Copia simple:** Copy of an *escritura* without signatures.

**Corral:** Farmyard.

**Cortijo:** Farmhouse or house on a *finca* (farm).

**Cosas comunes:** The parts of a community development that are owned communally.

**Cosas privativas:** The parts of a community development that are owned privately.

**Costa:** Coast.

**Cuarto:** Room.

**Cuarto de baño:** Bathroom.

**Cuarto grande:** Large room.

**Cuenta corriente:** Bank cheque (current) account.

**Cuota (de participación):** An owner's share (expressed as a percentage) of a community development, used to calculate his percentage of community fees.

**Declaración de obra nueva:** Declaration and registration of a new property (or part of) or development to a notary.

**Declaración de obra nueva y división horizontal:** Declaration of a new community development.

**Demanda:** Lawsuit.

**Demanda de desahucio:** Eviction order.

**Denuncia:** A formal complaint made to the authorities, e.g. the police.

**Departamento de extranjeros:** Foreign residents department, e.g. at a town hall.

**Dependencia:** Outbuilding.

**Depósito:** Tank, e.g. for water.

**Depósito de garantía:** Guarantee or security deposit.

**Derecho de paso:** Right of way.

**Derechos reales:** Real property rights.

**Desván:** Loft.

**Diputación:** Delegation.

**Dirección:** Address.

**Divisas:** Foreign currency.

**Doble cristal:** Double glazed.

**Domiciliación de pagos:** Standing order, e.g. for payment of utility bills.

**Domiciliación bancaria:** Direct debit.

**Domicilio fiscal:** Main residence for tax purposes.

**Dormitorio:** Bedroom.

**Dormitorio principal:** Master bedroom.

**Ducha:** Shower.

**Dúplex:** Maisonette.

**Edificio:** Building.

**Electricidad:** Electricity.

**Embargo:** Embargo on a property for unpaid debts such as a mortgage or property taxes.

**Entrada:** Hallway. Also the down payment on a home, the balance of which will be paid by a mortgage. The *entrada* isn't returnable if the buyer withdraws from a purchase.

**Equipados:** Equipped.

**Escalera:** Stairway.

**Escritura (pública) de compraventa:** Notarised deed of sale.

**Espacio para piscina:** Room for a pool.

**Estanco:** A tobacconist (seller of rental contracts and other official documents and *papel del estado*).

**Estatutos:** Statutes, rules or by-laws, e.g. of a community development.

**Estudio:** Study/studio apartment.

**Expediente:** The dossier on a property.

**Expediente de dominio:** Proof of domination, i.e. a document proving ownership of property or land when an *escritura* doesn't exist or has been lost.

**Factura:** Bill or invoice.

**Ferretería:** Hardware store or ironmongers.

**Fianza:** Security deposit.

**Finca:** Farm or farmhouse. Generally used to refer to any rural property outside a town or village.

**Finca urbana:** Town property.

**Fontanería:** Plumbing.

**Fosa séptica:** Septic tank.

**Frigorífico:** Refrigerator.

**Fuente:** Spring.

**Garaje:** Garage.

**Garaje doble:** Double garage.

**Garantía:** Guarantee, warranty.

**Gastos:** Fees or expenses.

**Gastos de comunidad:** Community fees.

**Gastos excluidos:** Not including expenses.

**Gastos incluidos:** Including expenses.

**Generador:** Generator (electricity).

**Gestor:** A licensed professional who acts as an intermediary between private individuals and government departments such as the tax office and social security.

**Gestoría:** A *gestor's* office.

**GIPE:** Initials of the *Gestor Intermediario en Promociones de Edificiones*, an association of real estate professionals.

**Granero:** Barn.

**Granja:** Farm or farmhouse.

**Guarda:** Keeper or guard.

**Habitación:** Room.

**Habitación principal:** Master bedroom.

**Hacienda:** Property, farm. Also the tax office, now officially replaced by the *agencia estatal de administración tributaria*, although *hacienda* is still used by most people.

**Hectárea:** Hectare or 10,000 square metres (2.471 acres).

**Hipoteca:** Mortgage.

**Honorarios:** Fees.

**Huerto:** Orchard.

**Importe:** Amount.

**Impuesto:** Tax.

**Impuesto sobre el Patrimonio:** Wealth tax, commonly referred to simply as *patrimonio*.

**Impuesto municipal sobre el incremento del valor de los terrenos:** See *plus valía*.

**Impuesto sobre Actividades Económicas (IAE):** Business tax or licence for business people and

professionals (which replaced the former fiscal licence) abolised for most small businesses in 2003.

**Impuesto sobre Actos Jurídicos Documentados:** Tax on 'documented legal acts' roughly equivalent to the stamp duty charged in some countries. This tax is levied at 0.5 per cent on all new property transfers.

**Impuesto sobre Bienes Inmuebles (IBI) Rústica/Urbana:** Annual property or real estate tax (replaced the *contribución territorial rústica/urbana*).

**Impuesto sobre Construcciones, Instalaciones y Obras:** Tax on 'construction, installations and work' levied on all building work requiring a municipal licence.

**Impuesto sobre el Patrimonio y sobre la Renta de No Residentes:** The tax declaration (form 214) for both wealth and imputed letting tax for non-residents owning property in Spain.

**Impuesto sobre la Renta de las Personas Físicas (IRPF):** Income tax.

**Impuesto sobre sociedades:** Company or Corporation Tax.

**Impuesto sobre sucesiones y donaciones:** Inheritance and gift tax.

**Impuesto sobre Transmisiones Patrimoniales (ITP):** Transfer tax (payable when buying a resale property).

**Impuesto sobre el Valor Añadido (IVA):** Value added tax.

**Informe urbanístico:** A certificate from the local town hall stating what can be built on a plot of land.

**Inmobiliaria:** Estate agent's office.

**Inquilino:** Tenant.

**Inspección:** Property inspection or survey.

**Interior:** Hinterland, i.e. not on the coast (also interior of a house).

**Inventario:** Inventory.

**Invernadero:** Conservatory or greenhouse.

**IVA:** *Impuesto sobre el Valor Añadido* (value added tax).

**Jardín:** Garden.

**Juzgado:** Court or tribunal.

**Ladrillo/ladrillos:** Brick/brickwork.

**Lago:** Lake.

**Lavadero:** Laundry or utility room.

**Lavadora:** Washing machine.

**Ley:** Law.

**Ley de arrendamientos urbanos:** Law governing property rentals.

**Ley de costas:** Coastal building law which governs construction in coastal areas.

**Ley de Propiedad Horizontal (LPH):** Law of horizontal division of a community development defining the legal rights and obligations of owners.

**Licencia:** Licence.

**Licencia de apertura:** Business opening licence.

**Licencia fiscal:** Business licence.

**Licencia de obra:** Building licence.

**Licencia de primer ocupación:** Licence required for the first occupation of a building, necessary to have an electricity meter installed.

**Llave en mano:** Ready to occupy, i.e. a fully built and decorated property.

**Localidad:** Location.

**Lujo/lujoso:** Luxury/luxurious.

**(En) mal estado:** Dilapidated (in bad condition).

**Mantenimiento:** Maintenance.

**Mármol:** Marble.

**Mensualidad:** Monthly payment, e.g. for a mortgage.

**Memoria:** List of materials and specifications for a building job.

**Memoria de calidades:** Building specifications, e.g. for a house, which must form part of the architect's plans.

**Metros cuadrados:** Square metres.

**Muebles:** Furniture.

**Modernizado:** Modernised.

**Moqueta:** Fitted carpet.

**Mudanza:** Move house.

**Multipropiedad:** Timeshare.

**Municipio:** Municipality.

**Muro:** Wall.

**Nevera:** Refrigerator.

**NIE:** See *Número de Identificación de Entranjeros.*

**NIF:** See *Número de Identificación Fiscal.*

**Nota simple:** Extract of the property register showing a property's details (such as the owner) and whether any encumbrances (debts) are registered against it. Also a copy of property deeds.

**Notario:** Notary public. The legal professional who handles the conveyancing for all property sales in Spain (similar to a British solicitor or an American property lawyer).

**Número de API:** The *Agente de Propiedad Inmobiliaria (API)* registration number of a real estate agent with the local college of estate agents.

**Número de Identificación de Entranjeros (NIE):** Fiscal or tax identification number required by all foreign property owners in Spain.

**Número de Identificación Fiscal (NIF):** The fiscal number which all Spaniards have (the same number as their identity card and passport numbers).

**Obra con garantía:** Work/construction guaranteed.

**Ocasión:** Bargain, special offer.

**Oficina de rentas y ventas:** Sales and rental office.

**Padrón municipal:** List of inhabitants, e.g. in a municipality.

**Papel de estado:** Tax stamps (literally 'state paper') issued in various denominations for the purpose of making official payments to government offices, e.g. to apply for a residence permit. Sold by *estancos* (tobacconist shops).

**Parabólica:** Satellite dish. In property advertisements it refers to a development or urbanisation with satellite TV.

**Parcela:** Building plot.

**Parcialmente construida:** Partially constructed or completed.

**Pared medianero:** Party wall.

**Parquet:** Wooden floor.

**Patio interior:** Central courtyard of a house.

**Patrimonio:** Wealth tax.

**Peligro:** Danger.

**Permuta:** A contract whereby two parties agree to exchange properties, usually with one party paying the other a sum to compensate for the difference in the properties' values.

**Piscina:** Swimming pool.

**Piscina climatizada:** Heated swimming pool.

**Piscina comunitaria:** Communal (shared) swimming pool.

**Piso:** Apartment, floor (of building).

**Piso piloto:** Show apartment.

**Plan parcial:** Plan of building plots, e.g. in a community development or a municipality.

**Planta:** Floor.

**Planta baja:** Ground floor (USA: first floor).

**Plaza:** Town square, often abbreviated at *plza*.

**Plaza mayor:** Square at the centre of many Spanish cities, often totally enclosed and arcaded.

**Plus valía:** A tax on the increase in land value. Officially called *impuesto municipal sobre el incremento del valor de los terrenos*.

**Poder:** Power of attorney or proxy.

**Poder especial:** Limited power of attorney.

**Poder general:** General power of attorney.

**Policía municipal/local:** Municipal or local police.

**Policía nacional:** National police.

**Ponencia de valores:** The official table of values used by local municipalities to assess the *valor catastral* of a property.

**Portero:** Caretaker or doorman, e.g. of an apartment block.

**Potencia:** Power rating, e.g. of a home's electricity supply.

**Pozo:** Well.

**Pozo negro:** Cesspool.

**Precio:** Price.

**Presidente:** Chairman, e.g. of a community development.

**Préstamo:** Loan.

**Presupuesto:** Estimate.

**Primera copia:** Signed original of the *escritura* or a certified copy.

**Primera línea de mar:** Front line sea position, e.g. on the beach.

**Procurador:** Barrister.

**Promotor:** Developer, e.g. of an urbanisation.

**Propiedad:** Property.

**Propiedad rústica:** Rural property.

**Provincia:** Province, e.g. Malaga.

**Pueblo:** Village.

**Pueblo blanco:** White village, e.g. a village in Andalusia with whitewashed houses.

**Puerta:** Door, gate or portal.

**Puerta blindada:** Armoured door, e.g. a high security front door of an apartment.

**Puerta de cristal:** French window.

**Recargo:** Surcharge.

**Recaudación municipal:** Municipal property tax (rates) office.

**Recaudación provincial:** Provincial tax office, e.g. for business tax.

**Recibo:** Receipt.

**Recién:** Recent, new.

**Reformada:** Reformed, e.g. modernised.

**Registro de la propiedad:** Property registry.

**Rejas/Rejillas:** Iron security grilles or bars, e.g. on windows and patio doors.

**Renovado:** Renovated.

**Renta:** Earnings or income.

**Reposición bancaria:** Bank repossession.

**Representante fiscal:** Official fiscal (tax) representative.

**Residencia:** Residence card or permit.

**Residencia habitual:** Main residence.

**Residente:** Resident (with a *residencia*).

**Responsabilidad civil a terceros:** Third party or public liability.

**Restauración:** Renovation.

**Retención:** Withholding tax. Also the 10 per cent of the sale price that must be retained by the buyer (in lieu of taxes) when a non-resident sells a Spanish property.

**Riesgo a terceros:** Third party liability, e.g. for household insurance.

**Río:** River.

**Rústica:** Agricultural property.

**Sala de estar:** Living room, lounge.

**Salón:** Lounge, living room.

**Salón-Comedor:** Combined Lounge and dining room.

**Salón de juegos:** Entertainment room.

**Segunda residencia:** Second or holiday home.

**Seguridad social:** Social security.

**Seguro:** Insurance.

**Seguro de hogar:** Household insurance.

**Seguro de viaje:** Travel insurance.

**Señal:** Deposit.

**Sistema de seguridad:** Security system, alarm.

**Solar:** Plot of land.

**Solería de mármol:** Marble floors.

**Solario:** Solarium/sun roof or deck.

**Sótano:** Cellar, basement.

**Subasta:** Auction, e.g. of property.

**Subasteros:** People who band together people to buy properties at auction at low prices and resell them at huge profit.

**Subrogación forzosa:** 'Compulsory substitution' where a lender offering more favourable mortgage terms or interest rates takes over an existing mortgage.

**Suelo rústico/urbano/urbanizable:** Agricultural land (*suelo rústico*), building land (*suelo urbano*) and land that can be changed from agricultural to building land (*suelo urbanizable*).

**Taller:** Workshop.

**Taller del constructor:** Builder's yard.

**Tasa:** Fee.

**Tasa Anual Equivalente (TAE):** The effective annual interest rate, e.g. for a mortgage, after interest is compounded and all commission and fees are included.

**Tejado:** Roof.

**(por) Temporada:** Temporary or short term, e.g. a seasonal property rental contract.

**Termo:** Water heater.

**Terreno:** Land, plot.

**Terreno rústico:** Agricultural or rural land.

**Terreno urbanizable:** Building land with an approved *plan parcial*.

**Terraza:** Terrace.

**Testamento:** Will.

**Tipo de interés:** Interest rate.

**Todo confort:** All mod cons.

**Todos los gastos:** All fees or charges, e.g. in a property purchase contract.

**Tranquilo:** Quiet.

**Transferencia:** Banker's order.

**Traspaso:** Lease or transfer of property.

**Trastero:** Storage room.

**Tribunal de expropriaciones:** Special court to decide disputes over expropriation of property.

**Ultimo piso:** Top floor.

**Urbana:** Urban. Also the colloquial name for property tax.

**Urbanismo:** Urban development office.

**Urbanización:** Urbanisation or housing estate. A community development.

**Urgente:** Urgent.

**Usufructo:** A life interest, e.g. in a property.

**Vado permanente:** Keep clear. No parking zone, e.g. in front of a private entrance or garage.

**Vallado:** Fenced in, e.g. a garden.

**Valor catastral:** The fiscal or rateable value of a property fixed by the local municipality, on which property taxes (IBI) are calculated.

**Vecindad:** Neighbourhood.

**(Se) Vende:** For sale.

**Vendedor:** Vendor or seller.

**Ventana:** Window.

**Vídeo portero:** Video entrance security system.

**Viejo:** Old.

**Vigas de madera:** Wooden beams, beamed ceiling.

**Visado:** Visa.

**Visado de residencia:** Visa required for a non-EU national to take up residence in Spain.

**Vistas al campo:** Country views.

**Vistas de la costa:** Coastal views.

**Vistas al mar:** Sea views.

**Vivero:** Garden centre.

**Vivienda de Protección Oficial (VPO):** Subsidised housing.

**Vivienda:** Dwelling.

**Vivienda habitual:** Primary or main residence.

**Vivienda secundaria/viviendas de vacaciones:** Second or holiday home.

**Zona verde:** Green zone where no building is permitted. Also refers to gardens, lawns and other 'green' areas.

# INDEX

# LIVING AND WORKING SERIES

**Living and Working** books are essential reading for anyone planning to spend time abroad, including holiday-home owners, retirees, visitors, business people, migrants, students and even extra-terrestrials! They're packed with important and useful information designed to help you **avoid costly mistakes and save both time and money.** Topics covered include how to:

- Find a job with a good salary & conditions
- Obtain a residence permit
- Avoid and overcome problems
- Find your dream home
- Get the best education for your family
- Make the best use of public transport
- Endure local motoring habits
- Obtain the best health treatment
- Stretch your money further
- Make the most of your leisure time
- Enjoy the local sporting life
- Find the best shopping bargains
- Insure yourself against most eventualities
- Use post office and telephone services
- Do numerous other things not listed above

**Living and Working** books are the most comprehensive and up-to-date source of practical information available about everyday life abroad. They aren't, however, boring text books, but interesting and entertaining guides written in a highly readable style.

**Discover what it's really like to live and work abroad!**

Order your copies today by phone, fax, mail or e-mail from: Survival Books, PO Box 146, Wetherby, West Yorks. LS23 6XZ, United Kingdom (☎/📠 +44 (0)1937-843523, ✉ orders@ survivalbooks.net, 💻 www.survivalbooks.net).

# BUYING A HOME SERIES

*Buying a Home* books are essential reading for anyone planning to purchase property abroad and are designed to guide you through the jungle and make it a pleasant and enjoyable experience. Most importantly, they're packed with vital information to help you **avoid the sort of disasters that can turn your dream home into a nightmare!** Topics covered include:

- Avoiding problems
- Choosing the region
- Finding the right home and location
- Estate agents
- Finance, mortgages and taxes
- Home security
- Utilities, heating and air-conditioning
- Moving house and settling in
- Renting and letting
- Permits and visas
- Travelling and communications
- Health and insurance
- Renting a car and driving
- Retirement and starting a business
- And much, much more!

*Buying a Home* books are the most comprehensive and up-to-date source of information available about buying property abroad. Whether you want a detached house, townhouse or apartment, a holiday or a permanent home, these books will help make your dreams come true.

**Save yourself time, trouble and money!**

Order your copies today by phone, fax, mail or e-mail from: Survival Books, PO Box 146, Wetherby, West Yorks. LS23 6XZ, United Kingdom (☎/▤ +44 (0)1937-843523, ✉ orders@ survivalbooks.net, ▣ www.survivalbooks.net).

# ORDER FORM

## ALIEN'S GUIDES / BEST PLACES / BUYING A HOME / DISASTERS / WINES

| Qty. | Title | Price (incl. p&p)* | | | Total |
|---|---|---|---|---|---|
| | | UK | Europe | World | |
| | The Alien's Guide to Britain | £5.95 | £6.95 | £8.45 | |
| | The Alien's Guide to France | £5.95 | £6.95 | £8.45 | |
| | The Best Places to Buy a Home in France | £13.95 | £15.95 | £19.45 | |
| | The Best Places to Buy a Home in Spain | £13.45 | £14.95 | £16.95 | |
| | Buying a Home Abroad | £13.45 | £14.95 | £16.95 | |
| | Buying a Home in Britain | £11.45 | £12.95 | £14.95 | |
| | Buying a Home in Florida | £13.45 | £14.95 | £16.95 | |
| | Buying a Home in France | £13.45 | £14.95 | £16.95 | |
| | Buying a Home in Greece & Cyprus | £13.45 | £14.95 | £16.95 | |
| | Buying a Home in Ireland | £11.45 | £12.95 | £14.95 | |
| | Buying a Home in Italy | £13.45 | £14.95 | £16.95 | |
| | Buying a Home in Portugal | £13.45 | £14.95 | £16.95 | |
| | Buying a Home in Spain | £13.45 | £14.95 | £16.95 | |
| | How to Avoid Holiday & Travel Disasters | £13.45 | £14.95 | £16.95 | |
| | Renovating & Maintaining Your French Home | Autumn 2003 | | | |
| | Rioja and its Wines | £11.45 | £12.95 | £14.95 | |
| | The Wines of Spain | £15.95 | £18.45 | £21.95 | |
| | | | | **Total** | |

Order your copies today by phone, fax, mail or e-mail from: Survival Books, PO Box 146, Wetherby, West Yorks. LS23 6XZ, UK (☎/▤ +44 (0)1937-843523, ✉ orders@ survivalbooks.net, 🖥 www.survivalbooks.net). If you aren't entirely satisfied, simply return them to us within 14 days for a full and unconditional refund.

Cheque enclosed/please charge my Amex/Delta/MasterCard/Switch/Visa* card

Card No. _ _ _ _   _ _ _ _   _ _ _ _   _ _ _ _

Expiry date _____   Issue number (Switch only) _____

Signature _____   Tel. No. _____

NAME _____

ADDRESS _____

_____

* Delete as applicable (price includes postage – airmail for Europe/world).

Swiss customers can order from Bergli Books, 4001 Basel (☎ +41 (0)61 373 2777, ▤ +41 (0)61 373 3778, ✉ info@bergli.ch, 🖥 www.bergli.ch).

# ORDER FORM
## LIVING & WORKING SERIES / RETIRING ABROAD

| Qty. | Title | Price (incl. p&p)* | | | Total |
|---|---|---|---|---|---|
| | | UK | Europe | World | |
| | Living & Working Abroad | £16.95 | £18.95 | £22.45 | |
| | Living & Working in America | £14.95 | £16.95 | £20.45 | |
| | Living & Working in Australia | £14.95 | £16.95 | £20.45 | |
| | Living & Working in Britain | £14.95 | £16.95 | £20.45 | |
| | Living & Working in Canada | £16.95 | £18.95 | £22.45 | |
| | Living & Working in the Far East | Winter 2003 | | | |
| | Living & Working in France | £14.95 | £16.95 | £20.45 | |
| | Living & Working in Germany | £16.95 | £18.95 | £22.45 | |
| | Living & Working in the Gulf States & Saudi Arabia | £16.95 | £18.95 | £22.45 | |
| | Living & Working in Holland, Belgium & Luxembourg | £14.95 | £16.95 | £20.45 | |
| | Living & Working in Ireland | £14.95 | £16.95 | £20.45 | |
| | Living & Working in Italy | £16.95 | £18.95 | £22.45 | |
| | Living & Working in London | £11.45 | £12.95 | £14.95 | |
| | Living & Working in New Zealand | £14.95 | £16.95 | £20.45 | |
| | Living & Working in Spain | £14.95 | £16.95 | £20.45 | |
| | Living & Working in Switzerland | £16.95 | £18.95 | £22.45 | |
| | Retiring Abroad | £14.95 | £16.95 | £20.45 | |
| | | | | **Total** | |

Order your copies today by phone, fax, mail or e-mail from: Survival Books, PO Box 146, Wetherby, West Yorks. LS23 6XZ, UK (☎/▤ +44 (0)1937-843523, ✉ orders@survivalbooks.net, 💻 www.survivalbooks.net). If you aren't entirely satisfied, simply return them to us within 14 days for a full and unconditional refund.

Cheque enclosed/please charge my Amex/Delta/MasterCard/Switch/Visa* card

Card No. _ _ _ _  _ _ _ _  _ _ _ _  _ _ _ _

Expiry date _____  Issue number (Switch only) _____

Signature _____  Tel. No. _____

NAME _____

ADDRESS _____

_____

\* Delete as applicable (price includes postage – airmail for Europe/world).

Swiss customers can order from Bergli Books, 4001 Basel (☎ +41 (0)61 373 2777, ▤ +41 (0)61 373 3778, ✉ info@bergli.ch, 💻 www.bergli.ch).

# OTHER SURVIVAL BOOKS

Survival Books publishes a variety of books in addition to the *Living and Working* and *Buying a Home* series (see previous pages). These include:

**The Alien's Guides:** *The Alien's Guides to Britain* and *France* provide an 'alternative' look at life in these popular countries and will help you to avoid the most serious gaffes and to appreciate more fully the peculiarities (in both senses) of the British and French.

**The Best Places to Buy a Home:** *The Best Places to Buy a Home in France* and *Spain* are the most comprehensive and up-to-date sources of information available for anyone wanting to research the property market in France and Spain and will save you endless hours choosing the best place for your home.

**How to Avoid Holiday and Travel Disasters:** This book is essential reading for anyone planning a trip abroad and will help you to make the right decisions regarding every aspect of your travel arrangements and to avoid costly mistakes and the sort of disasters that can turn a trip into a nightmare.

**Retiring Abroad:** This is the most comprehensive and up-to-date source of practical information available about retiring to a foreign country and will help to smooth your path to successful retirement abroad and save you time, trouble and money.

**Wine Guides:** *Rioja and its Wines* and *The Wines of Spain* are required reading for lovers of fine wines and are the most comprehensive and up-to-date sources of information available on the wines of Spain and of its most famous wine-producing region.

**Broaden your horizons with Survival Books!**

Order your copies today by phone, fax, mail or e-mail from: Survival Books, PO Box 146, Wetherby, West Yorks. LS23 6XZ, United Kingdom (☎/▤ +44 (0)1937-843523, ✉ orders@ survivalbooks.net, 💻 www.survivalbooks.net).